WOMEN AND ALCOHOL

CONTEMPORARY AND HISTORICAL PERSPECTIVES

Moira Plant

FREE ASSOCIATION BOOKS • LONDON / NEW YORK

Published in 1997 by
Free Association Books Ltd
57 Warren Street, London W1P 5PA
and 70 Washington Square South
New York, NY 10012-1091

A CIP record for this book is available from the British Library

ISBN 1 85343 363 2 hbk

ISBN 1 85343 364 0 pbk

Produced for Free Association Books Ltd by
Chase Production Services, Chadlington OX7 3LN
Printed in the EC by J.W. Arrowsmith Ltd, Bristol

We have a duty to show our daughters that the world we live in is our own very personal world. Some of the parts that we see as important are such because we have, for different reasons, focused on them and then unintentionally handed our telescopes or microscopes to our daughters. It is our task to help them understand this, to make it clear to them that these are *our* telescopes and microscopes: they do not necessarily have to take them. They can make their own viewing aids, hopefully something that gives them an even broader view so that they are not restricted by our blindness, but are able to see further, with a wider vision and more intense colour.

But how does a woman with a drinking problem, whose world is negative, without even much hope, focused on little other than the next drink, impart any of these opportunities to her daughter? A woman who lives in fear of the demons without and within, who does not even recognise that she is looking through a glass darkly but knows she feels lonely and isolated.

This book is dedicated to my daughter, Emma, my god-daughter, Rowan and to my mother Jessie.

Contents

Preface

The subject of alcohol consumption by women has been the focus of interest, concern and even hysteria for centuries. During recent decades, this topic has fostered a series of 'moral panics'. The latter have periodically been fostered by the mass media and by the ignorance and prejudices of a world in which there persists a chronic antipathy towards the use of alcohol by women.

This book presents a review of some of the key issues related to alcohol consumption and alcohol-related problems in women. At the outset, it should be emphasised that women are generally more likely than men to abstain from drinking alcohol. Moreover, most women who do consume alcohol generally drink in moderation and without serious adverse consequences. Most female drinkers consume markedly lower quantities of alcohol than do their male counterparts. Alcohol-related problems are serious and widespread in many societies. Such problems inflict great misery and sometimes premature death. The seriousness of such problems does not require exaggeration. At the same time, a growing body of evidence also supports the conclusion that low-level alcohol consumption has a protective effect in relation to mortality from such conditions as heart disease. Accordingly, this book does not concentrate solely upon the ill effects associated with heavy or inappropriate drinking by women. A much broader perspective is offered. This examines not only the epidemiology of recent patterns of alcohol use and alcohol-related problems by women in different cultures, but also the historical, moral and social context in which such drinking occurs. The following text presents a discussion of the widespread and persisting ambivalence or hostility in many cultures towards the relation of women and alcohol. This important theme is highlighted with reference to religious and social pressures, gender roles and stereotypes and the widespread assumption that the psychoactive drug ethyl alcohol is a 'disinhibitor', or facilitator of unrestrained and 'wanton' behaviour. A historical and cross-cultural perspective is presented. The ambiguity accorded to alcohol consumption by women in both industrial and developing societies is contrasted with both the normative nature of female drinking in many contexts and the dominant role of women as producers and retailers of alcohol in many developing societies.

The attention of this book is not restricted to alcohol-related problems amongst women. However, a wide-ranging review is presented of the physical, psychological and social harm associated with heavy or 'problem' use of alcohol by women. Research into the effectiveness of various clinical approaches to alcohol problems amongst women is reviewed, together with the merits and limitations of different approaches to counselling women with such problems.

Acknowledgements

Many people have assisted with the production of this book. The author is particularly indebted to Christine Thornton of the Alcohol & Health Research Group for her valuable assistance. Special thanks are also due to Gill Davies, Managing Director of Free Association Books, with whom the author has had the pleasure of working for many years. Sandy Gordon is thanked for his friendship and support. The exercise of reviewing the material cited and writing this book was generously supported by the Portman Group, the Scotch Whisky Association, William Grant and Sons Ltd, the Hope Trust, the Bank of Scotland, the Bill Kenyon Education Trust and an anonymous charity. The views expressed in this book are solely those of the author.

Those who have assisted with the production of this book include the following: Sue Baker of Alcohol Concern, London; Dr Kim Bloomfield of the Free University, Berlin; Dr Jan Gill of the Alcohol & Health Research Group, Edinburgh; Dr Tom Greenfield of the Alcohol Research Group, Berkeley, California; Professor Nick Heather of the Centre for Drug and Alcohol Studies, Newcastle Upon Tyne; Dr Harald Klingemann of the Swiss Institute for the Prevention of Alcohol and Drug Problems, Lausanne; Dr Marsha Morgan of the Royal Free Hospital, London; Margaret Nicholson and Wendy Mill of the Department of Psychiatry Library in the University of Edinburgh; Emma Plant; Catherine Redford; Lee Rocha-Silva of the Human Sciences Research Council, Pretoria; Professor Eric Single of the Canadian Centre on Substance Abuse, Toronto; Dr Betsy Thom of the Centre for Research on Drugs and Health Behaviour, London; Chris Thurman of the Brewers and Licensed Retailers Association, London; Dr Ien van de Goor of the Addiction Research Institute, Rotterdam; Drs Sharon and Richard Wilsnack of the University of North Dakota School of Medicine, Grand Forks and the members of the International Research Group on Gender and Alcohol (IRGGA) of the Kettil Bruun Society for Social and Epidemiological Research on Alcohol. Thanks are also due to all the members of the Alcohol & Health Research Group in the University of Edinburgh, for friendship, support, encouragement and for countless cups of tea.

Thanks are due to the following for permission to reproduce some of the illustrations contained in this book: The Bridgeman

Art Library, London; Paul Popper Ltd, Northampton; the Wellcome Centre for Medical Science (Medical Photography Library), London and the Zero Tolerance Campaign, Edinburgh District Council Women's Committee.

Finally, and most importantly, I thank my husband, Martin. Without his support, encouragement and energy this book might never have been completed. The patience and understanding he has shown has been constant and I appreciate it enormously.

The Author

Moira Plant has been engaged in research and clinical practice in relation to women and alcohol since 1970. She gained her PhD in 1984 for her work on drinking in pregnancy. She is Deputy Director of the Alcohol & Health Research Group in the Department of Psychiatry in the University of Edinburgh. Her numerous publications include the books *Women, Drinking and Pregnancy* (1985) and *Risk Takers: Alcohol, Drugs, Sex and Youth* (1992). She is author of a World Health Organization report, *Women and Alcohol*. Moira Plant is a former member of the co-ordinating committee of the Kettil Bruun Society for Social and Epidemiological Research on Alcohol. She worked as senior nurse and therapist in the Alcohol Problems Clinic in the Royal Edinburgh Hospital between 1970 and 1992. She has been a member of the training team of the Diploma in Counselling at Heriot Watt University's Moray House Institute of Education since 1992 and also works as an independent counsellor and trainer. She served as a member of the (UK) Governmental Committee on Women and Alcohol 1991–92. She also recently chaired a European expert working group on alcohol and pregnancy. She has served as a temporary adviser to the World Health Organization. She is a frequent lecturer and broadcaster and is a member of the International Advisory Board of the *Journal of Substance Misuse for Nursing, Health and Social Care*.

1 A Contemporary Perspective

Alcohol has been used since prehistoric times and has long been established as the most widely used psychoactive (mind-altering) drug in many societies. Patterns of alcohol consumption vary enormously between people in different cultures and regions. In some countries there is strong disapproval of drinking, backed up with severe penalties for those who infringe control laws. In other countries, alcohol use is legal, widespread and enjoyed. Most of those who drink usually do so in moderation and without associated problems. However, some drinkers do suffer from harmful consequences or inflict damage upon others by their consumption of alcohol. Because alcohol use is so widespread, the problems associated with heavy or inappropriate use are often on a large scale. It has long been apparent that neither alcohol consumption nor alcohol-related problems are the sole preserve of males. Women have been consuming alcohol and suffering from their own drinking, or that of others, for a very long time. Even so, it is evident that in general women are less likely than men to drink at all and those who do consume alcohol, generally drink smaller quantities than their male counterparts. In consequence, women are less likely than men to be recorded as experiencing problems attributable to their drinking. Although men are inclined to drink more heavily and to suffer higher rates of problems than women, alcohol use by the latter has rightly been acknowledged as a matter for enquiry and concern. This chapter sets out to provide a general introduction to what is now a very extensive and steadily burgeoning literature about the use of alcohol and patterns of alcohol-related problems amongst women. It has been 'normal' for women to drink in many societies for at least much of the present century, if not long before. Even so, this subject has frequently been distorted by prejudice, hostility and double standards.

Drinking Patterns

There is a huge body of information about drinking patterns in many industrial countries. Most of this information has been generated during the past two or three decades and relatively little comparable evidence is available from developing countries, even though alcohol is used extensively in some and drinking is on the increase in others. Drinking habits are as varied as human culture itself (Pittman and Snyder 1962, Pittman and White 1991, D.B. Heath 1995). In some societies the consumption of alcohol holds a central place in religious ceremony. In others it is an integral component of social activity, and major events, such as births and marriages, are invariably accompanied by alcohol consumption. More commonly, alcohol is a normal, albeit secondary, feature of social gatherings and relaxation. In some cultures, for example, the very invitation to 'have a drink' is generally interpreted as a reference to an alcoholic beverage.

Ethyl alcohol, the only type of alcohol that is safe to drink, is a depressant drug. Its consumption commonly produces a feeling of relaxation. The disinhibiting effects of alcohol are commonly assumed to suggest that it is a stimulant, which it is not. As with many other types of drug, it is possible for alcohol use to produce problems, including both psychological and physical dependence (addiction). Fortunately, most drinking is restrained and controlled and alcohol consumption is widely accepted, at least by adults, or those above the legal age of alcohol consumption and purchase. In many European countries alcohol use, either in the home or in taverns, inns or other establishments, was widespread by the Middle Ages. In Britain, for example, alcohol consumption was extremely high judged by modern standards. Men were reported not uncommonly to imbibe quantities such as two gallons (16 pints/8 litres) of ale each day. Warner (1992) noted that 'the heaviest alcohol consumption was evident in northern Europe and that the English were by far the heaviest drinkers'. This author also commented that although women in medieval England did consume alcohol, they rarely did so in taverns.

The Industrial Revolution was accompanied by the rapid growth of large cities. In Britain this period was accompanied by the eighteenth-century 'Gin Epidemic' and with the decline of the image of the urban inn to that of a disreputable establishment, often linked with cruel sports and prostitution as well as heavy drinking. Concern about alcohol problems in Britain reached a peak in the nineteenth century, when an influential temperance movement developed. Public and political concern and the introduction of licensing regulations to restrict the availability of alcohol, probably combined with other factors, resulted in a fall in alcohol consumption levels from around 1876. It should be noted that many of the problems associated with the city tavern were simply the problems of a society in transition, even though there is no doubt that heavy drinking contributed to and exacerbated such problems. During the twentieth century alcohol consumption has fluctuated markedly in many countries. During the two world wars consumption levels fell considerably. Since the Second World War levels of per capita alcohol consumption have risen in many parts of the world. This reflects increased disposable incomes and the availability of an ever greater range of types of commercially produced beverage alcohol. An indication of the extent of the evident international variation in levels of alcohol consumption is provided by Table 1.1. This presents details of recorded per capita alcohol consumption levels in 36 countries between 1970 and 1993. As the table indicates, there is a considerable difference in national levels of per capita consumption. In 1993 this ranged from 2.9 litres in Mexico to 12.3 litres in France. This information provides a useful indication of the scale of international differences. Even so, this type of information requires to be qualified by a number of considerations. First, most alcohol is consumed by males even though in many countries women play a major role in producing alcohol. Second, per capita levels of national consumption do not give any information about the proportions of men and women, young and old who drink or who abstain from doing so. Only some countries are included in this table, many others are not. Even some of those which are included have few reliable figures available. In addition these figures presented do not take account of the consumption of unofficial, home-made or illegal alcohol. It is acknowledged that in some countries, such as Norway or South Africa, for example, this may be considerable. As noted by Ambler (1990):

> According to a contemporary report by an African researcher, 'forbidding illegal brewing in Lusaka is now a political matter since women feed their own families, pay rent and supplement their husbands' income on the African beer they brew'. (p. 305)

It was also reported that during the 'Gorbachev Experiment', which greatly reduced legal vodka production in the former USSR, the production and consumption of home-made alcoholic drinks reached massive proportions. In many areas of Eastern Europe, the demise of the USSR has been followed by the development of what some commentators have termed a 'wild market' in alcohol. It has been reported that there are large-scale black markets operating in some countries, so that in countries such as Lithuania, Latvia, Russia and the Ukraine, official figures are no longer a very useful guide. Swiatkiewicz (1995) has noted that in Russia, illegal alcohol production has developed on an 'industrial' scale. Alcohol consumption is banned in some Islamic countries, but even in these

Table 1.1 Alcohol Consumption Per Head in Selected Countries (1970–93) (Litres of 100% alcohol)

Country	*1970*	*1975*	*1980*	*1985*	*1989*	*1990*	*1991*	*1992*	*1993*
Argentina	–	–	11.5	8.8	7.6	7.6	8.2	7.8	7.7
Australia	7.8	9.2	9.4	9.2	8.6	8.4	8.1	7.8	8.3
Austria	10.3	11.0	11.0	11.3	12.0	11.9	12.1	11.9	11.8
Belgium & Lux	9.0	10.6	10.9	10.6	9.6	11.1	10.6	10.8	10.6
Brazil*	0.7	1.0	1.3	1.4	2.4	2.5	2.3	2.0	2.0
Bulgaria	6.7	8.2	8.7	8.8	9.3	9.4	8.2	7.1	6.0
Canada	6.4	8.3	8.7	8.0	7.8	7.3	7.0	6.5	6.2
China	–	–	–	–	–	–	–	–	3.2
Chile*	5.6	5.4	6.4	5.5	4.2	4.5	4.5	4.5	3.3
Colombia**	1.4	1.4	1.8	2.3	2.4	2.5	2.1	1.4	1.7
Denmark	6.8	8.8	10.9	10.6	9.6	11.1	10.6	10.8	10.6
Finland	4.3	5.9	6.1	6.3	7.7	7.8	7.5	6.9	6.8
France	17.2	17.0	15.6	13.8	13.2	12.6	12.4	12.1	12.3
Germany	12.0	13.1	13.3	12.5	12.0	11.7	11.6	12.3	11.9
Greece	–	–	–	–	7.0	7.5	7.2	7.4	6.2
Hungary	9.9	11.0	12.9	12.6	11.7	12.2	12.1	12.2	10.7
Ireland (Rep.)	5.9	7.8	7.4	6.6	7.0	7.3	7.3	7.5	7.3
Italy	16.0	14.9	13.9	12.5	9.8	9.5	9.0	8.4	8.0
Japan***	4.8	5.4	5.6	6.1	6.2	6.5	6.5	6.7	6.8
Mexico	1.9	2.0	2.5	2.5	2.3	2.7	2.9	2.9	2.9
Netherlands	5.5	8.6	8.6	8.3	8.0	8.1	8.1	8.2	7.7
New Zealand	6.3	7.8	8.2	8.0	7.9	7.9	7.4	7.5	7.4
Norway	3.6	4.3	4.6	4.1	4.2	4.1	4.0	3.8	3.8
Poland	5.1	6.9	8.4	6.7	6.7	6.7	6.3	6.1	6.0
Portugal	9.8	13.1	10.8	12.9	10.3	9.7	11.7	10.7	11.4
Romania	5.8	7.3	7.6	7.4	6.8	8.5	8.6	8.7	8.6
Russia	–	–	–	–	–	–	6.2	5.8	5.9
Spain	12.0	13.9	13.5	11.8	11.1	10.8	10.4	10.2	9.7
South Africa	3.0	3.6	3.8	4.2	4.8	5.1	5.0	4.9	4.6
Sweden	5.8	6.3	5.6	5.3	5.9	5.8	5.9	6.0	6.0
Ukraine	–	–	–	–	–	–	–	–	–
UK	5.3	6.8	7.3	7.2	7.6	7.6	7.3	7.1	7.0
USA	7.0	7.7	8.1	7.8	7.2	7.4	6.9	6.8	6.6
USSR	6.5	6.6	8.5	7.1	3.8	4.8	–	–	–
Venezuela*	2.6	2.5	3.8	3.1	3.2	3.4	3.8	3.8	3.9

* Beer and wine ** Beer only *** Including sake

Source: Brewers and Licensed Retailers Association (1995, p. 78)

some alcohol consumption does take place often extremely covertly. This is generally unrecorded unless in relation to convictions for law breaking. These facts are not reflected by the type of information depicted in Table 1.1.

Finally, such figures do not provide any information about detailed drinking patterns, for example, the frequency and quantity that is consumed by different sub-groups of people within any given country. To obtain this type of information it is necessary to examine surveys and other more detailed sources.

Detailed surveys of drinking habits have been carried out in a number of countries. These provide an invaluable picture of what people *report* drinking. Such surveys have produced a wealth of information. Nevertheless, their coverage is often limited by non-contacts and refusals and some of those who do take part may provide inaccurate information because of poor recollection or by intentionally under-reporting or over-reporting what they have been drinking (Midanik 1982a,b, Plant, Peck and Samuel 1985).

Learning About Alcohol

> Gone are the days when young girls used to cook like their mothers but nowadays they drink like their fathers. (14-year-old South African). (Rocha-Silva, de Miranda and Erasmus 1996)

In societies in which adults consume alcohol, children appear to derive strong impressions about its use from an early age. Jahoda and Cramond (1972), from a study of children in Scotland, concluded that even children as young as five are able to differentiate alcoholic from non-alcoholic drinks and that young children are beginning to form impressions about adult drinking. Casswell et al. (1983), describing a New Zealand study, reported that eight- and nine-year-olds were more likely to record adverse consequences, such as intoxication, rather than positive effects, when asked to comment on adult drinking. Jahoda and Cramond also found that young girls were more likely than boys to deny that their parents drank alcohol. Moreover these authors concluded that young children of either gender were more inclined to disapprove of drinking by females than by males. A more recent British study has indicated that such prejudice persists. Indeed, this study suggested that girls were even more disapproving of female drinking than were boys (Fossey 1994). It is interesting to consider what the origins of this disapproval might be. It is probable that young children pick up their hostile view of female drinking from the adults around them. While children appear often to hold a negative view of alcohol, by the onset of adolescence, this view is reversed and is replaced by more positive attitudes. In particular, it has been noted that teenagers generally regard alcohol as desirable, a symbol of maturity and sociability (Davies and Stacey 1972).

In Britain, for example, it is not uncommon for children to be allowed to taste alcohol while quite young, often at the age of nine or ten. Most of these early experiences are facilitated by parents or other adult relatives (Plant, Peck and Samuel 1985). The minimum legal age for alcohol consumption (outside licensed premises) is five, so it is not illegal for children above that age to taste alcoholic drinks. 'Regular' drinking amongst teenagers in the UK begins to become established at around 13–14 years of age and above and becomes increasingly commonplace amongst older teenagers. Younger teenagers are likely to drink at home or with family members. Older teenagers are increasingly likely to drink outside their parental homes, with friends, and often to consume alcohol in licensed premises, while legally under age to do so (May 1992, Plant and Plant 1992, Lister Sharp 1994). Surveys indicate that teenage boys are more likely to drink than teenage girls and that the males also consume greater quantities of alcohol. For example a Scottish survey of 15- and 16-year-olds found that 54% of males and 43% of females had consumed alcohol in the past week. The mean level of alcohol consumption amongst those who had drunk in that period was 18 units for males and 9 units for females. (A 'unit' or standard UK drink contains 7.9 grams or one centilitre: equivalent to a standard half pint of beer/lager/cider or a single public bar measure of spirits or a glass of wine. It should be noted that a standard UK drink is smaller than those in some other countries. For example, a standard drink in the US contains 14 grams, while those in Canada are 13.6 grams and those in Australia and New Zealand contain 10 grams of alcohol (Stockwell and Single 1997).)

Loretto (1994) has compared the drinking patterns of 11–12 and 15–16-year-old Scottish secondary (high) school students with their counterparts in Northern Ireland. This showed that girls were significantly less likely than boys to have consumed alcohol recently, but the gender difference was especially great in Northern Ireland. A survey of teenagers in the Western Isles of Scotland (Anderson and Plant 1996) showed that 19% of girls and boys had never drunk alcohol. This is a very high level of abstention, which is atypical of the UK as a whole. This study, like that by Loretto, also indicated that females were significantly less likely than males to have drunk recently. Most of those surveyed reported drinking only modest quantities. Even so, a remarkably polarised pattern of drinking and non-drinking was evident. While a high proportion reported being non-drinkers, at the other extreme, a high proportion also reported having consumed considerable quantities of alcohol. Amongst the drinkers, 32.3% of girls and 38.8% of boys reported having consumed 11 units or more on their last drinking occasion. These are far higher proportions than had been reported by teenagers in earlier British surveys (Plant et al. 1991, Plant and Foster 1991, Anderson and Plant 1996). A UK-wide survey of 15- and 16-year-olds (Miller and Plant 1996) showed that only 5.8% of respondents had never consumed alcohol. Many of the non-drinkers attributed their abstention to religious beliefs, often Muslim. Girls reported significantly lower levels at last occasion's alcohol use than boys. Girls also reported having first tried beer and wine later than boys. In addition, this study found that girls in Northern Ireland were less likely to drink than those in England, Scotland and Wales. The proportions of abstainers in this study were: 15% (Northern Ireland), 6% (England), 4% (Scotland) and none in Wales. Over three-quarters of these young women reported having experienced intoxication and more than half had consumed five UK 'units' consecutively within the previous 30 days. A study of drinking by British teenagers (excluding Northern Ireland) has been described by Goddard (1996). This and other British studies, showed that most teenagers had not drunk heavily in the previous week. Even so, a minority did report consuming considerable quantities. Boys were twice as likely as girls to report having consumed 15 units or more in the past week. Goddard further noted:

> These differences in alcohol consumption between boys and girls are consistent with differences established in surveys of adult drinking behaviour – young men aged 16–17 drink roughly one and a half times as much as young women of the same age. (p. 6)

A Dutch study by van de Goor (1990) examined situational influences on adolescent drinking behaviours. This work supported the conclusion that a number of environmental factors influenced drinking patterns. These included music sound level in bars, day of the weekend and the composition of drinking groups. This study also showed that adolescent girls drank 25–30% more slowly than the boys. The drinking environment appears to have considerable importance in influencing alcohol consumption patterns (Graham 1985, Graham and Homel 1996). This is referred to further in this chapter and in Chapter 7.

Goddard reported that the average number of drinks consumed among teenagers increased rapidly with age. A similar trend has also been noted by other authors (Plant, Peck and Samuel 1985, Anderson and Plant 1996). Goddard found that rather fewer teenagers in Scotland had drunk in the previous week than had done so in England and Wales. She also found that both girls and boys in Scotland were more likely to have consumed spirits than their counterparts in England and Wales. Teenagers of either gender who drink heavily are also more likely than others to smoke tobacco and to use illicit drugs. This conclusion is supported by many studies (Plant and Plant 1992). Information from a survey of 14–16-year-old school pupils in England showed that heavier drinkers, both females and males, were more likely than others teenagers to have most recently drunk with friends rather than with parents. Heavier drinkers were also especially likely to have last drunk outside their homes and in licensed premises, even though those surveyed were all under age for this activity. Female heavy drinkers were less likely than other females to report that their parents or guardians would object to their consuming alcohol with a meal. There is some evidence that female drinkers 'mature' or at least reach an adult drinking level earlier than young males. A Scottish follow-up study (Plant, Peck and Samuel 1985), indicated that females aged 19–20 consumed no more in the past week than they had when surveyed at the ages of 15 and 16. In contrast male drinkers in the same study had increased their previous week's alcohol consumption by a third. These findings could reflect the earlier maturation of young women, combined with the fact that some 15–16-year-old females drink with older males. Against this, the study did not demonstrate that 15–16-year-old females were more likely than males of the same age to have been drinking in bars.

It should be noted that in the US the minimum legal age of alcohol consumption or purchase has been raised to 21. In spite of this, recent studies have shown that drinking is widespread amongst US teenagers and especially in the age range 18–20 years (Johnson et al. 1994). A South African survey of black youth indicated that 34–51% of those in a number of different groups (urban, rural, squatters) of young women were abstainers. Urban women were the most likely to drink and females were more likely than males to drink either wine or cider. Drinking amongst young women was associated with a number of social occasions:

> Female drinkers in the age group 18–21 years were especially those who reported that they attended *festivities*/gatherings (such as birthday parties, weddings, and the unveiling of tombstones) in the 12 months before the survey. (Rocha-Silva, de Miranda and Erasmus 1996: 43)

Risk Taking and Sexual Behaviour

As described above, there is evidence to support the conclusion that young men and women who drink heavily are also more likely to smoke and to use illicit drugs. This phenomenon has been noted for a considerable time (Goode 1972, Plant 1975). Jessor and Jessor (1977), commenting on mainly US evidence of youthful risk behaviours, including drinking and illicit drug use, described a 'Problem Behaviour Theory'. This suggested that young people raised in homes characterised by heavy or problematic drinking, illicit drug use or criminality, for example, would be at heightened subsequent risk of engaging in similar risk behaviours themselves. Many other studies have also noted an association between youthful heavy drinking and other forms of drug use. Moreover, as noted above, there is evidence that individuals may be adversely affected by parental heavy drinking or alcohol-related problems. One review of this topic concluded:

> The epidemiologic evidence from several countries shows significant points of agreement. Problem drinking by a parent markedly increases health risks to children and adolescents. Such risks include diminished intellectual capacity and development, increased neuroticism, and a wide range of psychological and behavioral disorders.
>
> Parents who drink excessively are also likely to have children who experience long-term adverse consequences. These include heavy and problem-causing psychoactive substance use, criminality, suicide, depression, personality disorders and psychological and behavioral disturbances. Parents who drink heavily are also especially likely to produce children who subsequently abstain from alcohol or drink only lightly. (Plant, Orford and Grant 1989: 433)

This will be discussed further in Chapter 4. The connection between levels of alcohol consumption and other forms of risk or health-related behaviour has been the focus of considerable attention. This has been given a major impetus by the advent of the HIV/AIDS pandemic and by suspicions that drinking might increase the chances of people engaging in unsafe sexual behaviour. In fact, fear of loss of control has been highlighted as an important reason why females might avoid drinking heavily. In a sexual context, there is sometimes fear that drinking might foster disinhibition which in turn might promote the risks of pregnancy or sexually transmissible disease (Room and Collins 1983). The historical background to women's drinking is discussed in Chapter 2. Ridlon (1988) has made the following comment on the antiquity of the alcohol–sex connection in a paragraph entitled 'Sexual promiscuity: the drunken slut':

> From the beginning of civilization, there has been a connection between drinking and involvement with sex. Wine drinking by women was punishable by death in early Rome because it was believed to be linked directly with adultery. It was feared that if a woman opened herself to one male vice, drinking alcohol, she might open herself to another, sexual promiscuity. (pp. 27–8)

An influential US study by Stall et al. (1986) indicated that gay men who had preceded sex by drinking or using drugs such as marijuana (cannabis) were more likely to have engaged in 'high risk' sexual activities than men who had not drunk or used drugs immediately prior to sex. This study raised the spectre of vastly heightened levels of sexual risk-taking by females as well as males as the direct result of commonplace recreational drug use. The publication of these results led to an upsurge in attention to the possible role of alcohol consumption in relation to risk taking, and in particular to sexual behaviour and the risks of HIV/AIDS (Robertson and Plant 1988, Leigh 1990a, Morgan-Thomas 1990, Plant and Plant 1992, Donovan and McEwan 1995, Stall and Leigh 1994, World Health Organization 1994a, Plant 1996, Rhodes 1996, Traeen and Kvalem 1996). Overall, this now considerable body of evidence has produced rather surprising results. The main two general conclusions are, first, that amongst heterosexual women and men, those who drink more heavily are more likely to have early sexual experience, to have sex with a greater number of partners and to have unprotected sex. Results amongst gay men are more equivocal in this respect. Second, it appears that most studies, though by no means all, have found that drinking prior to sex does *not* make an individual more likely to take risks. These conclusions may appear confusing. They imply that some people are in general more predisposed to take risks and that these women and men are more likely to take a number of risks in different areas of their lives. Conversely, people who do not normally take risks will not start to do so simply because they have been drinking. A host of cultural and psychological factors influence both drinking and sexual activity. Drinking, illicit drug use and sexual behaviour are associated with a number of lifestyle factors, as emphasised by Traeen and Lewin (1992). The latter include peer group affiliations, smoking, level of education and the frequency of visiting places such as bars or discotheques. Traeen and Kvalem (1996) concluded that amongst Norwegian teenagers sex under the influence of alcohol was associated with failure to use contraception. These authors make a number of pertinent comments on their findings: 'the consumption of alcohol before sexual intercourse is not in accordance with the socially accepted sexual script' (p. 1004). These authors further noted:

> The results showed that girls who had problems enjoying sexual intercourse were more likely to have consumed alcohol prior to the intercourse, and less likely to have used contraception, than girls in general. That girls who have problems enjoying intercourse drink alcohol before sex may reflect a belief that alcohol enhances sexual pleasure. (p. 1005)

This view echoes that of Klassen and Wilsnack (1986) who suggested that females who view alcohol as disinhibiting may consume it to become more free sexually. This issue will be discussed further in Chapter 4. A report by the World Health Organization (1994a) acknowledged that the possible connection between drinking and sexual risk-taking was not an easy one to understand. It also concluded that women might be at increased risk of HIV infection in drinking situations because of:

> complex gender and power dynamics at play in social and sexual contacts. Males may assume that female intoxication is associated with sexual promiscuity and that drinking makes females more vulnerable. (p. 16)

The relationship between sex and drinking is complex. In many cultures drinking is linked with sexual encounters, or at least the search for sexual partners, for a host of social as well as psychological reasons. Some drinking establishments have explicit sexual functions and cater for specific sexual orientations or tastes. It is commonplace for dating to involve alcohol consumption (Cavan

1966, Audience Selection 1993). Many people believe that alcohol is a sexual disinhibitor, and that as such, its use will relax themselves or their intended partners. Studies in the US and Britain have indicated that many young women and men believe that they were more inclined to take sexual risks after drinking than they would otherwise have been (Hingson et al. 1990, Bagnall and Plant 1991a). Leigh (1990b) has reported that gay men and lesbians have stronger expectancies of reduced nervousness and increased riskiness than heterosexuals.

A number of studies have found that drinking is more common in initial sexual encounters than in those with established sexual partners (Temple and Leigh 1990). As Traeen and Kvalem (1996) have commented:

> Drinking in sexual contexts allows interaction by affecting the tension that may be present in the script. Drinking and/or intoxication may be of importance for feeling 'swept away', and being 'swept away' may allow a kind of 'time out' where the probability of engaging in unprotected sexual intercourse increases. In this situation, the function of alcohol may be to loosen and stretch the valid norms and rules prescribed by this sexual script. In other words, the important function of alcohol in sexual scripts may be to overcome the rules that otherwise would inhibit behaviour. (p. 1004)

Wilsnack and Wilsnack (1995) found from US surveys in 1981 and 1991 that approximately 60% of female drinkers reported that drinking reduced their sexual inhibitions. Heavier drinkers were especially likely to give such reports. These authors also note that female drinking appears sometimes to be linked with a number of sexual problems. These are discussed further in Chapter 3.

Some degree of risk-taking in various forms is a normal human activity. This very normality poses real problems for prevention and health education and these are discussed in Chapter 7 of this book. It is clear that a minority of adolescent females and other young women do drink heavily and thereby expose themselves and others to the risk of harm. It should be emphasised here, and it is elaborated below, that most of the 'alcohol problems' that afflict the young relate not to chronic heavy drinking, but to periodic heavy drinking and intoxication. Even the majority of females who generally drink in moderation may occasionally drink heavily. Some young women do so on a regular basis.

Adults

In many societies, drinking by women has not had general social support, even though females often had a major role as alcohol producers and sellers. Such traditional disapproval has, for example, been noted in Nigeria (Ikuesan 1994), Lesotho (Mphi 1994), Ecuador (Pacurucu-Castillo 1994) and Japan (Goto 1994). Even so, in many countries in which female drinking has not been considered acceptable, recent social, economic and educational changes have often been accompanied by evidence that women are becoming more likely to drink. In some countries drinking is viewed as an integral part of 'modernisation' or 'westernisation'. Such developments have been noted in countries in Africa, Central and South America and Asia, Chile (Cárdenas 1995), China (Kua 1994), and Mexico (Medina-Mora 1994).

As already noted, surveys universally indicate that when females do drink, they generally consume less than males. Wilsnack and Wilsnack (1995) have summarised a considerable body of evidence thus:

> In all countries and historical periods for which there are general population survey data, the two strongest predictors of drinking behavior are gender and age. Men consistently drink more than women, and the young drink more than the old. Meta-analyses from 39 general population surveys in 15 countries show that in every country represented, women were less likely than men to drink, to drink frequently or heavily and to report drinking-related problems. Although gender differences are robust, levels and patterns of women's drinking vary greatly between nations and within nations over time. Societies also show different levels of concern about women's drinking behavior at different periods in their history. (p. 30)

As noted above, in some societies, drinking by women has never been viewed in a positive light. Ikuesan (1994) for example, has commented that in Nigeria:

> Drinking has never been part of the acceptable social image of women; and even while it may be said that the present apparent increase in female drinking could be associated with modernisation and western influence, much of such drinking, especially among rural dwellers and illiterate females, is still somewhat occasional, private and low-profiled. (p. 942)

Gender differences in drinking habits are universally evident. These have been illustrated by many studies. A British survey of people aged 18 and above (Foster, Wilmot and Dobbs 1990), showed that while 7% of males were non-drinkers, 12% of women did not drink. In addition the proportions of males consuming larger quantities of alcohol exceeded those of females. This study also confirmed the existence of regional variations of 'heavy drinking' by females and males. The highest proportions of such female drinkers were in the outer south-east and north-west of England, while the lowest proportions were in East Anglia, Scotland and Wales.

Drinking habits of women in the US have been reviewed in detail by Wilsnack and Wilsnack (1995). They concluded that the proportion of women who drink has fallen slightly during the 1980s: 'women drinkers drank less frequently and had fewer episodes of heavy drinking' (p. 29). These authors noted that although there was great mass media concern about drinking by US women in the 1970s, evidence from surveys suggest that their alcohol consumption was relatively unchanged during this period, except for a small rise in alcohol use by those aged 35–64. They also concluded that there was no evidence of a convergence in female/male rates of drinking or heavy drinking. They cited evidence by Williams and DeBakey (1992) that there was a move towards reduced alcohol consumption in the US in the later 1980s at a time when that nation's per capita consumption was falling. US surveys conducted between 1971 and 1991 show that a substantial minority, in the region of 20–27% of younger women, did not drink, while 2–7% were variously defined as being 'heavy drinkers'. Levels of abstaining were much higher amongst older women. For example, a 1991 study (Wilsnack et al. 1992), found that amongst women aged 50–64, only 54% were drinkers, while amongst those aged 65 and over, only 30% were classified as being drinkers.

There is evidence from surveys of an increase in levels of daily alcohol consumption amongst women in Western Australia, South Australia and New South Wales between 1977 and 1983 or 1985. This increase included younger females drinking at what were defined as 'hazardous levels'. It was also noted that older females in Western Australia and South Australia were drinking less beer and that women in South Australia aged between 25 and 64 were consuming less fortified wine than comparable women had been in 1977 (Corti and Ibrahim 1990). A further major study of women in Australia indicated that 87% of those surveyed had at some time drunk alcohol. This indicated that the heaviest drinkers were those aged 17–24 (Fleming 1996).

Recent evidence indicates that there has been an increase in alcohol consumption amongst British women. Information derived from General Household Surveys shows that, over the period from 1984–94 the proportion of women aged 18 and above drinking more than 14 UK 'units' of alcohol each week had risen from 9% to 13%. The overall pattern of women's consumption during this period is shown in Table 1.2.

Table 1.2 Previous Week's Alcohol Consumption Amongst British Women (1984–94) (%).

Units	*1984*	*1988*	*1992*	*1994*
None	13	12	12	14
Under 1	24	23	23	21
1–7	41	40	39	37
8–14	14	14	15	15
15–25	6	7	8	9
26–35	2	2	2	2
36+	1	2	2	2

Source: Bennett et al. 1996, p. 124.

Information from the 1994 British General Household Survey further indicated that there were only modest regional differences in the proportions of women who were classified as heavy drinkers. Even so, there was rather more variation in the proportions who were classified as non-drinkers. These ranged from 10% in East Anglia to 20% in Greater London. The latter probably at least in part reflects the presence of women from Asian backgrounds. Not surprisingly, heavier drinking was more commonplace amongst women who were single than amongst those who were married, widowed, separated or divorced. Heavier drinking, both amongst females and males, was most commonly found amongst those in households headed by professional and managerial workers. Consistent with this fact, heavier drinking was also most common amongst those whose households had the highest incomes. Amongst women in full-time paid employment the greatest proportion who were relatively high alcohol consumers were those on the highest incomes. The same was also true amongst males. The highest mean alcohol consumption, 17.5 units, was evident amongst unemployed women, while the lowest was amongst a group classified as 'economically inactive individuals'.

Even so, the highest proportion of heavier drinkers was amongst women who were working full time. This study examined the relationship of the self-image of their alcohol consumption to details of what they had, in fact, been drinking. This analysis revealed that women who reported drinking 'quite a lot' or 'heavily' were indeed those with the highest levels of previous week's consumption (Bennett et al. 1996).

Occupation

It has already been stressed that drinking habits vary between different social groups. These variations are evident amongst different occupations (Plant 1979). A number of commentators have remarked upon the fact that, in many countries, social change has included an increase in the numbers of women in paid employment outside the home. Such transition has been accompanied by alterations in the often extremely subservient role of women. Kua (1994), for example, has reported: 'whereas in the past Chinese women would drink only occasionally in the home during festivals, today many working women frequent clubs, pubs and other drinking places' (p. 957).

Information related to occupational differences in liver cirrhosis rates and other 'alcohol-related' deaths is cited later in this chapter. This section examines some evidence from surveys of women in specific occupations. US survey data, reviewed by Wilsnack and Wilsnack (1992) suggested that women employed away from home reported higher rates of drinking and are more frequent drinkers than those who worked at home ('home-makers'). Even so, these two groups did not differ in relation to levels of heavy drinking. These authors further concluded that evidence suggested that women working outside the home were more likely to drink, not due to stress, but because of their greater access to alcohol. Some investigators have found that women are likely to drink more if they work in male dominated occupations. There is evidence to this effect, note Wilsnack and Wilsnack, from the former Czechoslovakia, Finland, Norway and the US (Haack and Hughes 1989, Hammer and Vaglum 1989, La Rosa 1990, Haavio-Mannila 1991, Kubicka et al. 1991). A survey of qualified female Scottish nurses (Plant, Plant and Foster 1991), indicated that those working in psychiatry were significantly more likely than either surgical or medical nurses to drink heavily or to smoke tobacco. It should be noted that psychiatric nursing in the UK includes a higher proportion of male nurses than medical and surgical nursing. Another Scottish study examined drinking patterns amongst female and male prostitutes in Edinburgh (Morgan-Thomas, Plant and Plant 1989, Plant 1990, M.L. Plant 1990). This showed that the women who took part in this non-random exercise included many who were heavy drinkers. Tobacco smoking was virtually universal and illicit drug use, though mainly confined to non-injected substances, was commonplace. These findings are consistent with other evidence indicating that there is a clear occupational norm that promotes the use of alcohol and other drugs. Most of the women interviewed in the Edinburgh study came from lower socio-economic backgrounds and most had left school early and without educational qualifications. This study also noted that many of those working in the sex industry often meet clients in locales such as bars, clubs or other licensed premises. Other recent British studies have drawn attention to frequent heavy drinking amongst female prostitutes in Liverpool (Morrison, Ruben and Wakefield 1994) and London (Gossop et al. 1994). The role of the bar as a sexual meeting place has been noted by many commentators (Cavan 1966, Goldstein 1979, McLeod 1982, Weisberg 1985, Plant 1996).

People drink for many reasons, including availability, social pressure and enjoyment. Two of the leading researchers into issues related to women's drinking have made the following comment about the possible association between work and women's drinking:

> When trying to explain how women's employment affects their drinking behaviour, oversimplified theories produce weak and inconsistent results. Recent research casts doubt on any simple ideas that paid employment is hazardous for women's mental health and drinking, or that paid employment is beneficial for women's mental health and drinking, or that stressful jobs increase women's risk of problem drinking. (Wilsnack and Wilsnack 1992, p. 172)

These authors emphasise that the possible impact of paid employment on women is influenced by many factors and is likely to vary markedly in different situations. The possible connection between employment and alcohol problems is discussed later in this chapter.

The Elderly

In recent years, a number of commentators have reported evidence on drinking and alcohol-related problems amongst elderly people.

Graham et al. (1995) have noted:

> It is a general finding across surveys of older people that females are more likely than males to abstain, that male drinkers consume more alcohol and that drinking declines as people age (Adams et al. 1990, Adlaf et al. 1989, Smart and Adlaf 1988, Sulsky et al. 1990, Welte and Mirand 1992). Corresponding to alcohol-use patterns, older people and females report fewer problems than do males in all age groups (Graham et al. in press, Hilton 1987, Welte and Mirand 1992). (p. 333).

A considerable body of evidence now exists about alcohol use by elderly people (Beresford and Gomberg 1995, Wilsnack et al. 1995, Adams and Smith Cox 1995). Several studies, as noted above, show that drinking declines with age, so that rates of non-drinking are much higher amongst the elderly than amongst younger adults. The elderly are also less likely than young adults to be heavy drinkers (Cahalan and Cisin 1968, Smart and Liban 1981, Adams et al. 1990, Fillmore 1987). Set against this body of evidence, some studies have found a rather different pattern. Adams and Smith Cox have drawn attention to a longitudinal US study by Gordon and Kannel (1983). This showed an increase over time in alcohol consumption levels of all age groups. This rise was also reflected, but to a lesser degree, amongst those aged 60 and above. This study coincided with rising levels of per capita alcohol consumption in the US at the time (see Table 1.1). Clearly, the elderly are likely to be influenced by national trends in alcohol consumption due to economic factors or social habits. Their drinking should, therefore, be considered in this general context (Beresford and Gomberg 1995). This topic is considered further in Chapter 4.

Alcohol Problems

Some of those who consume alcohol do so with harmful consequences. The rest of this chapter attempts to provide an introduction to evidence on the pattern of such problems. These are indicated by surveys and from information about alcohol-related morbidity and mortality. Evidence about clinical populations, women receiving treatment or counselling for alcohol-related problems, is considered in Chapter 6. It should be emphasised that 'alcohol problems' come in many forms. They include physical and psychological problems, illness, dependence, premature mortality, accidents and injuries, social and economic harm as well as that within the family or workplace and involving public disorder. Alcohol problems involve individuals, their associates and entire societies. The type of international variations in alcohol consumption that exist have been referred to earlier in this chapter and are indicated, though only in a partial way, by Table 1.1. As noted earlier, since the break-up of the former USSR, illicit alcohol production has escalated in an uncontrolled way and in some places, on a massive scale. It has been suggested, for example, that illicit alcohol consumption in Poland might be 4 litres per head (Lehto 1995). Lehto and Moskalewicz (1994) have reported that illicit alcohol production has been accompanied by the sale of drinks that are frequently toxic and contain dangerous contaminants. Instances of alcohol poisoning have been a regular feature of drinking in societies in which legal supplies are highly restricted or banned completely (see Figure 1.1). Such poisoning, sometimes with fatal consequences, has been reported in recent years from localities such as Iran and 'dry' states in India.

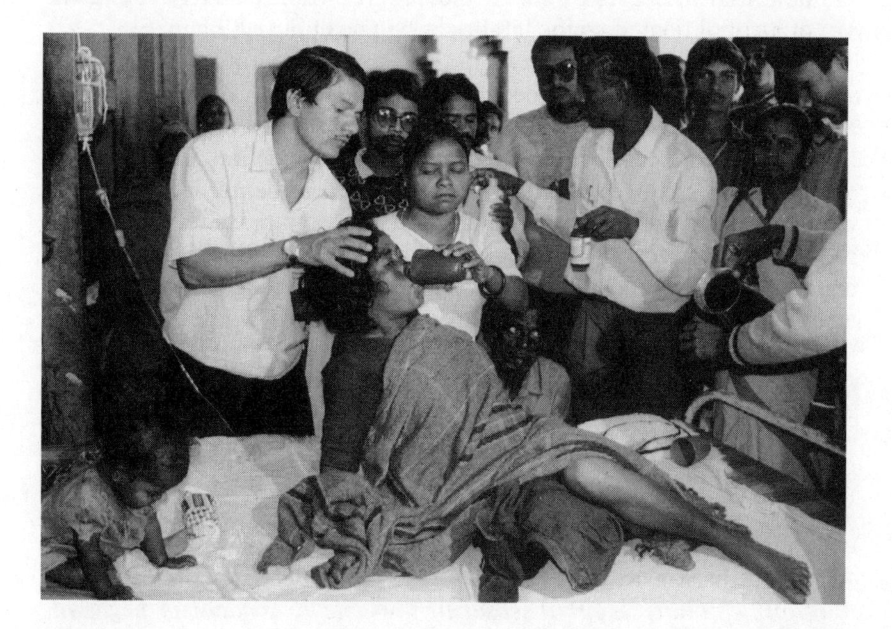

Figure 1.1 A victim of adulterated liquor is treated at Nawadha town hospital in the northern Indian state of Bihar. More than 50 people were killed after consuming adulterated cheap locally-made liquor, sometimes laced with methyl alcohol. Source: Popperfoto/Reuter.

It is very difficult to evaluate the economic costs associated with alcohol problems. Many such costs are intangible in financial terms, or are simply not recorded. A meticulous and balanced overview of the relative costs associated with alcohol, tobacco and illicit drug use in Canada has been produced by Single et al. (1996a,b). The authors of this review stated:

> It is estimated that 6,701 Canadians lost their lives as a result of alcohol consumption in 1992. The largest number of alcohol-related deaths stem from impaired driving accidents. It is estimated that 1,021 Canadian men and 456 women died in motor vehicle accidents as the result of drinking. Alcoholic liver cirrhosis accounted for 960 deaths and there were 908 alcohol-related suicides. Many of these deaths involved relatively young persons. Due to the high incidence of alcohol-related accidental deaths and suicides, the number of potential life years lost is relatively high at 186,257 (134,495 for men and 51,762 for women). This represents 27.8 years for each alcohol-related death. Motor vehicle deaths represent 22% of all alcohol-related deaths and 33% of potential life years lost – an indication of the relatively young age of alcohol related traffic fatalities. (Single et al. 1996b, p. 5)

Single and his colleagues also noted that in 1992 in Canada there were 29,602 alcohol-related hospitalisations for women and 56,474 for men. Most of these were for accidental falls, alcohol dependence syndrome and motor vehicle accidents. The authors concluded that the overall total costs per capita in Canada were $336 for tobacco, $265 for alcohol and $48 for illicit drug-related expense, a total cost of $649 per person. The greatest share of these costs, 51.8%, were associated with tobacco, while 40.8% were alcohol-related and 7.4% were associated with illicit drugs. These costs were equal to 2.7% of Canada's gross domestic product. Single and his colleagues (1996b) have drawn attention to the fact that, for some people, alcohol consumption is beneficial, rather than harmful, to their health:

> the use of alcohol is associated with decreased levels of coronary heart disease at low levels. *Indeed, the net number of deaths from coronary heart disease attributable to alcohol is negative: that is, more deaths are prevented than caused by alcohol.* However, this is small comfort to the families of those who die as the result of their misuse of alcohol. (p. 3)

These authors have elaborated on the balance between the adverse and positive effects of alcohol consumption:

> It should also be noted, however, that alcohol prevented 7,401 deaths in 1992 (5,162 males and 2,239 females). This includes deaths due to ischaemic heart disease (4,205 deaths prevented), stroke (2,265 deaths prevented), heart failure and ill-defined heart conditions (183 deaths prevented), and from various other causes (47 deaths prevented). Thus the number of deaths averted by the use of alcohol is greater than the number of deaths caused by alcohol use. However, alcohol-related mortality frequently involves young adults while the benefits of low level consumption to preventing heart disease generally involves the preventing of loss of life among older adults. Thus, the years of potential life lost due to alcohol (186,257) is more than twice as large as the number of years of potential life saved by the benefits of alcohol (88,656) ... With regard to morbidity, while alcohol accounts for approximately 86,000 hospitalizations in 1992, it is estimated that 45,414 hospitalizations (31,270 for males and 14,114 for females) were prevented by low level alcohol use in the same year ... Therefore the number of hospitalizations caused by alcohol far outnumbers the number prevented by alcohol. (Single et al. 1996a, p. 33)

This debate on the effects of alcohol will be discussed further in Chapter 3.

Young People

As noted above, during the teenage years alcohol consumption becomes increasingly widespread, so that in some countries the great majority of people are drinking regularly by the ages of 16–17, if not earlier. Surveys show that many young people periodically drink to intoxication and that some experience a range of adverse consequences associated with their drinking. It is emphasised that most of the 'alcohol problems' experienced by the young are attributable, not to chronic, prolonged, heavy drinking, but to periodic high intake. Accordingly, there are low levels of recorded alcohol dependence or liver disease among young people. An example of the type of information that has been produced by surveys of teenagers is a Scottish study already cited (Plant, Peck and Samuel 1985). This collected self-report details from 15- and 16-year-olds.

Seventy per cent of male and 61% of the female drinkers reported having experienced at least a degree of intoxication, while 25.5% of males and 22.6% of females reported having experienced a hangover in the past six months. Substantial minorities, 40.2% of males and 28.9% of females, indicated that they had experienced stomach upsets due to drinking and 2% of either gender reported missing time from school because of drinking. Some survey respondents also reported experiencing a variety of health and social problems because of their drinking. These ranged from having been advised by a doctor to drink less to being criticised for their drinking or having disagreements with parents because of their drinking. A small minority of the female drinkers surveyed reported having been worried about their drinking (3.5%), or having experienced what they regarded as alcohol problems (4.4%). The overall levels of problems reported by the females in this study, as in other studies, were generally lower than those amongst males. The latter are invariably shown by surveys to drink more than females. A number of British studies have found that 'low level' adverse consequences are commonplace amongst teenage drinkers. Marsh, Dobbs and White (1986) found that even amongst 13-year-old drinkers, the majority reported having been 'a little bit drunk' at least once in the past year. Only amongst Scottish girls was such experience confined to a minority, albeit a sizeable one (46%). By the age of 18 years, 53.59% of females had been drunk at least once in the past year. These authors also concluded that adverse consequences were frequent. This study showed that younger adolescent girls were more likely to report ill effects from drinking than were older girls. In addition, 14- and 15-year-old girls reported as many adverse consequences as boys of the same age. These investigators highlighted the fact that the pleasure and discomfort derived from teenage drinking were closely linked:

> The greater the degree of social enjoyment that adolescents recalled being associated with an evening's drinking, the more likely it was to have been followed with a disagreeable combination of sickness, incapacity and regret. Such symptoms, when they occurred often to adolescents, were closely associated with examples of antisocial behaviour when they too occurred. (p. 45)

As emphasised by Single et al. (1996a,b), a high proportion of alcohol-related traffic deaths in Canada involve young people. This appears to be true in other countries in which alcohol use is widespread. Nevertheless in many industrial countries there has been a marked decline in alcohol-related driver deaths. In Britain this has been particularly apparent amongst younger drivers. Between 1979 and 1989, for example, the proportion of car and other motor vehicle drivers killed in road accidents who were over the legal blood alcohol limit fell from 34% to 11% in the age group 16–19 years and from 42% to 24% amongst those aged 20–29 (Department of Transport 1990).

Adults

As stated periodically throughout this book, rates of most alcohol-related problems are lower amongst women than they are amongst men. A perceptive comment on this fact has been made by Fillmore (1987):

> The relative absence of heavy and problem drinking in women, compared to men, has rested on the observations that women, in this and other societies, occupy social roles which are subordinate to men, the power relations are asymmetrical, the roles of homemaker and mother are not conducive to drinkers, and the privileges of women's roles do not include drunkenness (and, in some cases, drinking). In sum, this series of explanations have suggested that women have had to swim against a tide of social norms which prevent excessive drinking. (p. 809)

Fillmore (1987) has reported that women differ from males in the development of their drinking careers and the development of alcohol problems. She noted that across most of the life course, men exhibit more alcohol involvement than women. This difference is particularly evident amongst those in their twenties:

> However, in the 30s the sex-ratio for incidence converges. This is because women are 'late bloomers' in comparison with men with regard to developing the patterns and problems measured. Men report higher levels of duration of the measures in the 40s and 50s, while women in their 30s are more likely to do so. Thus, for women the emergence and persistence of frequent and frequent heavy drinking and alcohol problems appears to occupy a smaller 'temporal space' in the life course. (p. 809)

The characteristics of problem-drinking women in clinical settings are discussed elsewhere in this book. Even so, it is useful to consider some of the available evidence related to the adverse consequences of drinking by women. As the review by Single et al. (1996a,b) has so well illustrated, with Canadian information, females constitute a minority, but a substantial one, of those whose alcohol consumption involves adverse, sometimes serious or fatal, consequences. The importance of alcohol-impaired driving has already been noted. In Britain convictions for this offence rose from 5925 in 1958 to a peak of 113,906 in 1988. Since that date there has been a decline in such convictions in England and Wales. Convictions in Scotland had been in decline since 1980. In 1993 the British total was 86,910. During the period 1958–93 the proportion of those convicted of alcohol-impaired driving who were women rose from only 1.3% to 7% (Brewers and Licensed Retailers 1995, p. 65). Figures such as these are a useful indication of the scale and trend of a problem. They do, however, also reflect police policy and changing access to motor vehicles by women drivers. In relation to drunkenness women also constitute a minority of those who are convicted. During 1992 a total of 5536 women were convicted of this offence. These accounted for 8.1% of the 68,770 people who were convicted in that year. In Scotland women constituted 11.1% of those convicted of drunkenness in 1993. It should be noted that drunkenness convictions in Britain rose during the 1960s and 1970s. In England and Wales the rate of such convictions has declined since 1989. In Scotland it has been falling since 1975 (Brewers and Licensed Retailers 1995).

It is not easy to make international comparisons between rates of alcohol-related problems. Methods of collecting and recording information differ considerably, as does the provision of health and social services or the operation of law enforcement within different jurisdictions. One indicator of alcohol-related problems is available which does provide some useful information; this relates to liver disease and cirrhosis. Table 1.3 illustrates how gender rates of mortality from these causes vary in different countries. As this shows, such rates are generally much higher for men than for women. They also have a clear association with national per capita levels of alcohol consumption – high consumption countries such as France have higher liver cirrhosis rates. The latter are associated with prolonged heavy drinking.

As the figures in Table 1.3 show, there is considerable variation in national liver disease and liver cirrhosis mortality rates. Particularly disturbing are the exceptionally high levels recorded in Hungary, where alcohol problems have been reported to be widespread and increasing rapidly (Varvasovsky 1996).

Table 1.3 Deaths from Chronic Liver Disease and Cirrhosis (1991–95) (Rates per 100,000 population)

Country	*Year*	*Females*	*Males*	*Total*
Albania	1992	3.6	8.3	5.8
Argentina	1991	3.5	15.0	8.9
Australia	1992	2.3	7.6	4.9
Austria	1993	9.8	29.7	18.9
Bulgaria	1993	4.5	22.4	13.0
Canada	1992	3.4	8.3	5.7
China*	1992	8.8	17.6	13.1
China**	1992	6.3	13.3	9.7
Czech Rep.	1993	6.0	18.8	12.0
Finland	1993	3.9	11.1	7.3
France	1992	6.6	16.8	11.4
Germany	1993	9.5	22.9	15.7
Greece	1993	2.7	9.0	5.6
Hong Kong	1993	4.2	10.3	7.4
Hungary	1993	31.4	93.9	60.0
Ireland	1992	1.4	3.1	2.2
Israel	1992	3.9	7.8	5.7
Italy	1991	9.3	22.2	15.2
Japan	1993	4.3	12.7	8.3
Kazakstan	1993	0.0	22.1	8.8
Lithuania	1993	4.5	10.7	7.2
Mauritius	1993	3.3	36.8	19.2
Mexico	1992	14.5	54.6	33.6
Netherlands	1992	2.6	4.8	3.6
New Zealand	1992	1.7	3.5	2.5
Norway	1992	2.2	4.5	3.3
Poland	1993	5.0	14.0	9.1
Portugal	1993	9.9	30.7	19.3
Puerto Rico	1992	7.3	29.8	17.8
Singapore	1992	2.0	6.2	4.0
Slovenia	1993	17.2	43.5	29.0
Spain	1991	6.8	20.9	13.4
Sweden	1992	3.0	6.4	4.6
Switzerland	1993	3.7	8.6	6.0
UK–England	1995	5.5	8.4	6.9
UK–N.Ireland	1995	3.9	4.1	4.0
UK–Scotland	1995	9.4	14.4	11.8
USA	1991	5.0	11.2	7.9

* selected rural areas ** selected urban areas

Source: World Health Organization (1994b), Registrar General for Scotland (1996), Northern Ireland Statistics and Research Agency (1996) and Office for National Statistics (1996).

It has been noted that rates of heavy drinking and alcohol problems are particularly high amongst women who have never married, the divorced and the separated. However, it is also noted that age confounds such differences: 'the young are more likely to have drinking problems and to be never-married, while the aged are more likely to abstain or drink little and to be widowed' (Wilsnack and Wilsnack 1995, p. 40). These authors have provided an invaluable and detailed review of evidence on the profile of women with alcohol problems. They cite US studies which suggest that such problems are especially commonplace amongst women who are cohabiting. They suggest that cohabitation rather than marriage might be an ambiguous, stressful state or that it might involve partners who are more likely than husbands to 'model and encourage heavier drinking'. They also note that unmarried women might be less tied to traditional norms related to female drinking than women who are married. Wilsnack and Wilsnack (1995) also note that most US surveys have shown that heavy or problem drinking is especially prevalent amongst women who are divorced or separated. They emphasise that such evidence fails to indicate cause and effect. Even so, they cite evidence showing that divorce predicted subsequent increases in drinking amongst females. Considering available evidence, including their own substantial research, they concluded: 'It appears that marital dissolution can have several different relationships with women's problem drinking, depending on the marital and drinking histories preceding the break-up' (p. 41).

The survey of Australian women by Fleming (1996) has been cited above. Using an assessment scale known as the AUDIT, over a third of the women in that study were categorised as 'hazardous' drinkers, 4% were classified as drinking 'harmfully' and 1% were classified as being 'dependent'. The highest proportions of hazardous, heavy or dependent drinkers were amongst those aged 17–24 years. Older females had lower rates of such 'problematic' drinking. This study also indicated that the heavier drinkers were more likely to be single and in a de facto relationship. Fleming also noted:

> The percentage of Australian women scoring positive on the AUDIT is lower than that reported by Holmila's studies of Finnish women. She found between 9 and 10% of women aged 20–64 scored 10 or more on the AUDIT (Holmila 1993, 1995). (p. 1331)

Romelsjö and Lunberg (1996), reviewing Swedish evidence, have reported that alcohol-related deaths amongst women have increased more rapidly than amongst men. Moreover, the women most at risk in this respect were those 'outside the labour market'.

It has often been noted that women are not supposed to lose control. Ikuesan (1994), writing about drinking by women in Nigeria, has noted:

> Suffice it to say that in Nigerian society, alcohol is seen as a social drink and alcoholic intoxication is pardoned only as a masculine feature. The woman is idealised and her role in the total social scheme is circumscribed, with alcohol being no part of the picture ... A woman who misuses alcohol, therefore, would be regarded as having betrayed her sanctity and as having fallen from a glorious Olympian height to the level of the gutter. (p. 942)

The same author goes on to note that disapproval of problematic drinking amongst Nigerian women exists in the context of their major role in the production of traditionally brewed rural alcohol. Ikuesan observed that alcohol problems amongst Nigerian women are rare, but that there has been a 'silent increase' in alcohol use, and its associated problems, amongst women. Nigerian women who do develop alcohol problems are subject to stigma and insult. The position of women with alcohol problems in Lesotho has been discussed by Mphi (1994). This author notes that there is a vicious circle in which women are brewers and sellers of alcohol and sometimes become heavy drinkers because of pressures exerted by their husbands. The subordinate position of females in this society causes further hardships. However, the possession by women of skills such as brewing and making pots may be all that stands between a family and starvation. A woman with drinking problems is likely to be stigmatised and rejected by her family.

> When angels fall, they fall disturbingly far ... A woman known to be abusing alcohol is seen as degraded and is regarded as an irresponsible woman. Such a woman brings shame not only on herself, but on her entire family, so much so that her children will at all times carry this shame into adulthood and will be stigmatised as being 'children of an irresponsible woman'. (p. 946)

The position of Ecuadorian women with drinking problems has been described by Pacurucu-Castillo (1994). This commentator has noted that westernisation in that country has made the norms about female drinking more flexible, but that female intoxication or alcohol dependence are still regarded as being shameful. Women with alcohol problems are frequently beaten and abandoned by their spouses. The severe disapproval of female problem-drinking is also a feature of Japanese society. Goto (1994) has reported that few female problem-drinkers are identified in Japanese hospitals. This, it is suggested, reflects the fact that few Japanese women develop such problems and that those who do are subject to great hostility.

Victimisation and Sexual Problems

The topic of sexual risk-taking has been considered earlier in this chapter. Many commentators have highlighted evidence suggesting that women who drink heavily are at risk from violence, including sexual, assault and abuse. First, heavy drinking has often been linked with the perpetration of assault and abuse. Men and women who drink heavily or who are alcohol dependent may be more likely to inflict such violence upon others (Collins 1982, Pernanen 1991, Odujinrin 1993, Bergman and Brismar 1994, Spacarelli et al. 1994, Turnure and Young 1994). The victims of violence are also especially likely to have been drinking (Lindqvist 1991). Many studies have noted an 'association' between drinking, especially heavy drinking, and violence.

The relationship between alcohol consumption and behaviour is complex. It is influenced by many factors, including social and contextual factors. Women in bars or other public places may be vulnerable to attack from strangers, but those in the home are vulnerable to assault from fathers, partners or other family members. It is possible that males may perceive women who have been drinking as easier prey for assault, sexual or otherwise. As noted earlier in this chapter, it has been suggested that drinking women are sometimes viewed by males as being more likely to be sexually available or acquiescent. Hamilton and Collins (1982) have stated that the involvement of alcohol in family violence ranged from 6% to 67% and that such involvement was generally lower in relation to child abuse than in relation to wife beating. They concluded that alcohol might sometimes be a causal factor in violence, but that there was little to explain how alcohol might influence family violence. There is evidence to suggest that individuals who have been subject to abuse or violence when young or earlier in their lives are at risk from the subsequent development of alcohol problems (Kilpatrick et al. 1992, Ireland and Widom 1994, Christensen 1995, Arellano 1996).

Wilsnack and Wilsnack (1995), have commented:

> physical and sexual victimization in childhood increase women's risks of later alcohol abuse in ways that are not explained by family histories of alcohol problems or by other background factors. (p. 49)

There appears to be a connection between heavy and problem drinking in women and sexual dysfunction. Wilsnack and Wilsnack (1995), reviewing evidence on this topic, concluded that: 'Amongst the heaviest drinkers, drinking may be both an attempt to self-medicate sexual problems and a cause of worsened sexual difficulties' (p. 48). These topics are discussed more fully later in this book. General population survey information described by the Wilsnacks (1995) showed that a high level of sexual dysfunction was the best predictor of continued heavy drinking amongst women. These authors also found that: 'problem drinkers who divorced or separated between 1981 and 1986 were more likely to report remission of problem drinking if their 1981 marriages had been sexually dysfunctional' (p. 48).

Alcohol Problems in Lesbian Women

A number of studies have concluded that gay men and lesbians have high rates of alcohol problems (McKirnan and Peterson 1989, Paul, Stall and Bloomfield 1991). Even so, as Wilsnack and Wilsnack (1995) have commented, some of the earlier findings in this connection were certainly distorted by the fact that some of these studies were carried out with individuals who had been contacted in bars. More recent investigations have also found rates of heavy or problem drinking to be higher amongst gay men than amongst heterosexuals. The Wilsnacks noted that little recent research has been focused on lesbians. However, they cited a Chicago study by McKirnan and Peterson (1989) which found that lesbians, though not heavier drinkers, reported experiencing more alcohol problems than heterosexual women. The Wilsnacks also noted that in both their study and that in Chicago, lesbian drinking did not decline amongst older women as it generally does amongst heterosexuals: 'In fact, daily drinking in the national lesbian sample *increased* with age, from 3% of women aged 17 to 24 to 21% of women aged 55 and older' (p. 48).

A number of factors are likely to foster heavier drinking

amongst gay men and lesbians. In most societies, such people are the victims of hostility, prejudice and often severe discrimination. Homophobia is widespread and in many settings, gay and lesbian people have responded to this by developing their own social groupings and meeting places. The latter often include bars, clubs or other licensed premises in which regular/heavy drinking is likely to be encouraged, or at least accepted. Leigh (1990b) found that lesbians and gay men who were heavier drinkers appeared inclined to believe that drinking would affect their sexual behaviour. The Wilsnacks have commented that it is not easy to identify specific risk factors associated with lesbian heavy drinking or alcohol problems. They noted that the Chicago study indicated that alcohol problems amongst gay men were associated with alienation and discrimination, but no such connections were evident amongst lesbians. The Wilsnacks (1995) cite evidence showing that 'alcohol abuse' amongst lesbians has been associated with 'underemployment, a heavy drinking partner, physical or sexual abuse, and a relationship of violence' (p. 48).

Occupation

As already noted, drinking habits have long been noted to vary amongst those in different occupational groups. Occupational variations have also been reported in relation to rates of alcohol-related problems (Plant 1979, Hore and Plant 1981). The 'conventional' picture is that males in jobs such as alcohol production and distribution, the hospitality industry, medicine, the armed forces and in seafaring have high rates of liver cirrhosis, mainly attributable to heavy drinking. Recent information for women in England and Wales has shown that high rates of mortality from alcohol-related causes was evident amongst those in artistic and literary occupations, publicans and bar staff and, curiously, hairdressers. The types of mortality that were cited in this context were cancer of the oral cavity, pharynx, oesophagus, liver, larynx; liver cirrhosis, and other alcohol-related diseases. Accidents were also included, primarily falls on stairs (Drever 1995).

The Elderly

One recent review of drinking amongst elderly people in the US concluded that as many as 10% were 'heavy' or problem drinkers.

The commentators also noted that as the numbers of elderly people are increasing, there is likely to be an increase of people in this group who drink heavily or develop problems. They also draw attention to the fact that the proportion of the population who are female increases with age due to the earlier average mortality of men (Adams and Smith Cox 1995).

Conclusions

There is now a huge and rapidly expanding literature related to the consumption of alcohol by women and its associated problems. This chapter has only made direct reference to a tiny part of this massive and daunting body of work. In spite of this, it is hoped that the material presented above will have provided the reader with an introduction to some of the issues as well as some of the evidence that has been accumulated on this topic over recent years. It was a common lament at conferences that 'very little has been done on women and alcohol'. This is clearly no longer the case, in many industrialised countries at least. Social, political and economic changes have in many places released greater economic freedoms for women. In spite of this, women's social, political and economic positions are generally secondary to those of males. While, in many contexts, women have greater access to alcohol, more purchasing power with which to buy it and more freedom to drink it, double standards persist. The latter often involve the supposition that a drinking woman might be sexual 'fair game' as well as extreme prejudice and discrimination if women drink heavily, become intoxicated or develop alcohol problems. It is clear that, in general, women are more likely than men not to drink at all. Those women who do drink generally consume much less than men. Females also experience much lower general rates of 'alcohol problems' than males. The rest of this book will attempt to consider some of these issues related to drinking and its associated consequences in women.

2 Alcohol Throughout the Ages

As noted in the previous chapter, alcohol consumption has long been a feature of many societies. Evidence that wine was in ancient use has been reported from the archaeological remains of a Neolithic village in northern Iran dated around 5400–5000 BC (McGovern, Glucker and Exner 1996).

The Roman Empire was a wine drinking culture. The Romans carried and planted the vine all over Europe, as they invaded and settled. They worshipped Bacchus, the god of wine. In relation to women, as noted by Purcell (1994):

> The most detailed account is to be found in the encyclopaedia of Pliny the Elder, the *Natural history* (xiv, 89–90): 'It was not permitted to women at Rome to drink wine. We have found among the collections of useful examples the case of the wife of Egnatius Maetennius who was clubbed to death by her husband for drinking wine from the jar: he was acquitted of her manslaughter by Romulus. Fabius Pictor wrote in his *Annals*, of a lady who broke the seal on the cupboard in which the keys of the wine-cellar were kept, and was compelled by her relatives to starve herself to death. Cato wrote that this was the reason why close relatives give women a kiss – to see if they smell of wine ... Domitius ruled as judge that a woman appeared to have drunk more wine than could be excused for medicinal reasons, without the knowledge of her husband, and fined her of her dowry.' (pp. 195–6)

This differentiation between the medicinal use of alcohol and its more common recreational consumption is found throughout history.

In Ancient Greece women were often portrayed in comedy as drunks (Just 1991). The belief that women who were intoxicated could be regarded as funny, is probably equivalent to historically later cartoons and impersonations in which characteristics, physical or otherwise, are exaggerated. However, it is rare in most 'Western' countries today for the character of a drunken woman to be viewed as a figure of fun. Words used now would be those such as pathetic, sad, even disgusting, but not funny. At that time according to Just (1991): 'Dipsomania was seen as the standard female vice' (p. 163).

Ehrenberg (1974) cited by Just (1991, p. 186) suggests another reason: 'The countless suggestions in comedy of women's love of drink, however much exaggerated, cannot have been without some real basis; wine might be a consolation in their frequent loneliness' (p. 202). The relationship of women and wine was also found in Greek classical plays. As noted by Just (1991) in relation to Dionysos: 'In the classical period Dionysos was honoured as a god by all ... in myth it was women who first felt Dionysos' power' (p. 253).

Just continued, describing the Bacchai of Euripides:

> For Pentheus, the Theban women's worship of the new god is but an excuse for some drunken libidinous orgy: I happened to be away out of the city but reports reached me of some strange mischief here, stories of our women leaving home to frisk in mock ecstasies among the thickets on the mountain, dancing in honour of the latest divinity. A certain Dionysos, whoever he may be! In their midst stand bowls brimming with wine. And then, one by one, the women wander off to hidden nooks where they serve the lusts of men. Priestesses of Bacchus they claim they are, but it's really Aphrodite they adore. (p. 253)

It is interesting how it seems more acceptable to be 'into Bacchus' than into the idea of free love. This seems to be a case of the lesser of two evils. It would appear that this view of women was common, that any combination of women and wine was automatically wrong and the outcome would be in some way bad. Links were made with Artemis, the most popular Greek goddess whose followers were seen as following nature and its cycles, leaving behind the social mores of the time.

Roman women were involved in the day-to-day running of taverns. At that time these establishments were clearly identified as the place to find women working in the sex industry (Purcell 1994, p. 203). In view of the social position of women at the time it is interesting that females used their housewifely skills to manage public places where wine and sex were both for sale.

The linking of wine and sexual behaviour was also evident in Greek comedies like Aristophanes. As noted by Dover:

> A famous passage from Hesiod (fr 275) relates the story in which Zeus and Hera ask Tiresias (who had been both man and woman) which sex got the most enjoyment from sexual intercourse. The answer was that men got one-tenth and women nine. (Just 1991, p. 159)

Toussaint-Samat (1994), another commentator, has written:

> According to Greek myth Dionysus transformed himself into a bunch of grapes to seduce Erigone. She later hanged herself beside the tomb of her father Icarus the first person in Attica to welcome the new god and introduce the drinking of wine. (p. 248).

However the general belief that alcohol led women into sexual abandonment was clear, as noted by Juvenal: 'When she is drunk what matters to the Goddess of Love? She cannot tell her groin from her head' (Purcell 1994, p. 200). It is interesting to think that this type of phrase would now be more commonly used about men. Even so, the 'flavour' is different. Today it might fit with the image of the macho man and be accepted. At the time of Juvenal this was not the case.

Women were excluded from many rituals due to the fact that most of these involved the drinking of undiluted wine which they were forbidden to consume. It is possible that this was because of the belief that women had magic powers and that if wine was imbibed by these already powerful and mysterious people then the spiritual/religious link between women and the gods would make men powerless. There were, however, a few cults founded by women. The cult of Bona Dea, the goddess of women, is one of the better known of these. The sacrifices carried out by this cult excluded men and it appears as though wine was also drunk, sometimes to excess. As noted by Scheid (1994): 'all the sources portray the cult of Bona Dea as an upside-down world in which women assume masculine roles' (pp. 392–3). This cult included a number of different rituals including sacrifice (of a sow) and the drinking of wine. The drinking of undiluted wine was forbidden and so in a wonderful loophole wine was simply called something else, in this case 'milk'. As noted by Scheid:

> the sacrificial banquet during which the matrons partook of the meat and wine that feel to them as sacrificial celebrants ... matrons were reputed to help themselves to a beverage they were normally forbidden to drink. (p. 392)

A more serious issue about the exclusion of women from sacrificial ritual was the fact that these times were for the benefit of the community. The exclusion of women thus meant that they were prevented from having a public voice or being visible at this level.

The practice of religious sacrifice in some countries often involved women, particularly young 'virgins', who were put to death to appease or please the gods.

Women's ritual and sacrifice have been linked both in myth and reality. Maize can be used as a base for bourbon whiskey. However, the Indians of Peru drank a beer made from germinated maize. In New Mexico the Ashiwis, ancient forebears of the Zuni Indians, told a story of the maize maidens who were very beautiful. They lived with their tribe underground.

Women were also believed to have magical powers in relation to growing crops. This probably comes from the ability to give birth. Again, as noted by Toussaint-Samat:

> if he is Peruvian he leaves his wife to sow the seed, for ever since the time of the Incas and even before, women have had the power of guaranteeing the best crops, especially after the first wife of the Great Inca sprinkled *chicha*, beer made from germinating maize, on the fields as a sacrifice. (1994, p. 168–9).

This issue of different strengths of beverages did not seem to be taken into account by the Romans (Jellinek 1976, p. 649). Given their history of travelling and conquering other lands, the production of beer would have been of little use to them at such times. They needed a beverage which was portable, relatively potent and could be preserved: wine.

Indeed, the Romans viewed countries where the preferred forms of alcoholic beverage were different from their own, as somehow of a lower order. For example, they held the Germans in contempt for drinking beer. The fact that the German people drank greater quantities of their beverage of choice led the Romans to dismiss them as drunkards. The most common family drink in Germany at the time was honey mead, a beverage traditionally made by the women. The Germans, clearly not too concerned about the Romans' view of them, retaliated in kind: 'Against wine there was first some resistance among the Germans. Caesar said that they prohibited the importation of wine fearing that it would make the men effeminate' (Jellinek 1976, p. 649).

One possible reason for concern about heavy drinking was the risk of men becoming incapacitated and being taken and sold into slavery. Even so, wine did begin to become more popular and by the beginning of the third century was being consumed in Germany by the more affluent. As often occurs throughout history, the beverage choice of the rich was related not only to the drink, but also to its rarity. Examples of this are champagne, tea, coffee and chocolate. Distilled spirits were less common and were often used for medicinal purposes. One of the traditional roles of women was the distillation of these tinctures and other healing compounds. Women were also the custodians of knowledge of the uses of these medicines. In Germany at this time brandies had quite a strong following as a medicine. Yet interestingly, as noted by Jellinek: 'Some legislation of that century indicate that brandy was used in the adulteration of wines' (1976, p. 650).

The nobles at this time and for the next few centuries were often a relatively responsible, benevolent force, and women were a powerful presence at all social gatherings. Their attendance acted as a social control. It was common for both women and men of rank to drink wine and have a 'night cap'.

Women have for centuries been involved in the process of brewing; it was part of the housewife's duties. As noted by Toussaint-Samat (1994): 'A ninth century text specifies *uxor conficit bracem* (the wife makes the mash)' (p. 180). However, they were not involved with wine making. This was regarded as the 'skilled' domain of the men.

The social order between the crown and the nobles continued to break down and extremes began to emerge. The position of high-born women became that of idealised, often untouchable, beings giving ribbons as favours to knights who fought in tournaments. The men regarded power and virility as their goals and drinking games became a demonstration of these. Some historians view this as the beginning of the rise in drunkenness which culminated in the sixteenth century in Germany. It is interesting to speculate as to whether the shift from a position of respect and acknowledgement to some degree of equality between the sexes, when both men and women had a 'night cap' of wine, to a more single-sex culture, was perhaps also a reason for the increase in male drinking at the time. The mutual support of the sexes, at least amongst the nobility, was being replaced by male domination. Indeed, there are some recorded instances of alcohol being used by families to 'encourage' daughters to behave in the way their parents wished. This was exemplified by the case of Christina of Markyate, as described by Amt (1993). This young noblewoman, born late in the eleventh century, wished to enter religious orders. Her family, however, did not agree with this and tried to encourage her to marry an eligible young man. Christina refused and the family used increasing pressure to force her to change her mind:

> The more her parents became aware of her persistence in this frame of mind, the more they tried to break down her resist-

> ance, first by flattery, then by reproaches, sometimes by presents and grand promises, and even by threats and punishment. (Amt 1993, p. 138)

On one occasion she was chosen by the family as cup bearer at a large gathering. The story continues:

> They hoped that the compliments paid to her by the onlookers and the accumulation of little sips of wine would break her resolution and prepare her body for the deed of corruption ... Against the urge to drunkenness, she opposed her raging thirst. (Amt 1993, p. 138)

It is important to remember that wine was also an essential element in the preparation of many medicinal remedies. In the twelfth century alcohol was used for everything, including 'foulness of the breath':

> 'tops of myrtle be grated and cooked in wine until reduced to one half. Let the wine be drunk on an empty stomach', to deafness, 'take the cooked fat of fresh eels, juice of caprifolium, juice of Jove's beard, and a handful of ant's eggs ... After cooking add vinegar or wine in sufficient quantity to make it more penetrating. Pour it into the sound ear and stop up the defective ear'. (Amt 1993, p. 106)

A book on everyday life in an English country house of the twelfth century shows the importance of alcohol in the daily diet:

> In the cellar or storeroom ... pure wine, cider, beer, unfermented wine, mixed wine, claret, nectar, mead, ... pear wine, red wine, wine from Auvergne, clove-spiced wine for gluttons whose thirst is unquenchable. (Amt 1993, p. 151)

Amt (1993) also reported that even swollen tonsils were treated with alcoholic beverages: 'Mugwort grated ... mixed with wine and cooked in honey' (p. 106).

A contemporary, Ullrich Von Lichtenstein, was saddened by what he regarded as the decline of this life in the latter part of the thirteenth century. He felt that the power and respect given to women, in the form of social controls, were diminishing and the attraction of drinking wine, alone or in the company of other men outside the home, was increasing.

Figure 2.1 An old woman attempting to cure her corns by drinking brandy while her feet are plunged in salt. Wood engraving reproduced courtesy of the Wellcome Institute Library, London.

Wine was also used in cleaning and stain removal. Keeping rich, heavy fabrics even vaguely sweet smelling took a great deal of time and effort. In a book entitled *The Householder of Paris* written anonymously as *A Manual for His Wife* around 1392, the remedy for oil or grease marks was given: 'Take wine and heat it until it is warm, and set the stain to soak in it for two days, if the stain is not gone have more wine prepared' (Amt 1993, p. 327).

Interestingly, this manual also gives advice to newly married women on how to treat their servants. In relation to feeding them, it recorded:

> have them seated at table, and give them to eat one kind of meat only, but plenty of it, and not several varieties, not dainties and delicacies; and order them one drink, nourishing but not intoxicating, whether it is wine or something else, but not several kinds ... Forbid them to get drunk, and never allow a drunken person to serve you nor approach you, for it is perilous. (Amt 1993, p. 328)

This control of the servants' behaviour is more prescribed and overt, but it was in keeping with the role a wife and mother had within her own family.

The size of task of brewing should not be underestimated. In large houses this was an important part of the housewife's duties. As can be imagined, accidents did happen:

> on 2 Oct. 1270 Amice daughter of Robert Bellamy of Staploe and Sybil Bonchevaler were carrying a tub ... in the brewhouse ... when Amice slipped and fell into the vat. Sybil immediately jumped towards her, dragged her from the vat and shouted; the household came and found her scalded almost to death. A chaplain came and Amice had the rites of the church and died by misadventure about prime the next day. (Amt 1993, p. 189)

Clearly brewing in at least some large houses was not carried out in small quantities.

The French heroine, Joan of Arc, was partial to wine in the form of sops – 'soaked bread'. Her favourite way of partaking of this was: 'wine put in a silver cup, into which she put only half the amount of water, and five or six sops, which she ate, and she ate nothing else' (Toussaint-Samat 1994, p. 276).

In the fourteenth century the Plague hit Europe bringing with it terror and death. People tried to protect themselves, denying their vulnerability and later rejoicing at their escape by gathering luxury goods around them. They grasped possessions in an attempt to feel protected against the 'Black Death'. For emotional support they grasped each other and then, fuelled by excesses in drinking and eating, tried desperately to celebrate life and laugh at death. Alcohol acted as an anaesthetic, removing the fear of their own mortality and the pain and sadness at the loss of loved ones. Other epidemics devastated populations throughout this time and even much later. As noted by Malcolm (1986) describing a smallpox epidemic in Ulster (Northern Ireland) in 1750:

> The increasing consumption of spirits by the young and by women particularly alarmed Henry. Most of the children of the lower people, who were seized with it first, died; which was occasioned by an unhappy practice of giving the children whiskey in order to strike out the pox as they termed it. (p. 43)

Religion was a source of support and strength to the people in many ways. Some were more practical than others in relation to health, for example encouraging the populace to drink ale. The positive part of this suggestion was that because ale was made with water which had been boiled the risk of diseases such as cholera was diminished (Toussaint-Samat 1994, p. 181). Alcohol, in the form of ale and wine, was an accepted part of the diet in both monasteries and convents. As again noted by Toussaint-Samat: 'there were nunneries where the holy sisters allowed themselves seven litres a day' (1994, p. 181). This led to a number of regulations being included in the monastic rules. One of the earliest of this kind was written in France and stated:

> let none of the sisters secretly buy wine or in any way obtain it; but if any does receive some wine, let the porteresses receive it in the presence of the abbess or the prioress, and let them hand it over to the winemistress. (Amt 1993, p. 226)

The rules went on to note: 'it will be the concern of the holy abbess to provide such wine as shall soothe those who are ill or who were raised more delicately' (Amt 1993, p. 227).

However, some of the senior members of the order were not in control of the convents. In 1249 on a visit to La Salle-aux-Puelles, a convent near Rouen, the Chaplain and the Cardinal Protector reported: 'The prioress is drunk nearly every night' (Amt 1993, p. 249).

By the fifteenth century the French writer Christine de Pizan opened up the question of the difference in perception of women between the two genders (Anderson and Zinsser 1990). Similarly, writing of an earlier period, Just (1991) described the role of women in Athens. He believed that it was 'not so much the mistakenness of presenting a male view of women, as the mistakenness of not recognising its relativity as a male point of view' (p. 3).

However, in some ways he falls into the very trap which he describes. He appears to have only partial awareness of how power affects, and is perceived by, the less powerful. For example he stated:

> before one could confidently talk of oppression, or of treatment constitutive of contempt, it would be necessary to know whether the restrictions imposed on women contravened or frustrated their own desires: whether women resented their situation and felt themselves underrated or even despised. (1991, p. 6)

This view has to be questioned, however. Generations of women have been seen and treated in such a way as to make it difficult, if not impossible for them to believe that there may be other options. Exercising choices depends not only on what may be offered, but also on a person's belief that they have a right to choose. Discussing the writing of the history of women, Duby and Perrot (1994) made the point that so little is known.

> The tenuous traces they have left did not originate with themselves – nothing knowing, nor ever letters reading – but were filtered through the gaze of the men who held the reins of power, defined official memory and controlled public archives. (p. ix)

However, as always in countries where there was some respite from the terror of the plague and war, life went on as usual. In London regulations governing the quality of produce were well established.

> Alice, wife of Robert de Caustone, appeared before Adam de Bury, the Mayor, and the Aldermen, and before them acknowledged that she had sold ale in a measure called a 'quart' that was not sealed; and also, that in the same measure there was put pitch, one inch and a half in depth. (Duby and Perrot 1994, p. 204)

The penalties for such infringement could be severe: 'for the falsehood and deceit aforesaid, it was adjudged by the Mayor and Aldermen, that the said Alice should undergo the punishment of the pillory for women ordained' (Duby and Perrot 1994, p. 205). To ensure that people would know the reason for her punishment the measure she used was tied to the pillory beside her.

It appears that by this time it was acceptable for women in England to be selling ale outside the home, and to take the consequences. What had started as a housewively task had become a trade. During the fifteenth century in Germany there is evidence of women actually training men in some of the arts of brewing (Amt 1993, p. 208).

However, by the seventeenth century this began to change. In the introduction to a reprinted version of Alice Clark's book *Working Life of Women in the Seventeenth Century* (1992), Erickson stated:

> Brewing was originally an exclusively female domestic trade; in the 1620s and 1630s it was monopolised in large scale production by men, with the specific encouragement of a government which wanted to control the taxation of ale and beer. However this monopolisation did not come out of the blue. Antagonism towards brewsters, or female brewers, is evident from at least the late middle ages. (p. xxxi)

However, in some countries, such as Africa, brewing remained the domain of women.

Figure 2.2 Native South African women brewing beer by their huts. Coloured lithograph by G.F. Angas (1849) reproduced courtesy of the Wellcome Institute Library, London.

The idea of legislation to control excessive drinking was developing in a number of countries. Patterns of consumption were giving cause for alarm even amongst the men. Ruling bodies in different countries were becoming concerned about the increase in drunkenness in the general population. One popular custom was the practice of toasting people's health. Each member of the group had to drink any toast proposed by another individual. To refuse was an insult not treated lightly. This had such a potentially wide-ranging effect that, as noted by Jellinek (1976): 'men of low alcohol tolerance sometimes declined to accept an invitation to a princely court unless they were given a document exempting them from the obligations of pledging the health' (p. 654).

Perhaps the power that women had in the past, to control excessive drinking by their very presence, was welcomed by men in ways which were never acknowledged. However, the power was gone, as were the women, to their homes. Indeed, in Germany at this time legislation was in place to make certain inns identified for the use of particular groups such as craftsmen's guilds. Women had gradually been excluded from the social heavy drinking within the home but the separation went further and men began to move outside the home into clearly identified groupings and places. Even so, German laws of the sixteenth century, which introduced measures designed to curb drunkenness, showed that this behaviour was not uncommon amongst women.

William Whately in 1617 is quite clear on the subordinate status of women in relation to men: 'The whole duty of the wife is referred to two heads; the first is, to acknowledge her inferiority; the next, to carry herself as inferior' (Keeble 1994, p. 151). William Gouge, writing five years later, brought the not inconsiderable weight of the Bible to bear, to inform women of their wifely duties:

> Object 2. But what if a man of lewd and beastly conditions as a drunkard, a glutton, a profane swaggered, an impious swearer, and a blasphemer, be married to a wise, sober, religious matron, must she account him her superior, and worthy of a husband's honour?
> Answer. Surely she must. For the evil quality and disposition of his heart and life doth not deprive a man of that civil honour which God hath given him. (Keeble 1994, p. 156)

Religion is a continuing powerful force in moulding societies. According to the 'Authorised' King James' Bible of 1611: 'A drunken woman and a gadder abroad causeth great anger, and she will not cover her own shame' (Keeble 1994, p. 79). Again the link is, however Freudian, with sexuality: 'She will open her mouth, as a thirsty traveller when he hath found a fountain, and drink of every water near her; by every hedge will she sit down, and open her quiver against every arrow' (Keeble 1994, p. 79).

By 1684, when John Gough wrote his *Academy of Complements* for the use of 'ladies and gentlewomen' he noted a popular proverb of the time: 'A woman and a glass are ever in danger'. Whether this reference related to a wine glass or a mirror is not stated (Keeble 1994, p. 76).

According to Madame de Pompadour, champagne was 'the only wine a woman could drink without looking ugly' (Toussaint-Samat 1994, p. 285).

Duby and Perrot (1994) wrote of the lack of writings by women. They stated: 'If we are to hear women's voices directly, they must first have access to the means of expression: gesture, speech, writing. Literacy is essential' (p. xiii).

Literacy was regarded as undesirable, even damaging, in women. Sadly, this is reminiscent of the situation in contemporary Afghanistan, as well as a number of other countries. In April 1645 John Winthrop wrote in his journal about the wife of the Governor of Hartford upon Connecticut. He described her illness and the reason for it. He stated the woman was:

> fallen into a sad infirmity, the loss of her understanding and reason, which had been growing upon her diverse years, by occasion of her giving herself wholly to reading and writing, and had written many books. (Keeble 1994, p. 46)

He concluded:

> if she had attended her household affairs, and such things as belong to women, and not gone out of her way and calling to meddle in such things as are proper for men, whose minds are stronger, etc., she had kept her wits. (Keeble 1994, p. 46)

The belief that a woman could write creatively under the influence of alcohol or other mind-altering substances was rare. One of these unusual examples was the case of Virginia Woolf (1984) who, in her writings such as *A Room of One's Own*, gave a personal understanding of women and drinking. This was portrayed, not negatively as described by many male writers, but in a positive light. However, it was a long time before women would take the equality issue into the realms of drinking and even then it was only women who were seen as so far removed from normal life that it somehow did not shake the status quo. One good example of this was Simone de Beauvoir. As noted by her biographer (Bair 1990) in relation to alcohol: 'Her capacity was enormous: while others fell into drunken stupors, she was still strong enough to walk back to her hotel, and the next day sober enough to keep her daily schedule' (p. 286).

In 1849 the famous woman author Charlotte Brontë published *Shirley*, albeit under a pseudonym. This book about life in Yorkshire at a time of great social change gives a fascinating insight into country life. In one incident involving a leading character she disperses a crowd by suggesting it was not a holiday. At their question, did she not think they deserved a holiday?:

> *'Never,'* was the prompt answer; 'unless,' added the 'Mistress' with a smile that half-belied the severity of her speech, 'unless you knew how to make a better use of it than to get together over rum and tea, if you are women – or over beer and pipes, if you are men, and *talk* scandal at your neighbour's expense' (1981, pp. 355–6).

Around this time in Britain, the famous artists Cruikshank and Hogarth were producing etchings highlighting the dangers of drunkenness, both to the individual, the family and the social structure

Figure 2.3 The effects of temperance on a man and his family. Lithograph c.1840, after Gunthorp, reproduced courtesy of the Wellcome Institute Library, London.

Figure 2.4 A convalescing woman trying in vain to rouse her slumbering hired nurse while the cat scavenges her food and the candle sets light to the carpet. Coloured etching by N. Heideloff, 1807, after T. Rowlandson, reproduced courtesy of the Wellcome Institute Library, London.

of the country. Almost invariably women were seen as the victims of the excesses of their husbands and fathers.

There were some women who succeeded in becoming well known for their expertise. However, some of these were well known not only for their skills. Mrs Mapp was famous in the reign of George II for setting bones. However, she was described by Gordon (1993) as: 'dressed in a loose-fitting robe-de-chambre, and manifesting by her manner that she had partaken somewhat too freely of Geneva water' (p. 102). Others, like the carer illustrated opposite, were often paid in food and drink. Unfortunately, they were sometimes paid while on duty, leaving the patient at risk. This was exactly the stereotype of the drunken nurse so often depicted by Dickens and others.

By the 1840s many women were travelling from what was then called 'Great Britain' to be with their husbands in the British Empire. There were guide books to help them live in a different country and to cope with the often arduous travelling involved in getting there. As noted by MacMillan (1988): 'ladies Cabin Baggage include ... a provision basket, with such comforts as biscuits, Bovril, whisky or brandy, and a spirit lamp for brewing up cups of tea' (p. 21).

Ladies were encouraged to take a variety of things with them when they were travelling in the countryside of India; these included 'Two pints of beer' (MacMillan 1988, p. 72). The women's drinking did not go unnoticed by other visitors to the country. A French officer noted with surprise the 'enormous quantity of beer and wine absorbed by young English women, so pale and delicate in appearance' (MacMillan 1988, p. 51).

A combination of the climate, the constant risk of uprising, boredom and what appears to be a much more relaxed attitude to drinking was noted to affect these women:

> The author of *Real Life in India*, published shortly before the Mutiny, described what could happen to a woman: 'she falls victim to indolent habits and coarse indulgences, the sylph-like form and delicate features which distinguished the youth of her arrival are rapidly exchanged for an exterior of which obesity and swarthiness are prominent, and the bottle and the *hookah* become frequent and offensive companions'. (MacMillan 1988, p. 80).

No mention of the constant childbearing and alienation which was the lot of these women. Interestingly, other women seemed more understanding: 'Mrs Ashmore in the 1840s, noticed ladies quietly downing glass after glass of champagne in an effort, she thought, "to remove the extreme depression and lassitude which are induced by the climate".' (MacMillan 1988, p. 88). This isolation and loneliness was the lot of many women in different countries. It is not surprising that, in relation to heavy-drinking husbands, a number of women worked on the principle, 'If you can't beat them, join them'.

Figure 2.5 A woman sits drinking as a man sleeps with his head on the table beside her. Engraving by L. Duval, nineteenth century, reproduced courtesy of the Wellcome Institute Library, London.

During the time of the British in India, the custom was such that even at the midday meal, large quantities of wine were often consumed. Because of alcohol's dehydrating properties, it is difficult to imagine how these women were able to remain healthy. In Britain at this time, women were drinking mainly tea with the occasional afternoon snack of cake and wine. However, the less well-to-do women in the UK were probably more likely to frequent the smaller gin shops of the time.

Figure 2.6 Three women in a gin shop divert the landlady's attention while a match boy steals her money. Mezzotint, c.1765, reproduced courtesy of the Wellcome Institute Library, London.

The traditional view of spirits as being the main alcoholic beverages used in India is based on the idea that these types of drinks survived the journey better, but for women, they did not seem to be used commonly. In this way the differences between women's drinking and men's drinking remained. It is possible that then, as now, the view that you will not develop a drinking problem unless you drink 'strong spirits' allowed British men in India to ignore any possible problems their wives may have been developing with alcohol.

However, sometimes circumstances developed in which it became impossible to ignore the fact that a woman's drinking was causing problems. In a book entitled *Mad Tales from the Raj: The European Insane in British India 1800–1858* (Ernst 1991), one solution was noted. A private clinic in Calcutta, a 'lunatic asylum' run by

Beardsmore, was a place where relatives could be sent when they became unmanageable at home. According to Ernst success of this institution 'owed much to the apparent need to "accommodate female Patients (sic) and others wishing to avoid public Exposure (sic) of a family misfortune"' (p. 121). The question of whether problem drinkers would be placed in such an institution was partly answered: 'If it is true that somatic diseases, malnutrition and alcoholism accounted for the majority of deaths and hospital admissions: then hospitalisation in the asylum on the account of mental illness was a comparatively rare occurrence' (p. 168).

To grasp the sense of how women were viewed at this time in history it is also helpful to examine the medical, as opposed to the psychiatric, literature. Women were not only victims of their male relatives but, according to the experts, at the mercy of their weak bodies. Treatments for 'women's troubles' were common and many of them sound quite barbaric now. In 1890, Dr W. Goodell, Professor of Gynaecology at the University of Pennsylvania, wrote about the abuse of uterine treatment through mistaken diagnosis. He stated:

> While the treatment of uterine diseases received a great impulse from the writings of Simpson in England, Kiwish and Scanzoni in Germany, and of Huguier and Recamir in France, it is to Bennet that we chiefly owe the common use of local applications and the popularisation of the speculum. Bennet as early as 1843 in French and 1854 in English published his work on *Inflammation of the Uterus* of which the last edition was 1861. In it he contended that the inflammation of the cervical canal is the main factor in female diseases ... and that the inflammation, being limited to the cervical canal, can readily be dislodged by strong caustics. (Goodell 1890, p. 78)

Goodell waxed lyrical about this marvellous new treatment:

> The profession was fairly taken by storm; the effect was as electric as the appeal of Maria Theresa to Hungarian nobles. From the Arctic to Antarctic oceans, from the Mississippi to the Volga, countless speculums of varied form leaped from their bags and flashed in sunlight boreal, tropical and meridian. Cauterise actual and potential, applied to actual and potential uterine sores, became the order, in fact, the ruling passion of the day ... Bennet, the medical Frankenstein, had evoked a monster which could not be curbed, and for five and thirty years the speculum ran riot. (1890, pp. 78–9)

He goes on to list the wide and varied illnesses and diseases associated with this treatment. According to many physicians, and even by:

> specialists working in other fields of Medicine, these organs are too wrongfully made the scapegoat for headaches and nape-aches, (sic) for spinal-aches and back-aches, for weakness of vision, for aural disturbances, for sore throats and weak lungs, for irritable hearts and also for a host of so-called uterine symptoms. (1890, p. 79)

Goodell's turn of phrase is refreshingly different. Describing a case of cervical fistula, a surprisingly common complaint of the time possibly due, at least in part, to the numerous pregnancies and deliveries, he stated: 'this small fistula has no more to do with the lady's general ill-health than the earring holes in her ears' (1890, p. 81).

He also acted as a consultant to various organisations and seemed to take what would now be described as a holistic view. In the case of a highly reputable boarding school for girls where an above average number of them experienced amenorrhoea or menstrual irregularities, Goodell stated:

> so many girls missed their monthly periods that the family physician of several of them wrote to me asking whether it were possible as their patients averred, 'that as their clothes were laundried (sic) in the building something was given in their food or their drink to produce the effect, for the purpose of saving the laundress the disagreeable task of washing the napkins'. My reply was, that if laundresses were acquainted with a drug that could arrest menstruation, they knew more than the profession: and that his patients had lost their monthly periods, not from secret drugs, but from loss of health due to an unwholesome system of education. (1890, p. 82)

Sometimes history repeats itself. With comments like those above one may be tempted to think that here was a forward-thinking man who could aid women in the struggle to be treated as equals. Sadly, this was not the case; his description of an 'unwholesome system of education' seems to be one which involves young women using their brains and becoming involved in 'intellectual rivalry'. Dr Goodell's main point was that much of the diagnosis of uterine disease would, more accurately, have a psychological as opposed to a physical component. For the women the choice was often of an illness which their husbands would be forced to accept unquestioningly, albeit in a rather embarrassed way, but which for the women would relieve them of the 'distasteful physical side of marriage' which, through multiple pregnancies, led to risk of their health and their very lives. Given the length of time, historically that this idea lasted, it is interesting to speculate whether there was some almost covert sexual issue in the medical profession which reinforced this.

There were a number of cases noted in the *Alienist and Neurologist*, an American journal of the time. Under the title 'Viscious therapeutics', it described: 'neurotic mammary tumours removed by uterine massage. An orgasm was produced by the manipulations' (*Alienist and Neurologist* (henceforth *AN*) 1890b, p. 254). The editorial continues: 'It degrades both physician and patient ... When, oh! when, will this needless and harmful, handling of the female genitalia cease?' (*AN* 1890b, p. 254).

Dr Goodell continued to write prolifically on the theme of diseases of women; in an editorial in 1894 he wrote:

> In the treatment of the diseases of women, at the present time, there seems to me to be tendency to lay too much stress upon lesions of the reproductive organs. Too little heed is, therefore, given to the nerve elements of women's diseases, and as a natural sequence the surgical feelers and antennae of the medical profession, always too keenly sensitive, vibrate vehemently at the approach of an ailing woman. This trend of the profession to appeal to the knife as the great panacea for women's diseases, is seen everywhere. (*AN* 1894b, p. 395)

From early history alcohol has been used in a number of conflicting ways in medicine – as an antiseptic, an anaesthetic and often as a medication. It is in this latter area that the greatest confusion arises. In 1886 a Dr Brosius presented a paper at the 'International Psychiatrical Congress' which described some of the broad range of uses of alcohol in nervous or 'psychiatrical' diseases:

> (1) The moderate indulgence in spirituous liquors is in itself never hurtful in psychoses or nervous diseases. (2) Larger doses (a pint of Rhine wine, sherry, etc.) are comparatively certain calmatives and even hypnotics in states of excitation. (3) In all patients refusing nourishment, in dyspepsia, and especially in paralytics, alcohol is a respiratory nutriment, (sic) as defined by Binz. (4) In all cases of withdrawal after morphinism, bromin-

ism, etc., to prevent collapse, a liberal administration of alcoholic beverage is necessary. (1886, p. 506)

It must remain open to question how many women developed problems with alcohol iatrogenically after some of these treatments. Although Brosius recommended high doses of alcohol, he also noted reservations about beverage type: 'Wine and beer, but not whiskies or cognacs (on account of the poisonous amyl-alcohol contained in them), are to be employed' (1886, p. 506).

As noted by Rehman (1986), British psychiatrists also had conflicting views on the uses of alcohol: 'Clouston [1904] also recommended the use of alcohol, sherry and port were freely prescribed as stimulants' (p. 112). However, Tuke, in charge of the famous York retreat in 1865, 'did not propose the use of stimulants as he believed they aggravated mania. He, however, found a limited amount of wine or whisky and large doses of morphia, beneficial in melancholic cases' (Rehman 1986, p. 112).

Again, what seems to make the difference is not only the dose, but also the beverage type. The view that some types of alcoholic beverage were health conferring, while others were potentially harmful, recurs periodically throughout history. This subject has received serious attention in the twentieth century and is discussed further in Chapter 3. Alcohol was also used for many physical ailments as well as infections such as cholera and tuberculosis. Nevertheless, according to many nineteenth-century temperance tracts, it was the responsibility of the doctors that so many people were 'taught the common use of distilled spirits ... the people did not drink them until the doctors had long given them freely as medicine' (Colman 1870, p. 18). These same doctors were requested, indeed, almost commanded, in the temperance literature to 'find some other way of treating their patients, and do not sanction the use of this terrible poison' (Colman 1870, p. 18).

Trotter, who was famous for closing 200 gin shops in Plymouth when he was stationed there, wrote *An Essay, Medical, Philosophical, and Chemical, on Drunkenness.* In it he noted one of the more unusual features of excessive drinking, that of spontaneous human combustion. It is interesting to note that the majority of cases involved women. In graphic detail, he described how over 15 women from different countries died in this way. His general observation was that there was a relationship with age: 'the combustion took place only in women far advanced in life. The Countess of Cesena was 62 years of age; Mary Clues, 52; Grace Pitt, 60; Madame de Boiseon, 80; and Mademoiselle Thuars, more than 60' (1981, pp. 86–7).

Figure 2.7 In a Café, or The Absinthe, c.1875–76 by Edgar Degas, reproduced courtesy of Giraudon/Bridgeman Art Library.

By the beginning of the nineteenth century women were beginning to be seen in the pub. It has already been noted in Chapter 1 that this was not always regarded as being a respectable type of establishment. As described by Barr (1995):

> Women were among the principal customers of the eighteenth century dram shops, and appear in the early nineteenth century to have transferred their patronage to the gin palaces. In 1828 the French sociologist Gustave d'Eichthal described these female patrons as 'a sight to be seen as they gulp down their glasses of gin, whisky, toddy and cheap brandy'. (p. 181)

This was not so common in some areas in the US. Even so, Rorabaugh (1979) has reported: 'eastern ladies drank in mixed company ... at pioneer dances the whiskey bottle was ... passed pretty briskly from mouth to mouth, exempting neither age nor sex' (p. 13). According to Rorabaugh, women would also drink when at the public baths. As noted by Powers (1995), between 1890 and 1920 women began to be seen more regularly in saloon bars. Many saloons had side doors recognised as the entrance for ladies. Powers noted: 'Through this portal passed a great many working class women ... Some were attracted by the free lunch' (p. 46). So this was not the case of sex workers (prostitutes) looking for clients, as so many myths state, but simply local women wishing to relax. Even so, it certainly was the case, then as it is now, that sex workers plied their trade in the local bars.

Interestingly, a number of temperance tracts written about the same time quote a figure of two thousand doctors who recommended total abstinence from alcohol. In 1866 the Ladies' Metropolitan Temperance Union met in Dublin, Ireland. By 1877 the Rev. David Macrae wrote a 'Temperance Catechism'. His reply to the question, referring to 'Intemperance in the Highest Circles' was:

> But surely ladies have not so fallen? Alas yes! in numberless cases. In one American asylum for the victims of drink (the asylum of Binghamton) more than 2000 of the applicants were rich men's daughters. (Macrae 1877, p. 9)

He was questioned whether the same was happening in England and Scotland. With regard to the latter country, women were again reported to be well represented amongst those with serious alcohol problems:

> Quite the same. Sherrif Bell declared in 1873 that he had received almost innumerable applications for persons, some of them belonging to the highest classes, to know what they were to do with relatives (in many cases ladies) who had become habitual drunkards, and were a horror to their friends. (Macrae 1877, p. 9)

Figure 2.8 A drunken man surrounded by women in a dingy alehouse. Lithograph, c.1840, after T. Wilson, reproduced courtesy of the Wellcome Institute Library, London.

The temperence movement would probably have been astounded by the representation of the 'Obliging Bar-maid' illustrated below.

In the same year in Ohio, USA, the Women's Crusade began, which would, a year later, become the Women's Christian Temperance Union (WCTU). As noted by Musto (1996):

> Opposition to alcohol legitimised women's participation in national political life. Because women had been relegated to defence of the home, they could reasonably argue that they had a duty to oppose alcohol and saloons – which were efficiently separating men from their paychecks and turning them into drunken menaces to their families. (p. 67)

Figure 2.9 The Obliging Bar-maid: 'Do you like it mild, sir?' Lithograph, c.1825, reproduced courtesy of the Wellcome Institute Library, London.

This was true, but women were also pushed into the temperance issue by being told they were the guardians of future generations. Some women had their sights set higher – votes for women to give them power in the fight for equality in relation to property rights, health care for the poor, etc. Another concern was, as recorded by Lender (1981): 'one of the WCTU's chief objections to the liquor traffic was its supposed ability to draw women into organised vice and white slavery' (p. 448).

Even so, women still paid the penalties for their husbands' drinking. Describing the situation in western Canada around the turn of the century, Gray (1982) noted:

> The merchants knew, as they watched the workers staggering home long after dark, which wives would be in the next day tearfully to explain they would only be able to pay something on account instead of their full bill. The distraught women seldom confessed the real reason for their plight. That would have been akin to publicly confessing the man they had married was an irresponsible wastrel. So they made excuses! In a sudden emergency they needed medicine for sick babies, a relative had become hospitalized, or had died; sometimes hospitalized one payday and dead the next. (1982, p. 24)

This isolation, by keeping secrets, still continues for some women today. Nevertheless, women were closely involved with the temperance movement, and indeed, some of the most powerful statements came from works written by women. In 1880 a Miss Firth gave a speech at the Autumn Conference of the British Women's Temperance Movement held in Bristol. Her address was entitled *Brandy: What it is, What it Does and What it Cannot Do.* In it she tells of how 'dangerous Brandy is ... It is especially enticing, because so full of fragrance and aroma that it may be considered a kind of nectar.' She goes on to describe the use women made of this beverage:

> Frequently we hear a lady say, 'I always keep a little brandy at hand, it is useful if anything happens.' Another will add, 'Yes, and I never go from home without a little in my trunk.' At a quiet country railway-station, lately, two young ladies were walking to-and-fro, waiting for the 11a.m. train, as they passed me, the younger of the two said, 'Oh, I feel so seedy after last night's ball, I don't know what to do.' 'Why,' was her friend's reply, 'have a little brandy'. (Firth 1880, p. 7)

Two years later, in May 1882 at the same annual conference, Miss Moorhouse gave a talk on *The Effect of Alcohol on the Blood*. This impressive presentation, price 'One Penny or 6 Shillings per 100', even included diagrams of the effects alcohol had on the walls of the arteries and veins and goes on to describe the damage caused to the organs of the body through drinking. This powerful campaigner gave particular attention to a plea to women: 'Of course you never intend to be drunkards, but thousands of women once as pure and strong as you are have fallen victims to intemperance' (Moorhouse 1882, p. 16).

That same year in the city of Sydney, the first Australian branch was opened (Dillon 1985).

A number of publications from the British Women's Temperance Association were published in the early 1880s, many of them giving information on the use of alcohol in the home (Best 1880, Carpenter 1880, Docwra 1880, Kirk 1880a, b, Ridge 1880, Webb 1880). Plays were performed, such as *Where there's a Will there's a Way*, described as 'a temperance entertainment arranged for five characters' (Hickey 1880). Other authors attempted to impart warnings about alcohol through the use of poems or recitations as they were called.

Julia Colman of New York wrote of the history of the temperance movement in a small catechism on alcohol published in London, England in the 1870s: 'Temperance societies were started in America in 1826, and in England in 1834 ... The Bands of Hope were started in 1846' (1870, p. 15). Her accuracy in other areas is more suspect: 'Half an ounce of alcohol will kill a child of four years old' (1870, p. 7). Perhaps her historical dates also need to be questioned. She also stated that the first law passed in the US forbidding the sale of 'alcoholic liquors' was in Maine, and that hopefully the same would come to pass in the UK: 'Sir Wilfred Lawson has proposed in the House of Commons to allow any town or neighbourhood to forbid the licensing of public houses in its own district when two thirds of the inhabitants wish the sale of liquor to be stopped, but Parliament has not yet given its consent to this' (1870, p. 16).

As noted earlier, the use of alcohol in the treatment of psychiatric disorders was widespread. Professor Tamburini, speaking at the Psychiatric Society of Italy in 1890, described a case in which alcohol reportedly drove out the devil:

> Satan himself, who, as his victim, a very intelligent and a very good woman, repeatedly affirmed, had taken up lodging in the

> roof of her mouth. The demoniacal drama went on, little changed, for two or three years, despite her earnest prayers for relief, and despite those of the regular Sabbath Day preachers ... The matron of the asylum, a very kind and sensible woman, one morning asked me if I would have any objection to allow Mamie C. a glass of toddy at bedtime ... It was done accordingly but with happier result, for in about half a year the devil was driven out by another more potent than himself. (Tamburini 1890, p. 382)

Interestingly, Tamburini advised that the treatment should continue even after the relief of symptoms: 'I did not deem it wise to withdraw the guard. From the day that old Sooty withdrew I heard him no more' (Tamburini 1890, p. 383).

By 1884, when Magnan published his *Clinical Lectures on Dipsomania* he noted Hufeland's likening of dipsomania to nymphomania. Over the course of his lectures he then proceeded to give case histories of women 'dipsomaniacs', introducing the first case by noting:

> Menstruation and the menopause have been given a prominent place in the etiology of dipsomania. Without overestimating the importance of the menses in this disease, we must admit that they exert some influence. (p. 694)

By 1894 there were a variety of substances for the treatment of neurotherapy. These included cocaine, mercury, morphine, opium and Syndenham's laudanum, a one in ten mixture of wine and opium. This was later commonly used by women for a variety of disorders such as the 'neuralgias'. This group of illnesses included features such as pains in the head and insomnia and along with the highly controversial neurasthenia were treated with laudanum. The latter condition was described as 'a disease of civilization, occurring in city life, especially amongst those who lived luxurious lives' (Johnson 1884, p. 383). The treatment consisted of rest and diet. As noted earlier this definition of rest was much more extreme than would be prescribed today: 'Some patients were much benefited by total seclusion and cutting off all outside influences, as of papers, letters and friends, and perseverance in absolute rest' (Johnson 1884, p. 383).

Indeed, many people would tolerate it no better than Charlotte Perkins Gilman described so vividly in *The Yellow Wallpaper* (1899, reprinted 1981). In fact this treatment was so extreme that only the rich could afford it. Even in relation to diet the need for money was obvious: 'The patient should be over-fed according to the recommendations of Weir Mitchell ... they should eat plenty of meat – beef three times a day – but vegetables should be limited to one at a time' (Johnson 1884, p. 384). Dr Thomas Clouston, a famous Edinburgh psychiatrist, agreed with this 'Gospel of Fatness', writing: 'All acute mental diseases tend to thinness of body, and therefore all foods and all medicines and all treatments that fatten are good' (Ferguson 1892, p. 410).

One of the original tonic wines, devised by a chemist in 1863, contained the stimulant drug coca (from which cocaine is produced). It became popular as a restorative and was certainly acceptable for women to take. Amongst the many people who endorsed the product were Queen Victoria and the famous actress Sarah Bernhardt. It may have been this wine tonic or some other similar drink which, 40 years later, inspired the invention of Coca-Cola in Atlanta, Georgia (Barr 1995, p. 14). Indeed, as also noted by Barr, the original US drink was manufactured by 'a druggist called John Pemberton. It has been suggested that Pemberton was attracted to coca by the claim it could cure opium and morphine addiction' (1995, p. 14). Pemberton himself had a drug problem and hoped that this new drink could cure him of it. It is interesting to think that one of the most famous non-alcohol drinks in the world today was designed with the purpose of weaning people off opiates! It is also notable that a number of alcoholic beverages available during the later 1990s include gaurana, a mild stimulant, sometimes, and probably dubiously, reported to be an aphrodisiac. In view of the fact that alcohol is a depressant, it is possible that the effect of such ingredients is to cancel each other out.

As noted in Chapter 5, although America was not to enter a period of industrialisation until later than the UK, the women did take part in communal working. Writing of America at this time Rorabaugh (1979) stated: 'Whiskey accompanied traditional communal activities such as house raisings, land clearings and reapings. It was even served when women gathered to sew, quilt, or pick the seeds out of cotton' (p. 19).

The habit of beer drinking in Wales was still common at this time, mainly because it was the safest beverage to drink, but by the 1870s the temperance movement was beginning to take hold (Lambert 1983).

The most colourful temperance campaigner was probably Carry Amelia Gloyd, better known as Carry A. Nation, an American, twice-married woman. Her first husband was a problem drinker who died due to his drinking and left her with a daughter, who was 'physically and emotionally damaged' (Lender 1984, p. 361). Her second husband was a minister and lawyer. Carry's claim to fame comes from her habit of attacking drinking houses, not with words as other women had done, but simply by breaking them up with an axe.

Figure 2.10 Women eject a drunk and publican from a bar in a crusade against drunkenness. Wood engraving by A. Joliet, c.1875, reproduced courtesy of the Wellcome Institute Library, London.

The fact that these tonic wines were to be taken, often on a doctor's recommendation, for health and not pleasure led to their becoming popular with women and acceptable to society at large. However, even these tonics often contained a percentage of alcohol. The well known American temperance campaigner Lydia Pinkham, famous for her Pinkham's Tonic, spent most of her time denouncing the evils of drink and the rest, advertising and producing her highly popular remedy. A brief look at the *Anti-Saloon Year Book* of 1909 shows the alcohol content of some of these 'tonics'. Lydia Pinkham's tonic contained 20.6% alcohol. Some of the others were even stronger: Colden's Liquid Beef Tonic contained 26.5% alcohol and was advertised in the *Anti-Saloon Year Book* as 'recommended for treatment of the alcohol habit' (1909, p. 242). Amongst the strongest were Richardson's Concentrated Sherry Wine Bitters (37.5%), Parker's Tonic, described as 'purely vegetable' (41.6%), Boker's Stomach Bitters (42.6%), and Hostetter's Stomach Bitters (44.3%).

The habit of drinking Pinkham's Tonic continued into the twentieth century and actually expanded. By the 1920s in western Canada, Gray (1982) noted that young women going to dances would refuse to have a drink out of a partner's flask, but:

> If they were going to drink, they wanted something diluted, that tasted nice, or at least familiar – like Tanlac, Lydia Pinkham's, or the other alcohol based 'women's tonics' to which many of the older women were unawaredly addicted. (p. 54)

It is interesting to note that at this time, as today, alcohol was perceived, wrongly, as a stimulant. Ferguson in 1892, lecturing in the University of Toronto, presented a number of cases of insanity following exhaustion. One of the women presented was a case of typhoid fever. The treatment was a combination of chloral and 'alcoholic stimulants' (Ferguson 1892, p. 428). Confusingly, the purpose was to sedate. He goes on to expand on this and it becomes clearer: 'alcohol in large doses is a powerful narcotic' (p. 436).

It is important to be aware that at the time when prohibition was gaining popularity people really did see a difference between drinks containing alcohol taken for medicinal purposes and those taken for pleasure. In view of the increased cost of alcohol at this time, taking alcohol as a constituent of a tonic meant that it was affordable. The ban on alcohol in Atlanta, Georgia, which occurred in 1886, did not include these wine-based medicines (Barr 1995). Thus, even at a time when men were banned from drinking, women could still have their restorative tonics.

Indeed, this even gave a loophole to some of the temperance organisations. In Birmingham, England, a Female Temperance Society (1836) abided by the rules which included: 'We agree to abstain from all intoxicating liquors, except for medicinal purposes and in religious ordinances'.

Alcohol was still used as part of the treatment of choice for many conditions which were seen as particularly female; for example: 'for hysteria, the mixture of alcohol, valerian and antikamnia, to be given one teaspoonful 3 times a day' (*AN* 1893d, p. 311).

It must be borne in mind that this was the time when many substances which have subsequently come under much stricter control were used freely, such as maltine with coca wine: 'The Coca

Figure 2.11 A poster promoting women's restorative tonic wine.

boosts the patient and the Maltine furnishes the peg' (*AN* selections, 1894, p. 491). The 'peg' was the substance which prevented the patient's condition from deteriorating.

The American Medical Temperance Association first met in Washington on 7 May 1891 after a call from Dr N.S. Davis of Chicago:

> Having for its object to advance the practice of total abstinence in and through the medical profession and to promote the investigation as to the action of alcohol in health and disease and it aims as being a bond of union. (Davis 1891, p. 637)

The membership was open to all medical practitioners who were abstainers from 'all alcoholic liquors as beverages' (Davis 1891, p. 637). Dr Crowther, a noted alcohol specialist, agreed with the aims of the organisation and was quite clear about the need for members to be abstainers. Few modern medical practitioners would agree with his rather extreme view: 'It will be apparent that the last qualification is more or less a scientific necessity for working in this field ... unbiased by any personal considerations of custom or habit' (Davis 1891, p. 637). Indeed, the editor of the *Alienist and Neurologist* took him to task on this, rightly pointing out there were already clear biases:

> the society requires evidence of a bias in favour of total abstinence ... It is not at all apparent to us that this qualification is a 'scientific necessity for good work in this field'. On the contrary, it appears to us to be at variance with the liberal spirit of true science. (*AN* 1891b, p. 637)

In this same editorial we get some indication of the questions and issues around at the time:

> Provided the investigator will qualify as a total abstainer. He is *not required to sign any pledge, but if for any reason he ceases to be a total abstainer, he is expected to withdraw from the association;* and yet this association is considered by the *Journal of Inebriety* to be 'entirely independent of, any other object except the purely scientific question of alcohol'. (p. 638)

The editor is clear in his views:

> This is the illiberal spirit of fanaticism and will undoubtedly

> impair the usefulness of this body, divest it of all scientific character ... The time is ripe for an inquiry into the therapeutic and social dangers of unguarded alcohol, but pledges of abstinence as conditions preliminary to such inquiry are too unscientific and fanatical to be tolerated. (*AN* 1891b, p. 638)

There was the now common differentiation between the use of alcohol as a recreational beverage and as a medicine: 'The liberty of members to prescribe alcohol is entirely uncontrolled' (*AN* 1891b, p. 637).

In Germany the *Deutscher Verein gegen den Milsbrauch geistiger Getränke* (DV) (the German Association for the Prevention of Alcohol Abuse) had around 5400 women members. However, as noted by Roberts (1984):

> although women were taking an increasingly active role in temperance work after the turn of the century, the anti-alcohol movement never became a major vehicle for advancing feminist goals. Women were never really at the forefront of the German temperance movement, which knew no organisation comparable to Francis Willard's powerful Women's Christian Temperance Union in the United States. Ottilie Hoffman's German branch of the International Women's Temperance Union, the *Deutscher Bund Abstinenter Frauen* was but a pale imitation of its American parent. (p. 61)

This cycle is clearly noted by Roberts in relation to 'the working classes in nineteenth-century Germany'. When describing Germany after the First World War:

> The new treatment movement located the source of the problem not in social relations and cultural values or even in drink itself, as the classic temperance movement had done, but in individual predispositions that rendered some men and women unable to control their drinking. (1919, pp. 125–6)

During the First World War the British government was concerned about efficiency among the factory workers (Carter 1919). Early in the war years the issue of drunkenness amongst women was noted:

> The leniency shown to the wives of Service men sprang naturally from the goodwill towards men serving with the Colours ... in

> view of the danger that a conviction for drunkenness might imperil a woman's separation allowance, constables, instead of arresting a drunken woman, would often advise her to go home quietly. (p. 239)

This leniency did not continue, however, and it may be that what changed the attitudes was the increase in mortality from alcohol-related causes and, even more relevant, the deaths of babies from 'overlaying'. This latter was seen as due to maternal drunkenness.

However, the majority of the working classes used alcohol then as now, in moderation. A description of the women who sold fish on the streets of Edinburgh in the early part of the twentieth century was noted by Bone (1926):

> after their fish and oysters were sold, the Newhaven fishwives would meet at a rendezvous for a single dram, sally forth with empty creels, and march down Leith Walk in a breast, singing in full chorus 'The Boatie Row'. (p. 115)

The belief that there is a single, identifiable, cause of alcohol problems has now been around for many years. However, alcohol problems are associated with many factors, in particular, social and cultural attitudes to drinking and intoxication. Throughout the centuries there have been cycles pinpointing the reasons for alcohol problems: as the responsibility of the person, giving the 'alcoholic personality'; the beverage, which leads into temperance and prohibition movements; and society, which puts the onus on social deprivation, high rates of unemployment and poor health care. It is hoped this book will serve to emphasise that the aetiology of alcohol consumption and alcohol-related problems are complex and reflect many factors.

3 Physical Effects

The issues which will be discussed in depth in this chapter include the key physiological factors which relate to women and alcohol. The gender differences in alcohol effects will also be discussed.

The physical effects of alcohol in women are complex issues and knowledge in this area has expanded dramatically over the last decade. Up until that point the majority of research work into the physical damage related to alcohol was carried out on male problem-drinkers. This was in part to do with the fact that there were more of them around and they were often captive populations either in general or psychiatric hospitals. As further expanded in Chapter 6, there were few women in alcohol treatment units, the ratio typically being about four men to one woman. Even if women did form part of a study group, surprisingly they were often not acknowledged. Even more irritating, when the subject group did include some women the analysis often did not contain any comparisons between the two groups. This led to possibly inaccurate conclusions about both groups. For example, if the study group comprises 50 women and 50 men and there is an increased risk of some factor: say 75% of the study group is at increased risk. It may be that this is made up of 37 women and 38 men, but it could also be made up of 4 women and 71 men. If the genders are not analysed separately then any interpretation would be based on inaccurate information. If the results are then used to inform policy decisions there could be far-reaching consequences. This related not only to research into treatment but also more generally to studies involving larger populations.

It is interesting to surmise why this happened. Certainly for many years most alcohol research was conducted by males. The proportion of female alcohol epidemiologists has now been on the increase, especially in the past 20 years. One of the reasons for the dearth of work on women was the problem related to follow-up. It is difficult enough to follow up a group of people who may change their address without informing the researcher, if they are also likely to change their names as well, the chances of being able to trace them for follow-up drops dramatically. These reasons are among my personal ones and some people may disagree with them.

Perhaps the main problem was that initially, people just did not think that there would be any differences between men and women in relation to the negative effects of alcohol. For example, if men developed alcohol-related liver damage and stopped drinking, unless the damage was severe, the liver would not continue to deteriorate. The reasoning was, why should women be any different? Work being carried out in the past few years is beginning to show us that this was an assumption and to some extent it was an inaccurate one. Although it is true to say that many alcohol-related physical problems are common to both genders, there are some, mainly hormone related, which are specific to women.

Genetics

The debate as to the power of a genetic component to alcohol related harm in general (Johnson, van den Bree and Pickens 1996) and for women in particular (Hill and Smith 1991) is still hotly debated. A review of this by Couzigou et al. (1993) noted:

> A single gene is unlikely to account wholly for the transmission of such a complex disorder as alcoholism. Most probably, different genes will be shown to affect different aspects of alcoholism and alcohol-related diseases. (p. 285)

Some studies suggest that although there is a genetic component, environment is probably a more powerful factor (Whitfield and Martin 1994). Others view it as a possible aid to prevention (Tarter 1995).

Gastro-intestinal System

The issue of why women develop alcohol problems at lower levels of alcohol consumption than their male counterparts has been debated for a number of years. Reasons given have ranged from, 'women have smaller brains so maybe the rest of their organs are smaller too', to, 'its all a male conspiracy to keep women powerless'. Neither of these statements is totally inaccurate; however, there are more consistent reasons. As noted by Dr Marsha Morgan, a UK liver specialist, women are more physiologically compromised by alcohol than men. There are a number of reasons for this, including gender differences in weight, tissue saturation, stomach enzymes and the proportion of fat to water in the body. Perhaps the most important general difference is the fact that women of the same weight and at the same dose of alcohol as men will have an alcohol tissue concentration one-third higher than men. This higher tissue concentration of alcohol in a woman's body means not only that her blood alcohol level (BAL) will be one-third higher for the same amount of alcohol, but also that the time it takes for her BAL to return to zero will be longer as the elimination curve will be one-third up on her male counterpart (Morgan 1996). Women have a lesser proportion of their body in the form of water and therefore, with a smaller body water, the alcohol is more highly concentrated (Marshall et al. 1983). Estimations of this factor are available (Watson, Watson and Batt 1980). However, work is in progress by Graham et al. (1996) on whether alcohol consumption measures need to be adjusted for gender differences, such as those mentioned above. At this point the answer would appear to be that this is not necessary.

In relation to the breakdown of alcohol, the initial steps in the process start in the stomach with the addition of the enzyme alcohol dehydrogenase (ADH). Women appear to have lower levels of this enzyme in the stomach and small intestine, therefore the first stage of the breakdown of alcohol in the body, the 'first-pass' metabolic process, does not start so early (Di Padova, Frezza and Lieber 1988, Roine et al. 1991, Seitz et al. 1993). In a small but detailed study by Frezza et al. (1990), alcohol dehydrogenase activity was measured by gastric biopsy as well as other less intrusive means. The subjects in this study consisted of problem-drinking women (n=6) aged between 17 and 52 years, and non-problem-drinking women (n=22) aged between 22 and 48 years. Six problem-drinking men aged between 45 and 61 years and 14 non-problem-drinking men aged between 26 and 53 were also included. Noting the ages of the women the researchers carried out the investigations on the premenopausal women during the second half of their menstrual cycles. As has been noted in other studies, few researchers have taken this degree of care. The authors noted differences between the genders with both groups of women having lower levels of ADH than their male counterparts. They reported:

These results indicate that the bioavailability of ethanol is much greater in women than in men, because women have less gastric first-pass metabolism of ethanol. This was associated with less gastric alcohol dehydrogenase activity in the women. Moreover, alcoholism was associated with a further decrease in gastric alcohol dehydrogenase activity; the first-pass metabolism was virtually abolished in the alcoholic women. (Frezza et al. 1990, p. 97)

This kind of information is important in many ways. It suggests that in relation to health education and primary prevention, acknowledgement needs to be made of gender differences. It also suggests that those working in the area of alcohol problem treatment should be aware that the women in their care, particularly if they relapse, may become ill faster, on smaller doses of alcohol than their male counterparts. Indeed, as noted by Frezza et al. (1990):

> These differences should be considered in the definition of safe levels of drinking for men and women driving motor vehicles or engaging in other activities requiring a high degree of attention or coordination (Dunbar et al. 1987). Moreover, the ingestion of equivalent doses of ethanol per kilogram of body weight can be expected to result in higher levels of ethanol in women than in men, not only in the systemic but especially in the portal circulation. Thus, in addition to the smaller volume of ethanol distribution, the decrease in first-pass metabolism and gastric oxidation of ethanol may contribute to the higher vulnerability to hepatic injury of women as compared with men who consume similar amounts of ethanol (Ashley et al. 1977, Krasner et al. 1977, Morgan and Sherlock 1977, Saunders et al. 1981, Norton et al. 1987). (p. 99)

In relation to age, some research has suggested that this reduction in gastric ADH appears to be greater in women who are under 50 years of age, that is, those who are pre-menopausal (Lucey et al. 1993, Seitz et al. 1993).

Other researchers have questioned these findings, highlighting the difficulty in separating out gastric and hepatic first-pass metabolism in humans and further suggesting that the rate of absorption may differ perhaps with beverage type (Thomasson 1995). However, studies with subjects who have had gastrectomies have indicated that it is the gastric metabolism and not that of the liver which is the key (Caballeria et al. 1987). Surgery for gastric ulceration is not uncommon in excessive drinkers. This may be relevant in relation to post-operative advice-giving with this group. Furthermore, a woman who is still menstruating and who has had gastric surgery will probably have an increased effect from even small amounts of alcohol (Van Thiel and Gavaler 1979, Tarter et al. 1991, Harris and Brunt 1995). There has also been some suggestion that cancer of the stomach may be related to the continual irritation of heavy alcohol consumption on the gastric mucosa (Doll et al. 1993).

Other issues relate to the speed with which the stomach empties, with some studies showing an increase in this process when alcohol is consumed (Kaufman and Kaye 1979, Lenz et al. 1983). Other studies, the greater number, show a delay in gastric emptying when alcohol is taken as an accompaniment to a meal (Barboriak and Meade 1970, Cooke 1970, Pfeiffer et al. 1992).

The effect of beverage type has also been described (Moore et al. 1981, Lenz et al. 1983, Singer et al. 1991, Pfeiffer et al. 1992). Roine et al. (1991) found no statistically significance difference between the blood alcohol levels (BALs) in 'fasting and fed' women and men given different beverage alcohols. However, in relation to bioavailability of alcohol they noted beverage differences:

> Our results demonstrate that the consumption of a concentrated solution of ethanol results in lower blood alcohol levels than does a dilute solution, when subjects are tested in the fed state. This effect is associated with more first pass metabolism and less bioavailability with the high ethanol concentrations. These findings now raise the issue whether ethanol in low concentration beverages such as beer and wine has a greater bioavailability than in distilled spirits. (p. 734)

These authors further noted in conclusion:

> Concentration of the ethanol consumed must be recognised as an important variable when different studies dealing with alcohol are compared. Furthermore it is important to note that after consumption of equal amounts of ethanol soon after a meal, BACs (and consequently the alcohol-induced impairment of motor and mental coordination) can be much higher with dilute than concentrated solutions. Up to now, it has been implicitly assumed that moderate drinking may be defined by the amount of alcohol consumed, regardless of the concentration of the beverage. Although the influence of congeners in alcoholic beverages needs to be assessed, our data reveal that equal amounts of alcohol result in different blood levels depending on the concentration. (pp. 737–8)

Even so, a number of studies into peak blood alcohol levels and gender differences have been carried out with conflicting results (Marshall et al. 1983, Hay et al. 1984, Goist and Sutker 1985, Brick et al. 1986, Van Theil and Gavaler 1988). These latter authors, in a thorough review, noted the importance of total body water (1988):

> Taken together, these data strongly suggest that sex differences in total body water, ethanol *Vdr* and the ethanol concentration-time AUC [mean blood alcohol concentration] can be accounted for as a consequence of the difference in body water content seen between the two sexes. These data also help to explain why women appear to develop greater degrees of hepatic injury than do men when their ethanol intake had been adjusted for body weight; in such circumstances, the peak blood alcohol concentrations achieved in women would be greater than those achieved in men. (p. 295)

The size of this difference was examined by Marshall et al. (1983) in a study on elimination of alcohol in relation to menstrual cycle and body composition. These authors concluded:

> The major sex difference in ethanol pharmacokinetics observed in the present study was that AUC, which is a measure of mean blood ethanol concentration, was 36% greater in females than in males. This implies that systemic exposure to ethanol following oral administration of a standard dose is considerably greater in females. The sex difference in AUC may have been due to male–female differences in oral bioavailability of ethanol or to differences in its volume of distribution. (p. 705)

The bacteria Heliobacter, which is more commonly found in men, can also 'mop up' alcohol, thus again reducing the amount of alcohol circulating in the blood system.

The speed with which the gut processes and excretes food waste is also affected by gender (Lucey et al. 1993). Women have a longer 'gut-transit' time than men. Factors which increase the length of time from food ingestion to excretion are strengthened even further in women at different phases in the menstrual cycle, for example immediately pre-menstrually (Van Theil et al. 1979, Wald et al. 1982). Evidence has also shown that the use of oral contraceptives has a delaying effect on this process (Jones and Jones 1977, 1984, Zeiner and Kegg 1981, Probert et al. 1995). This process is also delayed in pregnancy (Fisher et al. 1978, Wald et al. 1982). Interestingly, gastric transit time appears to increase after the menopause (Probert et al. 1995). From the above picture it appears that oestrogen and progesterone do slow down the speed with which the food is processed and passed through the gut. This is highlighted by the fact that in menopausal women the rate is faster. In fact, in the study by Probert et al., amongst the female subjects age emerged as the most influential factor, accounting for the greatest proportion of the variance. In relation to alcohol, this substance appears to increase gastric transit time in both women and men. In Probert et al.'s study, in women, alcohol came a close second to age in terms of predictive power. In men, alcohol was the major variable. The reason for the importance of these studies can be seen when the association between speed of gut transit time and such problems as cancer of the bowel and increased risk of gallstones is highlighted (Probert et al. 1995). However, the complexity again arises. The protective effect of alcohol on the production of gallstones has been found in a number of studies (Maclure et al. 1989, Maurer et al. 1990, La Vecchia et al. 1991). An Australian case control study (Scragg et al. 1984) stated:

> In summary, we found, in a large case-control study, that increased intake of alcohol was associated with a substantially decreased risk of development of gallstones. (p. 1118)

A study published more recently (La Vecchia et al. 1994), but using information from a 1983 Italian National Health Survey carried out about the same time as Scragg et al.'s study, included 2126 cases of gall bladder disease or cholecystectomy. In relation to gender the numbers were 1461 women and 665 men. One of the few weaknesses in the study was that the diagnosis of gallstones and subsequent operations for this condition was by self-report only. The authors concluded that alcohol consumption was clearly inversely related to the risk of gallstone production. They also noted that:

> The inverse relationship between alcohol and gallstone disease was somewhat stronger for females than males, but it was present in both sexes in the absence of significant interaction and was consistent across strata of age and body mass index. (p. 535)

It would appear that alcohol consumption is associated with a reduced risk of developing gallstones and that this association is stronger in women than in men.

As noted earlier in this chapter, the belief that women are more sensitive than men to the effects of alcohol grew from the mainly male literature. Some of the evidence for this view has been summarised above. However, the issue is not completely resolved. For example, why is it that women admitted to gastro-intestinal units are often more floridly ill than their male counterparts? There are a number of known reasons why this should be. There are physiological, but also psychological questions still to be taken into account.

A major contributory factor in alcohol-related liver disease is nutrition. As noted by Greco (1995):

> Large ethanol intake influences nutritional status: (a) it increases food intake by displacing other nutrients in the diet, (b) provokes gastrointestinal complications primarily involving the pancreas and gut, thereby causing either maldigestion or malabsorption of nutrients (p. 4)

In many countries women experience more problems related to poor nutritional intake than their male counterparts. This gender disparity occurs most frequently in the lower socio-economic groups. Poor nutritional intake is of particular importance for women with drinking problems because added to this scenario are the gender differences in pattern of drinking which are often evident. Wives or partners of male problem-drinkers are more likely to stay with their partners than male partners of female problem-drinkers. There are many advantages to the male problem-drinker in this pattern but few for the woman who looks after him, encourages him to eat well and will often go to great lengths to ensure that he maintains his nutritional intake. One of the common experiences is the woman who cooks for the family at the usual dinner hour and then will start cooking all over again whenever her husband comes home. Indeed, often one of the first lessons she may learn at self-help groups like Alanon is not to keep bending over backwards to accommodate her partner, because as long as she does so, he does not need to acknowledge that there are problems. It may be suggested to her that she cooks his meal at the same time as everybody else's and leaves it in the oven. When he arrives home four hours late he will notice something is wrong. There is sound advice in this. However, living with a problem-drinker is an exhausting and even frightening situation. Bringing him face to face with his behaviour may make him realise something is wrong; it may also unfortunately make him very angry. A woman who is worn down by her life and situation will need a lot of help to tolerate what may come of her husband's realisation, particularly if the thought that he has a problem with drinking makes him frightened. Often fear makes people angry and they may lash out at the person who brings them face to face with it. The husband of a problem-drinking woman is less likely to stay with his partner and therefore she has to feed herself, something which she may well not bother to do; even if she does cook something for herself, she may not bother to eat if there is no one around to encourage her to do so. One of the other ways in which problem-drinking men are more likely to eat better than their female counterparts is that when they return home from the pub or club they may well buy some kind of takeaway food. Adequate calorific intake is vital: the greater the intake, the better the protection from damage. The evidence shows that if calorific intake prior to admission for alcoholic hepatitis is recorded, the mortality rate for those with a calorific intake of less than 1000 is about 80%. For those with a calorific intake of more than 3000 the mortality rate is about 8%. This is the case for both women and men (Morgan 1996).

The view that women are more sensitive to alcohol than men has been around for a long time. Recent evidence, however, has enabled us to begin to understand why this is so and indeed to question some of the assumptions on which this kind of statement is based. For example, looking at women admitted to general hospitals with alcohol-related hepatitis, they are often more floridly ill than their male counterparts. (Harris and Brunt 1995).

Gavaler and Arria (1995), in a thorough review and analysis of the available evidence, concluded:

> Viewed together, these reports provide a strikingly consistent pattern spiced with statistical differences of reduced cumulative exposure to alcohol among females compared to males matched for stage of alcohol-induced liver disease. (p. 125)

As noted by these two authors, the first study to highlight a possible difference in gender susceptibility took place in 1945 in the US. Spain reviewed autopsy reports on 250 cases and found that the females died, on average, ten years earlier than the males.

Since this time, other findings have refuted these original ones. In Denmark studies on the incidence of male and female patients with alcohol-related liver disease showed peaks at 50–60 years of age (Prytz and Skinhoj 1980, Prytz and Anderson 1988, Almdal and Sorensen 1991). This is the case for both female and male patients. Studies have been carried out in a number of countries now. A Scottish study of alcohol-related liver disease (Hislop et al. 1983) noted that the women differed from the men in that they were less willing to disclose a history of problem-drinking and had a greater likelihood of a past psychiatric illness, usually alcohol related.

There is certainly evidence emerging about the possible effects of alcohol on hepatic protein metabolism. De Feo and colleagues examined the way that alcohol affects the breakdown of protein, the body's building blocks. This was a small study (2 women and 14 men) and was carried out literally under laboratory conditions to the point that the alcohol and food were given by naso-gastric tube. The results showed that although whole body protein breakdown was not affected by the consumption of alcohol, the breakdown of liver protein was affected adversely. The complex issue of beneficial versus damaging effects of alcohol are highlighted, as concluded by De Feo et al. (1995):

> it would be interesting to establish if the amounts of ethanol demonstrated to decrease the risk of myocardial infarction (25–40 g/d) (Gaziano et al. 1993) adversely affect hepatic protein metabolism similarly to the larger dose used in the present study. (p. 1478)

It is important to mention the 'larger dose' comment from these conclusions. The dose of alcohol given during the 'meal' was about 70g. This was seen by the researchers as 'an amount usual for many social drinkers'. In UK terms this is equivalent to approximately nine glasses of wine, not a typical quantity for a female to drink at one time. However, the study was carried out in Italy where this level of drinking may be more normal. The point is that scientists are constantly devising ways and means of measuring body indicators in a more sophisticated manner (Stanton and Spear 1990). Although the findings of this study may not affect the majority of social drinkers, it may be of great importance to the population of problem-drinkers whose increased, often acute, doses of alcohol on an already overworked liver may have a major impact. As a brief aside, these researchers have been very successful in controlling for many variables but do not appear to acknowledge that there may be differences between men and women in the process they were investigating so carefully. This study only included two women. Even so, an acknowledgement of the possible value of much more extensive research with women in this area seems to be missing.

The view of a causal relationship between alcohol, its breakdown products and liver disease is now well established (Lieber 1984, 1992). Once this mechanism occurs, the risk of other diseases is increased. As noted by Rodés et al. (1993) it is:

> unknown whether cirrhosis caused by excessive alcohol carries a

> greater risk of cancer development than cirrhosis caused by other factors (except for chronic hepatitis B infection, which results in a very high cancer risk). The high prevalence of antibodies against hepatitis C virus in alcoholic patients with liver cirrhosis and hepatocellular cancer (Bruix et al. 1989, Colombo et al. 1989, Chiaramonte et al. 1990, Kaklamani et al. 1991) suggests that this virus is responsible for the tumour. (p. 188)

The issue of alcohol's effect on the immune system has recently come in for increased attention, mainly due to the advent of HIV. Alcohol does appear to dampen the immune system, and this is mainly caused by the effect on lymphocytes, most powerful on T cells. Problem drinkers who develop infections often take longer to recover. Indeed, in some countries the incidence of tuberculosis is now increasing, often centred in pools of the homeless (Baker and Jerrells 1993). There is little evidence yet of gender differences, but this issue is now being addressed.

Examination of the possible impact of beverage type has brought conflicting results. However, in a letter published in the *New England Journal of Medicine*, Nanji and French (1984) noted that a proportionately greater number of women developed cirrhosis in countries where beer was the main alcoholic beverage consumed, compared to those in which wine was the most common beverage of choice.

In relation to the psychological aspects, the stigma of being labelled an 'alcoholic' or problem-drinker should not be underestimated. In this context it appears that women may, in retrospect, tend to report their problems related to alcohol as coming after the birth of their children. This may of course be the reality but it cannot be ignored that society in general frowns upon young mothers who drink excessively. Indeed in the UK any report of this could mean Social Services being called in with the possibility of the children being taken into care.

Coronary Heart Disease

Diseases of the heart and coronary arteries are more common in men than in women. For this reason it is not surprising that most of the research into this topic has related to males. However a number of case control studies (Klatsky et al. 1974, Stason et al. 1976, Petitti et al. 1979, Rosenberg et al. 1981, Ross et al. 1981, Jackson et al. 1991, 1992) and some cohort studies (Klatsky et al.

1981, Gordon and Kannel 1983, Colditz et al. 1985, Camacho et al. 1987, Stampfer et al. 1988, Klatsky et al. 1990) have been carried out with both genders or with women only. The majority of studies in this area come from the US, with a few from New Zealand. The ages of the study group participants ranged from 18 years (Petitti et al. 1979) to 80 years and older (Ross et al. 1981).

The vast majority of the studies have presented similar results. As noted by Renaud et al. (1993), in relation to coronary heart disease: 'The protective effect of alcohol seems to be present at all ages, in women as in men, whatever the length of follow-up (2–22 years), with other factors taken into consideration in addition to alcohol' (p. 82). In 1995 Grønbæk et al. reported findings from a large-scale prospective study of women (n=7234) and men (n=6051), aged between 30 and 70 years. The authors concluded:

> Low to moderate intake of wine is associated with lower mortality from cardiovascular and cerebrovascular disease and other causes. Similar intake of spirits implied an increased risk, while beer drinking did not affect mortality. (p. 1165)

The area of beverage specificity has been addressed in other studies but the findings have been inconsistent. Some studies noted wine being most beneficial (St Leger et al. 1979, Renaud and De Logeril 1992, Klatsky and Armstrong 1993). Freidman and Kimball (1986) reported wine and beer being more beneficial than spirits. Others found no difference by beverage type (Rosenberg et al. 1981, Klatsky et al. 1986, Stampfer et al. 1988). In a review of beverage type and potential differences in protective effects, Rimm et al. (1996) noted:

> Results from observational studies, where alcohol consumption can be linked directly to an individual's risk of coronary heart disease, provide strong evidence that all alcoholic drinks are linked with lower risk. Thus a substantial portion of the benefit is from alcohol rather than other components of each type of drink. (p. 731)

Beverage specificity aside, the consistency of these results is compelling. However, it must be noted that coronary heart disease in pre-menopausal women is relatively rare. For this reason the beneficial effects of small amounts of alcohol (about one UK drink a day) are at their most powerful in post-menopausal women. Gavaler and Van Thiel have suggested a reason for this. These two authors carried out a study of 128 non-problem-drinking, post-menopausal women. They found that the women who had a weekly alcohol intake of 4.8 US drinks (about 8.5 UK drinks) had significantly higher levels of oestrodial than women who were abstainers. As noted by Gavaler and Van Thiel (1992):

> these findings suggest that moderate alcohol use is an important factor for postmenopausal estrogen status and may offer a partial explanation for the reported protective effect of moderate alcohol consumption with respect to postmenopausal cardiovascular disease risk. (p. 87)

The potential benefits of hormone replacement therapy (HRT) to ischaemic heart disease have been noted (Bush 1990, Stampfer and Colditz 1991, Stampfer et al. 1991). In a study of 'well-to-do' white women, Ross et al. (1981) found: 'Our results suggest that oestrogen replacement therapy may protect against death from IHD (Ischaemic Heart Disease)' (p. 859).

Examining this issue from a different angle, Winkelstein (1995) re-analysed evidence from a case control study of women who had experienced a spontaneous abortion. The rationale was the possible connection between spontaneous abortion and deficiency of oestrogen. He found a clear association between women who suffered from myocardial infarction and a past history of spontaneous abortion. The women who had had between three and seven spontaneous abortions were more likely to experience a subsequent heart attack than those who had never had any miscarriages during their childbearing years. The importance of this latter study in the present context was that alcohol consumption levels were controlled for in the analysis.

Even so, there have been some recent studies which have examined the possible associations between protective effects and sex hormones in postmenopausal women and which have found no evidence of protective effects (Cauley et al. 1991, Cauley et al. 1994, Barrett-Connor and Goodman-Gruen 1995).

In some studies an association has been noted between alcohol consumption and exercise, particularly in a group or social situation (Gaziano et al. 1993, Barrett et al. 1995, Liao et al. 1995). Barrett and colleagues found that female drinkers, both moderate and heavy, were more likely to engage in regular physical activity than their non-drinking counterparts. These authors concluded:

> These data suggest that at least some of the apparent protective

effects of moderate alcohol consumption found in other studies may be due to differences between nondrinkers and drinkers with respect to physical activity and other health practices. (p. 9)

However, Wang et al. (1995) carried out a study of ten women ranging in age from 21 to 35 years. The exercise chosen was cycling on a stationary cycle. The results showed that after alcohol consumption there was a negative effect on the heart. Specifically, the strength of the heartbeat was diminished which led to an increase in the heartbeat to compensate for the reduced output. The point seems to be that drinkers who exercise are healthier but they should not drink immediately prior to, and certainly not during, exercise.

Even so, for problem-drinking women the picture changes dramatically. Chronic heavy drinking increases the risk of damage to the heart muscle resulting in the heart not beating effectively. This reduction in function relates to both cardiac output and the rhythm of the heart.

Some interesting points have been made on a possible gender bias in relation to delayed diagnosis and subsequent specialist treatment in this area (Ayanian and Epstein 1991, Steingart et al. 1991, Petticrew et al. 1993). It would appear that women may be less likely than men to be identified, accurately diagnosed and quickly hospitalised for treatment of this condition.

Hypertension

Research into hypertension has again been mainly related to men. However, studies which include both genders are now available from a number of countries (Harburg et al. 1980, Cooke et al. 1983, Fortmann et al. 1983, Gordon and Kannel 1983, Jackson et al. 1985, Paulin et al. 1985, Trevisan et al. 1987, Keil et al. 1989, Witteman et al. 1989, Dyer et al. 1990, Keil et al. 1991, Seppä et al. 1992, Seppä et al. 1996). This last study (Seppä et al. 1996), examined 297 women, the majority of whom (n=219) were originally part of a large-scale health survey of Finnish women aged 40–45 years. A further 78 problem-drinking women were included to facilitate comparisons. Interestingly, the results of this exercise differed from those of many other studies in that they did not show a J- or U-shaped curve picture. The latter indicates that abstainers and heavy drinkers are at the greatest risk. The moderate-drinking women that Seppä et al. examined did not show lower blood pressure readings than the abstainers. However, in agreement with other studies (Klatsky et al.

1977, Criqui et al. 1981, Gordon and Kannel 1983) a clear association between raised diastolic blood pressure (the lower of the two readings) and heavy drinking was shown to be present. The authors make the point that the pattern of drinking may be important in relation to their finding no association between moderate consumption and lower levels of blood pressure. The drinking pattern of the Finnish women was typical of that found in many northern countries, with almost all their weekly consumption being drunk at the weekend and little or no drinking taking place during the week. Other authors have also noted the importance of pattern as well as level of consumption (Criqui et al. 1981, Puddey et al. 1985). Another recent study carried out in Massachusetts (Gillman et al. 1995) with a group of 18- to 26-year-olds (n=177) set out to: 'examine the relationships of usual current alcohol intake with systolic and diastolic pressures among young adults' (p. 1106). The results reported by these authors noted that after controlling for a variety of confounding variables including family history of hypertension and smoking, the young women who had been drinking moderately (around 2 US units, 3.5 UK units a day), had the lowest blood pressure readings. The next lowest group were those drinking around one US unit (just over 1.5 UK units) a day. In the heaviest group of drinkers, there emerged the same association between higher consumption and raised blood pressure readings. As happens in so many studies, the pattern of drinking was flattened out by being dichotomised into daily or less than daily consumption. Seppä et al.'s comments, on patterns of consumption, remain relevant. However Gillman et al. (1995) concluded:

> Our findings of a J-shaped relationship, although not in agreement with all studies of alcohol intake and BP, may reflect an additional pathway by which light to moderate alcohol intake protects against coronary heart disease and death. (p. 1109)

There is evidence to suggest that arteriosclerosis can slowly develop over a 23–30-year period (Lynch et al. 1988). It will be interesting to ascertain whether the evident heavy drinking by some teenagers found in Gillman et al.'s study will have an impact on future risk of heart disease and stroke in this group.

The relationship between heavy alcohol consumption and high blood pressure is now seen as clear and causal. That is, heavy drinkers will more commonly have high blood pressure which appears to be attributable to their alcohol consumption. Confirmation of this link has been strengthened by a number of studies which show that a reduction in level of drinking also brings a fall in high blood pressure to a less risky level (Saunders, Beevers and Paton 1981, Potter and Beevers 1984, Keil et al. 1993). If, as the majority of studies suggest, the heavier drinkers in the population are at increased risk of high blood pressure and if this can be shown to be lowered by reducing alcohol intake, it is relevant to note some work carried out into alcohol withdrawal. Blood pressure readings, both systolic and diastolic, have been shown to be raised significantly during the phase of withdrawal. This increase seems to disappear after the withdrawal phase is over. The reasons for this are currently not clear, but there do seem to be gender differences in relation to hypertension in problem-drinking women and men. Problem-drinking women appear to be less likely than men to suffer from alcohol-related hypertension (Friedman et al. 1982, McMahon et al. 1984, Eisonhofer et al. 1985, Periti et al. 1988).

Some studies have been more robust than others. Differences in this respect have related particularly to measure of alcohol intake and inclusion/exclusion of confounding variables (see section on stroke). An example of the complexity of the issue was noted by McDonald et al. (1993):

> Since body fat distribution (rather than total fat or obesity) may be an independent risk factor for cardiovascular disease, hypertension, and diabetes, a study was carried out on 40,980 postmenopausal women to determine whether a correlation between alcohol consumption and waist/hip ratio (WHR) exists. It was found that WHR was obviously strongly related to BMI but was significantly and negatively associated with alcohol consumption, with the lowest WHR present in women who drank 2–7.4 g ethanol/day (Kaye et al. 1990). In Swedish women, however, alcohol consumption was positively associated with WHR (Lapidus et al. 1989), and no relation was found between WHR and alcohol consumption in a sample of Mexican and non-Hispanic women (Haffner et al. 1986). (p. 273)

Stroke

Cerebrovascular accident (stroke) can occur in two ways. A blood clot may develop or become lodged in one of the blood vessels in the brain. This cuts off the blood supply to the surrounding area, resulting in permanent damage (ischaemic stroke). This is by far the most common cause of stroke, accounting for over 80% of the total. The other type of stroke occurs when a blood vessel ruptures and subsequently bleeds into the brain (haemorrhagic stroke). The damaged vessel can be either within the brain structure or on the surface causing pressure and again resulting in damage to the brain itself. This accounts for the remaining proportion, less than 20%, of strokes. However, in terms of the possibility of a fatal outcome, haemorrhagic strokes carry the greater risk. In relation to haemorrhagic stroke, a number of studies – both prospective and case control designs – have included women. The prospective studies which included both genders ranged in sample size from 13,200 subjects (Grønbæk et al. 1995) to 859 (Khaw and Barret-Connor 1987). In between these two were a number of others differing both in size and geographical area (Peacock et al. 1972, Okado et al. 1976, Cullen et al. 1982, Omae and Ueda 1982, Tanaka et al. 1982, Boysen et al. 1988, Wolf et al. 1988, Klatsky et al. 1990).

The main large-scale prospective study of women was carried out by Stampfer et al. (1988). This study of over 87,000 nurses has already been discussed earlier in the chapter. In relation to stroke, Stampfer and his colleagues noted an association between moderate alcohol consumption and reduced risk of ischaemic stroke. This finding is consistent across the majority of studies. A number of case control investigations have also been carried out. (The studies cited include both female and male subjects: Peacock et al. 1972, Abu-Zeid et al. 1977, Petitti et al. 1979, Herman et al. 1983, Sacco et al. 1984, Taylor and Combs-Orme 1985, Von Arbin et al. 1985, Gill et al. 1988, Oleckno 1988, Gorelick 1989, Monteforte et al. 1990, Ben-Shlomo et al. 1991.) There have been weaknesses amongst studies of this type. For example, as noted by van Gijn et al. (1993) in their thorough review:

> Although it is important to adjust for the confounding effect of such factors as cigarette smoking, age, and sex in order to assess the independent effect of alcohol on stroke, the biases introduced by controlling for hypertension, which itself may be caused by the moderate to high alcohol intake, need to be considered. Therefore, by controlling for hypertension in the analysis, one may be 'over- controlling' for this effect, which may reduce the risk associated with alcohol. Control strategies initially should not include stroke risk factors that might serve as potential mediators of a causal association between alcohol intake and stroke. (p. 51)

It would appear, therefore, taking the body of evidence into account, that at low levels of consumption (between one and two UK units a day) there is a reduced risk of stroke caused by ischaemia. This may be attributable to the process whereby alcohol seems to prevent the platelets clotting. This will therefore reduce the risk of an ischaemic attack. There is some debate about how powerful the effect of alcohol is in this process. It does appear as though alcohol potentiates the effect of aspirin, the other commonly used drug for this condition (Deykin et al. 1982). However, there is some evidence that aspirin inhibits gastric alcohol dehydrogenase (ADH) activity (Roine et al. 1990). As has already been noted, this may be relevant for women. The negative aspect of this, of course, is that the same mechanism reducing platelet clotting, *increases* clotting time and therefore if bleeding, such as a perforated gastric ulcer or oesophageal varices, does occur, the risk of a poor prognosis is increased. There does not appear to be any added benefits from higher consumption levels with this type of stroke. As already stated, this is the commonest type of stroke, accounting for over 80% of cases. In relation to haemorrhagic stroke, the consensus view is that alcohol gives no protection at any consumption level. The clear balance of available evidence points to a positive association between stroke of this type and alcohol consumption. This association has been shown in some studies to have a dose response relationship (van Gijn 1993). As noted earlier, this is the less common of the two types of stroke. However, it is repeated that this also carries the greatest risk of a fatal outcome.

Some studies have examined risk factors associated with menopause from different perspectives such as nutrition (Gavaler 1993). That is, the use of hormone replacement therapy (HRT) and its effect on stroke (Gordon et al. 1978, Jick et al. 1978, Pfeffer et al. 1978, Bain et al. 1981, Ross et al. 1981, Stampfer et al. 1985, Paganini-Hill et al. 1988).

The possible effects of patterns of drinking have also been addressed. The results have not been consistent. Van Gijn et al. (1993) have commented: 'The conclusions reached by Camargo (1989) that: "The results of epidemiologic studies provide meagre evidence that recent alcohol use affects the risk of stroke" still holds true in 1992' (p. 59). Five years later, the picture does not seem to have changed.

The other issue related to alcohol in the area of the brain is that of gender differences in vulnerability to damage. Mann et al. (1992) carried out a study of 65 problem-drinkers (14 females and 51 males). There were differences in levels of consumption between the genders (women were lower) and also length of drinking history, with men drinking for about three times as long as the women – nine years and three years respectively. Variables such as body weight were taken into account. The authors concluded: 'After correction for body weight, the mean daily alcohol consumption did not differ significantly between the men and women' (p. 1052). However, the mean age of these women was 35.6 years. At least some of these would have still been menstruating, with the accompanied changes in hormone levels. This does not appear to have been acknowledged in this report. The authors concluded:

> By controlling for moderating variables such as age, mean daily alcohol consumption, liver dysfunction etc. the degree of brain shrinkage was found to be similar in men and women despite significantly shorter ethanol expositions in the women. (p. 1052)

This subject has also been examined in other studies with mixed results (Cala et al. 1981, Kroft et al. 1991).

As already indicated, one of the risk factors associated with a number of diseases, including breast cancer, is obesity. The results of surveys into the relationship between alcohol and obesity are inconsistent (see MacDonald et al. 1993). As in many areas the problem of conflicting and contradictory variables arises. An example of this is smoking. The confusion lies in the fact that smoking appears to be associated with lower body weight. However, smoking is also associated with consumption of alcohol in that heavier drinkers are also more likely to be smokers. As noted by MacDonald et al. (1993):

> Some reports found that in women, smoking reduces any body weight increase that may be due to alcohol consumption (Higgins and Kjelsberg 1967, Cooke et al. 1982, Fisher and Gordon 1985, Friedmann and Kimbal 1986, Schatzkin et al. 1987, Willett et al. 1987, Williamson et al. 1987, Stampfer et al. 1988, Colditz et al. 1991, Rissanen et al. 1991), while others found the opposite effect (Tofler et al. 1969, Gyntelberg and Meyer 1974, Lang et al. 1987, Trevisan et al. 1987). (p. 266)

Examining post-menopausal women, Kaye et al. (1990) found that those who did not drink were heavier in weight than those who did. Indeed, those who drank most weighed less. Other studies have shown similar findings (Jones et al. 1982, Williamson 1987, Colditz et al. 1991). However, confusion in this area remains and a number of the studies so far have failed to control for confounding variables in a satisfactory way, for example differences in eating patterns and lifestyles and even amounts of exercise.

Menstrual Cycle

The main hormones which are relevant to the physical aspects of alcohol and women are progesterone and the oestrogens – the hormones which change levels during the menstrual cycle. In many countries young women are now entering puberty at an earlier age; there is some evidence to suggest an association between higher oestrogen levels and early menarche. Due to the choice of delaying becoming pregnant, many women now experience a greater number of menstrual cycles uninterrupted by frequent pregnancies. They therefore also experience fluctuating hormone levels for a greater part of their lives than their forebears.

This area is a minefield of confusion and conflicting results (Gill 1997). There are a number of problems associated with the research, including difficulties in attempting to compare studies where phase of cycle, time of ovulation, and serum hormone levels have either not been noted or have been ignored. Indeed, in some studies it is not even clear whether the respondents actually are menstruating regularly or not. However, the work on levels and patterns of alcohol consumption in relation to menstrual cycle is ongoing (Välimäki et al. 1983, Croft et al. 1987, Allen 1996).

During their life courses, women may experience more transitions than are undergone by men. Their priorities may also change almost in line with these. Career and job opportunities may give way to family commitments. One thing that may not change, however, is a woman's sense of competition. The focus of the competitive urge may shift from self, in relation to promotion prospects, to children, and many women will recognise the pressure they put their children under to achieve. There is the risk that women who for whatever reason give up work to stay at home and care for their children may channel their own competitiveness through their children. This may be a very good reason for women not to stop working for long periods of time. Although both females and males experience puberty, women go on to a time when there is the possibility of producing children, then experience the menopause.

Clearly, most of these changes are hormone-related and this extremely complex physiological process has only recently begun to be examined in relation to how alcohol affects the system.

In 1976, a team of American scientists (Jones and Jones) carried out a small-scale, laboratory-based study on a group of normal-drinking men and women. The purpose of the study was to examine whether there are differences in blood alcohol levels (BALs) in men and women. To do this the researchers identified three points in the menstrual cycles of the female participants. All the respondents were then given comparable amounts of alcohol (measured per kilogram of body weight) which they drank within a short period of time. The results showed that for the men, their BAL was the same at each of the three times measured. The women were more interesting in that the BAL appeared to differ at each of the three points in the cycle. The lowest BAL was found at the first point measured which was when the women were menstruating; the next raised level was in the middle of their menstrual cycle, that is around days 12 to 14, and the highest BAL was found immediately before the next menstrual period. Interestingly enough, research has shown that women complaining of pre-menstrual tension have an increased risk of accidents at work and in the home at this time. The other measure taken at the time, that of absorption rates, showed that absorption of alcohol was faster at the final point of measurement, which was immediately pre-menstrually. For some years this was one of the few studies reported on this important topic. However, in the 1980s, a number of studies were carried out which did not produce the same results as Jones and Jones, finding no differences in BAL at different phases of the menstrual cycle (Mello 1980, Brick et al. 1986). By the 1990s a number of scientists still tried, unsuccessfully, to replicate the findings (Marshall et al. 1983, Sutker et al. 1987). The reasons for this are unclear but, as noted by Gill (1997), Jones and Jones' original study was flawed in its accuracy:

> No hormones were determined to confirm cycle phase designation. In this study of twenty women attendance was only requested at two or three times during the cycle. In addition six women failed to return for a second testing session. Thus in a significant proportion of the study participants, the length of the cycle may not have been confirmed by knowledge of the date of onset of the next period of menstrual flow. (p. 10)

The number of participants was small, yet even amongst 20

women there can be a great variation in length and regularity of their menstrual cycle.

As noted above, a surprising number of women do not have regular 28-day cycles. Metcalf and Mackenzie (1980) monitored menstrual cycles in 254 women within the age range 15–39 years. Of the women aged between 20–24 years only 62% ovulated in every cycle. There were a number of explanations given for this, for example student life, and living apart from relatives. However, it must be noted that these two variables at least may also be related to changes in behaviour, such as an increase in alcohol consumption.

The issue of menstrual cycle effects in general has become a more popular area for research with work on pre-menstrual syndrome (Ussher and Wilding 1992), physiological and psychological stress (Stoney et al. 1990, Weidner and Helmig 1990, Gallant et al. 1991, Girdler et al. 1993) and exercise (Choi and Salmon 1995a, b).

In relation to alcohol, studies have shown that women still experiencing their menstrual cycles who drink regularly have higher levels of oestrogens. Others have noted specific times when this may occur (Mendelson et al. 1987, Mendelson et al. 1988). The issue, noted earlier, of mood changes and menstrual cycle has led to the question of whether women will be more likely to self-medicate with alcohol (see Chapter 4).

Breast Cancer

This disease is probably one of the most frightening which can occur to a woman. It embodies the risk of disfigurement and possible death. It involves the fear of changes in intimate relationships due to scarring. In a world where perfection is so ardently sought, it can cause scarring at a level much deeper and more insidious than any operations or other treatment. It is because of all of these aspects that this particular issue and the work in this field deserves to be examined in detail.

Much has been written over the past few years about the relationship between alcohol consumption and breast cancer. The majority of studies show some association, albeit weak, between consumption of alcohol and breast cancer. However there are a number of issues which must be addressed, in relation to both collection and interpretation of these data.

In the early 1970s, two researchers reviewed evidence on alcohol and tobacco use and cancer mortality in the US (Breslow and Enstrom 1974). Their study investigated the possible associations between consumption of alcohol and tobacco with average, age-adjusted, annual cancer mortality statistics from 1950–75. Forty-one US states were included in this inquiry. The results showed a high level of association between alcohol consumption and cancer of the breast, liver and small intestine in women. The alcohol in this study was beverage specific; it appeared that beer was the type of beverage most clearly associated with these diseases. The authors warned of the need for caution in interpreting these results: 'the very lack of site specificity in the presumed effects of beer drinking argues against attaching too much etiologic significance to the findings discussed' (p. 638).

This type of conclusion is common amongst the study results. Harris and Wynder (1988), like many other researchers, found no dose response relationship and further noted: 'While these results do not entirely rule out a weak association between alcohol and breast cancer in certain subgroups, neither do they provide compelling evidence that alcohol has a role in the genesis of this malignancy' (p. 2867).

Since that time a number of studies have been carried out, some into unusual groups such as Phillips' analysis of Seventh-day Adventists (1975). This study showed a decreased risk of breast cancer in a group of women who neither smoked nor drank alcohol.

Two years after the publication of Breslow and Enstrom's study a letter was published in the *Lancet* questioning the link (Pochin 1976). This writer cited the rates of per capita alcohol consumption in 14 different countries (see Table 1.1, p. 4). The information considered was from the World Health Organization's statistics of 1965 and 1968 for adults aged 15 years and older. These, Pochin compared with mortality from breast cancer in these same countries: If there was a clear association between breast cancer and alcohol consumption levels, one would expect the countries with the highest alcohol consumption also to be those with the highest incidence of breast cancer. Many of the countries noted were wine producers and these were often the highest per capita consumers. France was then highest at 24.7 litres, with Italy at 18 litres and Portugal next highest at 17.6 litres (this situation has changed in recent years, as noted in Chapter 1). The lowest per capita alcohol consumption was Denmark at 7.5 litres, the Netherlands at 6.2 litres and Poland at 4.2 litres. Pochin went on to show that mortality rates from breast cancer did not show any positive association with per capita alcohol consumption. In fact, the highest rate of breast cancer was found in the UK at 40.6 deaths per 100,000. In relation to per capita alcohol consumption the rate for the UK at this time was 7.7 litres. Conversely the lowest breast cancer mortality rate (14.9) was found in Portugal which, as noted earlier was third highest in the per capita alcohol consumption table. Obviously there are difficulties in examining the data in this rather simplistic way. In all countries, most of the beverage alcohol is consumed by men. The proportion of abstainers in these countries is also relevant, perhaps particularly for women, where culture and society set powerful standards, and finally age is a factor which may be relevant. Even so, taking all this into account Pochin's point is an interesting one. An examination of more recent information on per capita alcohol consumption (see Table 1.1) and breast cancer mortality rates since 1987 confirms that there is no clear connection between these variables. For example, by 1992 some of the highest breast cancer rates are evident in countries such as Ireland (27.4), the Netherlands (26.7), New Zealand (24.0), Australia (19.4) and Canada (22.5). These are all only medium or low alcohol consumers.

Begg et al. (1983) detected a weak positive association between alcohol and breast cancer. These authors, in a letter discussing the work of Rosenberg et al., who had carried out a case control study published the previous year, stated: 'We feel that our results are considerably less supportive of the hypothesis that alcohol is a risk factor in breast cancer' (p. 294). The authors went on to highlight weaknesses in both studies:

> Moreover, inability to control for diet or other correlates of social class, either in our analysis or in the analysis of Rosenberg et al., is a serious drawback, especially since the relative risk estimates are not so far from unity that they cannot be easily explained by such confounding. (p. 294)

Some of these confounding factors have already been mentioned. Other positive associations have been found between breast cancer and diet (Byers and Graham 1984, Lê et al. 1986), particularly dietary fats (Assembly of Life Sciences 1983, Talamini et al. 1984, Wynder 1984, La Vecchia et al. 1987), tea and coffee consumption (Minton et al. 1979, Lawson et al. 1981) and oral contraception (Centers for Disease Control 1983, Meirik et al. 1986). Other studies have not done so (Rosenberg et al. 1984, Brinton et al. 1986). Some case control studies have shown a reduced risk of breast cancer in relation to cigarette smoking (Baron 1984, Kato et al. 1986, O'Connell et al. 1987). At high consumption, this protective effect of smoking will lead to even more confusion.

In 1977 the results of the third US National Survey were published, particularly examining occupation and industry (Williams et al. 1977). From the evidence generated by this large-scale study, the authors concluded:

> Breast cancer was more common among women who were teachers, other professionals and among those working in banking, real estate, accounting and insurance. Controlling for education did not affect these associations. Later age at first pregnancy is one breast cancer risk factor that may be found more often in such women. (p. 1149)

It should be noted that only 14% of women in this study listed recent employment. There may be a number of reasons for this, including the stage of their illness. Even so, another study by Talamini et al. in Northern Italy also showed 'teachers and other professional workers' (1984, p. 723) at increased risk compared to housewives. Given that age of first pregnancy is associated more with pre-menopausal breast cancer as opposed to post-menopausal breast cancer, another factor may have been age. Other variables associated with an increased risk of breast cancer include family history of breast cancer, early menarche, a history of benign breast disease, higher socio-economic status and obesity (Seidman et al. 1982, 1983). Since these initial studies, a confusing array of results have appeared. Some stated a clear association between alcohol consumption and breast cancer (Williams and Horn 1977, Byers and Funch 1982, Rosenberg et al. 1982, Lê et al. 1984, La Vecchia et al. 1985, 1987, 1989, O'Connell et al. 1987, Schatzkin et al. 1987, Garfinkel et al. 1988, Hiatt et al. 1988, 1990, McMichael and Armstrong 1988, Brandt et al. 1995). However, in many of these studies the associations were weak. As noted by Harris and Wynder (1988):

> Clearly when it comes to alcohol and breast cancer we are dealing with a weak association. Findings are not consistent from study to study. There is no definite dose response. The associations appear to be limited to certain subgroups, and there appears to be a lack of external consistency in that countries such as France and Italy, with the highest per capita intake of alcohol (16 and 12 l, respectively) do not have correspondingly high rates of breast cancer (about 16 and 15 deaths per 100,000). (p. 2871)

Other studies found no association of statistical significance (Paganini-Hill and Ross 1983, Webster et al. 1983, Lindegård 1987,

Adami et al. 1988, Schatzkin et al. 1989). At least two studies showed what could be a protective effect of small doses of alcohol. As noted by Rohan and McMichael (1988):

> When risk of breast cancer was examined across levels of daily alcohol consumption (irrespective of beverage type), women who drank less than about ¼ of a glass, between ¼ and 1 glass, and more than one glass daily had RR of 0.89 (95% CI 0.60–1.32), 0.99 (0.69–1.43) and 1.51 (1.03–2.23) respectively, compared to a risk of unity for non-drinkers. (p. 696)

It has been noted in Chapter 1 that the alcohol content of a 'unit' or a 'standard drink' varies in different countries. In relation to 'a glass' in this study, an Australian measure of alcohol contains 10 grams. This is slightly more than a UK unit at 7.9 grams and less than a US drink at 14 grams. The second study of Dutch women by Van't Veer et al. (1989), suggested that, in pre-menopausal women, alcohol in small quantities (between one and four grams daily) appeared to have a protective effect.

At higher doses of alcohol both the Rohan and McMichael study, and that by Van't Veer and colleagues, noted an association between alcohol and breast cancer, particularly in pre-menopausal women.

As noted by Seidman et al. (1982):

> Despite our efforts to determine risk factors for breast cancer, we have not appreciably increased our ability to identify substantial numbers of truly 'high-risk' women ... The fact that three quarters of all breast cancer cannot yet be attributed to any known specific causes is reason to increase our efforts to identify and quantify risk factors, and to seek effective means of intervention and control. (p. 311)

In 1988 Kelsey and Berkowitz commented:

> the American Cancer Society has estimated that only about one fourth of breast cancer cases can be accounted for by known risk factors ... much of the etiology is still unexplained and hitherto unidentified risk factors remain to be identified. Also, the mechanisms by which most of the established risk factors have their effects have not been elucidated. (p. 5615)

The situation nine years on does not seem to have changed a great deal.

As in any area of alcohol research, one of the 'gold standards' of methodological merit is the conduct of large-scale prospective (follow-up) studies. There have been large-scale cohort studies in this area but not all have been prospective in the true sense of the word. The first large-scale study, often described as prospective, was actually described by the authors (Hiatt and Bawol 1984) as 'a retrospective cohort study of over 95,000 women' (p. 676). What appears to have happened is that the women included in the study had been given regular health checks from 1964 to 1972 as part of the Kaiser Foundation Health Plan in Northern California. The authors identified those women who had developed breast cancer in the geographical area of California and traced back to find those who had been involved in the regular health checks. It is surprising how often this type of model is used and described as prospective, yet often the data collected on alcohol were not a priority at the time of initiation of the study and therefore the consumption measures may not be appropriate for the analysis which then is carried out. The results from this study noted:

> Women who had less than three drinks per day had no increased relative risk over non-drinkers. The results of this study might be explained either by an unrecognised carcinogenic effect of alcohol on breast tissue or confounding effect of other factors associated with heavy alcohol use. (Hiatt and Bawol 1984, p. 676)

Women who drank three or more drinks a day (the equivalent of 5 UK units or more) had an increased risk of breast cancer. This group constituted a relatively small proportion (5.2%) of the sample.

The second study (Schatzin et al. 1987) included 7188 women from the original National Health and Nutrition Study who later developed breast cancer. In fact this seems to be a similar model to Hiatt and Bawol's study. The study found that: 'The relative-risk estimate for any amount of drinking was 1.5 ... The estimates for three levels of consumption from lowest to the highest, were 1.4 ... 1.5 ... and 1.6, in comparison to no drinking at all' (p. 1169). However, yet again, information about important variables was not collected from the total sample. This is exemplified by the fact that, at baseline, details of tobacco smoking were only collected from 43% of the women and no details on family history of breast cancer and age at first pregnancy were collected at this time.

The third study, by Willett et al. (1987) is probably the most widely known of these investigations. This included 121,700 nurses who, in 1976, filled out and returned a postal questionnaire. This study did ask questions on risk factors for breast cancer such as: 'height, weight, age at menarche, menopausal status, age at first birth, parity, family history of breast cancer and personal history of benign breast disease and cancer' (p. 1174). When all these variables were taken into the analysis the relative risk for women drinking 5 grams to 14.9 grams per day (less than one to almost two UK units a day) was 1.3 compared to non-drinkers. Those women who were drinking 15 g or more a day (two UK units) had a relative risk of 1.6 compared to non-drinkers. Even so, a meta-analysis by Longnecker et al (1988) on available evidence concluded:

> There was a strong dose-response relation in both the case control and follow-up epidemiologic data ... We interpret these findings not as proof of causality, but as strongly supportive of an association between alcohol consumption and risk of breast cancer. (p. 652)

In this meta-analysis the relative risk of breast cancer for women who had consumed 3.5 UK units (2 US drinks, or 2.8 Australian drinks) a day was 1.4 compared to non-drinkers.

The final recent large cohort study is the only one of this type so far not to have been carried out in the US. This investigation, by Van den Brandt et al. (1995), included 62,573 women who took part in a study on diet and cancer in the Netherlands. The authors reported:

> the rate ratio for breast cancer in drinkers versus nondrinkers was 1.31 ... When separate alcohol intake categories were compared with nondrinking, the rate ratios were 1.30, 1.29, 1.28, and 1.72 for women who consumed ≤5, 5–14, 15–29, and ≥ 30 grams of alcohol per day, respectively ... The alcohol–breast cancer association was found to be stronger among women with a history of benign breast disease, women with a history of breast cancer among sister(s), and women with an early menopause, and it varied considerably according to age at first birth. These results support a positive association between alcohol and breast cancer among postmenopausal women. The increased risk was particularly found among women who consumed 30 grams or more of alcohol daily. (p. 907)

Other interesting findings from this study included no evident effect in any of the drinking groups for women who had received hormone replacement therapy (HRT) but an apparently stronger association between alcohol and breast cancer for women who had used oral contraceptives or those who smoked.

The majority of studies describe the elevated levels of relative risk of breast cancer by alcohol consumption. These range from 1.03 (Harris and Wynder 1988), through 1.08 (Simon et al. 1991), 1.09 (Byers and Funch 1982, Gapstur et al. 1992), 1.10 (Friedenreich et al. 1992), to 1.49 (Young 1989). These were the relative risks for women drinking 5 grams a day. At higher levels of consumption the Italian study by Talamini et al. (1984) showed a relative risk of 10.3 for women consuming 90 grams or more a day. This does suggest a dose response relationship, with women who drink more heavily being more at risk. As can be seen from the above list, the 'relative risk' factor is of great importance. Mantel (1988), a respected statistician, commented on two of the studies described above – Schatzkin et al. and Willett et al. – and stated:

> Epidemiologists have been warned not to take seriously demonstrations of relative risk unless they are at least 2.0 in view of the biases to which their investigations are frequently subject. However, the current investigations were done in such a way as to minimize bias, and for a disease like breast cancer which is of such great importance among women, an otherwise moderately high relative risk of 1.50 should be considered as being an extremely high relative risk. (p. 672)

However, Mantel went on to examine some of the issues discussed in this section and concluded:

> the two teams of investigators have failed to take into account the possible initial differences between drinkers and nondrinkers but have interpreted their results as though they came from ideal studies: they have failed to capitalize on the capability of cohort studies to yield results on other effects, possibly even beneficial effects of moderate drinking; they have rushed to judgement. (p. 675)

A good example of the confused thinking in this area is a letter by McMichael in the *Medical Journal of Australia*. He wrote of a study which he and his colleague Armstrong published and also of a meeting of the World Health Organization's International Agency for Research on Cancer which he had attended. McMichael (1988) reported:

> The meeting noted the significant positive association between alcohol intake and the risk of breast cancer in each of four large prospective studies and in seven of 13 case-control studies, while it recognised that the moderate increases in risk (up to doubling) were, in principle, compatible with confounding by some identified factor. The meeting concluded cautiously that, while the epidemiological data were suggestive of an alcohol-induced increase in the risk of breast cancer, a firm conclusion cannot yet be reached. (p. 422)

Then, for no apparent reason, McMichael takes a leap in logic:

> We are now on notice that alcohol, with its widespread consumption within our community, may be an important source of breast cancer risk. If no consistent countervailing evidence is published in the near future, it will become prudent, for the purposes of public health policy, to regard alcohol as a risk factor for breast cancer. (p. 422)

This is the kind of leap which can lead us down paths that wiser researchers would not tread. It is precisely the stuff beloved by the media under such tabloid banner headlines as 'Cancer Risk to Boozy Women' (*Daily Record* (Scotland) 1988). It also makes it much more difficult for more balanced views to be heard. Another example of this is a letter in the *Lancet* (Turner and Anderson 1990). The two authors noted the majority of studies showing an association, however weak, between alcohol consumption and breast cancer. They did not mention the number of studies showing no association. Indeed, in at least one of the studies mentioned by these authors (Harris and Wynder 1988) the original authors noted no consistent evidence of a dose response relationship and went further to note: 'While these results do not entirely rule out a weak association between breast cancer and alcohol in certain subgroups, neither do they provide compelling evidence that alcohol has a role in the genesis of this malignancy' (p. 2867).

There is obviously and for the best intentions, a real wish to search for any powerful causal links for breast cancer. It may be that alcohol has a part to play once the irreversible cell changes associated with cancer have taken place; that in some way alcohol may act as an irritant, rather than a causal mechanism. The difficulty with this scenario is the impossibility of predicting whether women with multiple risk factors such as family history, age at first pregnancy, would be wiser not to drink. As it stands at this point, it is neither scientifically wise nor humanely fair to magnify a weak association.

Finally a number of reviews on this subject have been published (Steinberg and Goodwin 1991, Plant 1992, McPherson et al. 1993). After a thorough review of the available evidence McPherson et al. (1993) concluded:

> A causative association of alcohol consumption and breast cancer cannot be confirmed but also cannot be finally excluded. However, all of the evidence would exclude a strong causative association. There is certainly the greatest possibility that the weak association found is an association only, a consequence of alcohol being related to a risk factor or factors that are as yet poorly understood or poorly measured. (p. 235)

There are a number of real problems in this area. I have highlighted some of these in a review (Plant 1992):

> First, regarding the reliability of alcohol consumption data, the greater the length of time between consumption and documentation, the greater the risk of inaccuracy.
>
> Second are the problems surrounding confounding variables, such as nutrition ... As stated earlier by Mantel it is possible that what many studies have used as confounding variables e.g. benign breast disease, may be 'reflections of the really true variables' (1988:675). If this is the case, then rather than clarifying, this would simply confuse the issue even more. The psychological factors which have been linked with the development of cancers over the centuries – such as depression often due to loss and anxiety, are also often the main reasons given by women as triggers for drinking which goes on to reach problem level status. Given the latency period between initiation of cancer and diagnosis, there may be some factor which led to the drinking, and therefore the imputed factor, and not the drinking, is the relevant variable.
>
> Third, the use of inappropriate controls, the use of patients with other hormone dependent cancers, such as endometrial cancers, or patients with benign breast diseases or whether the passage of time plays a part in the differentiation between benign and malignant.
>
> Fourth, although there is enough consistency in the results to suggest an association between alcohol consumption and breast cancer, there is little evidence of a causal link. It seems

> unlikely that further epidemiological studies to find a causal relationship will clarify this. So many of the studies have shown relative risks of less than 2.0 which, as noted by Harris and Wynder (1988) and Rosenberg et al. (1990), can only be seen as a weak association.
>
> Fifth, there is still no clear understanding of the mechanism(s) whereby alcohol consumption and alcohol's actions have effects on breast cancer. It may be that there are critical exposure times, e.g., times of increased or accelerated growth of breast tissue, e.g., during puberty ... or pregnancy. More effort is needed to assess this imputed factor. Perhaps the most difficult area is the latency period which, as already noted can range from 15 to 20 years. This problem has already been noted in the association between use of oral contraceptives at an early age ... or long-term ... and later onset of breast cancer. In conjunction with this is the issue of whether alcohol and its consumption is associated with the initiation of the disease or with the disease promotion. For instance, does something happen to change the cell irreversibly and then alcohol enters as one of the factors associated with the promotion of cancer? Many of these issues await clarification. (p. 122)

This latter point has also been addressed by Wynder (1984). Discussing the possible carcinogenic effects of diet, this author has written: 'the overall action of carcinogenesis may depend largely on promoting activity, and it is here that the carcinogenic process may be most susceptible to modification' (p. 174).

The issue may then be one of early identification however, effectively encouraging women to practise self-examination of the breast is difficult and available evidence on the effectiveness of breast screening is encouraging (Rogers 1990). The possibility of educating adolescent girls on how to practise self-examination has been discussed by Marino and Levy (1986) who described two US studies (Carstenson and O'Grady 1980, Honglandarom and Porter 1981). As noted by these two authors:

> Unfortunately, it is not easy to teach proficient breast self examination technique and successful lesion detection (Christopherson and Parker 1965, Foster and Costanza 1984, Friman et al. 1986, Grady et al. unpublished, Holleb 1985, Kegeles 1984). Self confidence in the ability adequately to detect changes in her breast have been demonstrated to be crucial to compliance (Alagna and Reddy 1984, Becker and Maiman 1980, Grady and

> Wolk unpublished, Kegeles 1984). It is even more difficult to evaluate compliance, although researchers have reported numerous possible methods (Howard 1982, Howe 1985, Turner et al. 1984). (p. 987)

Women who are Older

The age of menopause has remained remarkably constant over the decades. Lifespans have extended and so many women can expect to spend about one-third of their lives after the menopause. As more work is carried out into the relationship between alcohol consumption and hormone levels, the issue of hormone replacement therapy has been addressed by Ginsburg and colleagues (1995). These authors noted an association between alcohol consumption and a higher peak of blood oestrogen levels with 'Twelve healthy post-menopausal women' as the subjects. The latter individuals were all given oestrogens by the medium of applying skin patches. They noted that the peak serum oestrogen levels were higher when the women consumed alcoholic rather than non-alcoholic drinks. The authors suggested the interesting possibility that alcohol may decrease the women's physiological ability to excrete oestrogen. They also noted:

> Our findings raise questions about appropriate estrogen replacement dosing in various patient populations. Further work is needed to assess E2 levels and half lives in chronic alcoholics who use estrogen replacement and also in oral contraceptive users who drink alcohol. (p. 1230)

This is a good example of research working soundly: one group of findings replicated, and then used to set another series of questions.

Osteoporosis

Osteoporosis is a huge problem amongst older women. As noted by Liao et al. (1995), it 'is estimated that there are over 50,000 hip fractures in Britain per year; between one-quarter and one-third of the sufferers will die within 6 months and more than half of the rest will suffer pain or increased disability (Grimley-Evans 1990)' (p. 171). In an increasingly ageing population this can be a great burden on services in relation to health care costs.

The main measure for assessing the presence and degree of osteoporosis, is bone mineral density (BMD). This measurement enables an assessment of the risk of fractures. Heavy doses of alcohol, such as those found in binge drinking, can affect the way the body uses the calcium in the diet. By increasing the amount of calcium which is excreted in the urine the body loses this important substance (Laitenen et al. 1991). Bone mineral density is also affected by hormone levels, particularly levels of reproductive hormones. This issue of endocrine function in post-menopausal women is complex. The main hormone known to have a protective effect on women's health is oestrogen. As noted earlier, this hormone has a protective effect against such conditions as cardiovascular disease and cancers of the breast and uterus and also one of the major concerns for older women, osteoporosis.

At the menopause, either natural or surgical in the case of hysterectomy, the level of oestrogen falls. Studies have shown that it can be of great importance whether the ovaries are removed at the same time as the uterus if hysterectomy is performed. Women who have both ovaries removed have even lower levels of oestrogen. The other important aspect is that one of the main sources of androgens, which can be converted into oestrogens, are these small structures, the ovaries. In this respect alcohol may have a beneficial effect. Its consumption appears to be associated with an increase in levels of oestrogens (oestradiol) in the blood (Mello et al. 1989, Gavaler et al. 1993). This increase in oestrogens comes from one main process. In post-menopausal women, androgens are converted into oestrogens, thus prolonging the protective effect of oestrogen, albeit to a lesser degree. Alcohol appears to increase the conversion of androgen into oestrogen (Gavaler 1992). This process in turn affects BMD, as noted by Hill on a study of women in Finland (Laitinen et al. 1991):

> The effects of age and several physical and lifestyle factors on BMD were determined. BMD diminished with age, significantly so after menopause. However, when moderate users of alcohol were contrasted with abstainers, the postmenopausal women who had consumed alcohol showed a positive correlation between alcohol intake and BMD. Specifically the postmenopausal alcohol users had significantly higher BMD in the sites evaluated. The beneficial effects of moderate doses of alcohol on BMD was found only among the postmenopausal women, however. (Hill 1995, p. 186)

It should be stressed that this study relates to women who are drinking well below the level of what could be defined as problem-drinking. More recent research is cautious (Laitinen and Valimäki 1993). The picture for heavy drinkers changes. Calcium needs the presence of Vitamin D to enable the body to use it effectively. Metabolism of this vitamin, as with many others, is adversely affected by heavy drinking. In this way the ability of the body to use the calcium in the diet is effectively reduced (Bjorneboe et al. 1988). The increase in oestrogens noted above does occur in post-menopausal women who were problem-drinkers (Välimäki et al. 1983, Gavaler and Van Thiel 1992, Gavaler 1995). However, the advantages of this will be well outweighed by the damage associated with heavy drinking. In relation to osteoporosis, this will relate to such traumas as fractures due to falls and the resultant delayed healing, problems which are a well recognised part of problem drinking and advancing age (Hingson and Howland 1987).

It has been questioned whether prolonged heavy drinking damages the cells which form the bone matrix (Diamond et al. 1989, Pepersack et al. 1992, Bickle 1993, Bickle et al. 1993, Gonzalez-Calvin et al. 1993). From a laboratory-based study carried out by Klein et al. (1996), the authors concluded: 'These data confirm a direct inhibitory effect of ethanol on osteoblast proliferation without overt cellular toxicity that may in part explain the reduced bone mass observed in those who consume excessive amounts of alcohol' (p. 572).

Studies involving problem-drinkers who subsequently stopped drinking have shown that this damage may at least cease and may even improve with continued abstinence (Pepersack et al. 1992). As in other areas of work, studies can often raise as many questions as they answer. For example, in Klein et al.'s study they raised an issue of concern: 'The skeletal consequences of alcohol intake during adolescence, when the rapid skeletal growth ultimately responsible for peak bone mass is occurring, may be especially harmful' (p. 577).

The vast majority of the evidence for harm to bone formation has been found in heavy drinkers. It would be unwise to exaggerate the effects of youthful experimentation with alcohol. However, there is one particular group with which this issue may need to be seriously addressed: the group of adolescent young women with eating disorders whose possible excessive alcohol intake, added to the problems of the eating disorder itself, may put them at particular risk.

In view of the fact that osteoporosis is much more common amongst women than amongst men, it is interesting to note that a considerable amount of research into this topic appears to have related to males (De Vernejoul et al. 1983, Spencer et al. 1986, Crilly et al. 1988).

In a study of 9704 women aged 65 years or older, Nelson et al. (1994) examined neuromuscular and physical functioning and took lifetime histories of tobacco and alcohol use. The measurement of alcohol use over the lifespan was that described by Armor and Polich (1978 and Armor, Polich and Braiker 1980). This is a difficult phenomenon to assess and it is questionable whether it is possible to do so with any real degree of accuracy. We do not know enough about the changing patterns of women's drinking over the lifespan (Fillmore 1987). Each generation of women grow up with a different attitude to and experiences of drinking, both in relation to themselves and to their families, social contacts and 'significant others'. There may therefore be changes which may not at first be obvious. However, as noted by Nelson et al. (1994):

> Nondrinkers (including former and never drinkers) had worse performance on all but one measure of function compared with current moderate drinkers, after adjustment for age, history of stroke, BMI, clinic site, physical activity, and current and past smoking status. (p. 1828)

Reasons suggested for this vary but to a large extent relate to sociability and marital status. Sadly, it is probably true in many countries that as people become more infirm they may tend to withdraw from social situations. The subjects in the study by Nelson et al. were taken from a prospective cohort study of people with osteoporotic fractures. In this way again the link is made with calcium. Calcium is not only vital in the health of bones but also plays an important part in the transmission of nerve impulses and mechanisms of the neuromuscular system. It may be that deficits in this latter process explain in part the findings of this investigation.

Urbana-Márquez et al. (1995) compared alcohol-related muscle damage in problem-drinking men (n=100), and problem-drinking women (n=50) in Spain. Their results showed that:

> In summary, the fact that women in this study had about the same prevalence of cardiomyopathy as men, despite having consumed far less ethanol, is strong evidence for a greater female propensity to alcohol-induced cardiac damage. (p. 154)

Even in 1995 the view that tissue concentration etc. is greater in women has not been acknowledged by everybody. The final sentence of the Urbana-Marquez paper seems to carry a sense of regret: 'In any event, at least with regard to alcohol, the heart of a woman seems to be more sensitive than that of a man' (p. 154).

More research is still required to clarify the possible positive and negative effects of alcohol on physical health. The balance between the positive and negative effects of alcohol is an exciting and productive area for further research into gender differences. The fact that drinking might be beneficial as well as harmful is a key issue for future health promotional messages. The latter are discussed further in Chapter 7 of this book.

Even so, the fact remains that the majority of problems in most countries related to alcohol are not caused through prolonged heavy or problem-drinking, however that may be defined. They are caused by acute episodes of intoxication; for example a young person ending up in a wheelchair after being involved in a drink-related road traffic accident. Indeed, many of these tragedies involve young people. Sometimes the risky drinker is the casualty. Sometimes she or he is simply a casualty/victim of some other person's heavy or inappropriate consumption of alcohol. Women, often older women, may become trapped in a violent relationship and left without the power or strength to escape from it. The reality is that it is usually a woman who, willingly or unwillingly, has to bear the brunt of the effects of heavy drinking by a spouse or partner, or shoulder the burden of looking after an invalid, sometimes for many years.

4 Psychological Aspects

Attitudes to drinking and drinking habits involve a considerable number of psychological factors. This chapter reviews some of these in relation to drinking by women. During recent decades, the lives of women in many countries have changed dramatically.

A recent survey of adults in Britain was carried out in 1994–95 (Bennett et al. 1996). As noted in Chapter 1, this showed an increase in the proportion of women drinking over the 14 units a week level from 9% in 1984 to 13% in 1994. For the age group 65 years and over, the proportion has increased from 3% in 1984, to 7% in 1994. This is an interesting finding and would suggest that older women are now more in line with their younger counterparts. We are now beginning to see an effect of the acceptability of women drinking; these women were in their thirties when social changes in the 1960s enabled females to feel comfortable going into public bars. They are the first generation to grow up with the more relaxed culture.

Interestingly, in relation to self-image and drinking, the consumption levels of the women in the above study were compared with how the women viewed the amount they drank. In the groups of women drinking 15–25 and 26–35 UK units a week, 68% and 50% respectively described themselves as drinking a 'moderate amount' and 24% and 36% as drinking 'quite a lot'. In spite of the recent evident changes in alcohol consumption levels amongst women, a double standard still exists in relation to female drinking or intoxication. Gomberg (1976), writing of the different attitudes towards women and men drinking, referred to some of the early work by the distinguished US researcher, Genevieve Knupfer:

> Knupfer believes the relationship between drinking and women's roles involves two aspects, one relating to the division of labour between the sexes and impaired response to the needs of others, and the other relating to the loss of customary sexual restraints and inhibitions ... Knupfer makes an excellent point in regard to women's work role and alcohol. Her alcohol intake may not markedly lower the efficiency of a housewife in using a vacuum cleaner or washing machine or in cooking but it does impair 'precisely the quality of sensitivity to the needs of others' (Knupfer 1964) that we value in her familial role. (p. 126)

It is this very quality of being available for others, being open to help, support and encourage others, that makes women's relationship with alcohol so complex. Knupfer was right, women are not allowed to 'take time out' with alcohol the way that their male counterparts can and do. This is the case in many countries. As noted by Kua (1994): 'The problem of Chinese women who drink excessively is viewed more gravely because the stability of the home is in jeopardy – there is a tenacious belief that the sanctity of the family must not be tainted' (p. 957).

It has frequently been asked: 'Why do women drink?' However, the underlying enquiry seems more accurately to be: 'Why do some women drink too much?' Indeed, in some countries the wording of the question can make it even more difficult to answer. In Lesotho the question may well be: 'Why do you drink when you are a woman?' (Mphi 1994, p. 947). There is no simple answer. Indeed, we should not try to reduce the richness and complexity of human experiences and each individual's perception of them to simple answers. Trying to do so is more related to the enquirer's needs, than to the needs of the people with problems. Indeed, there is a risk that this leads to labelling people by type. This will be discussed later in this chapter.

Depending on the culture, the majority of women probably drink for the same reasons that the majority of men drink: that is, to enjoy themselves, have fun, feel part of the social group, relax, or give themselves a treat. Other reasons for drinking relate to religious and cultural norms. Drinking alcohol is above all a social behaviour, it bonds groups together (Heath 1995).

In a world where for many people anxiety and stress are at levels beyond which these are productive, alcohol is seen as one means of finding relief. As noted by Cowley (1992), Hippocrates stated that 'wine drunk with an equal quantity of water puts away anxiety and terrors' (pp. 1A–41S). The issue of anxiety and its relation to alcohol has been examined over many years (Polivy et al. 1976, Abrams and Wilson 1979, Wilson et al. 1989, Corcoran and Parker 1991, Abbey, Smith and Scott 1993, Allen 1995). The extreme aspect of anxiety, panic disorder, has been shown commonly to occur together with alcohol problems. Cowley's review (1992) suggested that the two problems may actually reinforce one another on a biological level.

There have been many attempts to produce simple explanations of drinking behaviours. For example, a number of authors have considered the question of whether stress, attributed to particular life events, may be an important factor in drinking patterns or problematic drinking. Obviously these differ with age, but traditionally for women, they are more often associated with relationship difficulties than for their male counterparts who cite factors such as job and financial difficulties. Other issues have included gynaecological problems, such as infertility, sexual difficulties and the menopause (Wilsnack 1984, Schaefer and Evans 1985, Wilsnack and Wilsnack 1995). However, Cooke and Allan (1984), commenting on the results of a Scottish study, concluded:

> no substantial relationship existed between the experience of life events and elevated alcohol consumption in a normal population. The life events hypothesis may have arisen because of the need for a 'special' explanation of female alcohol abuse. (p. 425)

In relation to areas such as infertility the question of cause and effect needs to be highlighted. The question of whether the drinking led to the infertility or the infertility led to the drinking has not been met with consistent answers.

The idea that women are more likely to drink in relation to issues such as loss of a particular role has now been well examined. There does appear to be an association between role loss and problem drinking. This loss of role can be anything from unemployment to the 'empty nest' syndrome (Curlee 1969), when the children leave home and the role their mother has carved out for herself suddenly vanishes.

An important theme of many studies into the psychology of drinking has been that of expectancy. This relates to the individual's belief that because they have had an alcoholic drink they will feel or behave in certain ways. For example, in relation to anxiety, De Boer et al. (1993) dichotomised the effects of alcohol on anxiety into pharmacological and expectancy-related aspects. This study included both women (n=32) and men (n=32). The authors concluded that: 'women who believed they had consumed alcohol, however, were less anxious than those who believed that they had consumed only tonic' (p. 123). This is an interesting finding because, although this reduction in anxiety may be what might be assumed to be the case, other studies have found that women were more likely to experience some degree of stress or anxiety related to drinking (Abrams and Wilson 1979, Sutker et al. 1982, Jones-Webb et al. 1996). Why the latter should be so remains in question, however. One possible explanation relates to the issue of control or loss of control. In many countries, a common reason given by women for not drinking heavily is the need to stay in control. It may be that some women believe that drinking at any level beyond minimal amounts incurs some potential risk. It is possible that for some women, past experience of unpleasant or dangerous situations when they have had too much to drink may affect later drinking and increase anxiety. Women with past histories of abuse for example, may feel that at all costs they must remain in control, and that means not taking the risk of becoming drunk.

An interesting study carried out in the Netherlands indicated that there were increased fear responses in women immediately prior to menstruation (van der Molen et al. 1988). This fear response also lasted longer than at other times in the menstrual cycle. Although van der Molen et al.'s study did not include alcohol, it gives perhaps an interesting view. Perhaps studies in the area of anxiety related to alcohol consumption now need at least to acknowledge the possibility that the time of the menstrual cycle may be a relevant variable (McLeod et al. 1994). One of the other areas of expectancy related to alcohol is that of sexual arousal (Goldman et al. 1987, Leigh 1990). As previously noted in Chapters 1 and 2, sex and alcohol have been inextricably linked for centuries, although the physiology and psychology seem to be at odds.

Physiologically, alcohol appears to dry up the vaginal secretions and thicken the cervical mucus. This may be related to alcohol's action on vaginal blood flow which is reduced with alcohol consumption (Wilson and Lawson 1976, 1978). Regardless of these and other physiological changes, many women believe alcohol makes them more able to enjoy, and engage in, intercourse. Obviously psychology can be more powerful than physiology. As noted in other areas, alcohol expectancy is important (Beckman and Ackerman 1995). According to Kline (1990) there is a commonplace expectancy that drinking increases sexuality and induces relaxation. Psychologically, this expectancy also relates to permission. Having had something to drink may, in some way, give women permission to behave in a way they want to but cannot when sober. Leigh found that in a group of women from a community study, those with the highest alcohol expectancies were more likely actively to initiate sexual encounters than those women who had lower expectations of the effects of alcohol (1990).

Female inhibition in this respect may be, at least in part, attributable to the old myths relating to 'fallen women'. The British in Victorian times were a good example of the powerful influence on women not to enjoy their sexuality. As noted by Stone (1977):

> for the first time in Western history there was a strong body of opinion which actually denied the existence of the sexual drive in

> the majority of women, and regarded the minority who experienced it to any marked degree as morally, mentally or physically diseased. A marriage manual of 1839 stated as a fact that sterility was caused by any female who displayed 'excessive ardour of desire', and advised that 'tranquillity, silence, and secrecy are necessary for a prolific coition'. (p. 54)

More recent work brings interesting light to bear on these views (Malatesta et al. 1982). As noted by Beckman and Ackerman (1995) of the Malatesta et al. study: 'As consumption increased, women ... also reported increased difficulty in having an orgasm and decreased orgasmic intensity' (p. 249).

It has also been shown that masturbation appears to cause uptake of acidity into the cervix thus decreasing the chances of pregnancy. Given that Victorian males were warned against any 'ardour of desire' in their wives, alcohol consumption by females might not have seemed so bad. Even so, both drinking and sexual arousal would have been a real threat to what they saw as a woman's main function in life, that of producing children.

There has been a growing body of work on the possible connection between sexual arousal and drinking by women (Beckman 1979, Covington and Kohen 1984, Peterson et al. 1984, Wilsnack 1984, Van Thiel et al. 1988). In a review by Crowe and George (1989), these authors concluded:

> on the strength of the available evidence: (a) alcohol disinhibits psychological sexual arousal and suppresses physiological responding, the former being stronger at lower doses of alcohol and the latter effect at higher doses: (b) although suppression is strictly pharmacological in nature, disinhibition appears to be both pharmacological (the result of cognitive impairment) and psychological (the result of socially learned expectancies) and (c) expectancies and cognitive impairment can disinhibit separately or jointly. There is also some evidence that alcohol can contribute to sexual arousal through misattribution or transfer of excitement. (p. 384)

It may be that, as is evident in relation to some physical problems, alcohol in small doses may be quite helpful to women who have mild sexual difficulties. Klassen and Wilsnack, in their national survey of American women, noted:

> moderate drinkers (consuming 4 to 13 drinks per week) scored lower than lighter or heavier drinkers on an index of female

> sexual dysfunctions (1986). Social restraints or personal inhibition may affect both sexual functioning and drinking among women who drink little or nothing. Amongst the heaviest drinkers, drinking may be both an attempt to self-medicate sexual problems and a cause of worsened sexual difficulties. (p. 48)

It must be noted that the upper limit of drinking in this study would, in relation to UK measures (23 units a week) be regarded as high.

Gynaecological problems are common in problem-drinking women (Jones et al. 1980, Perper et al. 1993, Lozina et al. 1995). Recent work has suggested that such females may find improvement in sexual function after a period of abstinence. This improvement can occur in as short a time as six months in women who are still experiencing menstrual cycles (Gavaler et al. 1993). For post-menopausal women the improvement seems to take longer, as noted by Gavaler et al. (1994): 'these findings suggest that alcoholic postmenopausal women abstinent from alcohol for longer than one year report greater satisfaction with the sexual aspects of their lives than women abstinent for a shorter period of time' (p. 269). It must be noted that the aspect of sexual relationships may depend on the past experiences of the women. It should not be assumed that someone who has long-standing sexual difficulties will find them disappearing if they stop drinking.

Alcohol is a central nervous system depressant; therefore it dampens response times. However, in relation to its impact on emotional state, alcohol will most commonly simply heighten the present mood of the drinker. Folk lore has it that certain drinks will make people behave in certain ways: 'Brandy makes you randy' (sexually aroused). Many people will tell you categorically that if they drink gin they will become depressed. However, as in many areas of alcohol consumption, whatever the reality, the fantasy and belief may be more powerful. If someone believes that a cool glass of white wine will help them relax, it probably will. If someone believes a glass of chilled lager on a hot summer's day will quench their thirst, then it probably will. The problem arises when someone believes that alcohol per se, or particular types or strengths of alcohol, will encourage *someone else* to behave in a particular way. This latter is associated with an important addition to women's own alcohol expectancies, that is the expectancies men have of expectancies of women who have been drinking.

A few years ago I was asked to do an interview for a television programme on beverage strengths. I asked for a pint of special lager to make the point that it is stronger than other lagers. The bar manager asked the barman for 'a pint of leg-opener'. The real risk in this kind of statement is the endless possible confusions. If a woman does want to have a sexual encounter then that is her decision. The problems can arise when both parties in the encounter tacitly transfer the responsibility on to the supposed disinhibiting effects of alcohol. This takes away the personal responsibility, something which should not be ascribed to an inanimate liquid such as an alcoholic drink. A study by George et al. (1988), examined perceptions of women's sexuality after drinking and the effects of the gender of the person who paid for the drink. Subjects were given a number of scenarios, for example a woman buying a non-alcoholic drink or alcoholic drink and a woman paying for the drink herself or a man buying the drink for her. Comparing these situations the woman drinking alcohol was described as:

> significantly more aggressive, impaired, sexually available, and as significantly more likely to engage in foreplay and intercourse. Perceptions of her sexual disinhibition and likelihood of sex play were significantly enhanced if the man bought the drinks. (p. 1295)

Women will not like this attitude, quite rightly, and many are fighting to change it, but women need to give clear messages that the above picture is inaccurate and that these kinds of assumptions do not belong in today's world. Men have been using alcohol for centuries to change their mood; there seems little reason to raise concerns and exaggerate the risks when women do the same thing.

However, in relation to problem-drinking women, there is a suggestion from some research that females are more likely than males to use alcohol to change negative mood (Olenick and Chalmers 1991, Grover and Thomas 1993, Rubonis et al. 1994). This may be of importance after treatment as it may carry an increased risk of relapse (Rubonis et al. 1994, Hodgins et al. 1995).

Sex-role conflict has also been examined in relation to women and drinking (Scida and Vannicelli 1979) and a number of studies have now been carried out into lesbian women in relation to their drinking (Bloomfield 1993, Hall 1993, Mays et al. 1994). Studies have also been conducted to examine lesbian women with alcohol-related problems, in relation to both the type of problems (Hall 1993, Savin Williams 1994) and the treatment (Deevey and Wall 1992, Hall 1994).

Young People

As noted in Chapter 1, the subject of adolescent (Petraitis et al. 1995), student drinking (Gleason 1994a, b) and the concerns raised for these groups have spurred a vast amount of research. Ohannessian et al. (1994) have stated:

> hassles may play an even stronger role during adolescence when the individual may be experiencing an array of stresses related to the developmental transitions required of adolescence (e.g. puberty, cognitive changes, alterations in family and peer relationships. (p. 761)

Many studies have examined different psychological aspects of drinking and problem-drinking at this time of life. These include factors associated with starting to drink (Montgomery et al. 1993, Tschann et al. 1994, Wilson et al. 1994), social skills (Hover and Gaffney 1991), risk/sensation seeking (Baker and Beer 1991, Rossow and Wichstrom 1994, Wiers et al. 1994, Patton 1995), the relationship with sexual risk-taking behaviour (Parker et al. 1994) and sexually transmitted diseases (Donovan and McEwan 1995, Fortenberry 1995), antisocial behaviour (Hesselbrock et al. 1992, Kosson et al. 1994) and aggression (Milgram 1993, White et al. 1993). This latter area of aggression is examined later in this chapter, but in relation to students, researchers have found it difficult to address the issue of gender differences in aggressive behaviour mainly because there are far fewer instances of female aggression. A review of studies on levels and consequences of alcohol consumption in college students by Brennan et al. (1986) noted:

> review of 21 studies of college drinking conducted between 1953 and 1984 found that ... Both men and women who were medium to heavy drinkers expected to experience more pleasure, sexual enhancement and aggressiveness after drinking than did light drinkers. (Milgram 1993, p. 55)

Other areas examined in relation to this age group include psychiatric concomitants, such as depression (Horwitz and White 1991, Van Hasselt et al. 1993), the effects of parental break-up (Doherty and Needle 1991, Billingham et al. 1993) and the effects of parental problem-drinking (Ullman and Orenstein 1994, Windle 1994). This latter aspect will be examined later in the chapter.

Studies of psychological aspects have examined adolescents in countries such as Australia (Winefield et al. 1992), Egypt (Soueif and Hannourah 1987), Greece (Madianos et al. 1994), Sweden (Persson et al. 1994), New Zealand (Connolly et al. 1994) the USA (Jessor and Jessor 1977) and the UK (Plant and Plant 1992). Research has also examined specific groups, such as students (Richman et al. 1992, Seda-Mendoza et al. 1992). Drinking patterns (Williams and Morrice 1992, Dick et al. 1993), have been noted along with levels of consumption (Wiggins and Wiggins 1992), place of drinking (Knibbe et al. 1991), and the effects of the mass media on these groups (Connolly et al. 1994). The transition from social to risk/problem-drinking (Prendergast 1994, Pulkkinen and Pitkanen 1994, Baer et al. 1995, Carey 1995), and the consequences of heavy drinking (Turnbell and Gomberg 1991), have also been examined, along with problem use (Farrel and Strang 1991, Tuttle 1993, Carey 1995, Smith et al. 1995). The assessment and diagnosis of adolescents with substance abuse problems (Murray and McMillan 1993, Osterling et al. 1993, Brown et al. 1994, Heck and Williams 1995, Rogers et al. 1995) are now recorded. Psychological differences between the genders have been investigated (Huselid and Cooper 1992, Gross 1993, Pope et al. 1994, Svenson et al. 1994).

The problems with outcome in relation to research have been described by Stinchfield et al. (1994).

Research into the effect of external influences on young people's drinking has produced mixed results. The influence of others (Brennan et al. 1986, Prentice and Miller 1993, Williams and Smith 1993), and of the situation (van de Goor 1990) have been investigated. A study by Bahr et al. (1995), examined a random sample of 27,000 adolescents. The authors concluded:

> The influence of family bonds is moderately strong but operates primarily through peers; adolescents with higher family bonds are less likely to have close friends who are involved with drugs. ... Family bonding appears to be an important social control mechanism that may decrease the risk of alcohol abuse among adolescents. (p. 457)

The difficulty about this factor is the degree of what is described as family bonding. In some cases, the closer the adolescent has been to her parents, the more she has to show she is moving away from them. For most parents the hope is that the grounding and love they have given their children may be enough, not to stop them finding excitement in risky situations, but at the end of the day, to find stable lifestyles after a period of experimenting. However, sadly, it sometimes does not work out that way. Some young women do suffer serious adverse consequences during the period of experimentation.

In a study by Harford and Parker (1994) on antisocial behaviour, family history and alcohol dependence, the authors examined data from the US National Longitudinal Survey. This survey was set up in 1970 to study the transition of young people into the labour force. It was a large-scale study with 12,686 respondents. Their results showed:

> there is a relationship between antisocial behaviors reported in 1980 by young men and women aged 15–22 years of age and the number of alcohol dependence symptoms reported by these same men and women in 1989, 9 years later. (p. 267)

The authors also noted that those young women and men who reported antisocial behaviour were not more likely to have come from a family with a history of alcohol problems. However, *severity* of antisocial behaviour during adolescence was associated with a positive family history of alcohol problems and the development of alcohol dependence problems in the group by then aged between 27 and 34 years of age. Weinberg et al. (1994) examined the relationship between adolescents' reports of parental drinking patterns and heavy use and misuse of alcohol in the adolescents themselves. These authors concluded:

> reported heavier drinking by parents appears to make a significant contribution to the risk of alcohol use and misuse in early adolescence. These findings appear to hold true for both mothers and fathers, whether drinking individually or together, and for boys and girls. (p. 101)

Adulthood

The transition from childhood, through adolescence, into adulthood can be exciting, painful, fun and terrifying. Some people move through it more easily than others. In an attempt to identify precursors to alcohol problems, Pulkkinen and Pitkanen (1994) examined a group of 196 males and 173 females during these transitions, that is, at the ages of 8, 14 and 26. They found that at the age of 8, aggression, low anxiety, problems with social relationships and poor school success were associated with alcohol problems in later life for men. Alcohol-related problems in women were also related to lack of success in school performance, but high anxiety was highlighted as a risk factor. This issue of anxiety will be discussed later in this chapter.

There are clear differences between the genders in relation to non-alcohol-related depression. Evidence is strong that from adolescence onwards women are more likely to experience depression. Prior to this time rates do not seem to differ greatly. A review by Nolen-Hoeksema and Girgus (1994) concluded:

> We suggest that the greater prevalence of pre-existing factors for depression in girls, in combination with the greater number of social and biological challenges that girls face beginning in early adolescence, leads to the emergence of substantial gender differences in depression. (p. 438)

The issue of mood changes in women is also related to menstrual cycle (Endicott 1993, Pariser 1993). Some studies have shown an increase in negative mood immediately prior to menstruation (May 1975, Wilcoxon et al. 1976); others have not been able to replicate these findings. Another consideration is whether the menstrual cycle affects the consumption of alcohol in women. Sutker et al. (1983) carried out a small study to assess the possibility that alcohol consumption may increase during different phases in the menstrual cycle. The authors concluded:

> The fact that this sample of healthy intelligent, working women drank alone and purposively to relieve tension and depression more frequently during menstrual flow suggests that such factors, especially when associated with elevated negative moods, may prompt maladaptive drinking patterns among heavier drinking samples. (p. 351)

Other studies have not shown this link. Even so, the comments of Sutker et al. on heavier-drinking women, rightly highlight the possibility that some individuals may sometimes drink in response to physical and emotional factors. Studies have been carried out with problem-drinking women (Podolsky 1963, Belfer et al. 1971), or women who seem to be at risk of developing alcohol-related problems (Charette et al. 1990). A more recent retrospective study by Allen (1996) involved a self-selected group of problem-drinking women (n=55), who attended a variety of alcohol problem clinics or drop-in centres. These women all completed a questionnaire with questions on their drinking histories. The point was, when these women were drinking, was there a particular time of the month when they drank more? Allen found that about one-third of her female subjects reported drinking more in the pre-menstrual phase and concluded:

> The practical import of the findings in the present study is that those counselling and treating alcohol-dependent women should be aware that they may be at increased risk of relapse or worsening drinking patterns at certain times of the month. The implications of this are that counsellors should be trained to ask directly about premenstrual drinking patterns and thereafter to work with the woman to reduce the risk by whatever means possible. These may include formal medical treatment for premenstrual symptoms as well as encouragement to make lifestyle changes to minimize stress at this time. (p. 147)

Factors that women perceive as contributing to their drinking problems include problematic relationships (Long and Mullen 1994, Lammers et al. 1995) and 'vulnerability' (Hill 1995).

The possibility of a link between alcohol problems and affective disorders has also been raised both in the problem-drinkers (Ross et al. 1988, Merikangas et al. 1990, Roy et al. 1991, Benishek et al. 1992, Coryell et al. 1992, Dunne et al. 1993, Rapaport et al. 1996) and their relatives (Schuckit et al. 1995). From the results of a study into alcohol problems and major depressive illness in female twins, Kendler et al. (1993) reached the following conclusion: 'Comorbidity between major depression and alcoholism in women is substantial and appears to result largely from genetic factors that influence the risk to both disorders, but common environmental risk factors also contribute' (p. 690). Interestingly, these authors go on to caution: 'Since the genders may differ both in the magnitude and in causes of comorbidity between alcoholism and major depression the results cannot be assumed to apply to men' (p. 696). It is surprising how often researchers and clinicians do not raise this important point in relation to results from studies on men being 'assumed' to fit for women.

The relationship between alcohol and other psychiatric sequelae has also been examined (Ojehagen et al. 1991, Struening et al. 1991, Dunne et al. 1993, Windle et al. 1995, Krausz et al. 1996) and in relatives (Bidaut-Russell, Bradford and Smith 1994, Bidaut-Russell, Smith and Bradford 1994).

The concept of personality has been debated in the alcohol literature over the years. One view was that there are a number of personality characteristics which are common to an end result of 'alcoholism', but these may be present in more than one personality type. Another view was that there was a particular type of personality which could be clearly identified and named 'addictive or alcoholic personality' (Zwerling and Rosenbaum 1959). Jellinek (1960), on the other hand, questioned whether problem-drinkers became more alike, almost by being shaped by the experience of being a problem-drinker. It must be made clear that at this time, the late 1940s and into the early 1950s, as noted by Cameron (1995), 'throughout the developed world, the disease concept of alcoholism was not just the leading theory in the treatment of alcoholism, it was regarded simply as the truth' (p. 5). This statement deserves attention. That it is true is not in doubt. It is the impact this had on what happened next, which requires examining. The real risk at this point was that people would simply accept this 'truth' that alcoholism was a disease and begin to tailor treatment programmes to fit with this concept. Sadly, this was in fact what happened. The close connection in relation to time between the re-emergence of the disease concept, (it had actually been around since the Middle Ages (Warner 1994)) and the 'alcoholic personality', reinforced the view that 'these people' were different. In terms of descriptions and treatment regimes, it also assumed they were male.

Just as part of human nature can reduce other people to objects to help contain fear and anxiety, so we can label people to show they are different and therefore we need not worry that we will become like them. They have a 'personality defect' or a type of personality which is different from one's own, and so everyone who is not in that group can relax.

Jessor's social psychological theory, first described in the early 1960s, expanded the personality theory to include social and cultural aspects. These studies by Jessor et al. (1968) showed significant positive association between low expectations of achievement and problem-drinking behaviour in college women. However, in a later study of high school students, Jessor and Jessor (1973) found this association between low expectations of achievement and problem-drinking to be present for both young women and men. By 1971 Jones, in a study of women problem-drinkers, noted a greater risk of depression and, in their adolescent years, a greater likelihood of their describing themselves as pessimistic and self-defeating. Jones also noted an increased likelihood in this group to act even more extremely in what they perceived as a feminine way. The advantage of this particular entity is the reassurance it provides that only those with this type of personality will develop alcohol problems. However, the majority of research into psychology of humans has added little to the puzzle of cause and effect related to alcohol problems. As noted by Bates: 'Nathan (1988), for example, concludes that it is primarily antisocial *behavior*, not antisocial *personality*, that has been consistently found to predict later alcoholism and drug problems' (1993, p. 53).

Available evidence has not supported the conclusion that only those with some unique personality develop alcohol problems (Fazey 1977). Anyone who drinks sufficiently heavily or inappropriately may do so. When the early lives of so many problem-drinkers, female and male, involve trauma, inconsistencies and confusion, it makes it extremely difficult to make close links with a particular personality, far less make a causal relationship. Rogers, a psychologist and psychotherapist, believed that people are born with many attributes but, because they have to live with a family, they generally adapt to 'fit in'. At best, the family encourages and nurtures individuality. Less fortunate children find themselves shutting off parts of themselves which are not accepted by other family members. They may ignore their own needs to the point that they truly believe they no longer have any and that their main aim in life is to help or look after others in whatever way they can. This process, according to Carl Rogers, occurs in all human beings, but in many countries female children have more powerful messages in this direction than male children. The young girl watches her mother and copies her, for good or ill. As she grows older she may learn never to question who she is, where she wants to go in her life, what kind of partner, if any, she wants to live with. Indeed, the latter is of great importance in women who later develop drinking problems. If she has not had the opportunity to explore who she is and how much of who she is has been pushed down to enable her to live in her family, she may have great difficulty in recapturing and integrating all of her personal identity. This may mean that the kind of partner she chooses may be more like her family than the person she would have chosen if she had had a more complete picture of her whole self. There are so many questions: Where are you in your life? Who are you with? How do you see yourself? How does how you see yourself, fit with the way you live your life?

Drinking History

There do appear to be different aspects of problem drinking which relate, as noted in Chapter 6, to age of onset. In relation to psychological aspects of problem drinking, females in their late teenage years or early twenties may have a very different profile from their older sisters with an average age of around 41 years. The differences include age of onset, by definition the former group have not been drinking as long as the latter. It may be that the younger age group are more severely damaged, not necessarily by their drinking but in their own psychopathology. In relation to treatment outcome also they may have less solid ground upon which to build because their drinking behaviour started while they were still going through the process of developing their own sense of who they are.

Different aspects of women's drinking have been noted (Sclare 1970, Wilkinson 1980, Ross 1989, Hesselbrock 1991, Bucholz et al. 1992). A recent study by Schuckit et al. (1995) studied problem drinkers using their relatives to collaborate reports of drinking behaviour. This group found that women did tend to have a slightly more telescoped history of drinking which started later in life around the age of 18.5 years and developed into identifiable problems sooner at about the age of 30 years. The equivalents for men were 17.5 years and 32.5 years. This was an important study and it was good to note that Schuckit et al. carried it out as a second step. The first phase had examined problem-drinking men. The second phase compared problem-drinking men and women who were all relatives of problem drinkers. There were a number of similarities between the genders with a generally similar path leading from mild to severe problems. Even so, the authors noted some differences in trends:

> the 69 women (43% of the 161 alcohol-dependent women) who reported that they hit inanimate objects or threw things while intoxicated experienced this event later in the progression of their problems related to alcohol than was true of the 180 of the 317 (57%) alcohol-dependent men who also reported this symptom. Similarly, women appeared more likely to report binges, craving alcohol when unable to drink and striking a family member at a later point in the course of their problems than men. (Schukit et al. 1995, p. 220)

The authors also noted some factors which occurred earlier for women in their drinking histories. These included: 'alcohol-dependent women reported experiencing driving and nondriving arrests, feelings of guilt and the formation of rigid drinking patterns earlier in their development of problems than their male counterparts' (p. 220).

A number of reviews have been carried out into the psychological aspects of problem drinking in women. The most recent of these include Gomberg (1993b), Quinby and Graham (1993), Hill (1995) and Fillmore et al. (1995). Researchers have also examined bio-psychosocial differences between problem-drinking and non-problem-drinking women (York 1995), differences between women in treatment and those who are not (Hanna 1991), women in prison (El-Bassel et al. 1995), gender differences (Dawson and Grant 1993, Patton et al. 1994, Schuckit et al. 1995) and different factors in relation to age (Gomberg 1995). Brennan et al. (1993) examined gender differences in relation to older problem drinkers and found that women in the group of 'late-middle-aged' had shorter drinking histories, drank less than their male counterparts and had fewer alcohol-related problems. These authors also concluded:

> Consistent with a gender role perspective on alcohol abuse, problem drinking women had more family related and fewer financial stressors than did problem-drinking men. Contrary to expectation, however, problem-drinking women reported more support from children, extended family members and friends than did problem-drinking men. (p. 781)

One of the major difficulties in this area is that of distinguishing cause from effect. After someone has been drinking heavily for a period of time, it may be difficult to differentiate between factors leading to such drinking, and those resulting from it. Obviously issues related to the distant past remain clear, but the question of whether something led to the drinking or was caused by it can be quite difficult to report. In an elegant study by Turnbull and Gomberg (1991), the authors noted nine factors related to the consequences of drinking: 'social withdrawal, sexuality, early effects [of drink related problems], maternal role, accidents, symptoms, work, illness, and relationship conflict' (p. 29). In this study, the age of the problem drinker did change the importance of some of the factors. For example, the women at both extremes of the age groups, the youngest and the oldest, were more likely to report symptoms as effects of the drinking being important. Women in the middle age-range were more likely to highlight accidents and issues related to their role as mothers.

Studies have also investigated the effects of having lived with a problem-drinking parent, in childhood (Sher et al. 1991, Garland et al. 1993, Zeitlin 1994), adolescence (Thombs et al. 1993, Windle 1994), amongst college students (Searles et al. 1993), and in adulthood (Black et al. 1986, Gravitz and Bowden 1986, Clair and Genest 1987, Harman and Arbona 1991, Donald et al. 1993, Schukit et al. 1994). The characteristics of problem drinkers with a family history of alcohol-related problems have also been the subject of a number of studies (Svanum and McAdoo 1991, Bucholz et al. 1994, Hill et al. 1994). The possibility of a parental history of heavy or problematic drinking being associated with chronic illnesses among young women has also been investigated (Radomsky 1992). A wider view of family problems related to and affected by alcohol problems has also been examined (Orford and Velleman 1991, Velleman 1992a,b, Sheridan 1995). It seems that young people can assess the drinking habits of their parents reasonably well for quantity and frequency (O'Malley et al. 1986).

In an interesting study on social support, family history of alcohol abuse and drinking behaviour, Ohannessian and Hesselbrock (1993) examined a mixed gender group of children of problem drinkers. The subjects of this investigation were found by asking problem drinkers in a treatment study if they had children who would be willing to participate. A control group of subjects with no family history of problem drinking was then used for comparison. The authors reported:

> Results from the present study suggest that social support from friends is more important in terms of moderating the relationship between family history of alcoholism and alcohol use in a young adult sample of children of alcoholics than did social support from family members. (pp. 1656–7)

There was a gender difference in relation to family history of alcohol problems. Young women who perceived little social support within the family, were those most likely to be concerned about their own drinking. This was an important study because it gave some possible future direction to helping people who have a known family history of drinking problems.

Sadly, for many the reality is that, just as a female problem-drinker and her partner tend to isolate themselves as the drinking escalates, so too do their children. The latter stop bringing friends home because they never know what condition the problem-drinking parent will be in and how embarrassing that could be for themselves and their friends. Then they may start to turn down invitations from their friends because they feel they cannot return the favour. The subjects in Ohannessian and Hesselbrock's study were in their thirties, but it is not difficult to see how this may have been a situation which had developed over the years to the point where making friends became increasingly difficult. Keeping family secrets is an isolating, lonely business. The authors also examined this group in relation to how they perceived and dealt with what they called 'hassles and uplifts' (Ohannessian et al. 1994). These were measured by giving the respondents a series of occurrences which they could either score as an 'uplift' or a 'hassle'. The results showed that this issue did not appear to be related to women's drinking in either those who had a family history of problem drinking or those who did not. However, another measure was also used, an optimism/pessimism score related to outcome expectancies. Amongst those women with a family history of problem drinking, those who were rated highly pessimistic in relation to outcome expectancies were those most likely to report alcohol problems. Conversely, those rating high on optimism were least likely to report alcohol problems. The authors noted:

> optimism appeared to protect [women with a family history of alcohol problems], but not [women with no family history of alcohol problems]. The difference may simply be attributable to the fact that [women with a family history of alcohol problems] have been exposed to parental problem drinking and have learned different behaviors (e.g. an optimistic attitude) that may assist in coping with their environment. (p. 760)

This may be true. Even so, it may also be a very 'skin deep' type of optimism. A behaviour which may have been born out of desperation, but which may also get in the way of their being rounded human beings who at times have problems where optimism may be an inappropriate response. This behaviour may prevent others reaching out to help the person who desperately tries to get on with their lives by denying that there is anything wrong. As noted earlier, this was an important study and could usefully be replicated on a larger, more ethnically and socially varied sample.

Jones and Zalewski (1994) examined the effects of parental drinking on the degrees of depression and shame found in women who were children of problem drinkers. The sample consisted of 30 adult children of problem-drinking parents matched to 30 adults with no family history of problem drinking. The women were self-selected having responded to a request to: 'Participate in a study of how lifestyles in women's families of origin affect how they see themselves and feel as adults' (p. 1604). The results of this investigation were interesting. The women who had experienced life as children of problem drinkers were significantly more likely to experience depression than their counterparts with no such family history. The former group were also more likely to have lost a parent before the age of 18 years, either through death or divorce. There was no difference between the two groups in relation to shame. The participants in this study were self-selected from a group of women who had all started psychotherapy within the previous six months; they were a group who acknowledged that there were clearly some areas in their lives which they felt needed to be addressed. Even so, the lack of significant differences in relation to this factor are perhaps worth closer consideration. It has been suggested that guilt is closely associated with depression. The definitions of guilt and shame and the possible differences between them are often debated (Lewis 1971). Guilt may be defined as related to an internal response to the person's own perceived negative behaviour, whereas shame relates more to a personal reaction to other people's view (an external view) of the individual's behaviour. According to the *Chambers Twentieth Century Dictionary*, the opposite of guilt is innocence. Shame, on the other hand, is related to incurring disgrace or dishonour (McDonald 1972). Most problem drinkers are more critical of themselves than anybody else could be, so the guilt/depression aspect may be powerful enough to 'swallow' the shame. For women in particular, this may be of major importance. Men with alcohol problems also feel intense guilt and shame. However, society in general gives males more positive messages about themselves as people than are generally available for females. Even if women problem-drinkers' feelings of worthlessness were the same as those of men, society would still give them more negative messages than those received by their male counterparts.

O'Connor et al. (1994) noted that women in treatment for drug problems were significantly more likely to score high on shame and depression using Tagney's (1990) Test of Self-Conscious Affect (TOSCA) and the Beck Depression Inventory (Beck et al. 1961). The authors question therefore whether the treatments based on confrontation are appropriate for women or whether they actually reinforce the views the women hold of themselves. O'Connor et al. also noted that 'the subtle power distinctions common in the traditional therapy relationship may also be felt by some clients as inherently humiliating' (p. 507).

Tweed and Ryff (1991) examined the psychological adjustment of a group of adult children of problem drinkers (n=114) and compared them with another group matched for socio-economic status (n=125). The authors commented that in relation to the measures of psychological well-being and personality development, the groups did not differ significantly. However, as noted by the authors, 'adult children of alcoholics scored significantly higher on the measures of anxiety and depression than did adults from non-alcoholic families' (p. 133). It seems that in some ways, although more prone to suffer from anxiety and depression, the coping mechanisms used by this group may have enabled them to live apparently ordinary lives. Of course, another more worrying possibility is that adults who, when children, lived in families with a problem-drinking parent may have used other mechanisms such as repression and denial to enable them to survive. The question has to be asked, at what cost to themselves? They have survived, and that in itself may have been no small task, but probably only through great personal hardship and loss. It is clear that for some people in this situation they repressed their own feelings and needs so severely that they have lost touch with the fact that they have any.

A patient with whom I once worked, when asked what she felt, replied: 'A feeling. Now what is that exactly?' This was not avoidance of a feeling she was aware of and unwilling to discuss. To this woman, the idea of having a feeling about anything, far less being asked what that feeling was, was complete anathema. Anxiety may be triggered if a client, such as the woman described above, begins to 'get in touch' with the feelings, the memories and the rawness that will still be there no matter how many years ago the experiences had occurred.

The concept of relapse is often discussed in relation to people with alcohol problems. It is vital to remember that one possibility, other than the definition of problem drinking as a 'chronic relapsing disease', is that going back into the memories and raw feelings of the past is something that has to be done with care and respect for the client. In fact they are going back into precisely the situation which may have been the original reason for their destructive drinking, and therefore one obvious solution to the pain and fear is to use the same behaviour again. When feelings get pushed down with memories, they often both emerge with the same intensity as that with which they were first experienced. Yes, the situation is different; no, they will not be hurt again by that person within the safety of the therapeutic relationship, but sadly the intensity of the feeling may well be there all over again. It is this trauma which makes it important for people working with problem drinkers to help contain the situation until it is resolved as far as possible by the development of a relationship which is built on trust. Of course this is the case for many people who come for help with childhood traumas, but for problem drinkers there is the added burden of what relapse may do to their present situation. The therapist's perception of relapse may also affect their view of the client and thus the therapeutic relationship (see Chapter 6).

In spite of this, the findings of Tweed and Ryff (1991) indicate that it should not be assumed that all children of problem drinkers are seriously traumatised by their early life experiences. However, this study did show that lower self-esteem was related to the degree of family dysfunction (see also Velleman 1992a, b). Werner and Broida 1991 found no significant differences in relation to parental problem-drinking and Bidaut-Russell, Bradford and Smith (1994) and Bidaut-Russell, Smith and Bradford (1994), in a small study, found that daughters of problem-drinking mothers were not significantly more likely than their brothers to experience psychiatric problems. This was interesting as most studies have suggested that women are affected more negatively than their male siblings. Such background factors may also exert a profound effect in adulthood (Lyon and Greenberg 1991, Domenico and Windle 1993).

The issue of aggression in women is becoming more widely researched. From Eileen Macdonald's book *Shoot the Women First* (1991), onwards, people are now acknowledging that women can be at least as aggressive as men. It would appear that in this, as in many other aspects of life, women have to be 'better' than men to be accepted. As noted by Macdonald (1991):

> [a] comment [was] made by a woman from the Italian Red Brigades to the effect that if a woman shows any hesitancy or expressed doubts, her wavering is taken far more seriously than it would be in the case of a male colleague. Women, then, have to be doubly tough, constantly on their guard against any emotion that might be construed as 'feminine weakness', and this might further explain why they are on occasion more ruthless. (p. 237)

However, in many countries, the only time it is acceptable for women to become aggressive is when protecting their children. There have been a number of studies carried out in relation to men and violence (Bushman and Cooper 1990). In general, the evidence suggests that the part played by alcohol is related to how drinkers perceive the risk of being physically hurt. There do, however, appear to be gender differences. This threat of physical harm is present for every male, drunk or sober, although it does appear as though alcohol in some way focuses the drinker to take note of the threatening cues rather than the complete picture. Women are more likely to continue to see the broader picture, leaving open the choice to calm down. In an interesting study carried out by Zeichner et al. (1994), male social drinkers were examined under laboratory conditions and placed in situations which were rated as either personally threatening or non-threatening. An example of a personally threatening situation was a negative comment taken from an earlier completed personality questionnaire (MMPI) accompanied by an electric shock. An example of a personally non-threatening situation was a positive comment taken from the same inventory again accompanied by an electric shock. The results suggested that those subjects who were given alcohol, as opposed to a placebo or a non-alcoholic drink, were more likely to focus on the negative areas and ignore others. This suggests that even men who drink heavily can differentiate between levels of personal threat. However, they are more liable almost to *choose* to focus on the area which will lead to, or allow them to display, a more aggressive response. The results in the above study as reported by the authors were:

> These findings concur with and refine previous models suggesting that alcohol focuses the drinker's attention to salient cues in threatening circumstances, thus increasing the likelihood of aggressive behavior. (p. 657)

The issue of alcohol and its relationship to aggression is a complex one. Even so, there are some points which have become clear. First, you do not find violence in a bottle. There is little evidence that alcohol *causes* aggression, even though heavy drinking is sometimes associated with such behaviour (see Chapter 1). However, as noted above, after drinking, men are more likely to focus on cues which are aggression related, for example, provocation and social pressure encourages aggressive behaviour (Taylor and Leonard 1983, Taylor and Sears 1988). Other studies have indicated that, again particularly in men, aggression related to intoxication is much more difficult to 'talk down' or successfully intervene in than non-intoxicated aggression. This is one of the reasons why work is now being carried out to reduce the opportunities for the initiation of aggression and the reinforcement of non-aggression (Taylor and Chermack 1993, Graham and Homel 1997). As noted earlier, most of the early research in this field related to men and a number of these, mainly laboratory based, studies have been criticised for this reason (Taylor and Leonard 1983, Gustafson 1985, 1986). Available evidence on the possible association between aggression and alcohol suggests that moderate doses of alcohol have not been shown to increase aggression in either females or males. As noted earlier, one of the main gender differences may be in perception and response to stimuli. In relation to women in particular, Gustafson (1991) noted:

> Women, irrespective of level of intoxication, prefer to exert influence on a male partner by using a nonaggressive alternative when such an alternative is available. Women do, however, increase their aggressive responding as a function of level of frustration, but never to the extent of becoming predominantly aggressive in their behavioral style. (p. 891)

This may be a point worth noting in the cases of women who, after long experience of abuse from a partner, eventually commit murder. This possibility may be borne out by another observation by Gustafson: 'this aggression seems to be of a calculated and cognitively controlled kind, since subjects took more time to decide their actions as numbers, intensities, and durations were increased' (p. 891). It will be remembered that he was commenting on the basis of laboratory based evidence but there is a chilling similarity between this last sentence and the descriptions given by women who have experienced years of violent abuse.

In a review of alcohol and aggression in women, Gomberg (1993a) noted a number of interesting points. In her review of the literature she described a study by Richardson et al. (1980) and stated: 'The authors of the study conclude that "the usual findings of female non-aggressiveness may be attributable to women's expectations of disapproval of aggressive behaviour"' (p. 90). However, examining some of the evidence in more detail raises some interesting points. In the above-noted laboratory based study by Gustafson (1991), college students aged between 19 and 50 years of age were divided into three groups: those given alcohol, those given a placebo and a control group. Gustafson concluded: 'Women do not increase their aggression as a function of alcohol in a situation with more than one response alternative available' (p. 886). Gustafson, like a number of earlier writers, highlighted the need to include gender differences when examining alcohol-related aggression.

There are many unanswered questions relating to women. For example, are women who have a more liberal view of the role of females more likely to become aggressive than their more traditional sisters? According to a study by Richardson et al. (1980), the answer to the latter question is 'no'. This group found that women with more liberal views in general were less likely to be aggressive than the women with a more traditional view of women's roles. It is interesting given the literature on problem-drinking women which suggests that their perception of the 'woman's role' is one of the traditional views of femininity. This fits with Gomberg's own study of problem-drinking women published in 1990. These females (n=30) were compared with a control group with no drinking problems (n=137) matched by variables such as age. About 50% of the problem-drinking group reported throwing things, or hitting their partners. This group were also more likely than the control group to report losing their tempers after drinking. There was a difference found in age, with the 20–29-year-olds being more likely to report physical violence (Gomberg 1993a).

Are women more aggressive towards men or towards other women? This question was addressed in a meta-analysis of 30 laboratory based studies (Bushman and Cooper 1990). The main analysis related to males; however, a secondary analysis included women. The authors noted: 'the sex of the target did influence alcohol-related aggression. When intoxicated, both men and women behaved more aggressively towards a female target than towards a male target' (p. 350). These authors went on to speculate as to the reasons for this conclusion. They suggested that alcohol is used as an excuse for a behaviour, that of violence against women, which is viewed by society in general as inappropriate.

The area of depression and violence has also been noted, for example in relation to suicide. It is well known that alcohol-related problems increase the risk of suicide and attempted/parasuicide markedly (Canetto 1991, Platt and Robinson 1991, Merrill et al. 1992, Murphy et al. 1992). In a study of 250 subjects by Merrill et al. (1992), the authors found gender differences in a number of variables, for example, levels of alcohol consumption and reported alcohol-related problems. The authors noted 15.5% of the women reported experiencing alcohol problems and concluded: 'Those responsible for assessing cases of attempted suicide should be adept at detecting alcohol misuse and instituting appropriate management' (p. 83).

Asking women about their alcohol consumption and any related problems is not a routine activity for many clinicians. It may be that the potential importance of this particular topic should be more clearly highlighted. A woman who has tried to harm herself often feels ashamed of her actions when she regains consciousness in a hospital bed. The attitudes of staff may even reinforce this belief. A woman with an alcohol problem often also feels ashamed of her actions. The combination of these two, at a time of particular vulnerability, may mean that the professionals have to be even more sensitive in their questioning. It would be sad if a possible alcohol problem was missed at a time when perhaps the very vulnerability would allow the beginning of a therapeutic relationship.

Violence Against Women

The topic of violence has already been raised in this book. However, for the vast majority of women the issue of violence is most likely to be related to someone being violent towards them. A study carried out by Miller and Downs (1993) compared groups of women, some of whom had histories of abuse and others who did not. These authors summarised that in relation to a number of types of violence, including mother to daughter, father to daughter, sexual abuse and partner violence, the women with alcohol problems were significantly more likely than others to report histories of violence directed at them. Women with drinking problems may enter into traumatic and violent relationships, or may use alcohol to deal with a relationship in which they feel powerless (Lammers et al. 1995). A surprising number of women and men have experienced incidents in their early life which have left them unwilling or indeed unable to trust in adult life (Downs et al. 1992). So often women in these situations will enter into relationships with men who will destructively remove any remaining belief they have in their own selves and their rights. These relationships can be destructive in many ways. Some of these are obvious, such as physical abuse and other forms of violence (Fagan 1993, Miller et al. 1993, Miller and Downs 1995), sexual abuse (Goodale and Stoner 1994), rape (Kilpatrick et al. 1992, Browne 1993), domestic violence (Miller et al. 1989, Pan 1994, Ramanathan 1996) and unnatural death (Klatsky and Armstrong 1993, Perola et al. 1994). In relation to the implication of alcohol to cases of sexual aggression, for example, rape, as noted by Crowe and George (1989):

> The actual association of alcohol with incidents of sexual aggression has been widely documented. Indeed, a large body of

> research has been dedicated to the investigation of alcohol as a moderating or mediating variable in occurrences of rape, but the only general conclusions reached have been that alcohol is somehow implicated in an alarmingly high percentage of cases of sexual aggression and that rapists who had been drinking often attributed their aggressive behavior to inebriation (Gebhard et al. 1965, Groth 1979, McCaghy 1968, Rada 1975, Scully and Marolla 1984). (p. 384)

Even so, other influential messages do not accept alcohol's role as any more than an association. During the early 1990s a campaign entitled Zero Tolerance was mounted in Britain. This was designed to highlight the harsh reality of violence against women. Amongst the statements included in campaign literature were some quotations from men who had been violent towards women. Some of these were frightening: 'She was drunk, she shouldn't be permitted to yell when she is sober "I was raped"'; 'I'm against hurting women. She should have resisted.' This very powerful visual campaign gave a sense of empowering women. Many of these campaigns sadly seem to leave women still feeling the victims and powerless.

The study by Bushman and Cooper noted above does raise other issues. For example, it is worrying that they seem to confuse association and cause in the relationship between alcohol and aggressive behaviour. In a prospective investigation into alcohol and unnatural death, Klatsky and Armstrong (1993) reported:

> Among people reporting six or more drinks/day, women and persons below 50 years of age were at especially high risk ... These data provide considerable detail about usual alcohol use and unnatural death. They point to special need for preventative efforts among young people and women, with particular attention to suicide and homicide. (p. 1156)

The authors note that these risk factors should perhaps be included when the issue of restricting the availability of gun licences is raised.

A study by Perola et al. (1994) of sudden death in Finland was carried out by reviewing 1658 autopsy cases, involving 485 females and 1173 males. The authors examined the cases for evidence of alcohol-related involvement and found, as others had before them, that the number of cases that had an alcohol-related component noted on the death certificate were far fewer than the number of cases which actually did have an alcohol component. Much of the

Figure 4.1 Zero Tolerance Campaign (Edinburgh)

alcohol-related disease was of relatively long standing. They also noted:

> The difference is most prominent in older males and in women of all ages. In the female age group 65 years and older, the differences were strikingly large: only a minority of cases with alcohol-related disease diagnosed at autopsy had an alcohol-related disease mentioned in the death certificate. An evident underdiagnosis of alcoholism thus seems to be a fact, especially for this group of older women. (p. 259)

Clearly, comparing autopsy results between countries is fraught with problems. However, it is probably fair to say that, in general, women will be more likely to be under-reported as suffering from alcohol-related disease than their male counterparts.

Eating Disorders

The literature on links between eating disorders and the abuse of alcohol and other substances has expanded over the last few years. In 1994 Holderness et al. reviewed 51 studies. They divided these investigations into groups. One group consisted of studies which had examined women with eating disorders who were also substance abusers, another group included studies on women who were primarily diagnosed as substance abusers with a secondary eating disorder. A third group included studies on the use and abuse of substances by the relatives of people with eating disorders. Holderness et al. concluded that there were a number of factors which seemed to cluster together. They could be covered under the headings of psychological, biological and environmental (Goldbloom 1993, Holderness et al. 1994a,b, Chandy et al. 1995). Specific sub-groups have also been examined, for example high school students (Striegel-Moore and Huydic 1993). Although the majority of the evidence available is from the US, evidence is also forthcoming from countries such as Japan (Higuchi et al. 1993, Suzuki et al. 1995) and from different ethnic groups within the US, such as Greek college students (Meilman et al. 1991). Family history of problem drinking has also been examined (Mintz 1995). Comparisons have also been made between women with eating disorders who have an alcohol problem and those who do not (Bulik et al. 1994) and with substance-abusing women with eating disorders in relation to exercise (Holderness et al. 1994a,b). The effects of food deprivation and severity of dieting in relation to alcohol consumption in this group has also been addressed (Krahn et al. 1992, Bulik and Brinded 1993). The extreme of eating disorder has also been noted, that of obesity (Mills 1992, King et al. 1996). The issue of eating disorders and other psychiatric diagnoses have also confused the picture, for example, borderline personality (Hamilton 1993) and self-mutilating behaviour (Cross 1991).

Child Abuse

Amongst the most extreme examples of violence is that of child abuse. There has now been considerable work on the issue of child abuse and alcohol (Swett and Halpert 1994, Williams 1994, Wilsnack et al. 1994). The early literature which began appearing in the early 1980s (Covington 1982, Schaeffer et al. 1985) compared two groups of women: those with alcohol and other drug problems and a matched group of women with none of these problems. Both these studies showed that the women with substance-abuse problems were more likely to have been abused. Even within the group of women who had been abused the histories were different. In the women who reported histories of abuse occurring earlier in life, at five years or younger (18.9% of the group), the abuse was more frequent and continued for a longer period of time. Covington also found the abuse to have been more violent and to have been carried out by more than one person. A paper by Browne and Finkelhor (1986) reviewed 27 studies. The subjects of these ranged from college students (Landis 1956, Finkelhor 1979, DeYoung 1982, Sedney and Brooks 1984, Seidner and Calhoun 1984), to more specific groups such as clinic populations, clients in therapy and prostitutes (DeFrancis 1969, Fields 1981). Seven years later, in 1993, Kendall-Tackett et al. reviewed 45 studies of children aged 18 and younger. This review was not specifically related to alcohol problems but rather examined general symptoms found in children who had reported episodes of abuse. These children were compared with children who had not been abused. The authors reported:

> sexually abused had more symptoms than nonabused children, with abuse accounting for 15–45% of the variance. Fears, post-traumatic stress disorder, behavior problems, sexualized behaviors, and poor self-esteem occurred most frequently among a long list of symptoms noted. (p. 165)

Research into child abuse has now been carried out into such varied areas as dissociative states (Mancini 1993, Zlotnick et al. 1995), psychological functioning (Fox and Gilbert 1994), short-term (Beitchman et al. 1991) and long-term effects (Beitchman et al. 1992). The issue of parental problem-drinking (Yama et al. 1992, Yama et al. 1993, Wiers et al. 1994, Chandy et al. 1995, Widom et al. 1995) has also been examined. As noted earlier in this chapter, sexual dysfunction and problems are relatively commonplace in problem-drinking women (Wilsnack 1984, Pinhas 1980, 1987, Beckman and Ackerman 1995, Lammers 1995a,b, Wilsnack and Wilsnack 1995).

In a thoughtful and analytical review, Hurley (1991b) compared women with past histories of abuse with women with substance abuse problems. This investigator detailed the profiles of both groups and found striking similarities. For example, traumatic disruptive childhood histories; difficulty in trusting people, especially in intimate relationships; low self-esteem, and the problems of shame and keeping secret the problem which prevents the much-needed help. Hurley expressed the view that 'it is generally accepted that alcoholism is an irreversible, progressive, potentially fatal disease' (p. 264). As noted elsewhere in this book, this view is not universally accepted and many commentators, including this author, do not agree with this suggestion. This view may be prevalent in some countries but is by no means seen in such simplistic and monochrome terms everywhere.

It would not be surprising if both the alcohol problem and the sexual difficulties were related to a past history of abuse (Mercy 1991, Swett et al. 1991, Bennett and Kemper 1994, Swett and Halpert 1994, Tschann et al. 1994, Windle et al. 1995).

As noted above, the literature is mixed on the increased risk of alcohol-related problems in adulthood in those who experienced childhood abuse of various types. Some studies have shown a strong association (Browne and Finkelhor 1986); others have not (Beitchman et al. 1992, Miller 1993). An interesting study carried out in the US (Widom et al. 1995) attempted to examine whether children who had been abused or neglected were at increased risk of developing alcohol problems in adulthood. The results highlighted the complexity of the issue:

> female victims of childhood neglect are at significantly elevated risk for alcohol problems in young adulthood ... we did not find a persistent relationship between victims of childhood physical or

> sexual abuse and alcohol abuse and/or dependence in women. (p. 213)

Earlier work had suggested that women problem-drinkers are more likely to neglect than to actively abuse their children. If this is the case, then Widom et al.'s study needs to be replicated on larger and more mixed populations. It is also the case, as the authors themselves noted, that more attention to this question may be useful in tailoring more effective treatment programmes.

This raises the difficulties that may occur when establishing a therapeutic relationship with someone who finds it so difficult to trust anyone. The issue of how to detect child abuse in populations of problem-drinking women has also been addressed (Simpson et al. 1994, Pearce and Lovejoy 1995), as have the implications for professionals working in the area (Janikowski and Glover 1994). The latter have acknowledged:

> it is important for counsellors to emphasize trust and to assure clients that all communications are kept confidential. Further counsellors should understand the role that shame plays in the incest history and acknowledge the agony of the experience. (p. 182)

Janikowski and Glover (1994) also note the very real problems for therapists working in this area:

> Many substance abuse therapists, because of their own discomfort and/or lack of familiarity with incest, never ask clients about sexual abuse or raise related issues that might lead to client disclosure (MacFarlane and Korbin 1983). Barnard (1989) argued that some clients may not disclose because they sense the counsellor's discomfort. (p. 182)

Historically, we know that even if the therapist can 'contain' and gently 'hold' the client in this trauma, pressure from colleagues can cause problems. Freud, who initially freely accepted his patients' histories, turned their truth into fantasy when his professional peer group put him under pressure. For many years people spoke of child sexual abuse only in terms of fantasy and complexes. It has taken a long time for some therapists to stand by what their clients say as the truth.

Even now, the spectre of 'False Memory Syndrome' can throw therapists into confusion. 'Did all these things really happen or am

I being deceived for some reason?' Perhaps even worse, some clients are told that the therapist they trusted is the one who is dishonest. This person whom they have begun to trust is trying to convince them that something traumatic happened of which the client has no memory. The possible cases of 'False Memory Syndrome' are drops in the ocean of the pain and terror of people who have been abused as children. However, in relation to child abuse and subsequent alcohol problems, the risk of relapse in either of these situations is greatly increased. Even so this is an area where the need to proceed cautiously with the client is paramount, there are still aspects of research into this area which need refining (Martin et al. 1993, Miller and Downs 1995).

Ethnicity

An issue which is beginning to receive more attention is that of the importance of ethnicity. An American study (Lillie-Blanton et al. 1991) comparing the differences between black women (the group consisted of American Indian, Alaskan, Asian, Pacific Islander and Hispanic women) and white women concluded that the black women were no more likely to have an alcohol problem than their white counterparts. The psychology of drinking amongst women in different groups has been examined, for example Latinos (Flores-Ortiz 1994, Marin and Flores 1994) Hispanic women (Lindenberg et al. 1994, Canino 1994, Hoffman 1994) Taiwanese (Cheng and Chen 1995), African American (Lozina et al. 1995), Mexican American (Corbett et al. 1991, Gilbert et al. 1994), Mexican (Medina-Mora 1994), Chilean (Araya 1994), Ecuadorian (Pacurucu-Castillo 1994), Nigerian (Ikuesan 1994, Omoluabi 1995), Japanese (Kitano et al. 1992, Hendry 1994, Higuchi and Kono 1994, Goto 1994, Suzuki et al. 1995), Chinese (Kua 1994, 1995), women from Myanmar (Phyu 1994), women from the former Soviet Union (Dragadze 1994, Davis 1994), Native American (Leung et al. 1993,) Peruvian (Yamamoto et al. 1993, Harvey 1994), Hualapai women (Teufel 1994). In addition, studies have also examined women from Fiji (Toren 1994), women in Scotland (McDonald, S. 1994) Canada (Adrian et al. 1995), France (McDonald, M. 1994b), Sudan (Huby 1994), Egypt (Neiuwkerk 1992), Greece (Iossifides 1992, Papagaroufali 1992), Kenya (Partanen 1991), the Czech Republic (Kubicka et al. 1991, 1993), Finland (Holmila 1995), Israel (Weiss 1991), New Zealand (Park 1990, 1995, Romans-Clarkson et al. 1992), the Netherlands (van de Goor 1990, Knibbe et al. 1991). Work on different cultures, including comparisons between men and women, has also been reviewed. In Australia (Hall and Hunter 1995), Canada (Cheung and Erickson 1995), Chile (Cárdenas 1995), China (Jiacheng 1995), Denmark (Schiøler 1995), Egypt (Ashour 1995), France (Nahoum-Grappe 1995), Germany (Vogt 1995b), Guatemala (Adams 1995), Honduras (Bustillo 1995), Hungarian Gipsies (Stewart 1992), Iceland (Ásmundsson 1995), Ireland (Peace 1992), India (Mohan and Sharma 1995), Israel (Weiss 1995), Italy (Cottino 1995), Malaysia (Arokiasamy 1995), Mexico (Rey 1995), the Netherlands (Garretsen and van de Goor 1995), New Zealand (Park 1995), Nigeria (Oshodin 1995), Poland (Moskalewicz and Zielinski 1995), Russia (Sidorov 1995), Spain (Gamella 1995), Sri Lanka (Samarasinghe 1995), Sweden (Nyberg and Allebeck 1995), the UK (Plant 1995), the US (Hanson 1995) and Zambia (Haworth 1995). For other recent reviews in this area see also Rouse et al. (1995), Edwards and Thurman (1995) and Barthwell (1995).

The issue of co-dependency has become a popular concept over the last few years. Indeed it is now described as a disease (Schaef 1986, Beattie 1989, 1992, Sheridan 1995b). Some workers have bravely questioned the validity of the concept (Harvey and Dodd 1993) – for a recent review see Brown (1991) and Rodney (1996) – but it must be remembered how difficult this is in a country, the US, which has invested so much into the concept. This, like the disease model of alcoholism, has been accepted as 'truth' and taken hold from there. One of the real problems with this dynamic is that anyone who tries to question it runs the risk of being targeted. People do not like their beliefs, however well or ill founded, to be challenged and if you have managed to get your life back together again with these beliefs it seems almost inhuman to question them. Even so, we cannot simply accept that because a concept works for some people it should be made into the truth. The main concern is that if it does not work for you, either AA, group therapy or the concept of co-dependence, then it is you who is denying, rejecting or as yet not ready to do the necessary work on yourself. To me this is a most destructive, dangerous idea and needs to be questioned seriously. In relation to this concept women are most often described as co-dependent with male problem-drinkers. Women with drinking problems, as has been noted many times in this book, are isolated, often lonely and very frightened. To isolate them more because they don't fit your view of the world is unfair, untrue and inaccurate. As noted by Appel (1988) in relation to co-dependency and other 'addictive' behaviours:

> Addiction then becomes a focus to make life meaningful. And it is with the support and emotional security that self-help groups provide that life, and especially those major transitions within one's life cycles, can be accepted, and living one's own life can become easier, if one is a member of a group of like-minded people. (p. 32)

Women who are Older

Aspects of ageing and drinking patterns have begun to be addressed. Women who are older have to deal with the myths and stereotypes placed upon them in their different societies. In some cultures older women are given more leeway in relation to drinking – for example, some areas of Kenya (Partanen 1991) – but this is not common. As noted earlier in this chapter, it may be that there has been a cohort effect in Britain and that women who are older are feeling more confident about drinking than their mothers or grandmothers did. In relation to problem-drinking women there are gender differences with age (Larimore 1992). A US study (Brennan et al. 1993) found that older problem-drinking women were more likely to use medication such as tranquillisers and antidepressants, be more depressed and be less likely to come forward for treatment than their male counterparts. The women were also more likely than the men to have started their problem drinking within the past two years (46% and 28% respectively). This group of 183 women also reported 'more support from children, extended family members and friends' (p. 781) than the men, whose main support seemed to be their wives. However if the women began to drink again they were likely to lose this support.

One of the few national surveys into drug and alcohol use in older women (aged 65 and over) has been carried out by Graham et al. (1995) in Canada. In relation to the differences between use of alcohol and prescription drugs, the authors concluded:

> Drinking was associated with being single, younger, not religious, in better health and smoking ... Use of psychoactive prescription drugs (especially sleeping pills) tended to be associated with being widowed, older, less educated, more religious, in poorer health, experiencing higher stress, having lower income, and less social support, smoking and use of other psychoactive prescription drugs. (p. 770)

Other issues related to women who are older include changes in mood, sleep patterns and sexual functioning (Gaveler et al. 1994, Stone and Pearlstein 1994, Wilsnack et al. 1995).

It has only been recently that the topic of homelessness in women has become the focus of research, in general (McCarty et al. 1991) and in relation to specific areas such as violence (Padgett and Struening 1992, Browne 1993), stereotypes (Geissler et al. 1995), comparisons between genders (North and Smith 1993), and the elderly (Rubington 1995). Homeless women with children have also been studied (Robertson 1991) as has the use of standard tests with this population (Drake et al. 1995). It has been noted how even among the homeless, women tend to remain isolated, as if, even then, the view of women being 'worse' than men remains.

5 Drinking in Pregnancy

It might seem strange to begin a chapter on pregnancy by examining the topic of infertility. Even so, this is what I propose to do. The topic of pregnancy is a thorny one for many women. There are so many 'dos' and 'don'ts'. Even down to different times of the month and different positions for intercourse to aid conception or ensure a child of a specific gender.

Over the centuries alcohol has been involved, both medically and socially, in relation to sex and pregnancy. A common finding in studies of problem-drinking women is the complaint of dysparunia or pain on intercourse; women experiencing this problem will also often report the use of alcohol helping ease the pain presumably by relaxing the vaginal musculature (see Chapter 4).

In the time of the Incas of Peru maize was one of the most, if not the most, important crop. As noted by Toussaint-Samat (1994):

> in the beginning of the world, maize fell as golden rain when the sun exploded. 'Oh lord, sorcerer prince, maize is truly yours', wailed the nation with one voice. Young mothers ran to the temple with babies on their backs for the sacrificial offering of children whose howls would attract the attention of the god throughout the day. (p. 170)

For centuries fertility has been celebrated and prayed for by women. The reasons for this are not surprising, apart from the joy of raising a family: many women's lives depended on producing children. One commentator, Pomeroy (1975), has written: 'Bearing children was the most important function of Spartan women' (p. 36). She also gives the reason: 'since the state was constantly at war and the production of warriors was of highest priority' (p. 36). Indeed, death in childbirth held equivalent respect to being killed in battle (Pomeroy 1975, p. 36). Infertility was, in some areas, as risky, if not more so than pregnancy. The Romans were clear that women should not drink when they were pregnant, as noted by Purcell (1994):

> Drunkenness, for instance prevents the retention of semen ... It affects digestion in the days after conception, ... It exacerbates

> the state (technically called *kissa* in Greek) of alternate craving and disgust for particular foods during pregnancy. (p. 201)

From the times of the Celts treatments for sterility survive. Interestingly often the treatment for irregular or scanty periods included the same ingredients as that for heavy periods, albeit given in different ways. Trotula of Salerno, a woman who wrote a great deal about the diseases of women sometime between the eleventh and thirteenth centuries, noted that for scanty periods the advice was: 'Let her drink strong wine, if she be without pain in the head and without weakness of muscles and without fever, because in all fever wine is injurious' (Amt 1993, p. 101). For heavy periods the recommended remedy was the same, wine, but the mode of administration was different:

> hot ashes mixed with red wine and blended together to form a soft paste. Make it into a small wedge, wrap it in a new linen cloth and insert it in the vagina while it is still hot. Or take sage and camphor, grind vigorously, make little curls of wine, cook over a hot brick and give it to the patient for the purpose of curbing the menses. (Amt 1993, p. 101)

Trotula also noted a link between emotions and menstruation; not in terms of a moveable uterus wandering lost around the body, but the way in which we would now accept, that of grief and other strong emotions affecting the monthly cycle.

The Spartans were well aware of the need for maintaining healthy young women, not primarily for their own sake, but for that of their future children. No difference was found in the care and nutrition of women who gave birth to girls as opposed to boys. However, in ancient Greece the situation was not so equitable. As noted by Pomeroy:

> This differentiation in nourishment could exist even for suckling newborn. The 'mothers' rations' awarded to Ionian women in 489 BC in Persepolis was exactly twice as much wine, beer, and grain for women who had given birth to boys as for those who had borne girls. (1975, p. 85)

Indeed this sense of looking after women in relation to their reproductive health has again being highlighted in modern Russia. A recent news item in the *British Medical Journal* noted that Russian women are prohibited from working in manual jobs involving heavy work as these are seen as harmful to their 'reproductive functions' (*British Medical Journal* 1996, p. 385).

There has long been a recognition that nutrition and general health could affect fertility. As noted by Rousselle (1994): 'Ancient sources speak more often of the male impotence caused by malnutrition than of the related amenorrhea in women' (p. 299). Even so it was believed that early marriage and the start of pre-pubertal sexual behaviour actually brought on menarche. According to Aristotle, bearing children was best left until later because the younger the woman the greater the chance of her giving birth to a girl (Pomeroy 1975). This author also noted: 'He (Aristotle) suggested that the optimum age for marriage was eighteen for women, thirty seven for men' (1975, p. 85). Rousselle also commented: 'Women, who lived with their husbands from the time they were twelve or sometimes earlier, were required to observe a strict diet and forbidden to drink wine' (1993, p. 323). It is interesting to speculate on why this was. Toussaint-Samat (1994) suggested: 'Symbolically wine was equated with blood. Women regarded as being essentially mothers, were figuratively committing adultery by drinking strange blood' (p. 266). The Romans had warnings from their deities. It was reputed that Vulcan, the Roman god of fire, was deformed because of his mother being drunk at the time of his conception (Heine 1981).

Pregnancy and childbirth have always carried a degree of risk. In Roman times the maternal mortality rate during childbirth was about 20% and the infant mortality rate was 200 per 1000 (Rousselle 1994). Over the centuries many cultures have tried to make the situation safer. Most of the care was concentrated on making the baby healthy, an admirable aim; however, it should be noted that the health of the mother often came second in the minds of the authorities. The mother was cared for and was adjured to care for herself, to ensure the birth of a healthy child. In some eras people even went so far as to legislate. In Sparta and Carthage laws were introduced forbidding newly wed couples from drinking (Haggard and Jellinek 1942, p. 210). The rationale for this may have been to prevent conception during intoxication. Given that this group were legally married and therefore well within their rights to start a family, it has been suggested that the reason was related to the health of the foetus. However, there are other views. Maguelonne Toussaint-Samat (1994) noted: 'Intoxication causes a form of delirium ... Delirium, especially the delirium of drunkenness, denotes possession ... possession implies violation, and a violated woman could never be regarded as chaste or pure again' (p. 267). She goes on to give another possible explanation: 'Who knew if such possession might not lead to the birth of a monstrous child whose father could be some licentious mythical creature, not the worthy *paterfamilias*?' (p. 267).

The people of ancient Sparta had marriage customs different from those in other parts of Greece, as written by Pomeroy (1975): 'the basic pattern was the familiar marriage by capture. One novel way was by shutting up young men and women in a dark room, each man leading home whichever woman he caught – sight unseen' (p. 37). One can only imagine the ways that women in that situation worked out who they wanted and how they paired with their chosen mates! Another way, deemed by Lycurgus to ensure strong healthy children, was to keep the husbands in the army from the time they married at 18 until the time they were 30. This meant that any meeting would be secret and therefore more exciting. (Pomeroy 1975, p. 38). Yet even for female children the period of early childhood was affected by their future childbearing function. As noted by Rousselle (1994): 'Doctors advised healthy families to mold infants' bodies with bandages during the first two months of life' (p. 299). This was the case for both female and male children, but there were differences: 'To reduce the circumference of a girl's shoulders and chest, her wet nurse or mother would bind them tightly, but the hips were left unbound to encourage a large pelvis. Boys' hips were bound' (Rousselle 1994, p. 299).

In German law of the sixth century the worth of women could be assessed in many ways. If a pregnant woman was murdered then the fine was more than three times that of the murder of a woman who had reached the menopause. Similarly the fine for the murder of a girl before menarche was one-third that for the murder of a woman who was breastfeeding a child (Amt 1993, p. 41).

The Franks, a German people who moved into Gaul in the fifth century, were more liable to levy fines for any crime. In relation to witches this meant: 'If a witch eats a man ... let her be held liable for 8000 denarii' (Amt 1993, p. 43). This was the same amount levied for the murder of a girl before menarche or a woman after the menopause.

Soranus of Ephesus described a syndrome which seems at least to be related to malformations caused by Vitamin D deficiency, known to us as rickets. This was a common sight amongst the children of Rome. According to Purcell (1994), the reasons given by Soranus were: '(i) that the city is perched up on open spaces through which cold water runs; (ii) that the women have sex too frequently; (iii) that the women are accustomed to make love when drunk' (p. 202). However, Soranus himself thought the reason had more to do with inexperience in swaddling the baby correctly.

Throughout the centuries suggested cures for infertility abounded. As can be seen from some texts, these were often unpleasant. William Sermon, writing in his *Ladies Companion* of 1671, recommended: 'take of the slime that a hare will have about his mouth when he eateth mallows, and drink it in wine; two hours after lie with your husband' (Keeble 1994, p. 25).

By the seventeenth century in England many of the wages of women living in rural areas were so low that they lived in a constant state of poor nutrition. It is possible that this state reduced their fertility and even if they did become pregnant, their poor nutritional status may have affected the health and survivability of their offspring. One commentator, Clark (1992), described this situation:

> Of those who reached maturity many were crippled in mind and body ... The sacrifice of the wage-earner's children was caused by the mother's starvation; vainly she gave her own food to the children for then she was unable to suckle the baby and grew too feeble for her former work. (p. 87)

The gender of the child was also of importance. Aristotle thought that young women were more likely to have boys because they were hotter than older women. Hippocrates stated that, 'if the right breast be harder than the left, the nipple hard and high' (Keeble 1994, p. 27), this indicated that the child would be a boy. Other ways of sexing the child were also related to the right side of the body with the *Ladies Dictionary* of 1694 suggesting that the right eye sparkled more than the left and that the woman always walked with putting her right leg first (Keeble 1994, p. 31). It is interesting to speculate whether the belief that left-handedness was somehow a bad sign, has its derivation in this long-held view that male is right-sided.

The topic of drinking and its relationship to foetal harm is a good example of how moral and medical issues can become intertwined, with each confusing the other. For centuries fertility, abortion of unwanted pregnancies, pregnancy and delivery were the domains of women. The latter were usually older relatives or village 'wise women'. However, as noted by Toussaint-Samat (1994):

> In fact the relationship between wine and the moon really is a strange one, and not solely a matter of legend, although the Egyptians too thought that Hathor, the gentle mother goddess who was crowned with the horns of the moon and the afterlife,

> midwife and consort of the old primordial god of heaven, Horus the nocturnal eye of Ra, was also the frenzied mistress of intoxication and wine. (p. 253)

The uses of alcohol were often medicinal, for instance as an antiseptic or to induce abortion. However, the role that drinking played was often confused. The use of alcohol as an abortive agent is a good example of this. In Roman times women were strictly forbidden to drink wine. There were a number of reasons for this (see Chapter 2) but one of these was the fact that wine was viewed as an abortive substance. Although some authors believe that even unwanted children in Roman times were carried to term (Rousselle 1994, p. 307), there was a recognised 'abortion wine' at this time cited by Dioscorides, a contemporary of Soranus. This beverage was made up of a number of herbs and plants such as squirting cucumber. It was recommended that these be grown near the grape vines so that the grapes would take up the substances and therefore be useful for unwanted pregnancy. Some of these plants have been shown to have contraceptive rather than abortive properties (Riddle 1992). It is interesting to think that this might have been the origin of the link between alcohol and abortion.

As noted by Warner and Rosett (1975) in their fascinating survey of the North American and British literature on the subject of drinking in pregnancy:

> Eighteenth-century obstetricians, however could not prohibit alcohol because they needed it as a drug ... As a result, obstetrical writers took an ambiguous position ... Edward Foster, a Dublin midwifery professor, stated in a 1781 work that uterine haemorrhage leading to miscarriage or abortion could result from 'the abuse of stimulants, vinous and other strong liquors,' but recommended alcohol as a pain killer during pregnancy and delivery. (pp. 1397–8)

These two opposing practices have been around for centuries. In the nineteenth century, the old wives' tale that a bottle of gin, 'mothers' ruin', and a hot bath induces abortion was just one of the ways attempted by desperate women to terminate unwanted pregnancies. As noted by MacMillan (1988) in the book *Women of the Raj*:

> The more usual alternative for women who did not want to produce one child after another was to try to bring on a

> miscarriage. Hot gin and quinine, violent exercise, or crawling upstairs backwards were all said to work. (p. 126)

It is sad to imagine how frightened these women must have been, often with little or no medical care, in a strange country and desperate to try to keep some degree of health by not being permanently pregnant.

Recently a number of studies have been carried out. Some of these have found an association between heavier drinking and spontaneous abortion (Kline et al. 1980, Sokol 1980, Harlap and Shiono 1981, Anokute 1986, Russell et al. 1988) and stillbirth (Kaminski et al. 1976). Other studies have not shown such a link either with spontaneous abortion (Wright et al. 1983, Halmesmäki 1989, Parazzini et al. 1990, Cavallo et al. 1995) or stillbirth (Kaminski et al. 1981, Marbury et al. 1983, Kaminski 1985). At this point the evidence is still inconsistent.

For desperate women who carried their babies to full term, Barr (1995), gave a vivid picture of the times for these women and their hapless children:

> In one case that came before the Old Bailey, a young woman named Judith Dufour had a two year old child housed in the workhouse, where he had been given a new set of clothes. The mother came to take him out for the afternoon. No sooner was she clear of the workhouse, however, than she strangled the child, stripped of the clothes, and threw the naked corpse into the ditch in Bethnal Green. She sold the clothes for 1s 4d; with the money she bought gin. (p. 190)

Deformities in children were regarded as being caused by various things and different measures were taken at different times. For example, the Greeks and Romans encouraged pregnant women to look at beautiful paintings and listen to music to prevent the birth of damaged babies. Other societies gave reasons for deformed children and thus showed ways of avoiding the heartbreak of giving birth to a damaged child. As noted by Keeble (1994), both the psychological and the physical were involved:

> for the woman's disposition and imagination were thought to have a powerful effect both upon conception and upon the development of the foetus. Monstrous or deformed were also attributed to copulation shortly before or during menstruation when the female seed had degenerated into a noxious state. (p.19)

Nicholas Culpepper supported this belief:

> imagination is the cause of monsters. For histories mention that women with child, by beholding men in vizards [masks] have brought forth monsters with horns and beaks and cloven feet ... And though doctors cannot cure monsters, they are to admonish women with child not to look upon monsters. (Keeble 1994, p. 30)

John Merrick, better known as 'The Elephant Man' whom, it is widely assumed, suffered from neurofibromatosis, believed that the growths on his face and body which eventually killed him were due to the fact that his mother had been frightened by a runaway circus elephant when she was pregnant. This was part of the myth which believed that women had babies which were deformed in a way which could be linked with a cause. Hence 'strawberry' birth marks came from eating too many strawberries and 'port wine stains' were attributed to drinking too much port. It could occasionally work the opposite way. In his *Histoire des Anomalies* Geoffrey Saint Hilaire notes:

> in the third year of the French Republic an infant was born with the representation of a Phrygian cap of liberty on the left breast, and to the mother the Government awarded the above sum (400 francs per annum), presumably for her patriotic thoughts! (Ballantyne 1904, p. 119)

In 1813 Trotter (whose classic writings were republished in 1981) wrote of the practice of adding opium to alcohol. He noted:

> when we consider that four grains of opium are sufficient, to double the intoxicating power of a gallon of porter, the article is still cheap enough to be used by the brewer, without subtracting much from his profits. (p. 46)

For this reason it is not surprising that descriptions of children born to mothers who drank alcohol heavily were very similar to those of children whose mothers used opium. Indeed, the reality was that the women probably consumed both substances at the same time, either in porter as noted above or in brandy, as well as taking additional opium (Berridge and Edwards 1981, Plant 1987).

Alcohol has also been used in cases of premature labour to *prevent* contractions and the early birth of the child. Indeed alcohol used to be put into intravenous drips to delay labour (Lele 1982). This is not too surprising as alcohol was given intravenously as a replacement for fat and carbohydrate when nourishment was needed in ill patients.

Many religious texts include some commentary on alcohol. The Old Testament of the Bible describes an angel advising Samson's mother about drinking during pregnancy, even noting beverage type and strength: 'beware I pray thee and drink not wine nor strong drink' (Judges 13:3). There is some question over what was meant by the term 'strong drink'; it may be that this related to beer brought to the area by the Greeks. The Talmud also notes the risks associated with drinking: 'One who drinks intoxicating liquor will have ungainly children' (Tredrea 1983, p. 4). Feldman (1927) has stated that the Talmud was even more specific: 'Rabbi Nachman claims that his daughters are beautiful because he is an abstainer but Rabbi Bibi's daughter needs cosmetics because her father is "a drinker"' (p. 121). Interestingly, complexion was also noted in a different way by Hippocrates who believed that if a pregnant woman had a bad complexion it meant that she would give birth to a female child. However if she had a clear complexion then the child would be male (Pomeroy 1975, p. 85).

Keeble (1994) has commented on how heat and cold were the decisive factors in determining the gender of the child:

> Males were the product of hot sperm from the right testicle deposited on the right (hotter) side of the womb, where the foetus was carried. Females, on the other hand were produced by cold sperm from the inferior left testicle, were debilitated by insufficient heat in the womb and were carried on the left side. (p. 18)

There was often confusion over what was named the 'nature–nurture' debate, with both sides of the debate having more than their fair share of fanatics. As noted by Warner and Rosett (1975), James Sedgewick, an apothecary, warned in 1725 that:

> half the train of chronical Diseases, with which we see children afflicted, are only the secondary Sighs, and Groanings, the evidential Marks, and reproaches, of parentive ill-spent Life ... These Consequences may, nay without doubt, will be brought on Infants, by the Debauchery of the Mother. So that from the whole, the Regulation of the Mother, during her Pregnancy, is an Affair of the highest Moment and Consideration. (p. 1396)

This idea of the 'regulation of the mother' began gently with the Greeks and the Romans, both of whom had clear views on how a woman should behave and conduct herself when pregnant.

In the late nineteenth century doctors were recommending: 'She should be guarded from exhausting work, alarms and annoyances, and kept in the healthiest and most cheerful condition' (Ireland 1894). Ireland, a physician from Edinburgh, went on to warn:

> The incitements now held out to women to share the work and anxieties of both sexes is dangerous both to themselves and their offspring. The mother should not seek to put her own nervous system into a state of morbid tension, nor withdraw for the use of her own overworked brain the nourishment needed for the brain of the child she is bearing. (p. 183)

Other professionals were even more ambitious. Punton wrote of the general practitioner's role in the prevention of insanity: 'By carefully directing the mental and physical life of a pregnant woman, he may form the future mental complexion of the unborn child' (1894, p. 65). Russell, in 1881, wrote:

> I could cite numerous instances showing the liability of transmitting to offspring the peculiar mental characteristics caused by inebriety. That which in the parent was merely a habit, becomes in the child an impulsive uncontrollable desire. (p. 630)

He placed responsibility on men, a shift from the idea that women are to blame: 'Could we lift the curtain and unveil the family history if some of our most distinguished men, we should be appalled at the fearful inheritance they have transmitted to their children' (p. 630).

In a well named article, 'Sentiment', Dr Augusto Tebaldi of Padua grouped together the

> children of drunkards, of epileptics and hystericals; offshoots of a diseased trunk; inheritors of an excitable and unsteady character; with violent propensities; incapable of early training ... these beings so sadly fated, frequently possess in early life, a rather brisk intelligence, but it soon becomes exhausted. (Tebaldi 1892, p. 635)

However, although the intelligence was noted to be easily exhausted, the main problem was:

> In the moral field appear outbursts of violence, unbridled passions, which either soon pass off, or sink into brutalism. These incomplete creatures, in whom the moral sense is wanting, [find] true and solid affection impossible. (p. 635)

During the 1880s Miss Firth, an outspoken temperance reformer, informed the annual conference of the British Women's Temperance League about a train journey she had made earlier that week:

> Two young ladies and an elderly gentleman were at one end of the carriage, then a mother with two children – one quite an infant – a middle-aged lady and another gentleman. I had not been seated long before the gentleman in charge of the two young ladies brought out his brandy-flask, and they all had some. The mother had a bottle of milk for her children's use. A little brandy had been put into it, and the last drop was eagerly drained by the elder child. The lady on my right, and the gentleman on my left, each had their refreshment in a flask of brandy. (Firth 1880, p. 7)

Miss Firth does not tell us what she said about this situation, but it paints a picture of an ease with alcohol and drinking it in a public place which, given the time, seems quite surprising. She is quite clear of the link between alcohol and damage to the offspring:

> Alcohol is specifically, and to all intents and purposes, a cerebral poison. Acting thus upon the brain it has a special tendency to produce insanity or mental debility, not only in the person who takes it, but its effects are found descending to the children of those who take it. (Firth 1880, p. 10)

Two years later Miss Moorhouse gave the annual address to the British Women's Temperance League in London. She quotes a number of famous medical men of the time, including a Dr Carpenter who stated:

> The result of the habitual employment of stimulants is to produce a modification of the nutrition of the nervous system ... These abnormal habitudes of nutrition tend to propagate themselves in the offspring. So that the children of a drunkard are born with an unnatural craving, or with a tendency to insanity or idiocy. (Moorhouse 1882, p. 10)

Dr W.F. Brown, known as the first 'Lunacy Commissioner' for Scotland, believed that:

> The drunkard not only enfeebles and injures his own nervous system, but entails mental disease on his family. His daughters are nervous and hysterical, his sons are weak, wayward and eccentric. (Moorhouse 1882, p. 10)

Some doctors in the US were also clear about the evidence of a connection between drinking and harmful effects on the children. Dr Collier of Chicago identified what he saw as the differences between the drinking habits of the mother and the father:

> If the drinking habits of the father have such an effect, how much worse when the mother is a victim to the vice, when, in the place of the holy and tender associations which usually cluster around the name of mother, the child has memories of excess and shame, and often cruelty. It is a miracle, indeed, if such a child escapes the ten thousand perils which beset him, and grows up a virtuous man. (Moorhouse 1882, pp. 10–11)

There was little gentleness in the accusations thrown at the mothers:

> Are we prepared to draw down upon ourselves the curse pronounced upon those who place a stumbling-block in the way of one of Christ's little ones? ... I would appeal especially to mothers, who are the creators of their children's future. How dare you expose the children you have brought into the world to such awful risks. How can you let them enter the race of life with such odds against them – those innocent little ones to whom you think you could lay down your lives? Can you not give up for them this one little indulgence? (Moorhouse 1882, p. 14)

Sir Francis Galton in 1889, wrote in his book *National Inheritance*:

> For example, a woman who was sober becomes a drunkard. Her children born during the period of her sobriety are said to be quite healthy: her subsequent children are said to be neurotic. The objection to this as a valid instance in point are many. The woman's tissues must have been drenched with alcohol and the unborn infant alcoholised [sic] during all it's existence in that state. The quality of the mother's milk would have been bad. (Galton 1889, p. 137)

Clearly he supported the view that maternal alcohol consumption during pregnancy is detrimental to the developing child. Indeed he notes that the issue does not appear to be one of genetics, another strongly held view at some periods, as he stated that the children born during the period of her sobriety are said to be 'quite healthy'.

Russell, writing on the psychological aspects of alcoholism in 1881, provided the following comment:

> No fact is better established than that the vice of intemperance, like other vices, and peculiar mental manifestations is due, in many instances, to hereditary transmission ... ..That which in the parent was merely a habit, becomes in the child an impulsive uncontrollable desire. (1881, p. 61)

Midwives and Wet Nurses

In Roman times many of the most skilled midwives would have been Greek (Pomeroy 1975, p. 169).

King (1994) has questioned the negative picture of the midwife. Quoting Evenden, she has stated:

> it is only the many centuries of bias in favour of male professionals which have led to the labelling of midwives in this period 'as generally incompetent illiterates', much the same could be said about accusations of drunkenness. (p. 118)

This is an interesting idea as it begins to address the issue of the threat midwives posed to the male medical profession. Indeed midwives did play very powerful roles at different times in history. As noted by King (1994):

> David Harley has recently re-examined sixteenth and seventeenth-century sources on witchcraft and has shown that, far from being accused of witchcraft, midwives were more likely to appear in the role of expert witness, using their knowledge of the normal female anatomy in order to detect witches marks. (p. 119)

This must have been a very difficult position to be in, given that so many of the so-called witches were often village women who were older and wiser than the rest. Midwives were also called upon to give evidence in the case of alleged rape (Harley 1994, p. 37).

Even before the seventeenth century, midwives in the UK were able to study from books written specially for them. From the knowledge we have now much of the information seems strange at best, and at worst inaccurate. One of the most famous books was probably written by Culpepper, a renowned herbalist, who wrote his *Directory for Midwives* in 1662. He noted the changes that occurred at puberty, known at that time as the 'terms': 'The terms commonly begin at fourteen and then the hair appears on the privities, [sic] the breasts swell and women begin to be lecherous' (Keeble 1994, p. 29). He went on to describe what he calls the 'Frenzy of the Womb' in this way: 'They are mad for lust, and infinite men, and lie down to them; and it differs from salacity in that there is no delirium' (p. 29). The causes were clear: 'hot meats spiced, strong wine, and the like, that heat the privities' (p. 30). This comment is one of countless in which alcohol consumption has been liked with disinhibition, sexual or otherwise. This topic has already been discussed in Chapter 1.

By the nineteenth century, as noted by MacMillan (1988) for British women in India, the most important part of being pregnant was to find the services of a competent midwife. If they were lucky they might get a good midwife from England:

> When Minnie Blane was expecting her first child, she wrote reassuringly to her mother in England that she had at last found a good midwife; 'Our great comfort is that she drinks neither wine, beer nor spirits of any kind. So many of these women do so excess'. (p. 126)

The Indian women who were employed to look after the children were also a cause for concern as rumours circulated amongst the British women that the *ayahs* gave the children opium to keep them quiet. However, things were not much better in Britain, where some of the poorer women who had to take the babies to work in the mills would sometimes give them opium to keep them quiet. The famous 'Godfrey's Cordial' was very popular for this purpose. For women who were not able to take their children with them to work the job of childminding developed rapidly (Parssinen 1983). The use of substances to keep their charges quiet was not restricted to the poor women. The lithograph depicted in Figure 5.1 shows what is described as a drunken wet nurse about to give the Prince of Wales (later Edward VII) a drop of alcohol as a horrified Queen Victoria and Prince Albert burst in on the scene.

The use of 'opiate-based children's quieteners' was common in Britain; this was apparently not the case in the US. The reasons

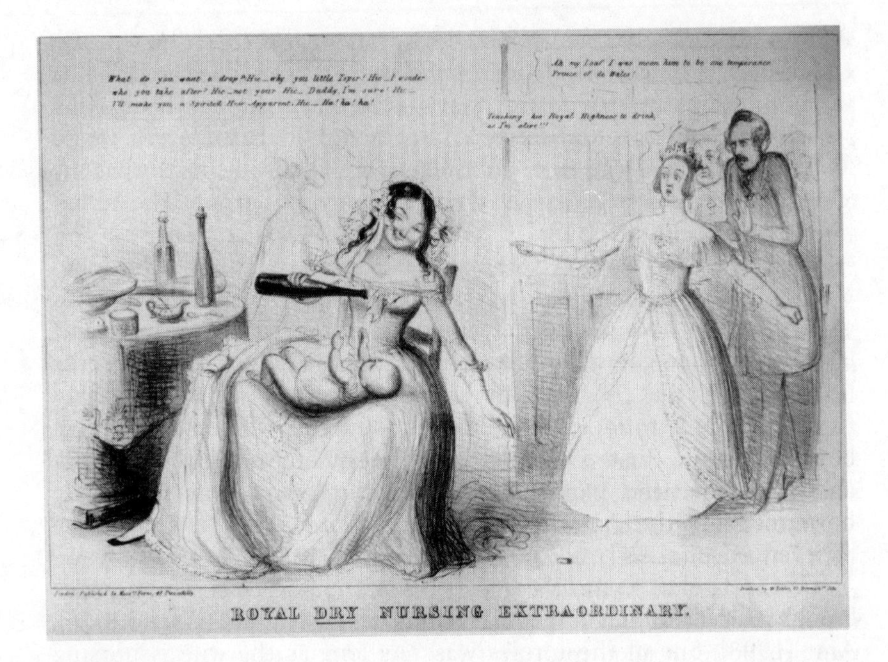

Figure 5.1 A drunken wet nurse about to give the Prince of Wales (later Edward VII) a drop of alcohol as a horrified Queen Victoria and Prince Albert burst in on the scene. Lithograph reproduced courtesy of the Wellcome Institute Library, London.

for this probably relate to the fact that at that time the latter was not a country where industrialisation had yet taken hold. Although opium was not therefore the risk it had become in Britain, morphia was being used for the purpose of quietening the children. As noted by Parssinen (1983):

> From analysis carried out over a period of years on 'Mrs. Winslow's Soothing Syrup', an infants' sedative popular in both Britain and America, it is clear that the morphia content varied from nil to one grain per fluid ounce. (p. 33)

In many societies, at different historical periods, upper-class mothers did not breastfeed their babies. Usually this task was the function of the wet nurse, a local woman who had recently given birth to a baby herself and was therefore able to provide the milk. Sometimes these women were chosen by the mother, sometimes they were already in the household as slaves. Yet not every physician agreed with this practice. As noted by Pomeroy (1975): 'The writings of Soranus, a physician of the second century AD ... declared that if the mother was in good health, it was better that she nurse the child' (p. 168). His reasons for this would not be out of place now: 'It would foster the bonds of affection.' This learned man also believed that the 'welfare of the mother take precedence over that of the infant' (Pomeroy 1975, pp. 168–9).

However, few women would behave in the way of the mythological picture of the Amazons who gave their children horses' milk to ensure that they would not grow large breasts. This was in part because breasts got in the way of using weapons. Indeed, some texts suggest that Amazonian women had their right breasts removed in order to facilitate more accurate aim when firing with a bow and arrow (Just 1991). However, it is interesting to speculate about whether the women were aware in some way of female hormones and the part they play in the 'weaker sex'; perhaps they believed that horses' milk might not contain these.

In the twelfth century *Book of Women* the Rabbi Maimonides brought together the family traditions of Jewish life. As noted by Amt (1993), one of those rules was: 'As long as the wife is nursing her child, the amount of her work should be reduced, while her maintenance should be augmented with wine and other things that are beneficial for lactation' (p. 288).

As with many occupations, there was a world of difference between the wet nurse of a wealthy family, at one extreme, and the wet nurse of the orphanages and foundling hospitals, at the other. The reality for the latter group was that they were at great risk of becoming infected by sexually transmitted diseases while breastfeeding (Hufton 1993, p. 38). This may have been one of the few means of earning money for these women but it put not only themselves but their families at risk.

In the seventeenth century the wives of husbandmen were reputed to be strong and healthy. 'Husbandmen' were a group of workers who had some land for which they paid rent and which they worked, but it was not enough to enable them and their families to survive. Therefore they went off to work leaving the women to tend the land. It was this picture of health, and the view that they had strong healthy children that made the women popular as wet nurses for the local richer women. One of the first references to the possibility that substances in the diet might affect the breast milk and therefore the child's digestive system, is to be found in *The Diseases of Women* written by Trotula of Salerno. On the subject of the choice of wet nurses she states:

> The nurse ought to be young and have a pink and white complexion. Let her not be too near to prospective parturition nor too far removed from preceding parturition. Let her not be dirty. She should have neither weak nor too heavy teats, but breasts full and generous, and she should be moderately fat. (Amt 1993, p. 105)

Trotula goes on to advise on the diet which will give the baby the best sustenance:

> If however the milk becomes thick, ... Compel her to exercise and she should be given vinegar syrup and light wines. If the milk becomes too thin let her nourishment be thick and substantial and have her rest more. If the child's bowels be loose, let foods which cause constipation be given to the nurse. (Amt 1993, p. 105)

A woman who finds a home willing to take so much care of her may seem lucky; however, it must be remembered that often this meant leaving her own children, one of whom would be very young, to go and live in the employer's house.

The issue of breastfeeding was debated in the British medical journal, the *Lancet*, in 1842 by Dr T. Beaumont, with the suggestion that alcohol passing through the breast milk was a cause of convulsions (Beaumont 1842, p. 342). Yet, five years earlier, temperance campaigners (Gourlay 1837) were having to answer questions put by nursing mothers: 'What are we to do about suckling? We are then obliged to take ale' (p. 75).

As noted by Kobler (1973), writing of the late eighteenth century in the US:

> Hard liquor had the endorsement of doctors, who prescribed it for practically every affliction from painful teeth in infancy ... ... rum and milk was a boon to pregnant women, as well as nursing mothers. (p. 26)

In fact, more recent work has explored this issue both in relation to alcohol and other drugs (Wilton 1992). It has been shown that alcohol actually inhibits the 'let down' reflex, the mechanism whereby breast milk flows into the breast to enable the infant to feed (Cobo 1973). This may be an issue for women who have difficulty feeding their babies. For many women, even those who have little difficulty with breastfeeding, there is often a problem with the early evening feed. The woman is tired, the other family members need feeding and the baby is hungry. It is at this time that women are sometimes recommended to drink some kind of fortified beer while they are feeding their babies. The rationale is that it helps the mother relax and this helps both mother and baby. This advice needs to be rethought with the above new evidence. Further to this is the possibility that alcohol may make the breast milk taste bitter.

This is useful information, but it should be borne in mind that there are probably many things which change the taste of breast milk, but like so many other substances, most of them have never been tested. This is one of the classic ways that women help each other, the information that some things like cabbage give babies wind and can make them colicky is often passed on in the same way now as it was centuries ago.

Treatment of Puerperal Mania

Dr Ferguson, teaching at the University of Toronto in 1892, suggested that alcohol was of great value in the treatment of puerperal mania:

> I am of the opinion that this is one of our best agents in puerperal mania. From four to eight ounces of brandy or whiskey, in the course of twenty four hours, have succeeded in relieving severe insomnia. I would recommend a trial in properly selected cases. No matter how difficult it may be to secure sleep in any given attack, press boldly on; and, once sleep has been secured, maintain a full allowance for a limited period. (Ferguson 1892, p. 436)

As noted by Rehman in relation to the treatment of puerperal insanity, many well known British physicians and psychiatrists also used alcohol as a treatment tool. Rehman, referring to Thomas Clouston, a famous Edinburgh psychiatrist, noted: 'Clouston [1904] also recommended the use of alcohol ... sherry and port were freely prescribed as stimulants' (1986, p. 112).

Interestingly, the other treatment favourite at the time was that of the 'Gospel of Fatness' where the patients were fed the most fattening foods with a great deal of meat and very few vegetables. It is not an exaggeration to suggest that some women at least may have started to drink 'for medicinal purposes' and gone on to develop difficulties. (See Chapter 2 regarding tonic wines.)

Interest in the topic of alcohol-related birth damage in the scientific community dropped in the first decades of the twentieth century. However, interest continued mainly in the US (Butler 1942, Warner and Rosett 1975) and also in Britain (Elderton and Pearson 1910). Ballantyne (1904), considering the results of a study carried out in Edinburgh, concluded: 'parental and especially maternal, alcoholism of the kind to which the name of chronic drunkenness or persistent soaking is applied is the source of both ante-natal and post-natal mortality' (p. 23).

The reasons for this are probably many and varied. In the US Prohibition had been introduced, and the First World War, followed by recession, coincided with a reduction in many scientific endeavours. The temperance movement was also still strong. However, there were a few papers published on studies related to this area (see Warner and Rosett 1975). There have periodically been reports by commentators who disagree with the view that heavy drinking in pregnancy is dangerous. In 1942 Jellinek and Jolliffe asserted that the idea of 'germ poisoning by alcohol in humans may be safely dismissed' (p. 162). Few clinicians or researchers agreed with them then and even fewer would do so now. However, as late as the 1950s and 1960s, some commentators have done so (Keller 1955, Montague 1965).

The Father's Role

The issue of 'hereditary alcoholism' has not always focused on the mother. Indeed, a number of experts in the field, including Rush, Morel, Magnan and Bevan Lewis, have suggested that it was the fathers' chronic drinking which led to the weakening of the children. As noted by Hughes in his address to the Mississippi Valley Medical Association on 9 October 1890, each subsequent generation was more severely damaged:

> If the first generation, as Morel has observed, shows immorality, alcoholic excess and brutal degradation, the second one will usually show, as he also observed, hereditary drunkenness, maniacal attacks and general paralysis or some similar psychopathic affection. The third generation may show sobriety, but instead of the transmitted drunkenness, the hereditary neuropathic perversion will probably reveal itself as Morel saw it, in hypochondria, mania, hypomania and tendency to homicide and suicide; and we shall see in the fourth and after-coming generations feeble intelli-

> gence, stupidity, early insanity and the beginning of the end of the family in extinction. (Hughes 1890, p. 545)

This is one of the clearest examples of the neuropathic degeneracy subsequent to 'ancestral alcohol excess' schools. However, in Hughes' rather emotive, flowery language:

> All alienists have confirmed this observation of Morel, and the fatal heritage of chronic alcoholic toxhaemia [sic] is proven upon those living within the walls of asylums for the insane the world over, and in every walk of life without and upon the cadavers of those who have died under the power of this neurotoxic force. (1890, p. 545)

This he calls the 'gospel of science'. Even so in all this, Hughes was actually writing about the harm due to the male drinker's family.

Russell, writing in 1881, stated: 'Could we lift the curtain and unveil the family history of some of our most distinguished men, we should be appalled at the fearful inheritance they have transmitted to their children' (p. 63). It is interesting to note that, intentionally or otherwise, Russell puts the responsibility for inheritance on to the father. The mother was not identified as having a role in this respect.

King Henry VIII of England confined his first wife – whom he divorced – in a nunnery and executed his second and fifth wives (his third wife died in childbirth; he divorced his fourth wife and his sixth wife survived him) because his need for a male heir was so pressing. Given the times and the uncertainty of the future for the Tudor dynasty, his behaviour needs to be judged by the often brutal standards of the time. However, it did not ever seem to be questioned that the reason for not having a healthy son was more to do with Henry than with his unfortunate wives. Indeed, things may have been different if he had had the opportunity to read the survey reported in the *Belfast Daily Telegraph* in 1988 and summarised by Alcohol Concern (1988):

> Heavy drinking fathers are more likely to have daughters than sons. The survey, apparently based on a study of thousands of birth certificates, found that men overindulging in alcohol had comparatively low levels of the male sex hormone testosterone; and that heavy drinkers produced more daughters than sons, with their babies tending to be smaller that average. Publicans,

barmen and other workers in the drinks industry have between six and 10 per cent fewer sons than other men. (p. 16)

This topic is again beginning to receive some attention and will be discussed later in the chapter.

Some of the first (recent) work into the possible impact of maternal drinking during pregnancy was carried out in France (Lecomte 1950, Rouquette 1957, Christiaens et al. 1960). In 1968 Lemoine et al. described 127 cases of alcohol-related birth damage. This group reported follow-up information about these children (Lemoine et al. 1992). Almost all of these original studies examined *parents alcooliques*. There was no question that it was the infants of problem drinkers who were affected. Soon after this Christy Ulleland (1972), a paediatric resident in Seattle, became aware of a group of babies who did not seem to be 'catching up' developmentally in the normal way. She checked through the case notes to try to identify any common factors and found one: all six mothers had been diagnosed as 'alcoholic'.

There have now been some large-scale epidemiological and case studies carried out in different countries (Mau and Netter 1974, Rosett et al. 1976, Streissguth 1977, Kaminski 1978, Sokol et al. 1980, Tennes and Blackard 1980, Davies et al. 1982, Hartwig et al. 1982, Kuzma and Sokol 1982, Gibson et al. 1983, Marbury 1983, Wright et al. 1983, Lumley 1985, Ioffe 1987, Plant 1987, Sulaiman et al. 1988). These have generally confirmed that birth defects are associated with *heavy* maternal drinking during pregnancy.

The diagnosis of Fetal Alcohol Syndrome depends on the presence of four categories:

1. Pre- and post-natal growth retardation: this includes intra-uterine growth retardation and babies who appear to be small-for-dates, that is, they are below average in length and weight for their gestational age. This short in length and light in weight pattern continues and these children are sometimes first identified in clinics where children were seen due to failure to grow within a normal range (Ulleland 1972).

2. Physical anomalies: the most well known of these are the specific cluster of facial features, which include short upturned nose, receding forehead and chin, asymmetrical ears, short palpebral fissures (the measurement between the inner corner of the eye and the outer corner of the eye). This latter measurement is difficult to assess and it is often the sense that the bridge of the nose seems to be broader

than normal which is first identified. The upper lip is narrower than normal and the measurement between the upper lip and the base of the nose is longer than normal. Although these features are often difficult to identify in different ethnic groups and do appear to fade as the child grows older, they can be an indication of less obvious brain damage (Majewski 1981).

3. Central nervous system dysfunction: the most obvious being the degree of mental handicap, cognitive disabilities, such as poor eye–hand co-ordination and hearing and visual deficits.

4. Finally, the mother of the infant has to have an identifiable alcohol problem. Note the term used is 'identifiable': this does not mean that a problem has been found, but rather that if information was collected on the mother's drinking, either in relation to consumption levels, patterns or both, a problem would be identified.

Jones and Smith, the two American dysmorphologists who gave the Fetal Alcohol Syndrome (FAS) its name did so in their paper published in 1973: 'a pattern of altered morphogenesis and function in eight unrelated children who have in common mothers who were chronic alcoholics during pregnancy' (Jones and Smith 1973, p. 1267). It is interesting to note that this latter point, 'chronic alcoholic', seems to have been missed out in the more recent descriptions of FAS. This is an extremely important point as it means that even if the mother is drinking heavily when she at first attends the ante-natal clinic, identification and help should be provided which could benefit both herself and her baby.

The term 'Fetal Alcohol Syndrome' was first used in 1973. In a paper published in 1981, the United States Surgeon General issued the following statement:

> Even if she does not bear a child with full FAS, a woman who drinks heavily is more likely to bear a child with one or more of the birth defects included in the syndrome. Microcephaly, which is associated with mental impairment, is one of the more common of these defects. Each patient should be told about the risk of alcohol consumption during pregnancy and advised to not drink alcoholic beverages and to be aware of the alcoholic content of foods and drugs. (United States Surgeon General 1981, p. 1)

It is important to examine more closely the knowledge of this subject at the time this report was published. The four main studies being conducted into the risks of drinking in pregnancy, all funded by the National Institute for Alcohol and Alcohol Abuse (NIAAA), were yet to be completed. Very little work had been carried out *prospectively* which could warrant this statement. Very little scientific evidence was therefore available with which to make these pronouncements. It was certainly a dilemma. If the United States Surgeon General (USSG) took the view, as appeared to be the case, that there was a real risk to pregnant women in general from even small amounts of alcohol, there was a responsibility to make this known. If small quantities of alcohol could damage the developing fetus then, even if only a proportion of pregnant women stopped drinking, hundreds of thousands of babies would be born healthier and lead fuller lives. If, on the other hand, this statement was issued and subsequently found to be unwarranted, not only would an equal number of women who had drunk alcohol during their pregnancy live a nightmare until the baby was born and found to be healthy, but it would affect the credibility of any future pronouncements. Problems of this type cannot be underestimated. Even small degrees of risk, if they involve hundreds of thousands of people, must be taken seriously.

However, the puzzle remains over the US Surgeon General's shift from the view that danger related only to 'a woman who drinks heavily' to asserting: 'Each patient ... advised to not drink alcoholic beverages and to be aware of the alcoholic content of foods and drugs.' The reasons for this shift appear unclear. Conversations with researchers in the US suggest that two issues may be relevant. One seems to be that the US did manage to avoid the horror of thalidomide. Although this seemed to be at least partly due to the slow speed of the Food and Drug Administration licensing, it nevertheless saved a lot of heartbreak. A second issue was that voiced by Dr Ruth Little, one of the main researchers working on the subject at the time: 'What is the benefit of drinking at all? That's what people should focus on rather than this frantic search for a safe level' (Kolata 1981, p. 642). This may seem a rather strange angle to approach the subject given that drinking is such an integral part of many cultures. However, it perhaps shows the kind of muddying of issues that besets the alcohol field. So often people do not stop at the evidence, or indeed even wait until the evidence is there, before going on to expound their own personal points of view whether they are relevant or not. Whether people in general and women in particular *should* or *should not* drink is not the point in this debate, but it highlights the direction in which the debate moved in the US. Other issues and rivalries which became clearer as time moved on were women versus men, researchers versus clinicians and health professionals versus the beverage alcohol industry. None of these were particularly new; however, they did nothing to elucidate this very important topic. Perhaps no one has expressed it more clearly than Edwards (1983):

> Alcohol problems notoriously attract absolutism, and covert moral stances easily become confused with medical advice. Threats to the unborn child excite particular anxiety. Lobbyists may seize on such an issue to manipulate support for a cause. Whatever the real biological problem, the story of the foetal alcohol syndrome might also profitably be studied in terms of what the sociologists would call the 'social construction' of a problem. (p. 248)

The other potentially more far-reaching aspect is how this kind of statement would affect people's trust in the government. As noted by Kolata (1981):

> Henry Rosett, Director of the Fetal Alcohol Education Program at Boston University of Medicine, says the government will lose credibility by crying wolf. Doctors won't believe this advisory. They are sceptical of simplistic propaganda. (p. 642)

The medical profession are not the only ones who might be sceptical. Take, for example, the 'Just Say No' campaign to stop children and young people taking drugs. Attempting to force complex human behaviour and needs into reductionist 'sound bites' is naive at best and positively destructive at worst. In relation to the 'Just Say No' campaign, the real risk was that the people who, for many reasons, had difficulty in saying 'No' to substances often saw themselves as so 'weak willed' that they had difficulty in going for help or even talking to their parents or friends. They often became more isolated, their low self-esteem was reinforced – 'I can't even "just" say no' – and they continued to move away from mainstream society, finding more in common with people on the drug scene.

The monochrome view of drinking in pregnancy, the pregnant woman's 'Just Say No' campaign, was also too simplistic. The topic of health education is considered further in Chapter 7. In the specific area of drinking in pregnancy there have been a number of different campaigns tried. Media campaigns to heighten awareness in the general population have been carried out in different countries: some have been evaluated; others have not (Minor and Van Dort 1982, Russell et al. 1983, Roman 1985, May and Hymbaugh

1989, Casiro et al. 1994). This short-sighted way of working becomes a serious concern when policy decisions start to be made with no knowledge of how effective a campaign has been. An example of a media campaign, 'Intoxication and Pregnancy', was launched in Norway in 1984 (Ihlen et al. 1993). This was directed primarily towards the relevant health professionals but also the general population. In the five-year period between the campaign and the follow up, the authors concluded:

> There was a significant reduction (50% decrease) in alcohol consumption among the second cohort of pregnant women compared with the first. Furthermore, we found an increase during the 5-year period in the number of persons with a restrictive attitude towards alcohol use during pregnancy. (p. 389)

The authors wisely note that 'it is hard to say anything about a causal relationship' (p. 389). Other researchers have not been quite so responsible.

An intervention aimed more specifically at pregnant women was launched in the US in 1995 (Reynolds et al.). Initially, a pilot study was carried out to develop the intervention and then the developed pack was used in two clinics, with a trial group and a control group. The authors concluded that the intervention had been successful: 'A higher alcohol quit rate was observed among the intervention participants (88%) than controls (69%). The effect was strongest with "light" drinkers, African-Americans, and non-Protestants' (p. 427). This was a brief intervention package and the authors suggest it may be useful in clinics where there is little time for staff to discuss issues with the patients.

As noted earlier, for the diagnosis of Fetal Alcohol Syndrome to be made the mother would have an identifiable alcohol problem. This does not mean that the problem will have been identified, but that if assessed the woman would be diagnosed. For this reason the treatment of pregnant problem-drinkers is similar to other groups in terms of the counselling, support factor. The issue of withdrawal is important, however. In research into drug-using women it has been shown that oxygen deprivation during withdrawal seizures may be as risky for the baby as the drugs themselves. Other problems include the substances with which the drugs are 'cut', many of which are more toxic than the primary substance itself. Finally, it is often very difficult to assess the actual amount of the drug, often there is very little of the active ingredient left. However, there is always the possibility that the dose will be purer and lead to peak doses of the substance entering the system. The issue with alcohol may not be so confusing, although a chaotic problem-drinker will find it virtually impossible to recall accurately how much she has drunk. Blumhagen and Little (1985) have commented that: 'reports of binge drinking were particularly unreliable' (p. 86). These are some of the main problem areas for treatment. Yet what about the ordinary pregnant woman attending an antenatal clinic? In the US the recognised recommendation would be to abstain completely. In the UK the likely advice would be to drink no more than one or two 'units' (or standard drinks), once or twice a week. A number of health education campaigns have been run by various organisations from government health departments to medical and health bodies. Media campaigns have also been used to heighten awareness and attempt to reduce consumption (Barrett et al. 1993). By 1989 the United States government had stated that by law all alcohol beverage containers must carry a warning label. An example of the wording contained in these labels stated:

> ACCORDING TO THE SURGEON GENERAL, WOMEN SHOULD NOT DRINK ALCOHOLIC BEVERAGES DURING PREGNANCY BECAUSE OF THE RISK OF BIRTH DEFECTS.

The value and impact of such statements are discussed further in Chapter 7.

There have now been studies carried out on a number of relevant areas such as pregnant women in different ethnic groups, black American (Jacobson et al. 1994) and African American (Oyemade et al. 1994); the attitudes of women and the professionals towards drinking (Lelong et al. 1995); implications for the professionals (Osborn et al. 1993), and maternal mortality (Raskin 1993).

In the past it was thought that the placenta was a barrier that somehow magically prevented anything damaging reaching the baby, but by 1904 Ballantyne reported that chronic drunkenness

> leads to that failure of the filter ... not only does the alcohol more readily pass through it itself, but it is also possible for other poisons, germs, and toxines [sic], to cross over into the foetal economy. (p. 65)

Other investigators have since continued this work (Idänpään-Heikkilä et al. 1971, 1972, Gartner and Ryden 1972, Waltman and Iniquez 1972, Mann et al. 1975, Baldwin et al. 1982, Fisher and Karl 1988, 1993). Fisher and Karl noted in 1993 that alcohol did affect the placenta by changing its ability to produce hormones. This in turn may affect the foetus adversely. *In vitro* studies of the umbilical artery suggest that alcohol may decrease the blood flow (Savoy-Moore et al. 1989).

Work has also been carried out into fathers' alcohol consumption, showing evidence of an association between such drinking and lower birth weight (Little and Sing 1987, Abel 1991, Sokol 1993) and increased risk of ventricular septal defect (Savitz et al. 1991). A new follow-up study has been set up in the US to assess the impact of fathers' drinking. The study, headed by Leonard, will follow-up children at 12, 18 and 24 months of age (RIA report 1995).

Other studies on problem-drinking women examine the issues such as accuracy of recall for consumption of alcohol and other drugs (Jacobson et al. 1991, Russel et al. 1991, da Costa Pereira et al. 1993). Studies have been made on the alcohol-related effects on early development (Jacobson and Jacobson 1991, Jacobson et al. 1993, Finnegan 1994, Nordberg et al. 1994), central nervous system deficits (Smith and Eckhardt 1991), and alcohol effects on reaction time of the fetus (Jacobson et al. 1994b). Fetal malnutrition (Fisher and Karl 1988) has also been examined, as have the issues of poor sucking response (Martin et al. 1979), neurobehavioural problems (Coles et al. 1985, Elsner 1995), craniofacial features (Rostand et al. 1990), and perinatal mortality (Finnegan 1994).

Effects of drugs other than, or in conjunction with, alcohol have also been examined in relation to the pregnant woman. These include tobacco (Cassano et al. 1990), and cocaine (Streissguth et al. 1991, O'Connor et al. 1993). Possible fetal/child effects of these drugs have also been evaluated. The drugs include tobacco (Cliver et al. 1992, Floyd et al. 1993, Orlebeke et al. 1994, McGee and Stanton 1994), caffeine and tobacco (Meyer et al. 1994), tobacco and marijuana (Fried 1993, Fried 1995), marijuana (Day et al. 1991, 1994, Chandler et al. 1996), cocaine (Strickland et al. 1993, Glantz and Woods 1993), methadone (DePetrillo and Rice 1995), opiates (Lindenberg and Keith 1993), and intravenous pentazocine and methylphenidate (Debooy et al. 1993). Prevention has also been described in relation to the use of different substances such as tobacco (O'Campo et al. 1992, Floyd et al. 1993, Valbo and Schioldborg 1993, de Vries and Backbier 1994, Haug et al 1994, Brosky 1995, Isohanni et al. 1995).

Programmes to reduce alcohol consumption in heavy-drinking women have shown to benefit the unborn child (Rosett et al. 1980). More comprehensive approaches to prevention are now being carried out (May 1995). The reasons for problem substance-use during pregnancy and post-partum have also been addressed, for example social stress (Lindenberg et al. 1994), and comfort (Collins et al. 1994).

Treatment

There are now a number of studies on identifying pregnant women problem-drinkers (Streissguth, Martin and Buffington 1977, Hinderliter and Zelenak 1993, Russell et al. 1994) and treating the pregnant woman with a drinking problem (Rosett et al. 1983, Finkelstein 1993, 1994, Finnegan 1994, Stevens and Arbiter 1995). The question of any potential risk to the baby has also been addressed (Blumberg 1974, Black and Meyer 1980, Ayoub et al. 1983, Shorkey and Armendariz 1985, Jacobson et al. 1993). Williams-Petersen et al. (1994) carried out a study into this area. The study consisted of substance users (n=25) and non-users (n=55). The majority of substance-using subjects in this study were drug users. There were some problem drinkers but the analysis did not appear to differentiate between them. Using the Milner inventory for measuring the potential for likely child abuse (Milner 1980), the substance users scored higher than non-users on the potential for harm to the baby. In relation to the distress section of the inventory, the authors noted:

> Over half the users scored higher than the upper 5% cut-off score for a clinically worrisome level of distress. Their scores indicated that these women felt angry, frustrated, mixed up, depressed, worried, fearful, rejected, and had difficulty in relaxing. (Williams-Petersen et al. 1994, p. 1639)

It is not difficult to see why this group of women scored high on this scale: experience has probably taught them that there was no reason to feel the future would be any better than the past. However, the issue here is the risk to the child. Williams-Petersen et al. stress that these women have not physically abused their children, although depending on the consumption levels of their continuing drug use, this may be questionable. The other issue highlighted by this group is that of social isolation: a risk factor for problem-drinking women is isolation. As noted in earlier chapters, at the point when she needs all the support she can get, the problem-drinking woman is likely to withdraw from her friends or, depending on her behaviour, have her friends withdraw from her. A number of studies have shown increased risk to the child if the parents are more socially isolated and Williams-Petersen et al. also commented on this problem. They found that the drug users who had high scores on social isolation also rated higher on potential for child abuse. Again, as noted in earlier chapters, given all the past experiences of many of the women in the substance-using group, it is not surprising to note that they measure low on self-esteem. Indeed, the authors reported that the main differences between the two groups of women related mainly to their views of themselves. It is important to note that the two groups, substance and non-substance users, rated similarly on areas such as affection for the baby, attitudes towards childrearing and external support. Even so, it is not difficult to see how a picture of risk to both mother and child begins to build up. Perhaps the most important part of this study is the clues it can give to helping both the mother and her as yet unborn baby. As concluded by the authors: 'What has been targeted in this study is a set of feelings about themselves which make this group of drug-using women at risk for maltreating their infants once they are born' (p. 1640).

There is a clear opportunity for helping these 'pairs of people'. It is of great importance to both mother and child to see that the child comes to no harm, but there has to be a better way to protect than simply removing the child and putting her in care. Of course, in extreme situations this may be necessary and, if so, it must be done as soon and as sensitively as possible. However, if it is possible to work with the mother ideally when she is pregnant, or even better, before she becomes pregnant, to enable her to develop a more gentle, forgiving view of herself, the outcome for both mother and baby may be much improved. It can almost be seen as working for both of them by concentrating on the one. There are many people who will not give women who are heavy or problem drug/alcohol users a chance. Some do so out of genuine concern for the baby. Others do so from high moral positions. However, no one has the right to dismiss another human being if that person wishes to seek assistance and support. Work like that of Williams-Petersen et al. may be what gives us the opportunity to help in more subtle yet more powerful ways for the good of both mother and baby. It should also be remembered that to treat problem-drinking or drug-using women with judgemental attitudes will mean the risk that they will withdraw from treatment rather than drug use, and any chance of helping the unborn child will be diminished (Poland et al. 1993, Nardi 1994). The effects on both mother and child of separation at birth are long term (Mundal et al. 1991).

It cannot be forgotten that problem-drinking women may be in relationships, however tenuous, with problem-drinking or drug-using partners. The possible impact on both mother and child of witnessing violent behaviour has been examined (Taylor et al. 1994).

Treatment programmes for older children and their mothers have also been examined (Metsch et al. 1995, Stevens and Arbiter 1995). Substance-using women of different age groups have also been examined, such as adolescents (Trad 1993). Cornelius et al. (1994), comparing drinking patterns in adolescent and adult women, concluded: 'Offspring of white adolescents, in particular, may be at higher risk for intermittent high peak alcohol exposure farther into the pregnancy than are offspring of older women' (p. 412). This may be an important aspect of health education, that of patterns as well as levels, of consumption.

Long-term Effects

Since the first of the recent work (Lemoine et al. 1968) there has been the opportunity to follow up the development of children who were diagnosed at birth as having FAS. The durations of such follow-up studies range from 8 months (Barr et al. 1984, Day et al. 1990), through 12 months (Fried and O'Connell 1987), 13 months (Gusella and Fried 1984), 18 months (Day et al. 1991, Forrest et al. 1991, Florey et al. 1992, Olsen 1994), 2 years (Fried and O'Connell 1987, Autti-Ramo et al. 1992), 3 years (Day et al. 1991), 3½ years (Olsen 1994), 4 years (Landesman-Dwyer and Ragozin 1981), 4 years 10 months (Greene et al. 1991a,b), 5½ years (Coles et al. 1991) pre-school (Schandler et al. 1995, Zucker et al. 1995) 6 years (Darby et al. 1981, Russel et al. 1991), 7½ years (Streissguth et al. 1990) and 14 years (Sampson et al. 1994, Streissguth et al. 1994). Few people would question the devastating effects of high doses of maternal alcohol consumption. However, the results are inconsistent in relation to the longer-term effects of lower levels of maternal alcohol consumption and it becomes increasingly difficult to find clear relationships with problems such as learning difficulties (Pihl et al. 1991).

Possible alcohol-related problems in these children as they get older become extremely difficult to view in anything other than vague associations. By the time the affected child becomes old enough to drink the factors associated with the way she or he is brought up will have far more impact than anything other than problem-drinking levels of maternal alcohol consumption (Emmelkamp et al. 1988, Bernardi 1989, Widom et al. 1995). Recent work on whether the gender of the problem-drinking parent makes a difference as a predictor of psychopathology in the adult offspring has not found this variable to make a significant difference (Belliveau and Stoppard 1995).

The policy implications have also been debated in the areas of alcohol and drug abuse (Abel and Sokol 1991, Besharov 1992, Garcia 1993, Schroedel and Peretz 1994). Yet some of the issues remain confused. In an editorial on preventing FAS, Blume (1996) noted three areas which a 'rational agenda' would include; the last two of these related to identification and referral of problem-drinking women, particularly in ante-natal settings, and education of health professionals in the same identification. These two make absolute sense. However, Blume's first point seems to follow the lines of the original United States Surgeon General's report, moving from the target group – that is, women with drinking problems – to all women. Blume suggested: 'Producing real change in drinking norms and customs for young women through curtailing beverage advertising and promotion and through relevant education (including "counter advertising")' (1996, p. 474). This statement seems even more surprising given that in 1991 Blume had written: 'we should be careful to state the basis on which the recommendation is made, and not to exaggerate the risk of small amounts of alcohol' (Kaskutas 1995, pp. 1538–9).

From where does this need to make sweeping statements originate? The majority of women in the US, as in most other countries, do not drink enough to put their babies at risk. In terms of attempting to change drinking norms, given the limited funds for health promotion, it might be more cost effective to concentrate in particular on reducing heavier and more damaging male alcohol consumption than to overemphasise that by females.

Fetal Alcohol Effects

The term Fetal Alcohol Effects (FAE) was brought in initially because it was thought that if heavy drinking caused severe damage, then, in dose response terms, lighter drinking would produce milder forms of damage. However, the reality now is that the term FAE has become a 'dumping ground' or repository for any odd feature that cannot be explained. Until we stop behaving so irresponsibly, we will continue to do women a disservice. However, the uncritical application of the term FAE also causes a great deal of trauma for women who have probably not drunk very much during pregnancy but now have to live with the message that they could have damaged their babies. Furthermore, and even more dangerously, it allows politicians and health policy makers 'off the hook' in terms of improving living standards and health care in deprived areas. To go along with this attitude is inappropriate. Many of the factors which contribute to fetal damage are as yet unexplained. We must not become lazy and unthinkingly attribute damage to alcohol harm when it may be related to other substances. If we do so we delay the discovery of these other damaging factors.

It is interesting to note that two of the most famous and longest standing members in this field, Lemoine (1994) and Jones (1994), have both recently been commenting on the above issue. As noted by Kaskutas (1995), Jones' most recent views were:

> [I] recommend that physicians document alcohol exposure *in utero*, low birthweight, and behavioral difficulties when they occur, but to avoid the F.A.E. diagnosis which carries an implication of causation. They are concerned because conclusive evidence that the effects are unique or due to prenatal alcoholism exposure do not exist. (p. 1540)

It is pleasing to note that Jones also stated:

> Citing inappropriate use of the term F.A.E. over the years, they argue that such overdiagnosis impedes the search for other causes of children's problems, frustrates any accurate assessment of the true magnitude of the problem caused by maternal consumption, stigmatizes mothers whose drinking may in fact not have damaged their children, and affects misdiagnosed children by lowering others' expectations of them. (p. 1540)

It is to be hoped that the standing of these people in the field may in some way redress the balance and aid in the clarification of this issue by careful investigation rather than building on ground which was shaky even in the beginning.

Problems in the methodology of studies in this area have been noted over the years (Sokol et al. 1992, Verkerk 1992, Fried 1995a) including the issue of prospective versus retrospective measurements of alcohol consumption. The problem of 'flattening' the consumption levels by adding total consumption rather than peak doses may be of particular importance in this field.

One of the real problems in this field is the difficulty in finding a large enough sample of heavy-drinking women to allow for sound analysis. In an attempt to enable this to be done, in 1984 work began on a collaborative project in Europe. This was an important step as the overwhelming evidence suggested that heavy alcohol consumption was related to adverse fetal outcome. The study was eventually funded after a great deal of negotiation in 1988 and data were collected in eight research centres: Denmark, France, Germany, the Netherlands, Portugal, Spain (two centres), and the UK. The study produced good reviews of general work in the field (Kaminski 1992, Larroque 1992) and also work on particular issues such as the impact of misclassification of alcohol consumption measures (Verkerk 1992), maternal alcohol consumption (Forrest, Florey and Taylor 1992), pregnancy outcome (Ogston and Parry 1992) and development at 18 months (Forrest et al. 1991, Florey et al. 1992, Parry and Ogston 1992). Florey et al. concluded that their results showed:

> an association between infant's body size and maternal alcohol consumption either before or in early pregnancy at levels of about 140 g/week or more ... There was no evidence that the development of children of mothers who drink at the levels observed in the studies was impaired either mentally or physically at age 18 months. (1992, p. 55)

Interestingly, the authors go on to suggest that women should not drink during pregnancy, but that if 'social pressure' makes this difficult, 'consumption should be restricted to no more than one standard drink a day' (p. S5).

The field of drinking in pregnancy is an emotive one. It is also one where some people are vociferous in their beliefs: sometimes these are based on fact; sometimes they are stated because no drinking during pregnancy seems a simple, straightforward message. However, many women drink when they are pregnant and although work is continually being published there is little evidence that small amounts of alcohol will harm either mother or baby. Wild stories of obstetricians being sued for millions and restaurant staff refusing to serve pregnant women in the US are viewed in Europe and elsewhere with a degree of puzzlement.

Women have the right to accurate information. They can understand and assimilate complicated messages if the messages are not simple. It is insulting to suggest otherwise. It is also unfair of governments and health workers to suggest that nothing but the alcohol is related to adverse fetal outcome. The truth is that social deprivation is a health issue and it has become too easy for people to say it is the woman's fault regardless of whether her living conditions are acceptable or not. Politicians should not be allowed to sit back comfortably when babies are being born damaged from women who may be trying against all odds to keep themselves and their offspring healthy in conditions which make it almost impossible. The evidence is clear: drinking to the point of having an alcohol-related problem is risky for both mother and baby (Abel and Hannigan 1995, Abel 1995). The chances of a problem-drinking woman giving birth to a Fetal Alcohol Syndrome child range from 2% to 26% (Abel and Sokol 1987). This is an unacceptably high figure. Given some of the problems such as difficulty in sleeping and feeding which these poor children experience, it can be seen that to a problemdrinker in this situation the pressure, tension and stress at times may be great enough to put the baby at risk from non-accidental injury. The little money there is in the health system could more wisely be spent on identification, treatment and continuing support of this group. Witch hunts in this field are unethical, and are likely to be counter-productive. People who already feel ashamed will not come forward if they think the reception they are going to get will be hostile. Efforts need to be made to raise awareness of staff in ante-natal clinics, family practitioner surgeries and alcohol problem treatment centres. Ideally, problem-drinking women should be given contraceptive advice to prevent pregnancy until they have dealt with their alcohol problem. It is simply not true to say that all problem-drinking women do not care whether they have a damaged baby or not, or that their drinking is more important to them than their unborn child. Having worked with a number of women who have given birth to damaged babies, the weight of guilt is immense. These women feel completely isolated; they are asked to attend support groups for mothers of children born with other forms of damage such as Down's Syndrome. Imagine how that feels – the other mothers may have no idea why they had a damaged baby, but the problem-drinking mother knows or fears only too well. This is a perfect example of being alone in a crowd.

6 Treatment Issues

The Roman jurist Ulpian, living in the second century AD, stressed the need for viewing problem drinkers as sick and diseased and therefore as people who needed special care in designated places (Crothers 1889a). As noted by Dr Robert Baker, Superintendent of the internationally respected York Retreat, in an address to the British Medico-Psychological Association:

> It was undoubtedly said and believed by them of old time that all insane persons should be sent to the wards of an asylum, but we, in these latter days, know of a more excellent way; we know, and are sure there are not a few persons, especially young people in a condition of temporary and incurable insanity who can be infinitely better and more wisely treated outside an asylum than in an asylum ward. Personally, I have always been profoundly impressed by this fact, so much so that my soul has sometimes been saturated with sadness in realising in all its intensity the inevitable annoyances of asylum life. (1893, p. 326).

These special places were often hospitals for the insane, one of the first recorded examples of these being in 491 AD when a hospital was established in Jerusalem. (Moulton 1890). However, women were not specifically mentioned in relation to treatment of the insane and it is likely that they were cared for at home. By the thirteenth century the French King James I passed a law decreeing that people who were known to have numerous episodes of drunkenness were to be admitted to hospital. There is little information on how successful this was but it demonstrated an awareness of the need for care rather than punishment (Tongue 1978). Other definitions for and beliefs used to explain drinking to this degree were common, particularly in relation to women. The confusion between the mad, the sad and the bad has been around for a long time. Morality and insanity took turns in being the rationalisation for women's behaviour. Jellinek (1960) noted, as he saw it, the need to differentiate between drunkenness and alcoholism:

> The alleged statements by St John the Damascene, and the enactments of an 'early Spanish king' on the disease nature of

> inebriety, are not invoked here as evidence as they turn out to refer to intoxication rather than alcoholism. (p. 1)

It is questionable whether this is an appropriate differentiation as most of the historical work in this area referred to repeated bouts of drunkenness and therefore would probably equate with a modern definition of a 'drinking problem'. Even into the twentieth century, many writers still have not differentiated between acute or periodic drinking problems and chronic problems. A study carried out in 1948 at Rutgers University in the US of a nationwide survey with a representative sample of women and men showed that: '58% saw no difference between an alcoholic and a person who gets drunk frequently' (Jellinek 1960, p. 183). By 1958 a similar study, again in the US (Roper et al. 1958), showed that in relation to someone whose drinking was causing problems in a number of different areas, 58% of people classed the drinker as 'sick' and 35% as 'morally weak' (Jellinek 1960, p. 183). It would be interesting to know how the same people would have responded if the question had been: 'Would you say that *she* is morally weak or sick?' Instead it was: 'If you knew someone who habitually drank so much that it affected his job and his relations with people, would you say that he is morally weak or would you say that he is sick?' (Jellinek 1960, p. 183). It would be interesting to note the possible differences in the proportion who chose which view, and whether the female respondents gave different responses from those provided by males.

The Nineteenth Century

In Morocco in the late 1880s an American doctor visiting Fez, one of the two capitals and the residence of the Sultan, described a 'house for the insane' which consisted of two levels. The ground floor held the male residents described as 'dangerous maniacs'. These 'maniacs' were imprisoned in boxes little more than a yard square arranged around a courtyard. Their necks were held in iron collars, 'of about the size of two hands. Each collar was riveted to a large chain, sealed to the wall.' There did not appear to be any care and they ate only when relatives or friends brought them food. The women were kept on the upper floor:

> however these were not insane. Some twenty women were crying and gesticulating, and as I could not explain to myself their presence I was informed that this storey of the house served as a

> prison for the street walkers of Fez. Below, the furious insane; above amorous insane. (*Alienist and Neurologist* 1889a,b, pp. 654–5)

In France during the 1880s, Magnan (1884), in his first clinical lecture in dypsomania, summarised the aetiology of problem drinking. He worked in the famous St Anne's Asylum in Paris. His clinical lectures were published over a period in the American journal, the *Alienist and Neurologist*. He wrote:

> Hufeland, Salvatori, Bruhl-Cramer, Erdman, and Esquirol call dipsomania a distinct malady – a monomania. The description of the attack alone is not enough – a complete history of the patient's disorder is necessary. Dipsomania then becomes one of a group of symptoms, occurring as phases of hereditary insanity. Causes other than hereditary have only a secondary influence. The attack of dipsomania is an attack of melancholia in outline. (p. 691)

Other physicians such as Salvatori, an Italian practising in Moscow in 1817, coined the phrase 'Oinomania'. Two years later a German physician, Bruhl-Cramar, minimised the idea of vice or mental disturbance but highlighted the 'overmastering and paroxysmal craving for drink' (Magnan 1884, p. 6).

Alcohol problems, then as now, were often associated with other conditions. In women the most common link was with hysteria. Dr Babinski in Paris described: 'A woman, 45 years of age, addicted to alcohol, subject to nightmare, and showing the signs of arteriosclerosis, was admitted to La Salpetrière in March 1886 in the service of M. Charcot' (1893, p. 275). The treatment, not surprisingly, given the fame of Charcot, in the early years was 'magnetism' which afforded some improvement. As time progressed and hypnotism became fashionable, the public exhibitions of hypnotism began to concern the medical profession in many countries. In 1890 the British Medical Association set up a committee to consider this topic. This body presented their report in 1892. This committee included some of the most famous names of the time in British medicine such as Clouston, Hack, Tuke, Conolly and Yellowlees. All of these people were renowned for their work in the field of psychiatry. Their report expressed satisfaction about the genuineness of the 'hypnotic state', but continued: 'no phenomena which have come under their observation however, lend support to the theory of "animal magnetism"' (*Alienist and Neurologist* 1893, p. 322). In relation to alcohol problems, the committee evaluated the use of hypnotism as a therapeutic tool and concluded: 'As to its permanent efficacy in the treatment of drunkenness, the evidence before the committee is encouraging, but not conclusive' (p. 322).

Committees were clearly no more willing to 'commit' themselves then than they are now. Furthermore they believed that hypnotism should be used only:

> for therapeutic purposes, its employment should be confined to qualified medical men, and that under no circumstances should female patients be hypnotised except in the presence of a relative or person of their own sex. (p. 322)

The latter comment is interesting because at that time it does appear as though this treatment was far more commonly used with women. This was in line with the ratio of 20 females to 1 male noted by Briquet in 1859 and later by Freud and Charcot. Briquet's study of 400 patients lasted over ten years, a formidable commitment. This provided an insight into some of the concerns about the proportion of female patients being hypnotised. As noted by Sulloway (1992):

> he was able to dismiss altogether the prevailing notion that hysteria was related to unsatisfied sexual impulses (he found that prostitutes suffered more than nuns), to disturbances of the womb, or to an exclusive etiology in the female sex. (p. 41)

People today may question the assumptions about different occupational groups in this statement, but the message is clear. As noted above, there was much debate during the 1800s about hysteria and its association with such disorders or behaviours as alcohol problems. One of the areas that caused discomfort was the issue of the possible link between sex and hysteria, just as at other times, there has been interest in whether there is an association with alcohol consumption and sexual behaviour. For this reason questions about hypnosis, one of the reputed commonest and most successful treatments for hysteria in the nineteenth century were often linked with anxiety about sexuality. Theodor Meynert, a famous Austrian neurologist and one of Freud's teachers, was vehemently against the use of hypnosis which he likened to a psychotic episode. As Sulloway (1992) noted:

> He (Meynert) believed that much of the basis of the hypnotic trance was sexual. By inhibiting the subject's higher cortical

> activity (and thus his conscious control over his body), hypnosis encouraged, Meynert argued, the involuntary release of sexual impulses in the subcortex. He therefore considered this method improper for general medical use. (p. 44)

The fear that alcohol consumption by women was sexually disinhibiting and the possibility that hypnosis might make matters worse were serious concerns at this time. It would be nice to think that such concern was motivated by interest in the safety of the female patient. However, it is much more likely that the principal regard was for a male medical profession being at risk from amorous female patients.

To some degree the treatment of alcohol problems varied by time, by geography and by culture. As noted earlier, the use of hypnotism was popular in France. Dr Auguste Voisin, physician to the Salpetrière in Paris, believed that it cured many ills, including, 'dypsomania and morphinomania'. However, other medical authorities of the time were less successful with hypnosis. Indeed, Giles de-la-Tourette (1890d), in an editorial, wrote that:

> those who were hysterically disposed, the majority of whom one imagines would be female, were made hysterical by frequent hypnotising. Of those who were already hysterical hypnosis may 'cure' the symptoms but this was not a true cure but rather that the symptoms moved to another area or organ of the body. (p. 429)

As noted in Chapter 1, the issue of the possible links between alcohol consumption and sexual behaviour have become a legitimate research topic since the advent of the worldwide AIDS epidemic. However, in relation to treatment populations, one of the evident difficulties that exists is the perceptions or misconceptions that many women, problem drinking or otherwise, have about alcohol and sexual behaviour. This link for problem drinkers can remain after alcohol withdrawal and treatment. One reason for this may be that for many women, the perceived association is not with sex per se but with comfort. The main need for some women is to be close to another human being, and, at the end of the day, such women may feel 'obliged' to have intercourse with a partner, however brief their acquaintance. If sexual behaviour is engaged in, this may serve to reduce a woman's view of herself and her own power even further. Many women in this situation are completely misunderstood. People make assumptions about them, use words such as 'promiscuous' and the constant link between alcohol and sex is reinforced. For the woman herself, the issue is both simpler and more complex. First, intercourse is often seen as the price she has to pay for the comfort and warmth she so desperately seeks. Second, many problem-drinking women believe they do not have the right to say 'no', particularly if the man tells the woman that she 'led him on' by her initial behaviour. Third, as with many women, she may have been raised to believe that other people's needs are more important than her own. Sadly, this can reach a stage where the woman cannot even recognise or allow herself to believe she has any needs. She may have pushed them down so far and for so long. She may have been told, often initially by parents, that: 'What you want does not matter.' Some of the most destructive relationships can occur when women who have heard these kinds of messages for so long that they believe them, meet men who bolster their own low self-esteem by bullying or belittling others, particularly women. Every part of her which she views as worthless and useless, actually feels comfortable with this type of relationship. The same negative parts resonate, are reinforced and then become magnified, when inevitably the relationship ends. The ending of the relationship is met often with resignation and, 'Well I knew it would happen, it always does.'

Although it sounds like a contradiction in terms, the issue of intimacy and the fear of it, is a common and paralysing factor for many problem drinkers, both female and male. Given that for many years the main form of treatment for alcohol problems has involved some form of group approach, many therapists just did not see how difficult it was being a member of a group. As the group became more cohesive the difficulties increased and the individuals who perhaps had the more extreme problems with intimacy, felt under more and more pressure to disclose personal details. As the group *norm* became that of disclosing increasingly intimate details, a normal part of the group process, then anyone not doing so almost by definition became *abnormal.* The isolation to which this may lead might re-create past experiences. The risk becomes that past strategies will then be used to deal with the situation. In this case, the possible 'past behaviour' would obviously be drinking. So, to the staff, the person has refused to take part in group discussions, denies having a drinking problem as she never talks of her past and has relapsed. It is not difficult to imagine the possibility that the woman would be discharged as being unwilling to enter fully into the treatment programme. Irvin Yalom, an American psychotherapist who wrote one of the most influential books on group psychotherapy (Yalom 1985), has suggested one way of dealing with the situation. When a group member manages, tentatively, to disclose something, the therapist can differentiate between what Yalom describes as vertical or horizontal disclosure. The tendency of the group members, is to move quickly into encouraging what he calls 'vertical disclosure': that is, asking questions which push the group member into revealing more deeply held secrets. The more helpful approach is to move horizontally, for example, asking questions around how it felt to tell the group; was the group's response what the person imagined or feared? What was it about the group at that time which enabled the person to talk so intimately? Yalom believes that in this way the group member is 'held', the difficulty in disclosing is acknowledged and the risk of moving too far too fast is lessened. Clearly, this example is relevant for anybody involved in running groups. It is of particular importance for people working with women problem-drinkers whose anxieties about how people see them and how they see themselves can be so powerfully negative. The main importance is the sense of taking a step into the group rather than standing on the sidelines becoming more and more isolated. Others have written of working particularly with groups of problem drinkers (Fox 1975, Kanas 1982, Khantzian et al. 1990, Vannicelli 1992). As noted by Kaufman (1994):

> The advantages of group therapy for Substance Abusers (SAs), as suggested by Vannicelli (1992), are as follows:
>
> 1. Groups reduce SAs' sense of isolation through the recognition that they are not alone and that they can be understood. This leads to instant, early bonding, with ties that develop increasing depth as a group becomes more cohesive over time. In the later stages, sobriety rather than the disease becomes the glue that holds the group together.
>
> 2. Groups provide ongoing support, safety and containment.
>
> 3. Groups instil hope by providing new members with access to longer-term members who are successful.
>
> 4. Groups permit members to learn from watching others. Many conflicts are more easily resolved by first watching and helping others work through them, then applying what is thereby learned to oneself.
>
> 5. Groups provide members with information about coping and

relapse prevention strategies, community resources, and support groups.

6. Groups permit members to model ways of communicating and interacting.

7. Groups provide a laboratory for the study of the members' actual here-and-now interactions, as well as a variety of transference reactions particularly those related to siblings. (pp. 177–8)

Although I am unhappy with the use of initials – they take away from the humanity of the person – the above description of group therapy by Vannicelli is one of the best acknowledgements of the complex interactions that occur when using this approach.

As noted above, for many people the very powerful aspect of working in groups is the sense of feeling you have something of value to share which may help others. You are not useless or lacking in experience. This factor can be very important for a woman problem-drinker. There is a negative aspect, however, and that is the relative ease with which many women will help others; it is almost second nature, and many females are taught to do so at a very early age. A major problem is to enable such women to help themselves or at least to begin to address their own problems.

The area of treatment is a good example of how male bias often became the norm. It often consisted of hospitalisation for a number of weeks. For many women this was not a viable option.

Most of the original studies on alcohol problems, physical, psychological and social, were conducted in Alcohol Treatment Units. This resulted in a number of distortions. First, the people admitted to hospital for alcohol problems fell into two categories; those so physically damaged due to their drinking and lifestyle that they were usually admitted to general hospitals with severe physical damage, either acute or chronic, and those who were admitted to Units for the Treatment of Alcoholism, as they were then called in the UK. The latter facilities were often highly selective and admitted only those problem drinkers who were likely to 'do well'. These included people who were still in stable relationships, who were in employment and who were not so physically damaged by their consumption that they could not take part in the treatment regime. Because most of these agencies worked using group therapy, this meant that people who were able to function socially as contributors to a group were verbally reasonably skilled. Such individuals also did not have any deficits, particularly brain impairment, which would affect the way they functioned in the group settings. Obviously this meant that these units could be selective in the people they admitted. They often came in for a great deal of criticism from the staffs of other neighbouring (or rival) treatment agencies. Such individuals understandably believed that they were often having to care for a number of the more disruptive and uncooperative problem drinkers who were excluded from group therapy. Many of these UK units were situated in psychiatric hospitals and there was often a degree of friction between staff in the different areas within such hospitals. A common point of debate was why the specialist treatment units took only the 'best' patients, by which was meant those with the best prognoses. This, of course, meant that the other wards had to take all the 'others', the patients who perhaps were in hospital because someone else wanted them to be there. The 'someone else' could range from a spouse to the police. However, the problem was that the patient may not have had any interest at that point in stopping drinking, or at least in remaining abstinent. It is interesting to think about how this split affected the view and behaviour of staff in general psychiatric wards in relation to problem drinkers. The reality was that even if the staffs of specialist units had wanted to admit all the problem drinkers referred to the hospital, they could not have done so.

As noted earlier, these units were mainly small. Indeed, they were often not even able to admit all the suitable candidates for their programmes. So what happened to these other patients? How did the views and behaviours of the staff in other wards, the staff who constantly felt imposed upon by these units, affect the patients' chances of appropriate treatment? Indeed, if a person was admitted to hospital determined to stop drinking and stay stopped, how did being in close contact with other patients who did not want to do so affect them? Anecdotal evidence suggests that this is a risky combination. It is not necessarily the case that the unwilling patients could make the enthusiastic ones change their future plans, but the pressure could perhaps make it difficult to use any group therapy sessions to the full. Staff in psychiatric hospitals are well aware of the pressures that can be brought to bear on patients to conform to what the strongest members of the patient group decide are the norms. For problem-drinking women in particular, these, usually mixed gender, wards may carry real threats of harassment from other patients. From male patients there may be the threat of sexual harassment and from female patients the kind of messages that reinforce a woman's negative self-image: worthless, useless, somehow an insult to womanhood. Add to this the possibility that the female problem-drinker may have a history of abuse. Try to imagine what it would be like sleeping in a room with other women, in a ward where the doors are not secure at night and where during the day strange people may behave in even stranger ways. This is often the situation for every person who enters a psychiatric ward, but it gives rise for concerns over which the staff, overworked and under pressure, may have little control. For this reason and also because of the staff's attitude towards problem drinkers, especially females, a woman may find it impossible to discuss her feelings with the staff. Add to this the possibility that the staff themselves may give covert messages of not being interested or caring and it is possible to see what a nightmare this can become.

In some ways it was understandable that these, usually small, units were selective about the admission procedure in that they were small, expensive to operate (the staff–patient ratio was often higher than in other wards), and there was a much greater blurring of roles between the different professional groups. Indeed, in the UK, these units were among the first examples of multidisciplinary teams outside more general Therapeutic Communities. However, as noted above, this meant that people actually had to be quite 'well' to be admitted. In view of the then prevailing beliefs about female problem-drinkers, having a poorer prognosis and being more defensive, it was not surprising that the ratio of men to women was about 4 to 1. Obviously the fact that there have always been fewer female problem-drinkers than males is a relevant factor. However, there were a number of other reasons for this and these affected every stage in the treatment of female problem-drinkers. First, the woman herself was probably no more likely then than now to be able to accept that her problem was alcohol related. Second, her family doctor was not even identifying the male problem-drinkers in the practice (Wilkins 1974) and therefore the chances of identifying a female were even smaller. Indeed, a recent Swedish study has shown that, at least in that country, this situation has not changed. As noted by the authors, Seppä and Mäkelä (1993): 'physicians identified as heavy drinkers only 64% of the men and 44% of the women with a positive self-report of heavy drinking' (p. 1381). Heavy drinking was defined as 140 g or more per week. It is also relevant to note that rates of identification varied between departments, with none of the heavy-drinking women (n=10) in obstetrics and gynaecology being identified. Given the quite high correlation between gynaecological problems and heavy drinking it would seem that education and training in identification may be worthwhile in this area.

Finally, even if she was identified and her family doctor sent her along to the nearest Unit for the Treatment of Alcoholism, she may have been less likely to be admitted. This may have reflected some unacknowledged bias on the part of the professional or the fact that she may have been more severely damaged by her drinking by this point and was therefore not deemed eligible. The other very real problem for her, if she had children, would have been that most of these units had set treatment regimes lasting from about two weeks for 'drying out' to twelve to fourteen weeks for an intensive psychotherapy programme. She was then in the impossible situation of having to think about what to do with her children. For many women in this situation, their children and their roles as mothers, although exhausting and at times terrifyingly large, were the only roles that they felt they had. How could a woman in such a situation give that up? It was often the case that her partner had already left her and her relatives and friends had given up trying to help. The latter might have tired of being used as donors of money used to purchase drink. The only solution was for the children to go into care. What kind of choice was that? Sometimes, to make it even worse, the staff would imply that if she was ambivalent about treatment, maybe she was not committed enough to the programme to be eligible for admission. For a male problem-drinker going into hospital, even for something as stigmatised as a drinking problem, there was often a real sense of relief for his partner and any children. The anxiety, often amounting to fear, which is a constant companion of partners of problem drinkers; the uncertainty and insecurity of never knowing whether they will come home drunk or sober and, if drunk, what minor irritation will she or the children commit to exacerbate an already tense situation? – to be free of that, even for a few days, is a relief. For the patient too, the feeling is controlled in a positive sense of being 'held' or 'contained' to relieve the sense of being out of control.

Other issues for a woman came into play when she was admitted. These often involved the way that the treatment was structured. One of the pioneering British agencies was the Unit for the Treatment of Alcoholism in Edinburgh. Now known as the 'Alcohol Problems Clinic', this was the first of its kind in Scotland. The treatment was said to continue 24 hours a day. The patient did not leave the unit for the first two weeks, the 'drying out' period, and the main treatment was group psychotherapy. The groups lasted from one to one and a half hours in length and after the first few days when patients felt physically quite ill these groups were often quite intense. In this unit there were few acceptable reasons for patients not attending groups. They had to be physically ill. If they just decided they did not want to attend the group then the group would come to them and would be held round the patient's bedside. Often the possibility of this was enough for the patient who would then join the group. In British culture there are few times when a woman is seen in bed and where intimate matters may be discussed. Although this is also true for men there is a precedent for female nurses taking care of men, the situation in which male nurses looked after female patients was relatively uncommon at that time. It is questionable whether anybody in that situation would be able to take part in any depth of therapy, particularly if the topics were related to sexual behaviour. Even with clothes on, groups may leave people feeling vulnerable, exposed and almost naked.

Within the structure and dynamic of a group there are many assumptions made about how people 'should' behave. These assumptions are based on the individual's perceptions and experience as well as factors such as age, gender, ethnicity and sexual orientation. The individual may also initially behave in a way which she or he perceived as the culture of the group. They will also be 'on their best behaviour' at first. This, however, will not last too long and one of the great benefits of group work is the opportunity to see how a member relates to others in the group in the 'here and now' when they 'forget' to behave in the way they think they should. In many cultures it is more acceptable for women to express their emotions than for men to do so. In fact it is even more complicated than this. Women may express certain feelings such as sadness and fear, but extreme degrees of these which in the past would have been called 'hysteria', will still cause discomfort in others. Men, on the other hand, may express feelings such as anger, but again, the degree is important. Anger can be a wonderful means of defence, it can cover up tears and fears and it can be very effective, keeping not only the group away from that person's feelings but also the person herself or himself. Due to the fact that it is less acceptable for women to exhibit anger, the more common defences for females are tears or silence. The latter is often interpreted as withdrawal from the group. Close observation may show that far from withdrawing from the group, a female member may be very involved in what is occurring, but she may not be contributing verbally. Although silence or tears can be successful ways of keeping the group at a distance they are also more easily interpreted by others as being signs of withdrawal. Anger or aggression often work by getting group members to withdraw from the person or not challenge them for fear of being hurt verbally or physically. This behaviour serves the purpose of enabling the aggressive individual to remain outside the group, but to unskilled therapists is sometimes not so easily identifiable as such. This is a problem not only for the individual concerned but may also be misinterpreted by the staff.

The other main problem for women in mixed-gender groups is one which also spills over into other areas of the treatment milieu. This is the issue of the perception of women's primary role being to look after men. This role is very powerful and may be accepted by both men and women. If this role is played then the women in the group may 'look after the men'. For example, as they are the ones who can express feelings more easily, they may become the group members who are the 'feeling carriers'. The women express their own feelings so the men do not need to do so. Indeed, the women may go as far as preventing the men from expressing their feelings when they see the struggle it may be for them to do so. This is a very complex role and also very disruptive for all group members. As noted earlier, even though women are 'allowed' to express certain emotions, in many cultures anger is not one of them, so the expression of feeling in the group is not balanced. Take the very destructive classic 'Jekyll and Hyde' character associated with alcohol problems. This depicts a person who is intellectually brilliant, polished, polite and well mannered – until he takes a substance which changes him into a monster, cruel, dangerous and out of control in both his behaviour and his emotions, particularly rage. The saddest and most destructive aspect of this 'Jekyll and Hyde' view is that it prevents an individual from ever becoming a complete person who has the ability to express every feeling – happiness, sadness, anger, fear. With this stereotype the person cannot be complete when they are sober; they have to be 'sweetness and light' and if they are not, then those closest to them may panic because they view it as the onset of a drinking bout. Everyone at some time experiences negative feelings. The skill for the problem drinker is often in learning how to express them in a way that can be heard. The challenge for the problem drinker's family is to recognise negative feelings without always regarding them as the beginning of something wrong. Conversely and particularly important for women problem-drinkers, is learning to express feelings without the fear that everyone will be damaged by them and also to be able to hear the expression of the feelings of others without believing that she will thereby be destroyed.

In addition to these factors, there is often another important problem which may compound difficulties. Some women have been taught from an early age that other people, particularly men, are more important than they are, that other people's feelings are more important than their own and that other people's needs are also more important. Put such a woman in a group and she will behave in the same way, often apparently very successfully. She will help and enable other group members to express their feelings and disclose their 'secrets'. She may well feel really good about it, she has learned that this is the way to be fulfilled, to feel useful. Yet she senses and then becomes more and more aware that although other group members may think she is great and tell her so, the staff members seem less happy with the way she is behaving. They may suggest that she is behaving in this way in an attempt to avoid her own feelings. The role she has been trained to play and has been playing most of her life is brought into question or directly criticised. The importance of such a situation should not be underestimated. When the ground you have been walking on, however drunkenly or unhappily, begins to shift under your feet it is terrifying and the first reaction is to try harder. The effect of this is to provoke more implied criticism from the staff. Many of the first UK treatment units worked on a 'semi-therapeutic community' basis. The patients were responsible for making their own beds and keeping the communal bedroom areas tidy. They were also responsible for buying, preparing and washing up after a supper meal. Again the issue of gender roles arises with the women patients either feeling secure in the role of looking after the men, or as they develop more of a sense of their own rights, they may become more and more resentful. Obviously the ideal is that these issues will be examined in the group and used to enable the patients to explore the roles they have adopted in their relationships and how these may have affected them adversely, for example in relation to the part drinking has played in their lives. However, when people are encouraged to examine long-standing behaviours they have to feel safe to do so. Given such complexities it begins to become clear that this is no easy task. As noted above, due to the prevailing gender ratio of an average of four men to one woman admitted to these units it was not uncommon to find a group comprised of one woman and nine men. It is not hard to imagine the isolation felt by the woman and the security she could find in 'playing mother' to all the 'boys'.

Another thorny subject in relation to the operation of mixed-gender groups is that of sexuality. Take the issue of multiple sexual partners. In many ways a woman is more likely than a man to be judged harshly for having multiple sexual partners. Groups and staff members are liable to react very differently to such reports from women or men.

Finally, another major problem relates to the difficulty that many problem-drinking women have with their own sexuality. Research has suggested that women with drinking problems report feeling more sexually attractive when they have been drinking (Beckman 1978). Their appearance is of great importance to them. They may be so out of touch with their inner being that the outside shell is polished to reflect rather than let people look for fear of them finding nothing.

The so-called 'talking therapies' have been used for treating problem drinkers for many years with varied levels of success. Freud interpreted alcohol problems as a fixation at the 'oral phase' of development. Jung took a broader view of problems in general. Melanie Klein and her colleagues devised a description of 'object relations theory'. Many of these views have now been challenged (Clare 1976, Masson 1990, 1992, Dryden and Feltham 1992, Hillman and Ventura 1992). By the 1960s, the so-called humanistic models had come into being. Carl Rogers developed 'non-directive' therapy which later became known as client-centred and now person-centred therapy (Rogers 1951, 1957, 1961, Brazier 1993). This model has specifically addressed the issue of women with alcohol problems (Hunt and Seeman 1990). Other models included Fritz Perls' Gestalt therapy (Perls 1969, Perls et al. 1974) and Reichian therapy (Reich 1951, 1972, West 1994) which led on to the newer and ever expanding innovative models such as Neuro-Linguistic Programming (Bandler and Grinder 1979, Grinder and Bandler 1981).

As noted above, many therapies do aid people with a variety of problems. However Transactional Analysis (TA), the model developed by Eric Berne (1961), with its emphasis on the three ego states of Parent, Adult and Child, has a book specifically about people with alcohol problems. *Games Alcoholics Play* by Claude Steiner (1971) has a front cover carrying the claim: 'This New Bestseller Now Offers The First Real Hope for Problem Drinkers'. The foreword, written by Berne noted:

> The word 'alcoholic' is only about a hundred years old (1856). It is one of those words ending in 'ic' used by clinicians to mean a non-person, like 'schizophrenic' and 'psychotic'. What Dr Steiner has done here is give back to 'alcoholics' their membership in the human race. (p. ix)

Claude Steiner wrote about Life Scripts. This concept, central to TA theory, is described as: 'A life plan, made in childhood, reinforced by parents, justified by subsequent events, and culminating in a chosen alternative' (Stewart and Jones 1991, p. 100). One of the interesting aspects of Steiner's book is the way he challenges the disease model of 'alcoholism'. It must be remembered that this concept is very powerful, especially in the US where 'Twelve Step programmes' and AA in particular, have for some time been the dominant approach to alcohol-problems treatment. These are also important in a number of other countries. During the 1960s 'Alcoholism Treatment Units' were established in many areas of the UK. Most of these were based upon the view that 'alcoholism' was an incurable disease, a belief popularised by AA:

> Like diseases, scripts have an onset, a course and an outcome. Because of this similarity, scripts have been mistaken for diseases. However, because scripts are based on consciously willed decisions rather than on morbid tissue changes, they can be revoked or 'undecided' by similarly willed decisions. Thus, I believe that a cured alcoholic (though he often does not choose to) will be able to return to social drinking, while the person who returns to uncontrollable drinking after one drink has been essentially unable to dispose of his script. (Steiner 1971, p. xvii)

Many adherents of the disease concept of alcoholism would be horrified by this description. Indeed Steiner acknowledged they would, but went on to state: 'It is important to distinguish between social drinking and the institutionalised alcoholism that passes as social drinking in our culture' (1971, p. xvii).

Yet what effect, if any, did this 'disease concept' have on women? Were the differences which have consistently appeared in the pages of this book taken into account? Were the perceptions of women and their view of the world acknowledged in this new 'disease'? Was the structure of this 'disease' even thought of in terms of differences between the genders or was it another example of maleness being the norm and therefore male perceptions and male structuralism dominating as so often in the past? As can be seen later in this chapter (Kirkpatrick 1986), these questions appear never to have been asked. Yet what if the female view of the world had been used as the norm? What if, instead of the need for guilt to be highlighted and used as a great weight to carry, the idea of nurturing and care had been emphasised? What if, instead of the powerlessness over alcohol which is such a cornerstone of Alcoholics Anonymous (AA), we perceived the problem as: 'I have a drinking problem that once had me?' (Kirkpatrick 1986, p. 161). If instead of: 'Humbly asking Him to remove our shortcomings' we said: 'I am a competent woman and have much to give others' (Kirkpatrick 1986, p. 161), where would people's view of alcohol-related problems be now? Perhaps the self-help group's time would be spent more on support and nurturing than on ever longer and more traumatic repetition of past difficulties. This process could be interpreted as implying that by simple repetition, such experiences are somehow transformed into something almost to be proud of; to be remembered, as though by not doing so, magically, uncontrollably, the behaviour would be repeated. Even that view expresses a sense of powerlessness which for many women can only reinforce their view of the impossibility of change. Over the years AA has been predominantly male orientated, yet in the famous 'Big Book' many of the stories are of women (Aaltonen and Mäkelä 1994).

There are signs from the recent literature that perhaps AA is now becoming aware of the need to acknowledge the distinctiveness of the female members of its organisation (Chrouser 1991, Clemmons 1991, Covington 1994). It is interesting to speculate as to whether this is in part related to the rise and spread of the women's movement, especially in the US. The title of some of the publications such as Clemmons' *Feminists, Spirituality and the Twelve Steps of AA,* would suggest that this may be the case. If so, this powerful message that women have a right to be in AA and that they are not abnormal because they do not have the same 'stories' as the men may even begin to transform the structure of AA over the next few years. Even so, in areas where AA has been adapted for different cultural groups there still appears to be little provision for women (Hoffman 1994).

The well known treatment programme of Alcoholics Anonymous has always been predominantly male. Views about AA are mixed, with some people experiencing a support and closeness they have never had before. Others view it in more sociological terms. As summarised by Donovan (1993): 'Alcoholics Anonymous is systematically organised around the processes of sacrifice, investment, renunciation, communion, mortification and transcendence' (p. 411). When this works it can be very powerful. Perhaps it would also be wise to caution that when it does not, it can be quite destructive, leaving people feeling guilty and alone against power. However, a study by Snow et al. (1994) in relation to maintenance of long-term sobriety concluded: 'women in the present study participated equally in AA in terms of exposure, frequency of attendance and level of affiliation' (p. 369).

By the 1980s in the US, 34% of the sample taken by the General Service Board were women (Weisner and Morgan 1992). According to these authors it is also increasingly possible for women to attend women-only groups; a move which may well increase the number of women using this service. In Switzerland this increase has also been noted (Klingemann 1992).

The use of traditional, and often ancient, methods is now gaining popularity. These include generalised healing (Meek 1986, Chishti 1988, Meadows 1992), the use of Visualisation (Gawain 1985, Markham 1989), those linking mind and body, and acupuncture (Brumbaugh 1993, Brewington et al. 1994) through Aromatherapy, Dreambody work (Mindell 1982) and Core Energetics (Cranmer 1994), looking at current problems in relation to past lives (Williston and Johnstone 1983) and Psychosynthesis (Parfitt 1990). Other methods include Transcendental Meditation both in treatment (Alexander et al. 1993, Murphy et al. 1986) and relapse prevention (O'Connell 1991), and relaxation training (Klajner et al. 1984). Even books on 'complete alternative cures' (McManus 1993) have been written.

More recently there has been a return by some of the more conservative psychotherapies to examine the role of the therapeutic relationship in a broader light (Budd and Sharma 1994, Bragan 1996). The list is almost endless, with new ways of working with and helping people growing at a phenomenal rate. Most of these therapies are used for a wide variety of health issues and the majority tend to view the person as a whole, not as someone with a specific 'disease'. For this reason treatment of alcohol problems will not be found, but treatment of individual aspects of the problem will. Others, such as Coggins' Native American Recovery Wheel (1990), are used, for example by Alcoholics Anonymous (AA). The use of acupuncture for the treatment of detoxification appears, on balance, to have been effective (Brewington et al. 1994). Some of these ways of working are sound and based on experience, evidence of effectiveness and skilled training. Others are used with little or no justification or training and the risks to the clients should not be ignored. The risk to the client is frighteningly well documented in relation to the so-called 'conventional' therapies. This is discussed more fully below. The aspect of treatment for women by women is now well recognised.

Gender-sensitive therapy has been discussed by several authors (Carter 1993, Schliebner 1994). In this treatment, 'The focus of therapy is on providing a caring, nurturing and empowering environment for women to become independent decision makers' (Schliebner 1994, p. 511). This fits well with the *raison d'être* of other organisations such as Women For Sobriety (Kirkpatrick 1986, Kaskutas 1994,) and more clearly identified feminist therapies (Bepko 1991, Clemmons 1991, Kaplan 1991, Van Den Bergh 1991, Abbott 1994). However, it is important to be aware of some of the issues around this. For many problem-drinking women the idea of feminism is one which ignores femininity. Given the often ultra-feminine stereotypes these women carry, any therapist has to be sensitive to this. We may not have negative views of problem-drinking women being worse than their male counterparts, but the woman may and we cannot ignore that. There are still a great many people treated by approaches such as psychodynamic psychotherapy, both individually (Bean 1981, Bean and Zinberg 1981, Dodes 1984, Brehm et al. 1993, Najavits and Weiss 1994) and in groups (Khantzian et al. 1990, Galanter et al. 1991). However, as with counselling for other problems, as noted by Howe (1993), what clients seek is: 'safe place to lower one's defences, be vulnerable and be held together while the rebuilding takes place' (p. 5).

It is often the case that the nearer the client gets to the pain, the greater the wish to run from it and the more nurturing the therapist needs to be, to 'hold' the client and contain the anxiety. It is amongst the most important times in therapy. Even so, as noted by Nelson-Zlupko et al. (1996) in a study of the perceptions of what was effective in the treatment regimes for women problem drug users:

> The gender, age, race and substance abuse history of the counsellor while viewed as important characteristics, were collectively perceived as less important than the extent to which the counsellor treated them with dignity, respect and genuine concern. (p. 55)

There were clear differences between the counsellors whom the clients reported had helped them and those who had not. Indeed, as stated by the authors of a study of 24 women who had been 'in recovery' for times ranging from 1 month to 68 months:

> According to the participants, 'bad' counsellors were described as poor listeners with little time to offer them, little respect and compassion for their clients, and an inability to individualise treatment plans ... 'Good' counsellors were described as caring listeners who treated participants with respect, believed in their strengths, viewed their clients as having multiple needs, and trusted in them. (Nelson-Zlupko et al. 1996, pp. 55–6)

These factors were not unimportant as these authors found that being looked after by a counsellor who fitted the description of 'bad' was associated at best with less participation in the treatment regime, at worst with withdrawal from the treatment programme. Clearly these factors are of great importance. However, a worrying aspect of the information given by the subjects in this study was the issue of sexual harassment by the counsellors. These women were asked about their experiences of treatment, some of whom had been in numerous programmes for their drug problem:

> Over half the study's participants described at least one episode of sexual harassment while talking of previous drug-treatment experiences. It is worth noting that respondents were never asked whether they had experienced sexual harassment, as that was not initially a central question of this study. (p. 56)

The effects of this trauma can be devastating for a woman in a therapeutic relationship:

> The quality of the relationship seems to me unquestionably the most valuable part of the experience. It provides the security and motivation indispensable for the more cognitive work in the therapy and for survival in the really testing moments. (France 1988, cited in Howe 1993, p. 25)

For women who have been in abusive relationships, often multiple relationships of this type, it can be difficult almost to the point of feeling it impossible, to be involved in something as intimate as therapy. It has to be remembered that having been abused not only breaks trust with people who are of the same gender as the abuser but also of the opposite gender also. To have been abused by a father, older brother or uncle may have been terrifying. The person's ability to trust has been damaged. However, what about the mother or aunt who did not protect them? People who have been abused can lose trust in everybody. It is for this reason that counsellors must not assume that a woman who has been abused will always want a female counsellor. Not being protected by her mother, when it is a child's right to that protection, can have as devastating an effect as the abuse itself. Add to this, in relation to problem-drinking women, the low self-esteem and even self-disgust; the inability to trust, not through choice, but based on experience, and you can begin to see just how complicated, fragile and tentative the first steps in therapy have to be.

According to Patrick Gannon, 'Addictions are the first cousins in the family tree of child abuse' (Gannon 1989, p. 116). The area of past sexual abuse has been referred to frequently in relation to present drinking problems, both in terms of the link between past experiences and present behaviour (Wallen and Berman 1992, Simpson et al. 1994, Pearce and Lovejoy 1995) and treatment (Janikowski and Glover 1994). Miller and Downs (1995) have stated: 'childhood sexual abuse and father-to-daughter violence were found to predict later alcohol problems' (p. 81). According to a study by O'Connor et al. (1994), women in a chemical dependency unit who reported histories of child sexual abuse were significantly more likely to score higher on measures of shame than those women without a history of such abuse. Therapists also need to be aware that women who have experienced ritual abuse may find it extremely difficult, if not impossible to take part in treatment programmes which include any part which, even vaguely, reminds them of the past terrors.

For women with drinking problems, particularly those who have a history of abuse, unethical and power-hungry counsellors and therapists can do untold damage. (Pope and Bouhoutsos 1986, Rutter 1990, Russel 1993). As noted by Jehu (1994):

> Bouhoutsos et al. (1983) found increased alcohol and drug use by victimised patients, and 43% of Vinson's (1984) subjects reported taking more pills, drugs or alcohol than usual. Briere (1992) refers to these substances as 'immediate painkillers' and lists their acute effects as 'temporary attenuation or elimination of dysphoria, inducement of some level of euphoria or relative well-being, interference with memory of painful events, [and] for some individuals provision of an opportunity to express painful affect (e.g. sadness, rage) that might otherwise be inhibited' (p. 59). (p. 108)

This seems to be a good description of some of the reasons people give for drinking at a level which could be classed as 'problematic'. Even so, if this is the possibility for clients who do not have a recognised alcohol problem, how much more destructive this behaviour would be for a woman who already drinks to use alcohol as a means of coping with life in general. Just as women who have been abused in early life are more at risk of using alcohol to cope, so women who have experienced this kind of trauma appear to be at greater risk of abuse by therapists (Armsworth 1990, Kluft 1990, Pope and Vetter 1991).

Although the belief that patterns from childhood may affect

later life may not be accepted by some people, it must be remembered that many current models of therapy are based on this premise. It is certainly true that many people, female and male, come from families which are no strangers to problems, powerful negative messages and conflict. Consider, for example, the description of what Gomberg (1976) describes as the woman with a 'high risk' of developing an alcohol problem:

> The alcoholic-prone woman begins significantly often with an early history of deprivation or trouble in early life in the form of death, desertion, or alcoholism among relatives. She develops into an isolated distrustful adolescent, fearful of dependence, rather pessimistic and depressed, often unpredictably impulsive and inadequate in frustration tolerance and defence mechanisms for coping with stress. The facade she presents is one of intense femininity and over identification with the female role. (p. 629)

A further description by Vogt (1987) of 29 problem-drinking women in Germany included a description of what she saw as two distinct types:

> Type 1, in which the women started to drink heavily only after the age 25 and in response to a life crisis ... The women live in a family situation and family marital quarrels frequently lead to violence against them. Nevertheless the women tend to feel responsible for the events and to have low self-esteem ... They have only frail social networks and support outside the family constellation. These women (Type 2) started drinking heavily relatively early in life. Most of them are divorced or never married ... they have experienced much physical and sexual abuse, most often from their male partners. They have inconsistent and contradictory self-images and fairly bad relations with their children. (p. 1)

Most of the above treatments or theoretical models have only approached alcohol problems as one of many difficulties. However, others, such as motivational interviewing, have focused particularly on people with substance abuse-related problems.

Over the years a number of myths have developed around problem-drinking women and treatment. These include the following:

1. Problem-drinking women are more difficult to treat than problem-drinking men.

2. Problem-drinking women are not so open, or even honest, as problem-drinking men.

3. Problem-drinking women have a poorer prognosis than problem-drinking men.

As noted by May (1991):

> A myth is a way of making sense in a senseless world ... Myths are like the beams in a house: not exposed to outside view, they are the structure which holds the house together so people can live in it. (p. 15)

If this is true, then what impact do these myths about problem-drinking women have on the women themselves, their relatives and even on the therapists who work with them? In fact what impact do they have on the whole community in which the woman lives?

The second myth relates to treatment outcome. As noted:

> Many of the studies on treatment either excluded women or have not differentiated between the genders ... Emrick (1974) reviewed 271 studies of which only 28 were gender specific. He noted that 25 studies showed women with a better outcome than men. More recently Vannicelli (1984) reviewed 259 studies of which only 23 were gender specific. Eighteen showed no difference in treatment outcome by gender, in four the women had the better outcome and in one men showed the better outcome. (Plant 1990, p. 22)

Patterson (1995) concluded: 'A review of published materials by Tonaetto et al. [1992] shows no sex differences in the outcome of treatment, but 72% of studies do not address gender' (p. 46). Surprisingly, this important issue is still not acknowledged in some studies. In a meta-analysis of controlled trails of alcohol-misuse treatments Agosti described 15 studies dating from 1973 (Gerrein et al.) to 1992 (O'Malley et al.). The sample descriptions range from 'mostly/majority male' (Wilson et al. 1978, Eriksson et al. 1986, Peachey et al. 1989) to 'Male 67%' (Longabaugh et al. 1983). Other studies had a greater proportion of male subjects or were all male. Agosti noted:

> Literature reviews of treatment studies have potential limitations: (1) reviewers may be biased against reporting studies with negative

> results; (2) there may be an absence of data, in published studies, to evaluate efficacy across a series of outcome variables; (3) reviewers may arbitrarily exclude studies from review; (4) reviewers may make biased interpretations of outcome; (5) reviewers may fail to assess the relationship between research methodology and outcome variables [Thacker 1988]. (1994, p. 760)

Nowhere in the paper is the crucial issue of gender differences acknowledged. This is even more surprising since (where noted) the most common concomitant psychiatric diagnosis is that of depression. As noted by Nixon and Glenn (1995):

> Of particular interest to clinicians and researchers has been the role that affective state, in particular depression, may play in the aetiology, course and outcome of alcoholism [Petty 1992, Ries 1993, McMahon and Davidson 1986, Murphy 1992, Roy et al. 1991] Petty in a review of the literature, found that between 10 and 13% of the alcoholics in any one study also suffer from depression. This review also indicated that not only were female alcoholics more likely to have a pre-existing depression, they were also more likely to develop depression following heavy drinking. (p. 289)

It seems such a waste not to make the most of the evidence on gender which is available, particularly when it covers such a wide range of time and treatment regimes.

The issue of self-esteem (Marr 1993) has already been discussed in Chapter 4. The development of measurements, such as the Rosenberg Self-Esteem (SES) in the 1960s (Rosenberg 1965), which have been used in both clinical and general populations, has enabled researchers and clinicians to compare populations of women (Kaskutas 1992, 1994, Graham et al. 1995). The Rosenberg instrument, made up of ten statements, is rated on a four-point scale ranging from 'strongly agree' to 'strongly disagree'. Studies on women problem-drinkers in treatment have shown that this group measures lower on the scale than problem-drinking men; that is, their self-esteem is lower. Importantly, it also shows that this particular group score lower than women in the general population (Beckman 1978). As noted by Guõmundsdóttir (1996) in her study of 74 hospitalised women problem-drinkers in Iceland: 'For the women in the study, the most frequent indicators of low self-esteem are that they wish they could have more respect for themselves, that they feel useless at times and no good at all' (p. 3).

The main usefulness of this scale is in follow-up studies. As noted by Graham et al. (1995b):

> Studies have shown the SES to be a particularly sensitive outcome measure with women substance abusers. Beckman found significant increases in the SES scores of both men and women alcoholics following treatment, with women showing a greater increase than the men. Kaskutas (1992) compared the effectiveness of two treatment programmes, Alcoholics Anonymous and Women for Sobriety (WFS), in increasing the self-esteem levels in women alcoholics. In each case, SES scores among women sober less than two months were compared to women sober for 11 to 13 months. Higher levels of self-esteem were evident for both groups of women sober 11 to 13 months, but greater increases in SES scores were found among women who attended Women For Sobriety. (Part 4, p. 50)

Many people have now noted the link between low self-esteem and guilt in problem-drinking women (Beckman 1978, Kirkpatrick 1986, Marr 1993). However, it is important to be aware of how paralysing and devastating this feeling is. It can prevent a woman reaching out to those near her who desperately want to help but do not know how. It can prevent a woman from accepting help when it is offered and indeed get in the way at almost any stage of treatment when she reaches another 'layer of the onion' of therapy. Perhaps the most destructive point at which guilt and low self-esteem take hold is if the woman starts to drink again. The risk of drinking always increases when a person takes another step on the path of therapy: if memories, buried for years, begin surfacing in the form of dreams or fragments of memories, the wish to 'drown' them again can become very strong. If the woman drinks she may feel so bad about it that she stops going for treatment, counselling or whatever help she was getting. At precisely the time when she needs to be cared for she cannot allow herself to feel she deserves it. I believe that this sense of guilt and self-disgust lingers far longer than the alcohol and can get in the way of treatment for quite a long time afterwards, perhaps even longer than the therapist realises.

An unusual but difficult problem which may arise at the point of relapse occurs if the woman attends a treatment session while she is intoxicated. Occasionally at this time she can begin to disclose some of the really painful areas which may so far have only been hinted at; perhaps not even that, but only a sense the therapist has that there may be more to come. If the relapse is in some part related to her moving deeper and getting in touch with the pain and fear then there is a possibility of disclosure occurring at this time. The problem is this: if the therapist quietly listens what does she then do with the information? At the next session, how much does the client remember about what she has disclosed? What effect would it have if the therapist disclosed to the client the contents of the last session? Would she feel relieved that at last it was revealed and move further into the therapeutic alliance or would she deny everything and become angry in her fear? These are the kinds of question which the therapist has to face, if the client's response to 'Do you remember what we spoke about last time?' is, 'Not a thing.' The situation is one where the therapist may be more aware of the intensity of the feelings and memories than the client is, in that she has now pushed them down again. This is one of the reasons for being very careful about seeing someone who is intoxicated. This is something that therapists often decide against; preferring instead to sit in a more relaxed setting and perhaps have a cup of tea or coffee, and thus clearly changing the usual situation. In this way the client is not rejected because of the drinking, but the drinking has changed the situation. It is important for the therapist not to reject the person while objecting to the behaviour. After the client has sobered up, it is important to take into account that, for the client, this may mean a time of moving away from the intimacy of the relationship. For the therapist, however, as the client climbs painfully out of the chasm of relapse, it may be a time when defences drop and steps can be taken towards greater understanding. It is a time of vulnerability for the client and it is vital that the therapist does not in any way abuse this. It is important to allow the woman not to feel crowded or even intruded upon. There is a very fine balance between nurturing and being perceived as smothering. However, the drinking episode and how the therapist responded to it will remain in the client's memory long after the therapist may have stopped seeing it as relevant. As noted by Howe (1993), there is often a wide gap between the client's perception of the relationship and that of the therapist, with the client being much more aware of the atmosphere of the relationship than the counsellor. Howe has described one therapist who seems nearer the client's perception:

> An exception to this rule is Peter Lomas, whose reflections on his own practice as a psychotherapist produced conclusions completely in tune with all that has been said so far by clients:

> 'the commonplace attitudes which are relevant to healing lie in the direction of warmth rather than coldness, trust rather than cynicism, closeness rather than distance, encouragement rather than discouragement, spontaneity rather than calculation' (Lomas 1981:6). He believes that people are helped by 'wisdom and love' and not by 'technique'. (p. 39)

For anyone, woman or man, who has started drinking and managed to stop and return to therapy they will be hypersensitive to the atmosphere. It is vitally important that the therapist has worked through her or his own feelings about the relapse with a supervisor or colleague as it is not possible to 'hide' the feelings. Experienced therapists may still go through a gamut of feelings about a client who drinks, but it is important to remember that however bad it feels for the therapist, it feels a lot worse for the client.

One aspect of relapse which is very important is that of the client 'testing out' the therapist's commitment to her by drinking. This is not conscious and many clients would not accept it as possible. However, it does happen and it can happen for a number of reasons. In a therapeutic relationship which has developed to the point where the client sees it as possible to have an intimate relationship, within the boundaries of therapy, this may suddenly become very frightening, even intrusive. Experience has shown them that the one way of being left alone, of going back to the 'devil you know', is to drink. Another reason for this happening is, as noted above, to see how the therapist will respond. The question, 'How much do you really care about me?' is asked non-verbally. Again this can be a difficult time for both the therapist and client. Colleagues and supervisors need to be sensitive to the therapist and support her or him in whatever decision is taken.

In the past few years there has been a deluge of reports on treatment issues for women. Such reports have related to identification, types of treatment such as self-help groups (Humphreys et al. 1991, Mäkelä 1991, Duckert 1993, Khantzian and Mack 1994, McCrady 1994) and also relapse prevention (Nurco et al. 1991), peer support (Roth and James 1994), community based treatment (Farid and Clarke 1992), therapeutic communities (Stevens and Gilder 1994, Tims et al. 1994, Stevens and Arbiter 1995) and, more recently, women participating in Employee Assistance Programmes (EAPs) (Reed 1994, Blum et al. 1995a,b). As noted by Blum et al. (1995b):

> These data indicate that EAPs are effective in sustaining the employment of most women with alcohol-related problems who seek

services from EAPs and that EAPs' goal of early intervention is especially realised among women with alcohol problems. Other conclusions include: women with alcohol problems do not enter EAPs through routes that are strikingly different from those of men; many of the gender differences that are revealed are associated with job status differences; employed women with alcohol problems are detached from nuclear families, with markedly low rates of current marriage; even when married, spouses are less likely to play a role in the referral of women with alcohol problems than the spouses of the men; and, there is no clear indication that women are the target of any form of discrimination in the process of EAP utilization. However women are considerably more likely to have less adequate insurance coverage, according to the EAP administrators' assessment reported at client intake, than their male counterparts, leading to treatment choices that may be less than appropriate. (p. 125)

It does appear as though the issue of status may also be a factor, again as noted by Blum et al.:

Blue-collar workers seem especially 'different' on a variety of measures. Of interest here is that for women, blue collar work is both lower status and non-traditional for women, bringing two intertwined dynamics into play. In general, upper-status employees seem to have a number of 'breaks' in the referral process. Here a germane consideration is the comparable status level between the employee referred to the EAP and the EAP counsellor. Greater social distance from lower level employees, perhaps coupled with gender differences, may lead to reactions by supervisors and subsequently EAP counsellors that might be viewed as less constructive than when this social distance is lessened among referrals from upper-organisational levels. (p. 54)

The evidence that upper-level employees may be given more leeway in relation to EAPs is clear. However, the suggestion that the reaction of counsellors to their clients may differ depending on the employee level is worrying. It would suggest that supervision of counsellors in this situation and good training are essential. The final issue in relation to EAPs is the evidence that women employees who suffer from a combination of alcohol problems and depression, experience particular difficulties in many aspects of identification and treatment compared to other women EAP users (Blum and Roman 1995).

Given all the above concerns women have about treatment,

confidentiality, staying at home for the children, and so on, the idea of treating people at home has begun to be seen as an important addition to the treatment armoury. The idea of helping people through the initial discomfort of withdrawal, by treating them in their own homes is now well established (Cooper 1994). The Home Detoxification Treatment programme run in Central Scotland has around 41% of its clients being women (Bennie 1996). It would appear that this may be an important way to enable women to get help early. The fact that the proportion of women is so high compared to other treatment programmes suggests this is a sensitive way to identify and treat women earlier.

The issue noted in Chapter 4 of alcohol problems being related to other types of difficulty or adverse life circumstances, has meant that research has also been carried out on such areas as dual diagnosis (Morris and Schinke 1990, Allan 1991, Ries 1993, Clark and Zweben 1994, Madden 1994, Haver and Dahlgren 1995, Rørstad and Checinski 1996, Ward and Goodman 1995), including affective disorders (Keeler 1982, Kendler et al. 1993), schizophrenia (Gottheil and Waxman 1982, Ries 1993, Krausz et al. 1996) and other issues such as antisocial personality and depression (Rada 1982, Hesselbrock 1991) and panic disorder (Cowley 1992) (see Chapter 4). A common problem for women problem-drinkers is that of multiple drug use. Often this is related to medication being given by family doctors who for whatever reason have not identified the alcohol problem. Treatment of women who are experiencing problems with polydrug use is now well documented (Kosten et al. 1991, Toneatto et al. 1992).

There has been a great increase in the application of behavioural approaches to the management of 'problem drinking' (Heather and Robertson 1981, Sher 1987, Sobell et al. 1988, Donovan and Marlatt 1993, Saunders 1994, Najavits et al. 1996). Motivational interviewing (Miller and Rollnick 1991) has become more common and appears to be of great value in the treatment of problem drinking. As noted above, some of the theoretical models for this have been around for some time, for example, aversion therapy (Lemere and Voegtlin 1950, Pomerleau 1982). This treatment sounds quite barbaric in retrospect. As noted by Pomerleau in 1982:

> The procedure first developed by Voegtlin in 1940 [Lemere and Voegtlin 1950] continues to be used: An emetine-pilocarpine-ephedrine mixture is administered intravenously; at the earliest sign of nausea the patient is given a drink of preferred beverage to smell and to taste, with additional drinks given over a 30-

> minute to 1-hour period as nausea and vomiting persist: booster sessions are given to patients whenever they feel a return of the urge to drink. (p. 1056)

More recently, advances in behaviour therapy, sometimes in conjunction with other models, have become one of the most successful ways of treating problem drinkers.

Rational Emotive therapy by Albert Ellis (Ellis and Whiteley 1979) is another example of a theoretical model which specifically addressed the issue of substance-abuse treatments, both in its own right (Ellis et al. 1988) and also in conjunction with behaviour therapy (Ellis 1982). Indeed, the US organisation Rational Recovery (RR) has based its 'twelve-step' programme on this theory (Trimpey 1989). The use of behaviour therapy in relapse prevention has been extremely important (Marlatt and Gordon 1985, Donovan and Chaney 1985). However, alcohol problems are not a single entity: what is an appropriate approach for one client may be totally inappropriate for another; this relates to gender as well as other factors. There will always have to be a balance. As noted by Saunders (1994):

> It is possible that the addictions field is on the verge of a third generation of treatments. The first generation, that of intensive, in-patient, psychotherapeutically based programmes is past. The second, a rebound into brief intervention for less chronic and less severe clients, while of considerable benefit ... risks resulting in the 'tough cases' being relatively ignored. However with the increasing acceptance of the cognitive-behavioural approach to the cost effective management of addictive behaviours, there may be a renewed interest in the intensive and long term management of difficult cases. (p. 170)

A close second to the behavioural approaches are the pharmacological treatments. One of the first of these was the use of the drug chloramid in the treatment of 'alcohol abuse' in the 1890s. This pharmacological hypnotic was mainly used to treat the insomnia often associated with withdrawal. However, the effects were uncertain and the use of this drug for women often caused dizziness, headaches, nausea and vomiting. In fact these symptoms were exactly those produced in the first types of behavioural approach such as aversion therapy noted above.

More recently interest has again arisen in this area (Liskow and Goodwin 1987, Deckert et al. 1992a,b, File et al. 1992, Grabowski and Vanderbos 1992, Gorelick 1993). The substances involved have included lithium (Litten and Allen 1991), busipirone (Bruno 1989, Malcolm et al. 1992), acamprosate (Lhuintre et al. 1990), naltrexone (O'Malley et al. 1992, Volpicelli et al. 1992) and the use of antabuse (Kristenson 1992, Larson et al. 1992, Lejoyeux and Ades 1993) and tiapride (Shaw et al. 1994) in relapse. In relation to gender differences in blood antabuse levels work by Helander et al. (1993) found no differences. As noted by Cantwell and Chick (1994):

> This is an exciting time in the development of new pharmacological approaches to alcoholism and rapid changes may be expected over the coming years. Medication alone however is unlikely to be a complete solution for a disorder in which psychological, biological and social factors are so intertwined. (p. 147)

Yet even within the pharmacological armoury there is now debate. A recent long-term prospective study from Austria of 270 hospitalised problem-drinkers, part of a multicentre study involving 4000 subjects from Austria, Switzerland and Germany, suggests that this particular treatment tool may be of more use to some people than others. Examining different 'sub-types' of problem drinkers, the group assessed the effectiveness of acamprosate and reported:

> Our findings demonstrate that these patient subtypes are relevant to outcome in trials of pharmacological agents. We strongly recommend subtyping alcohol-dependent subjects in future trials, because the usefulness of effective drugs could be overlooked when they are tested in a heterogeneous population. (Lesch and Walter 1996, p. 63)

Interestingly, the issue of gender is not even acknowledged and it is not possible, from the results presented, to ascertain whether women were included in the study. This type of deficiency has been highlighted by Gorelick (1993): 'An important focus of clinical research in the next decade should be erasing the current glaring gap of knowledge about pharmacological treatments of alcoholism in special populations such as women' (p. 425).

In the 1890s, as noted above, acknowledgement was paid to the possible gender differences in side effects. This is still of pressing importance. The idea of sub-types of problem drinkers is not new; the view of mad, bad or sad was probably among the first. Since then there have been a number, such as personality, in relation to treatment (Nixon 1993) and outcome (Donovan et al. 1988). Jellinek

(1946) preferred the labels Alpha, Beta and Gamma. His reason for letters of the Greek alphabet rather than names he explains thus: 'Letter symbols arouse perhaps less misgivings than names which may have different connotations for many students of alcoholism' (Jellinek 1960, p. 36).

As noted by Glenn and Nixon (1991), since Jellinek there have been other attempts to classify different sub-groups of problem drinkers:

> Knight discriminated between 'Essential' alcoholics, with early onset of severe alcohol abuse unrelated to environmental factors, and 'Reactive' alcoholics, who began to abuse alcohol later in life in response to stressors in the environment [Knight 1937]. Tarter et al. [1977] revised and extended these discriminations by devising a Primary–Secondary Scale focusing on behavioral characteristics of Primary alcoholics with onset of excessive drinking before age 40 (similar to Essential alcoholics), and Secondary alcoholics who began drinking at a later age in response to significant life stressors (similar to Reactive alcoholics). Goodwin [1979] and Stabenau and Hesselbrock [1984] as well as other researchers have suggested that there are at least two types of subtypes of alcoholics based on the presence or absence of psychiatric diagnosis of antisocial personality disorder. (p. 851)

Even so, the question remains (given that with few exceptions these sub-types were focusing totally on men), did they have any relevance for women? Furthermore, is it possible that it could even have been counter-productive for women to be 'typed' in this way if the labels did not fit? This was the issue that Glenn and Nixon addressed. Examining a sample of 51 women with a diagnosis of 'alcoholism', they tried to match these individuals to Cloninger's Type 1 and 2 sub-types (Cloninger et al. 1988, Gilligan et al. 1988). The women were divided into those with an early onset of alcohol-related problems (before the age of 25) and those with a late onset (after the age of 25). Glenn and Nixon found that these women did not seem to fit the Cloninger sub-types, but that they often had some of the features of one mixed with some of the features of the other. They concluded:

> The findings indicate that modification of the Cloninger classification criteria to reflect age of symptom onset regardless of symptom type provides better classification of individual female

> alcoholics and suggests that female alcoholics are represented in both Type 1 and Type 2 alcoholic subtypes. (p. 851)

Indeed, Glenn and Nixon go on to re-examine the literature on both male and female alcoholics and question whether the application of symptomatology without taking into account the age of onset of these problems is necessary.

Special Populations

Examples of 'special populations' of women include the elderly (Maletta 1982, Meyers et al. 1982, Nespor 1990, Miller et al. 1991, Robbins 1991, Osterling and Berglund 1994, Ward and Goodman 1995). Some investigators have an interesting concept of categories of society into which women fit. This is exemplified by Closser and Blow's (1993) paper entitled 'Special Populations: Women, Ethnic Minorities and the Elderly'. A follow-up study carried out by Brennan et al. (1993) of 659 subjects, of whom 183 were women, showed that:

> Compared with men, women consumed less alcohol, reported more recent onset of drinking problems, and experienced fewer alcohol-related difficulties. In addition, they more frequently used psychoactive medications and reported more depression. (p. 785)

These authors also reported that the problem this group of women share with females in the younger age groups is that they do not refer themselves to alcohol identified treatment agencies. The worrying aspect of this is that whereas younger women, particularly those with families, may well be in contact with health services for other family members if not for themselves, these older women may remain unsupported and therefore untreated for longer (Dunham 1986). As further noted by Brennan et al.: 'This reinforces the need for health care providers to be sensitive to evidence of alcohol abuse among their older clients' (p. 786).

Research in some countries has shown that drinking in the older population is often used almost as medication, for example with difficulty in sleeping or depressive mood. In a review by Glantz and Backenheimer (1988), the issue of an increase in use of prescribed medications in women who are older was examined. The authors concluded: 'elderly women appear to be at greater risk for physician-perpetrated drug abuse than any other age by gender group' (p. 3). These authors also noted the problem of an increased risk of drug–alcohol interactions in this group. It would appear relevant for family practitioners to be more aware of the risks of these issues and perhaps routinely take a drinking history before prescribing medication for older women. However, in localities as far apart as Israel (Weiss 1993) and the US (Gomberg 1995), there is agreement that although the prevalence of alcohol-related harm in the elderly is low, hospitalisation of this group, particularly for physical problems, is high. It is certainly true that older people in general and older women in particular are not seen as possible problem drinkers. An elderly female patient in a local Alcohol Treatment Unit was referred by her doctor only after the latter was alerted by a number of her neighbours. This 72-year-old woman, who lived in a building also containing seven other apartments, had each of her seven neighbours doing her shopping on a different day of the week. On her shopping list each week was a bottle of brandy. This meant that all her neighbours thought she was getting a bottle of spirits a week, which seemed a little high, but 'it helped her sleep'. However, she was getting a bottle of spirits each day. It was by chance that two neighbours met in the supermarket and the 'secret' was revealed. There are more and more concerns being raised about drinking and what constitutes a problem in the older age groups. Older people in many countries now live in sheltered or warden-assisted housing which means that although they live in their own apartments, there are sometimes quite a large number of other residents living in close proximity to them. The caretakers of these complexes are beginning to ask questions such as: 'Does this person have a drinking problem or is she/he just a bit unsteady on their feet?' 'How do I handle a situation when one of the male residents starts to drink and make awkward comments to the female residents?' The man may feel he is just being friendly but the woman may feel very threatened by it. As more older people decide this kind of accommodation is appropriate for their needs, this problem will become more common. There are measures specifically designed for assessing problems in an older population, for example, the Problem Drinking Index designed by Finney et al. (1991). However, it is clear that this will be a potential problem which has every chance of increasing in the future for purely demographic reasons in many countries.

Issues of race and ethnicity are also becoming of increasing importance (Clark and Zweben 1994, Comas-Diaz 1994, Mays et al. 1994, Jackson 1995, Rouse et al. 1995). As noted by Rouse et al. discussing the situation in the US:

> Some race/ethnicity differences in alcoholism rates and treatment effectiveness are due to socioeconomic factors. There is significant variability within as well as diversity between the ethnic/racial groups. Race and ethnicity are complex sociocultural phenomena. For example, an individual coming to the clinician may share African, Hispanic, Asian, and Native American heritages within herself or her family. (pp. 361–2)

A qualitative study by Saulnier (1996) of African-American women (n=12), concluded:

> Results suggest that the dual focus on individual and social issues, and the opportunity to simultaneously address racism, sexism, and classism in an African-American women-only alcohol recovery group was helpful. (p. 1259)

The added complications of problem drinking in the families of different ethnic groups has also been addressed (Barthwell 1995). The issue of sexual orientation has been examined in relation to factors which might contribute to problem drinking (Rothberg and Kidder 1992, Lewis 1993, Mays et al. 1994), treatment (Greene 1994), outcome of treatment (Kane and Rullo-Cooney 1991, Schneider et al. 1995) and needs in recovery (McNally and Finnegan 1992). Other special groups of women problem-drinkers include the homeless (Hall 1993a, Argeriou et al. 1994, Geissler et al. 1995, Gregore 1996), women who self-harm (Evans and Lacey 1992), who are offenders (Lex et al. 1990, 1991, Genteel 1994, Wiese 1995) and who are victims of violence (Martin 1993, Miller and Downs 1995). Victimisation may often lead to Post Traumatic Stress Disorder (PTSD) (Najavits et al. 1996). As noted by Miller and Downs (1995): 'there is evidence that women's experiences of violent victimisation are followed by symptoms of PTSD and that victimisation, PTSD, and alcohol problems are linked for women' (p. 96). The issue of training of professionals to identify and help children in this situation is vitally important (Alcohol Training Project 1996).

Family relationships have always been an integral part of the treatment of problem drinkers (Gomberg et al. 1991), such relationships prior to treatment (McKay et al. 1992), including problem-drinking parents (Svanum and McAdoo 1991) as part of treatment (Metsch et al. 1995), in relation to treatment outcome (Ravndal and Vaglum 1994), and to follow-up (McKay et al. 1992). The link between eating disorders and treatment of drinking problems has also been highlighted (Mitchell et al. 1990, Gordon 1991, Strasser et al. 1992, Walfish et al. 1992, Goldbloom 1993, Taylor et al. 1993).

Comparisons between therapies have also been studied (Miller and Taylor 1980, Latimer and Sweet 1984, McCrady et al. 1986, Kadden et al. 1994, McCrady 1994): psychiatric versus multimodal (Ojehagen et al. 1992) or combinations, for example, family therapy and twelve-step programmes (Schroeder 1991); pharmacology and behaviour therapy (O'Malley et al. 1992); and AA and psychotherapy (Rosen 1981, Dodes 1988, Khantzian and Mack 1989). A relatively new method, the biopsychosocial approach, seems to acknowledge more than many the complexity of the drinking process. As noted by Donovan and Marlatt (1993):

> This model holds that alcoholism is a complex disorder with multiple determinants and systems involved in its development, maintenance, and treatment. It suggests that the interaction among biological, physiological, behavioral, psychological, cognitive, and social factors must be considered. Furthermore there may be a limited degree of continuity between those factors that contribute to beginning drinking, to later stage drinking and to problem-drinking, to the maintenance of subsequent abusive drinking and the development of alcohol dependence (Zuker and Gomberg 1986). Thus one must consider the interaction of these multiple variables as they exert their influence at different stages of the drinking process. (p. 400)

This approach has been used in many areas of problem drinking such as prevention and treatment (Marlatt 1992), assessment (Donovan 1988) and relapse prevention (Donovan and Chaney 1985, Marlatt and Gordon 1985, Marlatt 1992).

The aspect of self-recovery or spontaneous remission, that is, recovery without any active treatment, is also interesting (Emrick 1975, Tuchfeld 1981, Ludwig 1985, Fillmore 1988, Tucker and Sobell 1992, Sobell et al. 1993). Some people appear to overcome drinking problems without recourse to formal 'treatment'.

Some of the themes touched on earlier in this chapter, such as the female problem-drinker's perception of herself and her problem, do appear to raise real gender differences. Women are more likely than their male counterparts to acknowledge they have a problem, more likely to recognise diffuse symptoms as a problem, but less likely to report that it is alcohol related. There are also gender similarities such as the fear of giving up the 'only friend I have'. Yet the knowledge that this same friend may be killing you is present for both. However, as stressed by Burman (1994): 'According to Hamilton and Volpe [1982/83] "Alcoholic women have difficulty seeing themselves as separate, autonomous individuals, and instead develop identities based entirely upon their relationships with others"' (p. 22). A vivid example of this for me was a patient in an alcohol treatment unit who, when I asked her to describe herself replied: 'Well, my husband always says ...'. Again I asked her: 'Can *you* describe yourself to me?' The reply came back: 'My son was saying just the other day that I ...'. Once more I explained I wanted to know how she saw herself, but she could not answer me. In fact the question alone seemed to puzzle her. Burman raises the issue of whether the commonness of a dual diagnosis, usually of depression, makes it even more likely that women come to be labelled as ill. This may be the case and most certainly suggests an increased risk of medication being given earlier than necessary. In the majority of cases, problem drinkers need to be clear of the withdrawal phase before the diagnosis of depression is given (Petty 1992). With the common knowledge that women problem-drinkers are more likely to have a clinically diagnosable depression, it may be that an assumption is made that: 'Since she is bound to be depressed we will start her on antidepressant medication right away.' This may not only be unnecessary but may give the message that the depression, a clinical entity, is the reason for the drinking problem. The message is: 'There is no need to look at where you are and how you got here, just keep taking the tablets and you will get better.' This message, in combination with the belief that 'alcoholism' is a disease, may reinforce the view that she is sick and other people will make her better. Her feeling of guilt and shame may in some way be soothed by this, an understandable wish, but, as described by Burman (1994):

> Instead of looking within herself for self-sustaining capabilities, she succumbs to the potential of others to 'fix' what is wrong in her life. This perpetuates the cycle of feelings of inadequacy and incompetence, while validating the need for others to take care of her. (p. 124)

This suggests that possibly, regardless of the external barriers to treatment (Allen 1994, Hagan et al. 1994, Metsch et al. 1995), the internal barriers may be at least as paralysing, if not more:

> These feelings of powerlessness and helplessness are generally pervasive, irrespective of racial or class backgrounds, and limit the

> capacity to overcome barriers and obtain needed supports and resources for satisfactory functioning. (Burman 1994, p. 122)

These external barriers and supports for women with drinking problems certainly vary between countries and regions. In the UK it may be a lack of appropriate services in an area; a family doctor who does not think of the possibility that a women may have an alcohol problem and, if she has a family, the lack of necessary support to enable her to attend appointments. In other countries such as the US, it may be a lack of adequate insurance cover, something which is more likely for employed women than employed men (Blum et al. 1995). Other reasons may include the fact that women are less likely to present at agencies which are seen to be alcohol identified (Hingson et al. 1980), are more likely to experience friends or relative being obstructive rather than supportive to the idea of treatment (Beckman and Amaro 1986), and are more concerned about what their doctors think of them and how a doctor's knowledge of the woman's drinking may harm that relationship (Thom 1986, 1987). As noted more succinctly by Thom (1995):

> Few studies have examined the issue in any depth. Existing research spans a time period of approximately 20 years; includes samples of women drawn from different cultures and social groups; consists mainly of women who have entered treatment thus missing those for whom the barriers are insurmountable; lacks standard or common measures; employs different theoretical approaches and is often not designed to investigate gender issues. (p. 24)

Thom (1995) has highlighted three issues common to much of the research carried out in this area: 'failure to recognise the problem, the perceived cost of taking action and the perceived acceptability of taking action' (p. 24).

Some other countries have also noted an increase in awareness of the need to service provision for women clients. For example, when describing the expansion of outpatient treatment in Austria, Eisenbach-Stangl (1992) noted:

> the extension of treatment attracted the socially more privileged and also women. As in other countries they were attracted especially by the exclusively outpatient treatment, with its relative anonymity and freedom from institutional restrictions. (p. 179)

The need for confidentiality has been highlighted in relation to women. It appears to fit with the fear of people's reaction and the feeling of shame often described by women. The other issue which makes outpatient treatment more attractive for women is related to the woman being the main child carer. Being admitted to a hospital in a patient treatment programme raises fears of the children being taken into care. For many problem-drinking mothers the only role they are clear about, however much they may resent it at times, is that of mother. To take that role away from them leaves them with no structure, no meaning to their lives.

The awareness of women problem-drinkers as a group with special needs has emerged since the early 1970s, either due to changing economic systems or expanding treatment programmes. This has been apparent in a number of countries such as the US (Weisner and Morgan 1992, Schmidt and Weisner 1995), Canada (Rush and Ogborne 1992), Austria (Eisenbach-Stangl 1992), Finland (Takkala and Lehto 1992), and Hungary (Elekes 1992). In relation to New Zealand, Stewart and Casswell (1992) noted:

> Factors that deter women from coming to treatment include shame because of societal double standards about women's drinking, unsuitability of mixed-sex programs in dealing with such issues as sexual abuse, and the difficulty that women with children have in reaching services (Johnstone and Hannifin 1987). In response to such factors, women-only programs have been established in many services, and may be run from a feminist perspective. Other services, established in the late 1980s, include a number of 'women for sobriety' self-help groups, a small residential retreat for lesbians, and two halfway posttreatment houses for women. (p. 141)

In Sweden the issue of compulsory admission has been noted. Rosenqvist and Kurube (1992) reported:

> Of 4200 abusers registered and in institutions at the end of 1987, some 250 men and 80 women, or 8% of all, had been compulsorily committed. The number of women had doubled since 1982. For the vast majority (80%) of the compulsorily committed, alcohol was the main drug. (p. 73)

Switzerland underwent a number of changes. As noted by Klingemann (1992):

> First admissions of women doubled between 1970 and 1980, probably reflecting a changed societal view of alcoholism in women, but also increased intake capacity from a new alcohol clinic for women in 1974 and extensions to other institutions. Supply may have partially increased demand. (p. 154)

It appears that in Switzerland, as in Austria, women, for whatever reason, were more visible in outpatient counselling services: 'Whereas in 1961 the ratio of women to men was 1:11, it increased to 1:8 by 1971 and to a remarkable 1:4 by 1981' (Klingemann 1992, p. 159).

The increase in admission for women was also noted in the former Yugoslavia. Lang and Srdar (1992) reported: 'between 1965 and 1985, male admissions increased almost fourfold and female almost sixfold. The age structure of females admitted remained stable (about 40% under 44 years)' (p. 61).

In the US, as noted by Schmidt and Weisner (1995), two main elements seemed to add strength and energy to the debate:

> First, controversy over women's substance abuse and 'fetal rights' proved a consistent theme throughout the decade: The 1980s began with debates over fetal alcohol syndrome babies and closed with a crisis over drug exposed infants [Noble 1993]. Second, there was a general expansion and diversification of substance abuse treatment systems over the course of the decade, evident in a doubling of national bed capacity and significant broadening in types of treatment modalities [Institute of Medicine 1990, Schmidt and Weisner 1993]. (p. 310)

A guide to improving women's access to alcohol services has recently been published in the UK (Alcohol Concern 1995). In relation to the question of prognosis, in a study of gender differences in inpatient treatment outcome by Schneider et al. (1995), the authors noted a number of areas in which differences were apparent. At three months follow-up, risk factors for women included being married (this was actually a protective factor in men), having less education and, importantly, self-reported symptomatology of psychological impairment. The latter appeared to be related to a longer drinking history. A major factor then was that the shorter the time between developing problems and starting treatment, the better the outcome. Given the already noted problems women have, both in self-acknowledgement of an alcohol problem and identification by professionals, this last result is worrying.

Finally, the last of the three myths mentioned earlier in this chapter was that women have a poorer prognosis than men. The most recent and important large-scale study, 'Project Match' (1997), has shown that there are few differences between treatment outcome. In fact, only gender is predictive of the proportion of days abstinent. Women do better than men. If this is indeed the case, another myth has been laid to rest.

7 Prevention and Health Education

As emphasised in earlier chapters, females are less likely either to drink heavily or with problems, than males. Nevertheless, both the consumption of alcohol and its associated problems, have been increasing amongst women in many countries. The increasingly normal use of alcohol by women reflects many changes. These include greater economic power, political and social freedoms and, in some contexts, the widespread perception that drinking is an integral facet of industrial or 'westernised' society. Thus, it has become increasingly acceptable for women to consume alcohol in many parts of the world – for example, Asia, Africa and South America – in which drinking by younger women has not been traditionally tolerated or condoned. Most of the women (and men) who drink generally do so in moderation and without harm. Some people derive health benefits as well as pleasure from their drinking. Even so, many drinkers of either sex periodically put themselves and others at risk by heavy drinking. Women are sometimes harmed by their own alcohol consumption. Many are also adversely affected by the drinking of males, including their own partners. As outlined in earlier chapters, 'alcohol-related problems' cover a wide range of adverse consequences. These include alcohol dependence, illness, premature deaths, accidents, public disorder and problems in the workplace, family and with relationships in general. Most types of alcohol-related problems are by no means a solely female preserve. Alcohol-related problems are widely acknowledged to constitute some of the greatest health and social concerns of humanity. The debate about how to prevent or curb such problems is probably as old as the use of alcohol itself. Alcohol is humanity's favourite recreational, leisure-enhancing psychoactive drug. Its use is greatly valued and esteemed. Because of its very popularity, the associated problems are also on a large scale. This chapter reviews the effectiveness of some past strategies designed to prevent or to reduce the level of alcohol-related problems. Whenever possible, attention is focused on issues or measures that are specific to women. Even so, much of what follows is as relevant for males as for females. The drinking habits of the genders are linked and shaped by many common influences. These include nationality, culture, language, religion, price, availability and disposable income.

Minimising Alcohol Problems

> No blueprint can be produced for a cut-and-dried preventive programme easily implemented all over the world. No vaccine is available to prevent inappropriate drinking and its consequences. (Grant and Ritson 1983, p. 187)

The best means of handling alcohol problems have often been hotly debated. Twentieth-century strategies to accomplish this aim have included the imposition of Prohibition in the US from 1920–33, the short-lived and unpopular 'Gorbachev Experiment' during 1985–87 in cutting vodka production in the former USSR and the introduction of prohibition in a number of Indian states such as Gujarat, Andhra Pradesh, Manipur and Haryana. Women, frequently the major victims of heavy drinking by males, have often played a leading role in campaigning for tighter controls on alcohol. This has recently been evident in India and, for example, in the foundation of the influential organisation Mothers Against Drunk Driving (MADD) in the US. In most countries in which alcohol is legal and widespread, policies to cope with alcohol problems have generally been far less draconian, designed to discourage or curb problematic drinking, rather than to discourage drinking in itself. The World Health Organization's Regional Office for Europe produced a *European Alcohol Action Plan* (World Health Organization 1994c). This stressed the reduction of national levels of per capita alcohol consumption as the key means of reducing alcohol problems in Europe. This emphasis has been called the 'Public Health Approach' to the control of alcohol problems. It had been expounded earlier by a number of commentators (Bruun et al. 1975, Edwards et al. 1995).

There is a clear relationship between national levels of per capita alcohol consumption and levels of many alcohol problems. Very few scientists now dispute the existence of such a connection. It is therefore legitimate for the reduction of per capita alcohol consumption to be considered as one possible approach to reducing levels of alcohol-related problems. Even so, the reduction of general levels of alcohol consumption does not appear to be either politically or socially popular in most countries. Godfrey (1997), for example, has acknowledged the possible value of using taxation to curb alcohol consumption, but has also stated: 'tax can be seen as a blunt instrument affecting all drinkers. Although the amount of tax paid will increase with the amount consumed and potentially with the problems caused' (p. 40).

The unpopularity of using tax to control general levels of alcohol consumption has led a number of researchers to emphasise a rather different, pragmatic, perspective called 'harm minimisation' or 'risk reduction'. Harm minimisation is not in opposition to what has recently been called the 'traditional public health approach' (Plant, Single and Stockwell 1997). It does, however, take as its principal aim, not the reduction of alcohol consumption per se, but the reduction of harmful drinking. It is important to emphasise that drinking is not in itself harmful, only certain patterns of drinking or levels of alcohol consumption at certain times, for example, when driving. Harm minimisation has been called 'sharpening the focus of alcohol policy' (Stockwell et al. 1996). It should be emphasised that this approach involves strategies which are likely to involve the reduction of some people's drinking. Moreover, such strategies have often also involved introducing restrictions surrounding the places in which alcohol is consumed or the use of other restraints upon drinking behaviour (Plant, Single and Stockwell 1997). Harm minimisation does offer a rather different approach from that outlined by Bruun et al. and other authors and, recently, by the World Health Organization (1994c). Even so, the latter has also outlined a number of approaches fully consistent with harm minimisation in relation to alcohol (World Health Organization 1994d, Ritson 1995). A number of harm-minimisation approaches have been suggested earlier by various authors (Tether and Robinson 1986). As emphasised by Plant, Single and Stockwell, harm minimisation has two major considerations. The first of these is whether or not a policy succeeds in reducing the harm associated with drinking. The second is whether or not a policy is politically or socially acceptable. The latter point has sometimes been criticised on the grounds that 'researchers should not take sides'. This view may be reasonable from the perspective of assuming that scientists are value free and influenced not by personal prejudices but only by available evidence, but fails to take account of the fact that alcohol-control policies have to operate in many different settings. However, the reality is that making assumptions can be dangerous and researchers are human beings. The best which can be hoped for is that these researchers will have some insight into their views. Some strategies are not likely to be popular or to be accepted in some countries, while they might be perfectly acceptable elsewhere. It is a poor policy that is not sensitive to such important considerations. To be successful, alcohol-control policies have to be tuned and adapted to the social contexts in which they are to be implemented and, even more important, sustained. In most countries, this involves creating and maintaining a supportive public and political sentiment towards specific policies. Such a sentiment is far more likely if there is available clear evidence of the production of a tangible benefit, such as the saving of lives or the reduction in accidents, injuries or public disorder. Such evidence needs to be highlighted and disseminated to key opinion formers as well as to at least relevant sections of the community or to the general population.

Some Prevention Strategies

It is probable that, human nature being what it is, some people will inevitably sometimes drink in potentially damaging ways. As noted by Grant and Ritson (1983), there is no clear and universally accepted means of preventing the many possible problems associated with heavy or inappropriate drinking. Even so, in societies in which alcohol is used, often with adverse consequences, there is experience of the use of a number of strategies to reduce such problems. A number of these approaches have recently been reviewed by Plant, Single and Stockwell (1997). Interested readers are referred to that book for a detailed consideration of a number of possible policy options. This chapter seeks only to provide a very brief and selective discussion of such approaches. Tether and Robinson (1986) have commented that:

> in every major area of contemporary life there are people getting into difficulties to a greater or lesser extent because of their alcohol consumption. It follows from this that there is in every area of contemporary life a *potential for prevention*. (pp. 4–5)

These authors presented a valuable guide for local action. This included consideration of the role of liquor licensing, work, education, the offender, helping professions, advertising and the media. The following section reviews a number of rather different policy options. These are not a comprehensive list of strategies, but are used to exemplify the type of approaches that have been adopted in some places.

Rigorous Enforcement of Existing Laws

In many countries, there are laws designed to curb some of the most serious types of problem associated with alcohol consumption. These include laws to regulate the sale and consumption of alcohol in licensed premises, and laws to curb alcohol-impaired driving. A classic study by Jeffs and Saunders (1983) has illustrated the type of gain that may be made simply by using existing legal powers and good community policing. They report that in Torquay, a coastal town in southern England, there were problems of aggression and violence in and around bars in the harbour area, popular with tourists as well as with local people. The police conducted a one-year experiment which involved informing bar owners and managers that the licensing laws were to be carefully applied. This involved regular police visits to bars with particular attention being shown to opening and closing times, under age drinking in bars and the service of alcoholic beverages to people who were plainly intoxicated. Jeffs and Saunders reported that during this period all arrests in Torquay declined by 21%. In a nearby comparison town there was no comparable fall. At the end of the experimental year, arrest rates rose again. This study was widely noted by researchers, but not, apparently, by the police, although this type of apparently productive approach had been adopted and maintained in Sussex, also in southern England. It is surprising, given the apparent success of the Torquay experiment, that it has not been far more widely adopted. A recent review by Lister Sharp (1994) concluded that there appears to be little interest in the United Kingdom to implement or enforce laws relating to either under age drinking in licensed premises or those relating to the service of alcohol to intoxicated patrons.

Drinking and Driving

In many countries alcohol-impaired driving became a major problem, especially in the economic boom decades after the Second World War. One response to this has been the introduction of blood and breath alcohol limits. A policy known as 'random breath testing' (RBT) was introduced in Finland in 1977. It has also been adopted in Australia. In both countries the introduction of RBT was followed by a marked fall in driver deaths attributable to alcohol impairment (Dunbar et al. 1987). Interestingly, the reduction of alcohol-impaired driver deaths has been noted in many industrial countries with a variety of different approaches to the problem of drunken driving (Stewart and Sweedler 1997). Clearly, in many countries public attitudes to drinking under the influence of alcohol have undergone a major transition in the last two decades. The driver who drinks is no longer a socially acceptable figure. This fact strengthens the hand of passengers and others who could be in a position to prevent intoxicated individuals from driving (Isaac et al. 1995). Even so, it is difficult to identify the specific factors that have led to this change in both attitudes and behaviour. RBT is not solely responsible, for similar improvements have been evident in the UK and other countries that do not operate RBT. Peacock (1992), for example, has concluded that the key factor in discouraging alcohol-impaired driving is the implementation of laws to restrict what can legally be consumed by drivers. Another important factor is the perceived extent to which laws to curb drunken driving are actually enforced. It should be noted that while women constitute a minority of those convicted of driving while intoxicated, they are in some countries a large and growing minority.

Reducing Aggression and Violence in Bars

An important study of Vancouver bars indicated that violence and aggression were associated with grimy, badly maintained and unattractive surroundings (Graham et al 1980). More recent Australian work has also indicated that aggression in bars is associated with lack of cleanliness (Homel et al. 1994a). These findings could reflect the fact that unattractive bars attract more violent patrons. Even so, Graham and Homel (1997) have stated that there is considerable scope for reducing the occurrence of violence in bars through their better organisation and design. These authors highlight the importance of 'creating a social atmosphere with clear limits' in bars. They note that: 'the physical environment provides patrons with the first indication of expected behaviour'. They further note that the following have been shown to be associated with aggression in bars:

> overall decorum expectations (rated from restrictive to 'anything goes'), swearing (especially abusive swearing), sexual activity among patrons, sexual competition, prostitution, drug use and dealing, male rowdiness, and male roughness or bumping. (p. 177)

The methods suggested by Graham and Homel to create safer bars include banning known troublemakers, recruiting and training bar 'peace loving' staff. Training the latter to refrain from serving people who are intoxicated is an important component of creating a safer bar environment. One example that has attracted considerable recent interest is the 'Surfers' Paradise Project'. This initiative was designed to curb disorder and crime in a popular Australian coastal tourist resort in which such behaviours appeared to be at a high level. The project involved mobilising licensing authorities, the police and bar owners and managers to participate in a carefully monitored scheme. It emerged that this initiative led to improvements in the way in which licensed premises were operated, together with a fall in aggression and violence (Homel et al. 1994b). It was further concluded that the Surfers' Paradise Project had not simply displaced problems to other nearby areas (Homel et al. 1994, Graham and Homel 1997). This issue of safer bars and training staff may be particularly appropriate in relation to gender differences (see Chapter 4).

Another potentially useful approach to reducing unacceptable behaviours in licensed premises is the adoption of server interventions or what has been called a 'Responsible Beverage Service'. Saltz (1997), reviewing such initiatives, has noted:

> At a minimum, server intervention refers to servers of alcoholic beverages making sure that no intoxicated or impaired customer is left to drive away in that condition. More generally, under the rubric of Responsible Beverage Service (RBS), it refers to the steps that servers of alcoholic beverages can take to reduce the chances that their patrons (or guests) become intoxicated in the first place. (p. 72)

Saltz has referred to O'Donnell (1985) who reported that around half those whose driving was above the legal blood alcohol level had been drinking in licensed premises. He also cites Mosher (1984) who has reported on legal precedents in Canada and the US which hold servers and licensees liable for financial costs when patrons, even though they were known to be intoxicated, were served alcohol and then inflicted harm on other people, for example, in driving accidents. Solomon and Payne (1996) have noted that Australian licensees have similar legal obligations to their Canadian counterparts in relation to bar-room safety. They also note that Australian courts have been reluctant to acknowledge that serving intoxicated patrons increases risks:

> Nonetheless, as we have discussed, such practices create an environment in which violence and injuries of some kind are likely, even if the specific incidents are not. Overcrowding, underage patrons, drinking contests, cheap drinks, and aggressive bouncers all contribute to this 'powder keg' situation. (p. 41)

Saltz has concluded that there is evidence that training programmes can succeed in equipping bar staff to intervene more often in situations of patron intoxication or disorderliness and to reduce levels of bar-room intoxication (Saltz and Hennessy 1990, McKnight 1993, Stockwell et al. 1993). Such initiatives clearly hold the promise of producing positive results. This type of approach would be of particular value if it could be adopted on a voluntary basis by the owners of licensed premises. Such a step would not need to be wholly altruistic, since bar servers and owners would be amongst those most likely to benefit from a reduction in violence and intoxication associated with drinking in bars, clubs and other licensed premises.

Reducing Injuries in Bars

In association with bar-room violence, there is an associated toll of injuries (Giesbrecht et al. 1989). One possible method of reducing such injuries, either accidental or the result of violence, has been suggested by Shepherd, a surgeon working in Wales, and his colleagues (Shepherd et al. 1990, Shepherd Price and Shenfine 1990, 1994, Shepherd, Huggett and Kidner 1994). These authors have drawn attention to the fact that in many British bars injuries have been sustained by staff and patrons as the result of the breaking of beer glasses. The latter are sometimes used as weapons in violent assaults. Shepherd and his colleagues have suggested that injuries might be reduced by the adoption of toughened or tempered glasses in bars. This view has been supported by a pilot study of 100 bars in Edinburgh. This indicated that tempered glasses were reported to be safer, more durable and associated with fewer staff injuries than untoughened glasses (Plant et al. 1994). Experimental work in the Department of Mechanical Engineering in the University of Edinburgh has confirmed the greater strength of tempered beer glasses. Tempered glasses are also less likely if they do break to shatter into dangerous, dagger-like shards (Plant and Mills 1994/95). In view of this compelling evidence, it would appear that tempered glasses offer one way in which the drinking environment could be made at least a little safer.

Services for 'Problem Drinkers'

Issues related to treatment and clinical services for women have been considered in the previous chapter. One of the main objectives of the varied specialist services available for people with drinking problems is to prevent further harm from drinking. For many people, their drinking careers do involve moving into and out of alcohol problems at different points in their lives. One recent book has reviewed the potential role of alcohol-problems treatment under the title of *Liberating Solutions* (Cameron 1995). As this book illustrates, one role that such treatment can serve is to help people at times of particular crisis, when the support of their families and friends may not be enough. It is emphasised that some people overcome their problems by cutting down rather than cutting out, drinking altogether. 'Changing from *determined drinker to ex-determined drinker* requires reassimilation of an existing set of cultural beliefs of drinking enthusiasts' (p. 241).

For those women who have already experienced problems because of their drinking, one obvious option is to seek assistance from some form of specialised agency. In many counties such agencies are available. In some, such as the UK, there is a wide range of different types of services in some areas. In many parts of the world, however, few if any such services exist and in some localities there may be little variety in those that do exist. As indicated by the previous chapter, a high proportion of individuals who do come to the attention of alcohol-problems treatment agencies appear to 'do well'. However, it must be remembered that women are less likely to go to an alcohol-identified agency, preferring to use other types of treatment/support organisations. Available evidence does not suggest that any particular approach to the treatment and management of alcohol problems is uniquely effective. A number of different methods appear to be productive in this respect. Accordingly, organisations of this type, together with the powerful role of families, friends and close associates, all have a potential for the prevention of individual alcohol problems. Other people can often help. It has long been acknowledged that women with alcohol problems may be less likely than comparable males to seek help or to be recognised as in need of support. Prejudices about female drinking might deter many women from contacting agencies that could help them to overcome alcohol problems. One clear educational priority, as noted by Beckman and Mays (1985), should be to educate and alert 'community gatekeepers' about alcohol problems in women. As suggested by Gearheart et al. (1991), key professionals such as family doctors need to be informed of signs that could indicate that females have alcohol problems. Such individuals should also be informed about the range of services available to help and support such women. Whenever possible, alcohol services should be outgoing and welcoming to women. This could, for example, entail organising opening hours to suit the needs of women in paid employment as well as those with children.

Alcohol Education

One of the most popular approaches to preventing or minimising alcohol problems is health education. In some countries considerable thought, effort and expense has been invested in producing and implementing alcohol education materials or campaigns. Health education of this type has wide appeal. It is relatively non-invasive, popular and is frequently a high-profile method of emphasising political commitment and concern about a serious problem. Many, probably most, alcohol education activities are not subject to any form of evaluation or assessment. It is frequently not possible to obtain the funding necessary to carry out such evaluations and it is also sometimes simply assumed that alcohol education is a reliable means of reducing or forestalling heavy or problematic drinking, especially if directed towards adolescents and other young people. It should be emphasised that 'alcohol education' involves an individual's continuing socialisation and lifetime's experiences about alcohol. Such experiences, as noted in Chapter 1, often begin at an early age and continue to change throughout a person's life. As shown by Jahoda and Cramond (1972), even very young children frequently have clear impressions about alcohol, derived from their perceptions and experiences related to drinking by parents or significant others. Such experiences begin to form before school attendance and continue to develop long after school. Accordingly, it is unreasonable and unfair to expect the school to be the sole purveyor of what is conventionally called 'alcohol education' when parents and other family members and other associates clearly have an important and often very negative and damaging role in this respect.

A high proportion of the alcohol educational materials that have been produced, at least in primarily English-speaking countries, appear to have been devised for use with teenagers and adolescents. What has all of this activity achieved? Fortunately there have been some detailed evaluations. Sadly, many commentators have reached the conclusion that alcohol (and drug) education has not been generally successful in reducing levels of alcohol consumption or illicit drug use amongst young people (Kalb 1975, Kinder, Pape and Walfish 1980, Schaps et al. 1981, Bandy and President 1983, Grant 1986,

Tobler 1986, Moskowitz 1989, Bagnall 1991, May 1991, Gerstein and Green 1993, Plant and Plant 1997). More alarming still, some studies have even suggested that exposure to alcohol or drug education might have *increased* rather than decreased, youthful alcohol and drug involvement. An example of the latter has been described by Hawthorne, Garrard and Dunt (1995). This assessment concluded that exposure to the large-scale and high-profile 'Life Education' programme in Australia was associated with raised levels of drug use. Hawthorne (1996) concluded that the programme had exerted no preventative impact in the state of Victoria. It had not altered drinking amongst girls, but 22% of boys' recent drinking was attributable to exposure to the programme. Hawthorne, Garrard and Dunt (1995) had earlier stated that their negative findings in relation to the Life Education programme suggested that alcohol and other substance education should be gender specific and should also be appropriate to the 'drug recruitment patterns' of the recipients. In the context of female drinking, health education could usefully provide information about gender differences in alcohol use and the effects of alcohol. Topics such as pregnancy, the biological effects of alcohol on females (including the effects of menopause) and sexuality should be considered. In addition, as the Australian findings have illustrated, initiatives should be devised, implemented and evaluated bearing in mind the possibility that alcohol education may have different effects on females from those on males. If this is the case, as highlighted by Taylor and Qi Wang (1988), then in future greater consideration should be given to the use of gender-specific educational materials and initiatives. There is other evidence to support the influence of gender, not only in the effect of specific messages, but in relation to the sex of the person providing or involved in the provision of the message. Bochner (1994), for example, reported that a study in New South Wales showed that teenagers responded better to same-sex role models than to others in relation to advertisements designed to reduce alcohol consumption. Taylor and Qi Wang also noted that, not only should educational initiatives take into account gender differences in drinking habits, but also the fact that rural/urban differences exist. Ethnicity is also an important factor. A number of agencies have already acknowledged the need for at least some specific information of this type. This has mainly been in the form of leaflets for women, or for pregnant women. There have been some educational intiatives especially for women, but, like most other ventures in this area, there is little evidence to suggest that even these have changed drinking behaviours (McMillan and Baldwin 1993, Shore 1993).

Providing people with information is no guarantee that they will change their behaviour in the desired direction. People drink and engage in other pleasurable, but potentially risky, forms of behaviour for many reasons. The aetiology of drinking and alcohol-related problems is complex and reflects many factors (Fazey 1977). A number of commentators have concluded that health education in this area should take account of such influences, and should go beyond the provision of factual information. Many educational initiatives have for a long time been devised in the light of this realisation. Sadly, there is little persuasive evidence that such ventures have achieved more than a very modest impact on behaviour (Bagnall 1991). More commonly, it has been reported that alcohol education may increase levels of knowledge/awareness or modify attitudes, but probably not for very long. The longer-term impact of many educational initiatives is simply unknown. In view of this rather depressing evidence, it is clear that expectations of what may be achieved by health education should be realistic, and probably fairly modest. People enjoy drinking and many, if not most, may be disinclined to imagine that they could ever become casualties because of this part of their lives. Mass media campaigns generally appear not to have influenced alcohol consumption. Even so, such campaigns might serve a useful purpose in influencing the climate of public opinion (Glicksman 1986, Douglas 1990 cited in Edwards et al. 1995).

As noted earlier in this book, the use of warning labels on alcoholic beverage containers was introduced in the US in 1989. One of these labels warns of the dangers of drinking and driving. Another states that:

> According to the Surgeon General, women should not drink alcoholic beverages during pregnancy because of the risk of birth defects.

As emphasised in Chapter 5, available evidence suggests that while heavy drinking during pregnancy is inadvisable, moderate drinking does not appear to cause birth defects. Accordingly, the precise nature of this message could be questioned. One of the hopes behind the introduction of these warnings would be that they might have an effect on the heaviest drinkers, because the latter would be most exposed to them (Kaskutas and Greenfield 1992, Kaskutas 1995). Greenfield (1997), reviewing evidence on the impact of the use of these labels, concluded that the use of these messages might have served to remind those most at risk to take precautions. Recall of the pregnancy warning was associated with conversations about drinking and pregnancy. Such conversations were more likely amongst those who were older and better educated. Greenfield also noted that pregnant women who remembered the pregnancy warning indicated that their maximum alcohol intake during pregnancy was less than the maximum they had consumed for the previous year. Given that this reduction in drinking is an acknowledged part of the change in drinking levels before and during pregnancy, this could not be taken as proof that seeing the warning label had led to decreased drinking. It is possible that pregnant women who were most aware of health issues were most likely to have noticed the warning. Greenfield also concluded that the message about drinking and driving had succeeded in reaching those most at risk, notably heavier drinking and younger males. However, Hankin et al. (1996) have questioned whether the usefulness of warning labels has reached its peak. This group noted that although drinking has decreased among women who were not drinking much, it appeared to have had little effect on women who were drinking heavily.

Some Practical Advice for Women Drinkers

There is no internationally generally agreed advice on what constitutes 'low risk' drinking. Several recent commentators have drawn attention to the fact that 'standard drinks' vary in different countries, as do weekly or daily alcohol consumption guidelines produced by a number of national health departments or other authorities. For example a standard drink or 'unit' of alcohol in the UK, as noted in Chapter 1, is equivalent to 7.9 grams of absolute alcohol. In Australia, Austria, New Zealand and Spain a standard drink is 10 grams. It is 14 grams in the US, 13.5 grams in Canada and no less than 19.7 grams in Japan (International Center for Alcohol Policies 1996, Stockwell and Single 1997). Official advice on what constitutes low-risk drinking also varies. Even so, it is generally acknowledged that females should be advised to drink substantially less, typically only 40–60%, than males. This differentiation is not, however, universal. In Canada and the Netherlands, for example, the same general advice has been given for drinkers of either sex. The advice accepted by most health professionals and researchers in the United Kingdom is for females to restrict their drinking to 14 units per week, while the recommended equivalent for males is 21 units (Royal College of Psychiatrists 1986). In the US, Canada and Australia official advice is for females to consume only one or two standard drinks per day and for males to restrict their consumption to between one (Canada) and four drinks (Australia).

In spite of the obvious variation in the precise advice offered in different national settings, it is possible to highlight a number of points that could be adopted as useful guidelines. First, the wording of health messages needs to be thought through. In many countries words such as 'recommended', or 'sensible', are used. Words which are almost guaranteed to make people react in a challenging way. Use of words such as 'responsible' may give people the sense that they are the only ones who can really be aware and take care with their drinking. Those who drink in moderation are far less at risk of experiencing alcohol problems than are those who drink heavily. Moderate drinkers, especially those who are middle aged or elderly, are also likely to derive a degree of health protection not evident amongst those who drink heavily and put their health and well-being at risk. Evidence does support the view that females are well advised to drink less than men. It is reasonable to endorse the type of advice already available for adult females, in good health, to generally keep within 'low risk' consumption levels of one or two standard (UK) drinks per day. It is also sensible for women not to drink every day and to avoid intoxication. There are also times when particular care should be taken. Pregnant women should consume only the equivalent of one or two UK drinks no more than once or twice a week or, if they prefer, abstain from alcohol completely. People who are driving, working or performing any task requiring care and precision should simply not drink while doing so or immediately before doing so. It is also important to take account of the fact that the effects of alcohol take some time to wear off. A UK standard drink of 7.9 grams, for example, requires about one hour to dissipate. Accordingly, any person who has consumed three standard drinks will be influenced by this for at least three hours. This should be borne in mind when planning activities such as driving or working.

As emphasised elsewhere in this book, most people generally consume alcohol in moderation and without harm. Advice of the type suggested above would, if followed, greatly reduce the chances of any individual experiencing adverse consequences from their personal drinking.

8 Conclusions

This book has ranged over a considerable number of issues. These have included drinking habits and evidence of patterns of alcohol-related problems, history, the physical effects of drinking beverage alcohol, psychology, pregnancy, treatment/clinical issues, prevention, harm minimisation and health education. I have presented the above material from the perspectives of my dual roles as a researcher and as someone who has worked with problem drinkers. Inevitably, the material considered has been selective and inevitably, the mode of presentation has been coloured by my personal views and experience. I hope, however, that I have succeeded in bringing together a considerable amount of information which for many, if not most, readers, will be new. The literature related to women and alcohol is now massive and continues to expand. It can no longer be maintained that, in the industrialised world, at least, little has been done to investigate drinking and its associated consequences amongst females. The 'research scene' has changed considerably in the past 20 years. There are now many active female clinicians, counsellors and researchers in the 'alcohol field'. These and heightened awareness amongst many of their male colleagues, have combined to ensure that alcohol use by women is now receiving, in some places at least, the degree of attention that it deserves.

Sadly, information about female drinking continues to be in scarce supply in many developing countries, although the same is often true in such settings in relation to men. The result of this is that, although some reference has been made to evidence from non-industrial countries, information from the former has been far less prominent in this book than that from countries such as the US and the UK.

From the material considered above, it is evident that there have been major changes in many countries in alcohol use by women. In both industrial and some non-industrial countries, female alcohol consumption has become far more commonplace and widely accepted. To a large degree, such consumption appears to be associated with more general changes in the social, economic and political power and freedom of women. The international picture is, it should be emphasised, far from uniform, and far from generally promising. In many countries women remain the victims of widespread institutionalised discrimination, and in some countries their position has been worsening. In recent years, the spread of religious fundamentalism in some countries has brought with it a direct and systematic attack upon the legal and social rights of women. In some localities, this has even involved closing women's schools, and banning women from being educated or working outside the home. This amounts to a return to the Dark Ages.

In association with increased drinking where this has been occurring, there has been an accompanying rise in rates of alcohol-related problems amongst women in many countries. In spite of the greater acceptance of drinking by women, double standards, prejudice and active discrimination persist even in many settings in which gender discrimination is not official policy, or is even illegal. Even in countries in which female drinking is well established and normative, greater antipathy exists to heavy drinking or the development of adverse consequences amongst female drinkers. The latter are more stigmatised than their male counterparts and there is often far less sympathy for them.

It has been emphasised throughout this book that most people who drink generally do so in moderation and without attendant harm. Women who drink, however, are vulnerable in a number of respects in which men are not, or at least only to a lesser degree. The most obvious of these is the widespread and persisting assumption that women who drink are likely to be sexually available and acquiescent. Second, there are a number of evident physical differences between females and males which justify advising women to drink less than men. Third, the important topic of pregnancy has received considerable concern. Not all that has been written about alcohol consumption by women has been reasonable or objective. Much has been biased and highly prejudiced or simply hysterical. Women, it should be emphasised, are not a 'high-risk group' for either heavy drinking or alcohol-related problems. In general, they drink far less than men and accordingly experience much lower rates of problems than males. Even in countries in which the gender gap in relation to drinking has closed, there remains a considerable disparity between the sexes. As noted several times in earlier pages, some women experience problems because of their own drinking. Probably a greater number are damaged by the heavy drinking of their partners or of others.

The issue of drinking during pregnancy has been considered in some detail in Chapter 5. Concerns about this topic are centuries old. During recent decades a considerable body of research has been devoted to this issue. As noted above, while heavy maternal drinking during pregnancy is associated with fetal harm, moderate and light drinking are not. The 'Fetal Alcohol Syndrome' is associated with a constellation of health and lifestyle factors for which heavy drinking is a marker, a proxy variable and only a single component. These factors include poverty, ill health, unemployment, social deprivation, heavy use of tobacco, illicit drugs, maternal age and a number of other variables. It is remarkable that the now considerable evidence on this topic continues to be distorted and inflated. This simply serves to frighten, intimidate and to mislead. Health messages should be couched in cautious terms, but they should not be either unduly alarmist or inaccurate as many in this area have been.

Virtually all contemporary social groups use some form of psychoactive drug for recreational or religious purposes. Alcohol is the most widely used of these and most alcohol consumption is associated with pleasure rather than problems. Drinking habits vary markedly between national and social groups, by area, ethnicity, religion and not least by gender. It is evident that the aetiology of both drinking and the development of heavy drinking are complex and that these cannot be explained in terms of any single, simple theory. There are vast differences between those who consume alcohol and between those who, at some time in their lives, may be harmed by their drinking, or by the drinking of somebody else. In view of the bewildering complexity of motivations for drinking and for the variations in patterns of drinking and alcohol-related problems, it is hardly surprising that no single treatment approach has emerged to be uniquely effective in enabling problem drinkers to cut down or discontinue their alcohol use. A number of alternative treatment approaches and philosophies exist and several of these clearly have merit. Indeed, many of those with alcohol-related problems overcome them without resorting to any type of formal professional help. The prognosis for people with alcohol problems is often favourable and available evidence does not suggest that women with alcohol problems have a poorer prognosis than men.

In spite of this, there are a number of factors which are likely to inhibit women with alcohol problems from seeking help and support. These have been considered in Chapter 6. Alcohol services invariably attract far more males than females. This fact is in itself a source of problems for women. In addition the way in which many services operate makes it difficult for many women, especially those with children or other family responsibilities, to attend or to fit into available programmes.

As indicated in Chapter 1, national patterns of alcohol consumption vary enormously (see also World Health Organization 1996). Even so, in all countries in which alcohol is consumed, some people (mainly men, but also women) consume it in ways that are potentially risky. Alcohol-related problems in their many forms inflict massive personal, social, health and economic costs on society, even if many of these are intangible or cannot easily be assessed (Godfrey 1997).

The problems associated with alcohol pose a major challenge for humanity. Can these be addressed in ways that achieve effective harm minimisation and without a major onslaught upon human rights? I have attempted to consider some of the issues around prevention and health education in the previous chapter. The general level of alcohol-related problems in a society are clearly linked with general levels of alcohol consumption. They are also very clearly linked with patterns of drinking. In theory, it would be possible for all drinkers to consume alcohol in moderation, in an enjoyable and harm free, even beneficial, way. Sadly, this is as yet an unattained ideal in many contexts. Past experience does, however, demonstrate that rates of alcohol problems can be reduced, especially if communities are sufficiently concerned to act to curb them. At times of national health crisis, this might lead to the use of measures designed to reduce all alcohol consumption. Even so, in most contexts and under most circumstances, such general measures lack appeal. Other, more focused, strategies are usually more acceptable and also more likely to be sustained. Health education is an important arm of prevention policy. Even so, it has not been demonstrated that alcohol education alone can be relied on to deter people from drinking heavily or in a risky manner. Accordingly, education has greatest promise to inform, rather than to change behaviours. It is likely to be of greatest value as a supporting arm of a range of policies to foster responsible, enjoyable drinking and to discourage or prevent heavy, risky or harmful drinking. To a large extent women drinkers require similar services and prevention initiatives to those likely to be of most use in relation to men. In spite of this, as I hope this book has emphasised, there are important differences in relation to many aspects of drinking by women in comparison to drinking by men. Accordingly, all major responses to 'alcohol problems' should be devised with particular attention, whenever appropriate, to the special characteristics and requirements of women as well as men. It can no longer be assumed that the sexes are identical in relation to drinking, or that females are an unimportant or tiny minority of drinkers. Moreover, it does appear likely that the freedom of women to drink and the decency with which alcohol problems are managed depend upon the preservation of the fundamental human rights of both women and men.

Epilogue

Some Thoughts and Questions

'Normal' Mother–Daughter Relationship

1. How does a daughter make sense of her mother's world?
2. How do her perceptions of that world differ from those of her mother?
3. Does the world look bigger?
4. Does her mother look bigger or smaller?
5. Does her mother make sense of the world?
6. Is her mother frightened of the world, and if so, why?
7. How do these perceptions and the way they may be communicated, impact on the daughter?
8. How do they affect the relationship with her mother?
9. How do they affect the part she wants to play, thinks she can play, in the world as she gets older?

'Problem Drinking' Mother and Daughter Relationship

1. How does a daughter live with and come to terms with the shame and guilt her mother feels?
2. How does a daughter live with and come to terms with the embarrassment of living with a problem-drinking mother?
3. Has the world damaged her mother?
4. Will it damage her?
5. Does she grow bigger to protect her mother from the world and the damage it has caused her?
6. Does she take on the world, perceiving it to be a hostile place with no one she can trust?
7. How is a daughter's view of herself as a woman affected by the way she sees her mother?
8. How is her view of herself as a woman affected by the way she sees other people treating her mother?
9. How is her view of herself as a woman affected by the way she interprets other people's perceptions of her mother?
10. If her mother tends to relate to men in a flirtatious way, how might the way in which men respond to her affect her view of them and her relationship with them?

Bibliography

The following references were invaluable in the writing of this book. Many, though not all, have been cited directly in the text.

Aaltonen, I. and Mäkelä, K. (1994) 'Female and male life stories published in the Finnish Alcoholics Anonymous journal', *International Journal of the Addictions*, 29: 485–495.

Abbey, A., Scott, R.O. and Smith, M.J. (1993) 'Physical, subjective, and social availability: their relationship to alcohol consumption in rural and urban areas', *Addiction*, 88: 489–499.

Abbey, A., Smith, M.J, and Scott, R.O. (1993) 'The relationship between reasons for drinking alcohol and alcohol consumption: An interactional approach', *Addictive Behaviors*, 6: 659–670.

Abbott, A. (1994) 'A feminist approach to substance abuse treatment and service delivery', *Social Work in Health Care*, 19: 67–83.

Abel, E.L. (1981a) *Fetal Alcohol Syndrome: Vol 1. An Annotated and Comprehensive Bibliography*, Florida, CRC Press.

Abel, E.L. (1981b) *Fetal Alcohol Syndrome: Vol 2. Human Studies*, Florida, CRC Press.

Abel, E.L. (1982a) *Fetal Alcohol Syndrome: Vol 3. Animal Studies*, Florida, CRC Press.

Abel, E.L. (1982b) *Alcohol and Reproduction: Bibliography*, Connecticut, Greenwood Press.

Abel, E.L. (1991) *Fetal Alcohol Syndrome*, Oradell, New Jersey, Medical Economics Books.

Abel, E.L. (1995) 'An update on incidence of FAS: FAS is not an equal opportunity birth defect', *Neurotoxicology and Teratology*, 17: 437–443.

Abel, E.L. (1997) 'Was the fetal alcohol syndrome recognised in the ancient Near East?' *Addiction*, 32: 3–8.

Abel, E.L. and Hannigan, J.H. (1995) 'J-shaped relationship between drinking during pregnancy and birth weight: re-analysis of prospective epidemiologoical data', *Alcohol and Alcoholism*, 30: 345–355.

Abel, E.L. and Sokol, R.J. (1987) 'Incidence of Fetal Alcohol Syndrome and economic impact of FAS-Related Anomalies', *Drug and Alcohol Dependence*, 19: 51–70.

Abel, E.L. and Sokol, R.J. (1991) 'A revised conservative estimate of the incidence of FAS and its economic impact', *Alcoholism: Clinical and Experimental Research*, 15: 514–524.

Abrams, D.B. and Wilson, G.T. (1979) 'Effects of Alcohol on Social Anxiety in Women: Cognitive Versus Physiological Processes', *Journal of Abnormal Psychology*, 88: 161–173.

Abrams, J. (1990) *Reclaiming the Inner Child*, London: Mandala, Harper Collins Publishers.

Abrams, R.C. and Alexopoulos, G. (1991) 'Geriatric Addictions', in Frances, R. and Miller, S.J. (eds) *Clinical Textbook of Addictive Disorders*, New York, Guilford Press, 347–365.

Abu-Zeid, H.A.H., Choi, N.W., Maini, K.K. et al. (1977) 'Relative role of factors associated with cerebral infarction and cerebral hemorrhage: a matched pair case-control study', *Stroke*, 8: 106–112.

Ada ıi, H.O., Lund, E., Bergstrom, R. and Meirik, O. (1988) 'Cigarette smoking, alcohol consumption and risk of breast cancer in young women', *British Journal of Cancer*, 58: 832–837.

Adams, P.L. (1987) 'The mother not the father', *Journal of the American Academy of Psychoanalysis*, 15: 465–480.

Adams, T.D. (1986) 'My gay Antonia: the politics of Willa Cather's lesbianism', *Journal of Homosexuality*, 12: 89–98.

Adams, W.I. (1995) 'Potential for adverse drug–alcohol interactions among retirement community residents', *Journal of the American Geriatric Society*, 43: 1021–1025.

Adams, W.L., Garry, P.J., Rhyne, R., Hunt, W.C. and Goodwin, J.S. (1990) 'Alcohol intake in the healthy elderly: Changes with age in a cross-sectional and longitudinal study', *Journal of the American Geriatric Society*, 38: 211–216.

Adams, W.L. and Smith Cox, N. (1995) 'Epidemiology of problem drinking among elderly people', *International Journal of the Addictions*, 30: 1693–1716.

Adams, W.R. (1995) 'Guatemala', in Heath, D.B., (ed.) *International Handbook on Alcohol and Culture*, Connecticut, Greenwood Press, 99–109.

Adlaf, E.M., Smart, R.G. and Jansen, V.A. (1989) *Alcohol Use, Drug Use and Well-Being Among a Sample of Older Adults in Toronto: A Preliminary Report*, Toronto, Addiction Research Foundation.

Adrian, M., Dini, C.M., MacGregor, L.J. and Stoduto, G. (1995) 'Substance use as a measure of social integration for women of different ethnocultural groups into mainstream culture in a pluralist society: the example of Canada', *International Journal of the Addictions*, 30: 699–734.

Ager, J.W. (1992) *Discussion: Statistical Analysis in Treatment and Prevention Program Evaluation*, Nida Research Monograph 117 ISS, 31–40.

Agosti, C. (1994) 'The efficacy of controlled trials of alcohol misuse treatments in maintaining abstinence: A meta-analysis', *International Journal of the Addictions*, 29: 759–769.

Ahlström, S. (1987a) 'Women's Use of Alcohol. in Simpura', J., (ed.) *Finnish Drinking Habits*, Helsinki, Finnish Foundation for Alcohol Studies.

Ahlström, S. (1987b) 'Young People's Drinking Habits' in Simpura, J., (ed.) *Finnish Drinking Habits*, Helsinki, Finnish Foundation for Alcohol Studies.

Akers, R.L., LaGreca, A.J., Cochran, J. and Sellers, C. (1989) 'Social Learning Theory and Alcohol Behavior among the Elderly', *Sociological Quarterly*, 30: 625–638.

Alagna, S.W. and Reddy, D.M. (1984) 'Predictors of proficient technique and successful lesion detection in breast cancer self-examination', *Health Psychology*, 3: 113–127.

Alaniz, M.I. (1994) 'Mexican farmworker women's perspectives on drinking in a migrant community', *International Journal of the Addictions*, 29: 1173–1188.

Alcabes, P., Vlahov, D. and Anthony, J. (1992) 'Characteristics of intravenous drug users by history of arrest and treatment for drug use', *Journal of Nervous and Mental Disease*, 180: 48–54.

Alcohol Concern (1988) 'Sex of babies affected by drinking', *Alcohol Concern* 16.

Alcohol Concern (1993) *Alcohol Education: Providing Training Courses on Women and Alcohol*, London, Alcohol Concern.

Alcohol Concern (1995) *Improving Women's Access to Alcohol Services*, London, Alcohol Concern.

Alcohol Training Project (1996) *Alcohol Issues in Child Protection*, Surrey, Wynne Howard Publications.

Alexander, C.N., Robinson, P. and Rainforth, M. (1993) 'Treating and preventing alcohol, nicotine and drug abuse through transcendental meditation: A review and statistical meta-analysis', *Alcoholism Treatment Quarterly*, 11: 11–16.

Alexander, H. (1890) 'Forensic relations of the puerperal state', *Alienist and Neurologist*, 11: 38–43.

Alienist and Neurologist (editorial) (1881) 'Oophorectomy for neuropathic conditions', January 2,1: 117.

Alienist and Neurologist (editorial) (1881) 'To prevent puerperal insanity', October 2,4: 693–694.

Alienist and Neurologist (editorial) (1886) 'Teaching the nature of alcohol', October 7,4: 708–709.

Alienist and Neurologist (editorial) (1889) 'The paraldehyde habit', 10,1: 113–114.

Alienist and Neurologist (editorial) (1889) 'The insane of Morocco', 10,4: 654–655.

Alienist and Neurologist (editorial) (1889) 'The alkaloid of testicular juice', 10,4: 666.

Alienist and Neurologist (editorial) (1890) 'The cure of the drunkard and the habeas corpus', January, 11,1: 118.

Alienist and Neurologist (editorial) (1890) 'Viscious therapeutics', April, 11,2: 254.

Alienist and Neurologist (editorial) (1890) 'The evils of hypnotism: Giles De La Tourette', July, 11,2: 428.

Alienist and Neurologist (editorial) (1890) 'Naptha Delirium', July, 11,2: 429.

Alienist and Neurologist (editorial) (1890) 'A merited tribute to Dr. Alice Bennett', October, 11,3: 628.

Alienist and Neurologist (editorial) (1891) 'A brush with the fair sex', January 12,1: 124–125.

Alienist and Neurologist (editorial) (1891) 'The American Medical Temperance Association', October, 12,4: 637–639.

Alienist and Neurologist (editorial) (1891) 'Common scolds', October, 12,4: 640.

Alienist and Neurologist (editorial) (1892) 'The state's protection of the victims of alcoholism', April 13,2: 258–259.

Alienist and Neurologist (1892) 'Impregnation of one sexual pervert female by another', July 13,3: 545–546.

Alienist and Neurologist (editorial) (1892) 'Alice Mitchell the "sexual pervert" and her crimes', July 13,3: 554–557.

Alienist and Neurologist (editorial) (1892) 'Hysteria and Hypnotism', July 13,3: 565.

Alienist and Neurologist (1892) 'The relations of pelvic disease to physical disturbances in women', October 13,4: 729–730.

Alienist and Neurologist (1893) 'The use of hypnotism among the insane', 14,2: 305–307.

Alienist and Neurologist (1893) 'Treatment for hysteria', 14,2: 311.

Alienist and Neurologist (editorial) (1893) 'Report on hypnotism', 14,2: 322–323.

Alienist and Neurologist (editorial) (1893) 'Treatment of the Insane Outside of Asylums', 14,2: 324–326.

Alienist and Neurologist (1893) 'Removal of the ovaries of the insane', 14,3: 486.

Alienist and Neurologist (1893) 'Menstruation', 14,3: 486–487.

Alienist and Neurologist (editorial) (1894b) 'Diseases of women', July 15,3: 395.

Alienist and Neurologist (editorial) (1894) 'Lombroso versus women', 15,3: 405–406.

Alienist and Neurologist (1894) 'Maltine and coca wine', October 15,4: 491.

Allan, C.A. (1991) 'Psychological symptoms, psychiatric disorder and alcohol dependence amongst men and women attending a community-based voluntary agency and an alcohol treatment unit', *British Journal of Addiction*, 86: 419–427.

Allan, C.A. (1995) 'Alcohol problems and anxiety disorders: a critical review', *Alcohol and Alcoholism*, 30: 145–151.

Allen, D. (1996) 'Are alcoholic women more likely to drink premenstrually?' *Alcohol and Alcoholism*, 31: 145–147.

Allen, D.G., Allman, K.K. and Powers, P. (1991) 'Feminist nursing research without gender', *Advances In Nursing Science*, 13: 49–58.

Allen, K. (1994) 'Development of an instrument to identify barriers to treatment for addicted women, from their perspective', *International Journal of the Addictions*, 29: 429–444.

Almdal, T.P. and Sorenson, T.I.A. (1991) 'Incidence of parenchymal liver disease in Denmark, 1981 to 1985: analysis of hospitalisation registry data', *Hepatology*, 13: 650–655.

Almedom, A.M., and Abraham, S. (1994) 'Women moral virtue and tchatchewing', in McDonald, M., (ed.) *Gender, Drinks and Drugs*, Oxford, Providence, Berg, 249–259.

Almog, Y.J., Anglin, M.D. and Fisher, D.G. (1993) 'Alcohol and heroin use patterns of narcotics addicts: gender and ethnic differences', *American Journal of Drug and Alcohol Abuse*, 19: 219–238.

Alpert, J.J., Day, N., Dooling, E., Hingson, R., Oppenheimer, E., Rosett, H.L., Weiner, L. and Zuckerman, B. (1981) 'Maternal alcohol consumption and newborn assessment; Methodology of the Boston City Hospital prospective study', *Neurobehavioural Toxicology*, 3: 195–201.

Ambler, C. (1990) 'Alcohol, racial segregation and popular politics in Northern Rhodesia', *Journal of African History*, 31: 295–313.

American Academy of Pediatrics, Committee on Adolescence (1987) 'Alcohol use and abuse: A pediatric concern', *Pediatrics*, 79: 450–453.

Ames, G., Schmidt, C., Klee, L. and Saltz, R. (1996) 'Combining methods to identify new measures of women's drinking problems', *Addiction*, 91: 829–844.

Amt, E. (1993) *Women's Lives in Medieval Europe: A Sourcebook*, London, Routledge.

Anderson, B.S. and Zinsser, J.P. (1990) *A History of Their Own: Vol 1: Women in Europe from Prehistory to the Present Time*, London, Penguin.

Anderson, F.W. (1933) 'A study of the sexual life in psychosis associated with childbearing', *Journal of Mental Science*, 79: 137.

Anderson, K. and Plant, M.A. (1996) 'Abstaining and carousing: Substance use among adolescents in the Western Isles of Scotland', *Drug and Alcohol Dependence*, 41: 198–196.

Anderson, K., Plant, M.A. and Plant, M.L. (1997) 'Associations between drinking, smoking and illicit drug use among adolescents in the Western Isles of Scotland: Implications for harm minimisation', *Journal of Substance Misuse*, submitted.

Anderton, D.L. and Bean, L.L. (1985) 'Birth spacing and fertility limitation: a behavioral analysis of a nineteenth century frontier population', *Demography*, 22: 169–183.

Andrews, B. (1995) 'Bodily shame as a mediator between abusive experiences and depression', *Journal of Abnormal Psychology*, 104: 277–285.

Andrews, B. and Brown, G.W. (1995) 'Stability and change in low self-esteem: the role of psychosocial factors', *Psychological Medicine*, 25: 23–31.

Angel, J.L., Kelley, J.O., Parrington, M. and Pinter, S. (1987) 'Life stresses of the free black community as represented by the First African Baptist Church, Philadelphia, 1823–1841', *American Journal of Physical Anthropology*, 74: 213–229.

Anglin, L. (1994) 'Self-identified correlates of problem alcohol and drug use with comparisons between substances', *International Journal of the Addictions*, 29: 285–302.

Angold, A. and Worthman, C.W. (1993) 'Puberty onset of gender differences in rates of depression: a developmental, epidemiologist and neuro-endocrine perspective', *Journal of Affective Disorders*, 29: 145–158.

Anokute, C.C. (1986) 'Epidemiology of Spontaneous Abortion; The Effects of Alcohol Consumption and Cigarette Smoking', *Journal of the National Medical Association*, 78: 771–775.

Anonymous (1881) 'A New Hospital in a New Field', *Alienist and Neurologist*, January:2: 283.

Anonymous (1890a) 'State Hospital for the Insane at Norristown P.A. – Tenth Annual Report', *Alienist and Neurologist*, July, 11: 478–479.

Anonymous (1890b) 'Chloralamide: A new hypnotic', *Alienist and Neurologist*, January, 11: 92–94.

Anonymous (1987) 'Historic trials: Montreal Tramways v. Leveille (1933) 4 DLR 338', *Human Reproduction*, 2: 349–359.

Anti-Saloon Year Book (1909), Massachusetts State Board Analyst Doc. 34.

Appel, C. (1988) 'From temperance to codependency or: The discovery of the invisible alcoholic researched in regard to the ideas about women and alcohol in the history of the USA since the 1970s', Paper prepared for Alcohol Research Group, Berkeley, California.

Appignanesi, L. and Forrester, J. (1992) *Freud's Women*, London, George Weidenfeld and Nicolson Ltd.

Araya, R. (1994) 'Women's drinking and society', *Addiction*, 89: 954–956.

Arellano, C.M. (1996) 'Child maltreatment and substance abuse: A review of the literature', *Substance Use and Misuse*, 31: 927–935.

Argeriou, M., McCarty, D., Mulvey, K. and Daley, M. (1994) 'Use of the Addiction Severity Index with homeless substance abusers', *Journal of Substance Abuse Treatment*, 11: 359–365.

Armor, D.J., Polich, J.M. and Stambul, H.B. (1978) *Alcoholism and Treatment*, New York, John Wiley and Sons.

Armstrong-Jones, R. (1923) 'Puerperal insanity', *Lancet* 1: 1297.

Armsworth, M.W. (1990) 'A qualitative analysis of adult incest survivors' responses to sexual involvement with therapists', *Child Abuse and Neglect*, 14: 541–554.

Arokiasamy, C.V. (1995) 'Malaysia', in Heath, D.B., (ed.) *International Handbook on Alcohol and Culture*, Connecticut, Greenwood Press, 168–178.

Arriaza, B., Allison, M. and Gerszten, E. (1988) 'Maternal mortality in pre-Columbian Indians of Arica, Chile', *American Journal of Physical Anthropology*, 77: 35–41.

Asch, S.S. (1985) 'Depression and demonic possession: the analyst as an exorcist', *Hillside Journal of Clinical Psychology*, 7: 149–164.

Ashley, M.J., Olin, J.S., Le Riche, W.H., Kornaczewski, A., Schmidt, W. and Rankin, J.G. (1977) 'Skid Row alcoholism: A distinct sociomedical entity', *Annals of Internal Medicine*, 137: 883–887.

Ashour, A.M. (1995) 'Egypt', in Heath, D.B., (ed.) *International Handbook on Alcohol and Culture*, Connecticut, Greenwood Press, 63–74.

Ásmundsson, G. (1995) 'Iceland', in Heath, D.B., (ed.) *International Handbook on Alcohol and Culture*, Connecticut, Greenwood Press, 117–127.

Assembly of Life Sciences, Diet, Nutrition and Cancer (1983) 'Executive summary of the report of the Committee', *Cancer Research*, 43: 3018–3023.

Atkinson, R.M. (1992) 'Treatment programs for aging alcoholics', in Beresford, T.M. and Gomberg, E.S.L. (eds) *Alcohol and Aging*, New York, Oxford University Press, 186–210.

Audience Selection (1993) 'Survey of sexual behaviour conducted for the UK newspaper the *Sunday Mirror*', 3 January, 25–27.

Audigier, J.C., Tuyns, A.J. and Lambert, R. (1975) 'Epidemiology of oesophageal cancer in France. Increasing mortality and persistant correlation with alcoholism', *Digestion*, 13: 209–219.

Autti-Ramo, I., Korkman, M., Hilakivi-Clarke, L., Lehtonen, M., Halmesmäki, E. and Granstrom, M.L. (1992) 'Mental development of 2-year-old children exposed to alcohol in utero', *Journal of Pediatrics*, 120: 740–746.

Avins, A.L., Lindan, C.P., Eludes, E.S., Clark, W. and Eiulley, S.B. (1994) 'HIV infection and risk behaviors among heterosexuals in alcohol treatment programs', *Journal of the American Medical Association*, 16: 515–518.

Ayanian, J.Z. and Epstein, A.M. (1991) 'Differences in the use of procedures between women and men hospitalised for coronary heart disease', *New England Journal of Medicine*, 325: 221–225.

Ayoob, K.T. (1996) 'Chronic overeating without obesity in children with developmental disabilities: description of a new syndrome', *Mental Retardation*, 32: 194–199.

Ayoub, C., Jacewitz, M.M., Gold, R.G. and Milner, J.S. (1983) 'Assessment of a program's effectiveness in selecting individuals "at risk" for problems in parenting', *Journal of Clinical Psychology*, 39: 334–339.

Babinski, H. (1893) 'Associations of hysteria with organic diseases of the nervous system, neuroses and other affections', *Alienist and Neurologist*, April 2,14: 272–283.

Babor, T., Brown, J. and del Boca, F.K. (1990) 'Validity of self-reports in applied research on addictive behaviors: Fact or fiction?' *Behavioral Assessment*, 12: 5–31.

Babor, T.F. and Lauerman, R.J. (1986) 'Classification and forms of inebriety: Historical antecedents of alcoholic typologies', in Galanter, M. (ed.) *Recent Developments in Alcoholism*, Vol. 4, New York, Plenum, 113–144.

Bachmann, G.A. (1990) 'Hysterectomy: A critical review', *Journal of Reproductive Medicine*, 35: 839–862.

Baer, J.S. (1993) 'Etiology and secondary prevention of alcohol problems with young adults', in Baer, J.S., Marlatt, G.A. and McMahon, R.J., (eds) *Addictive Behaviors Across the Life Span*, London, Sage Publications Ltd, 111–137.

Baer, J.S., Kivlahan, D.R. and Marlatt, G.A. (1995) 'High-risk drinking across the transition from high school to college', *Alcoholism, Clinical and Experimental Research*, 19: 54–61.

Baer, J.S., Marlatt, G.A. and McMahon, R.J. (1993) *Addictive Behaviors*

Across the Lifespan: Prevention Treatment and Policy, London, Sage Publications Ltd.

Bagnall, G. (1991) *Educating Young Drinkers*, London, Tavistock/Routledge.

Bagnall, G. and Plant, M.A. (1991a) 'AIDS risks, alcohol and illicit drug use amongst young adults in areas of high and low rates of HIV infection', *AIDS Care*, 3: 355–361.

Bagnall, G. and Plant, M.A. (1991b) 'Education on drugs and alcohol: Past disappointments and future challenges', *Health Education Research*, 2: 417–422.

Bahr, S.J., Marcos, A.C. and Maughan, S.L. (1995) 'Family, educational and peer influences on the alcohol use of female and male adolescents', *Journal of Studies on Alcohol*, 56: 457–469.

Bailly, R.C., Carman, R.S. and Forslund, M.A. (1991) 'Gender differences in drinking motivations and outcomes', *Journal of Psychology*, 125: 649–656.

Bain, C., Willett, W., Hennekens, C.H. et al. (1981) 'Use of postmenopausal hormones and risk of myocardial infarction', *Circulation*, 64: 42–46.

Bair, D. (1990) 'Simone de Beauvoir. A Biography', London, Jonathon Cape.

Baischer, W., Koinig, G., Hartmann, B., Huber, J. and Langer, G. (1995) 'Hypothalamic-pituitary-gonadal axis in depressed premenopausal women: elevated blood testosterone concentrations compared to normal controls', *Psychoneuroendocrinology*, 20: 553–559.

Baker, D. (1977) *Alcoholism: The Hidden Significance*, 2nd edn. Hertfordshire, Baker Publications.

Baker, H.S. and Baker, M.N. (1987) 'Heinz Kohut's self psychology: an overview', *American Journal of Psychiatry*, 144: 1–9.

Baker, K. and Beer, J. (1991) 'Self-esteem, alcoholism, sensation seeking, GPA, and Differential Aptitude test scores of high school students in an honor society', *Psychological Reports*, 69: 1147–1150.

Baker, L.W. (1892) 'Drug habituation', *Alienist and Neurologist*, April 13: 276–285.

Baker, R.C. and Jerrells, T.R. (1993) 'Immunological aspects', in Galanter, M. (ed.) *Recent Developments in Alcoholism, Volume 11: Ten Years of Progress*, New York, Plenum, 249–266.

Baldwin, V.J., Macleod, P.M. and Benirschke, K. (1982) 'Placental findings in alcohol abuse in pregnancy', *Birth Defects*, Original Article Series, 18: 3A: 89–94.

Bale, A. (1989) 'Hope in another direction: Compensation for work-related illness among women, 1900–1960: Part II', *Women and Health*, 15: 99–115.

Balla, A.K., Lischner, H.W., Pomerantz, R.J. and Bagasra, O. (1994) Human studies on alcohol and susceptibility to HIV infection', *Ale*, 11: 99–103.

Ballantyne, J.W. (1904) *Manual of Antenatal Pathology and Hygiene*, Edinburgh, William Green.

Bandler, R. and Grinder, J. (1979) *Frogs Into Princes*, Moab, Utah, Real People Press.

Bandy, P. and President, P.A. (1983) 'Recent literature on drug abuse and prevention and mass media: focusing on youth, parents, women and elderly', *Journal of Drug Education*, 13: 255–271.

Bannister (1886) 'Affinity of the insanely disposed for each other', *Alienist and Neurologist*, July 7, 3: 507.

Banyard, V.L. and Graham-Bermann, S.A. (1993) 'Can women cope? a gender analysis of theories of coping with stress', *Psychology of Women Quarterly*, 17: 303–318.

Barber, J.G. and Crisp, B.R. (1995) 'The 'pressures to change' approach to working with the partners of heavy drinkers', *Addiction*, 90: 269–276.

Barboriak, J.J. and Meade, R.C. (1970) 'Effect of alcohol on gastric emptying in man', *American Journal of Clinical Nutrition*, 23: 1151–1153.

Barger, J. (1991) 'Coping behaviors of U.S. Army flight nurses in World War II: an oral history', *Aviation, Space and Environmental Medicine*, 62: 153–157.

Barnard, C.P. (1989) 'Alcoholism and sex abuse in the family: Incest and marital rape', *Journal of Chemical Dependency Treatment*, 30: 131–144.

Baron, J.A. (1984) 'Smoking and estrogen-related disease', *American Journal of Epidemiology*, 119: 9–22.

Barr, A. (1995) *Drink: An Informal Social History*, London, Bantam Press.

Barr, H.M., Streissguth, A.P., Martin D.C. and Herman, C.S. (1984) 'Infant size at 8 months of age: relationship to maternal use of alcohol, nicotine, and caffeine during pregnancy', *Pediatrics*, 74: 336–341.

Barrett, D.H., Anda, R.F., Croft, J.B., Serdula, M.K. and Lane, M.J. (1995) 'The association between alcohol use and health behaviors related to the risk of cardiovascular disease', *Journal of Studies on Alcohol*, 56: 9–15.

Barrett, M.E., Wong, F.Y. and McKay, D.R. (1993) 'Self-reported alcohol use among women of childbearing age and their knowledge of alcohol warning labels and signs', *Archives of Family Medicine*, 2: 1260–1264.

Barrett-Connor, E. and Goodman-Gruen, D. (1995) 'Prospective study of endogenous sex hormones and fatal cardiovascular disease in post menopausal women', *British Medical Journal*, 311: 1193–1196

Barron, D.H.K (1976) 'Paul Zweifel, pioneer fetal physiologist. A centennary tribute', *Archiv Fur Gynakologie*, 221: 1–4.

Barthwell, A.G. (1995) 'Alcoholism in the family: A muliticultural exploration', in Galanter, M., (ed.) *Recent Developments on Alcoholism: Vol 12: Alcoholism and Women*, New York, Plenum Press, 387–407.

Barwell, R. (1886) 'Oophorectomy and insanity', *Alienist and Neurologist*, July 1, 3: 507–510.

Bates, M.E. (1993) 'Psychology', in Galanter, M. (ed.) *Recent Developments in Alcoholism: Volume 11, Ten Years of Progress*, New York, Plenum, 45–72.

Baum, A. and Grunberg, N.E. (1991) 'Gender, stress, and health', *Health Psychology*, 10: 80–85.

Baumbach, J. and Turner, L.A. (1992) 'Female gender disorder: A new model and clinical applications. Special issue: gender dysphoria: Interdisciplinary approaches in clinical management', *Journal of Psychology of Human Sexuality*, 5: 107–129.

Bayatpour, M., Wells, R.D. and Holford, S. (1992) 'Physical and sexual abuse as predictors of substance use and suicide among pregnant teenagers', *Journal of Adolescent Health*, 13: 128–132.

Bazopoulou-Kyrkanidou, E. (1992) 'Genetic concepts in Greek literature from the eighth to the fourth century B.C.', *Human Genetics*, 88: 500–507.

Bean, M.H. (1981) 'Denial and psychological complications of alcoholism', in Bean, M.H. and Zinberg, N.E., (eds) *Dynamic Approaches to the Understanding and Treatment of Alcoholism*, New York, Free Press, 55–96.

Bean, M.H. and Zinberg, N.E. (1981) *Dynamic Approaches to the Understanding and Treatment of Alcoholism*, New York, Free Press.

Beane, V.A. and Beck, J.C. (1991) 'Court based civil commitment of alcoholics and substance abusers', *Bulletin of the American Academy of Psychiatry and the Law*, 19: 359–366.

Beattie, M. (1989) *Beyond Codependency and Getting Better all the Time*, New York, Harper and Row.

Beattie, M. (1992) *Codependent No More: How to Stop Controlling Others and Start Caring for Yourself*, San Francisco, HarperCollins.

Beaumont, T. (1841–42) 'Remarks made in opposition to the views of Dr Clutterbuck', *Lancet*, 2: 340–343.

Beck, A.T., Ward, C.H., Mendelson, M., Mock, J. and Erbaugh, J. (1961) 'An inventory for measuring depression', *Archives of General Psychiatry*, 4: 561–571.

Becker, M.H. and Maiman, L.A. (1980) 'Strategies for enhancing patient compliance', *Journal of Community Health*, 6: 113–135.

Beckman, L.J. (1978) 'Self–esteem in women alcoholics', *Journal of Studies on Alcohol*, 39: 491–498.

Beckman, L.J. (1979) 'Reported effects of alcohol on the sexual feelings and behaviour of women alcoholics, and non-alcoholics', Journal of Studies on Alcohol, 40,3: 272–282.

Beckman, L.J. (1994) 'Treatment needs of women with alcohol problems. *Alcohol: Health and Research World*, 18: 206–211.

Beckman, L.J. and Ackerman, K.T. (1995) 'Women, alcohol, and sexuality', *Recent Developments in Alcoholism*, Vol. 12: New York, Plenum Press. 267–285.

Beckman, L.J. and Amaro, H. (1986) 'Personal and social difficulties faced by women and men entering alcoholism treatment', *Journal of Studies on Alcohol*, 47: 135–145.

Beckman, L.J. and Bardsley, P.E. (1986) 'Individual characteristics, gender differences and dropout from alcoholism treatment', *Alcohol and Alcoholism*, 21: 213–224.

Beckman, L.J. and Mays, V.E. (1985) 'Educating community gatekeepers about alcohol abuse in women: Changing attitudes, knowledge and referral practices', *Journal of Drug Education*, 15: 289–309.

Beeber, L.S. (1990) 'To be one of the boys: aftershocks of the World War I nursing experience', *Advances In Nursing Science*, 12: 32–43.

Begg, C.B., Walker, A.M., Wesson, B. and Zelen, M. (1983) 'Alcohol consumption and breast cancer', *Lancet*, 1: 293–294.

Beitchman, J.H., Zucker, K.J., Hood, J.E., Da Costa, G.A. and Akman, D. (1991) 'A review of the short-term effects of child abuse', *Child Abuse and Neglect*, 15: 537–555.

Beitchman, J.H., Zucker, K.J., Hood, J.E., Da Costa, G.A. and Cassavia, E. (1992) 'A review of the long-term effects of child sexual abuse', *Child Abuse and Neglect*, 16: 101–118.

Belfer, M.L., Shader, R.I., Carroll, M. and Harmatz, J.S. (1971) 'Alcoholism in women', *Archives of General Psychiatry*, 25: 540–544.

Bell, S.E. (1987) 'Changing ideas: the medicalization of menopause', *Social Science and Medicine*, 24: 535–542.

Belliveau, J.M. and Stoppard, J.M. (1995) 'Parental alcohol abuse and gender as predictors of psychopathology in adult children of alcoholics', *Addictive Behaviors*, 20,5: 619–625.

Benirschke, K. (1991) 'The placenta in the context of history and modern medical practice', *Archives of Pathology and Laboratory Medicine*, 115: 663–667.

Benishek, L.A., Bieschke, K.J., Stoffelmayr, B.E., Mavis, B.E. and Humphreys, K.A. (1992) 'Gender differences in depression and anxiety among alcoholics', *Journal of Substance Abuse*, 4: 235–245.

Bennet, A. (1890) 'Insanity as a symptom of "Bright's Disease"', *Alienist and Neurologist*, October, 11: 566–605.

Bennett, E.M. and Kemper, K.J. (1994) 'Is abuse during childhood a risk factor for developing substance-abuse problems as an adult?' *Journal of Developmental and Behavioral Pediatrics*, 15: 426–429.

Bennett, L.A. (1995) 'Accountability for alcoholism in American families', *Social Science and Medicine*, 40: 15–25.

Bennett, L.A. and LaBonte, M. (1993) 'Family systems', *Recent Developments in Alcoholism*, Vol. 11: New York, Plenum Press, 87–94.

Bennett, L.J. (1993) *Before the Mayflower: A History of Black America*, 6th edn. London, Penguin Books.

Bennett, N., Jarvis, L., Rowlands, O., Singleton, N. and Haselden, L. (1996) *Living in Britain; Results From the 1994 General Household Survey*, London, HMSO.

Bennett, P., Smith, C. and Nugent, Z. (1991) 'Patterns of drinking in Wales', *Alcohol and Alcoholism*, 26: 367–374.

Bennie, C. (1996) 'Reconsidering home detoxification for problem drinkers', paper presented at 22nd Alcohol Epidemiology Symposium, Kettil Bruun Society, Edinburgh,

Benoit, M. (1993) 'Impact of violence on children and adolescents: report from a community-based child psychiatry clinic', *Psychiatry*, 56: 124.

Ben-Shlomo, Y., Marklowe, H., Shipley, M. and Marmot, M. (1991) 'Stroke risk from alcohol consumption using different control groups', *Stroke*, 23: 1093–1098.

Benson, J.F. (1995) *Working More Creatively With Groups*, London, Routledge.

Bepko, C. (1991) *Feminism and Addiction*, New York, Haworth Press.

Beral, V., Fraser, P. and Chilvers, C. (1978) 'Does pregnancy protect against ovarian cancer?' *Lancet*, 1: 1083–1087.

Beresford, T.P. (1995) 'Alcoholic elderly: Prevalence, diagnosis and prognosis', in Beresford, T.P. and Gomberg, E.S.L. (eds) *Alcohol and Aging*, New York, Oxford University Press, 3–18.

Beresford, T.P. and Gomberg, E.S.L. (eds) (1995) *Alcohol and Aging*, New York, Oxford University Press.

Beresford, T.P. and Lucey, M.R. (1992) 'Ethanaol metabolism and intoxication in the elderly', in Beresford, T.P. and Gomberg, E.S.L. (eds) *Alcohol and Aging*, New York, Oxford University Press, 117–127.

Berg, S.L. (1993) *Jewish Alcoholism and Drug Addiction: An Annotated Bibliography*, Westport, Connecticut, Greenwood Press.

Bergamaschi, A., Zanetti, F., Stampi, S. and De Luca, G. (1995) 'Consumption, behaviour and knowledge with respect to alcoholic drinks in student nurses in the province of Bologna, Italy', *European Journal of Epidemiology*, 11: 185–191.

Berger, B.D. and Adesso, V.J. (1991) 'Gender differences in using alcohol to cope with depression', *Addictive Behaviors*, 16: 315–327.

Berger, D., Ono, Y., Saito, S., Tezuka, I., Takahashi, Y., Uno, M., Ishikawa, Y., Kuboki, T., Asai, M. and Suematsu, H. (1995) 'Relationship of parental bonding to child abuse and dissociation in eating disorders in Japan', *Acta Psychiatrica Scandinavica*, 91: 278–282.

Bergman, B. and Brismar, B. (1994) 'Characteristics of violent alcoholics', *Alcohol and Alcoholism*, 29: 451–457.

Bernard, J. (1981) *The Female World*, New York, The Free Press, Macmillan Publishing Co. Inc.

Bernardi, E., Jones, M. and Tennant, C. (1989) 'Quality of parenting in alcoholic and narcotic addicts', *British Journal of Psychiatry*, 154: 677–682.

Berne, E. (1961) *Transactional Analysis in Psychotherapy*, New York, Grove.

Berne, E. (1975) *What Do You Say After You Say Hello?* London, Corgi.

Bernheimer, C. and Kahane, C. (1985) *In Dora's Case: Freud, Hysteria and Feminism*, London, Virago Press Ltd.

Berridge, V. and Edwards, G. (1981) *Opium and the People*, London, Allen Lane.

Berry, L.G. (1977) 'Age and parity influences on maternal mortality: United States, 1919–1969', *Demography*, 14: 297–310.

Besharov, D.J. (1992) *Mandatory Reporting of Child Abuse and Research on the Effects of Prenatal Drug Exposure*, NIDA Research Monograph 117 ISS: 366–384.

Best (1880) *Medical Orders*, London, British Women's Temperance Association.

Bewley, C.A. (1991) 'Violence in pregnancy', *Midwifery*, 7: 107–112.

Bidaut-Russell, M., Bradford, S.E. and Smith, E.M. (1994) 'Prevalence of mental illnesses in adult offspring of alcoholic mothers', *Drug and Alcohol Dependence*, 35: 81–90.

Bidaut-Russell, M., Smith, E.M. and Bradford, S.E. (1994) 'Gender differences in lifetime psychiatric disorders between sons and daughters of alcoholic mothers: a pilot study', *Alcoholism, Clinical and Experimental Research,* 18: 224–247.

Bickle, D.D. (1993) 'Alcohol-induced bone disease', in Simopoulos, A.P. and Galli, C. (eds) *Osteoporosis: Nutritional Aspects*, Basel, Karger, 53–79.

Bickle, D.D., Stesin, A., Halloran, A.S.B. et al. (1993) 'Alcohol-induced bone disease: Relationship to age and parathyroid hormone levels', *Alcoholism: Clinical and Experimental Research*, 17: 690–695.

Billingham, R.E., Parrillo, A.V. and Gross, W.C. (1993) 'Reasons given by college students for drinking: a discriminant analysis investigation', *International Journal of the Addictions*, 28: 793–802.

Billingham, R.E., Post, J. and Gross, W.C. (1993) 'Parental divorce and the change in drinking behavior from high school to college', *Psychological Reports*, 1275–1281.

Bittles, A.H., McHugh, J.J. and Makov, E. (1986) 'The Irish Famine and its sequel: population structure changes in the Ards Peninsula, Co. Down, 1841–1911', *Annals of Human Biology,* 13: 473–487.

Bjorkly, S. (1995) 'Trauma and violence: the role of early abuse in the aggressive behavior of two violent psychotic women', *Bulletin of the Menninger Clinic*, 59: 205–220.

Bjorneboe, A., Johnsen, J., Skylv, N., Oftebro, H., Gautvik, K.M., Hoiseth, J., Morland, J. and Dervon, C.A. (1988) 'Calcium status and calcium-regulating hormones in alcoholics', *Alcoholism: Clinical and Experimental Research,* 12: 229–232.

Black, C., Bucky, S.F. and Wilder-Padilla, S. (1986) 'The interpersonal and emotional consequences of being an adult child of an alcoholic', *International Journal of the Addictions*, 21: 213–231.

Black, R. and Mayer, J. (1980) 'Parents with special problems: Alcoholism and opiate addiction', *Child Abuse and Neglect,* 4: 45–54.

Blakemore, K.J. (1990) 'Prenatal diagnosis: historical and futuristic perspectives', *Maryland Medical Journal,* 39: 325–329.

Blane, D. (1990) 'Real wages, the economic cycle, and mortality in England and Wales, 1870–1914', *International Journal of Health Services,* 20: 43–52.

Blankfield, A. (1991a) 'Genetic and marital status in alcohol dependent women', *Drug and Alcohol Dependence,* 27: 95–100.

Blankfield, A. (1991b) 'Women, alcohol dependence and crime', *Drug and Alcohol Dependence*, 27: 185–190.

Blennerhassett, R., Sohneider, A., Tubridy, P., Oloideain, D.S. and Shelley, R.K. (1993) 'Cognitive dysfunction in recently detoxified female alcoholics', *Irish Journal of Psychological Medicine*, 10: 6–8.

Blodgett, A.N. (1883) 'The management of chronic inebriates and insane drunkards', *Alienist and Neurologist,* January, 4: 36–57.

Blood, L., and Cornwall, A. (1994) 'Pretreatment variables that predict completion of an adolescent substance abuse treatment programme', *Journal of Nervous and Mental Disease*, 182: 14–19.

Bloomfield, K. (1993) 'A comparison of alcohol consumption between lesbians and heterosexual women in an urban population', *Drug and Alcohol Dependence*, 33: 257–269.

Blum, H.P. (1990) 'Freud, Fliess, and the parenthood of psychoanalysis', *Psychoanalytic Quarterly*, 59: 21–40.

Blum, T.C. and Roman, P.M. (1995) 'Women and Work', in Wilsnack, R.W. and Wilsnack, S.C., (eds) *Gender and Alcohol*, New Brunswick, New Jersey, Center for Alcohol Studies, Rutgers University.

Blum, T.C., Roman, P.M. and Harwood, E.M. (1995) 'Employed women with alcohol problems who seek help from employee assistance programs: Description and comparisons', in Galanter, M., (ed.) *Recent Developments in Alcoholism: Vol 12: Alcoholism and Women*, New York, Plenum Press, 125–156.

Blumberg, L.U. (1978) 'The institutional phase of the Washington Total Abstinence Movement. A research note', *Journal of Studies on Alcohol*, 39: 1591–1606.

Blumberg, M. (1974) 'Psychopathopology of the abusing parent', *American Journal of Psychotherapy*, 28: 21–29.

Blumberg, M.A. and Billig, O. (1942) 'Hormonal influence upon "puerperal psychosis" and neurotic conditions', *Psychiatric Quarterly*, 16: 454.

Blumhagen, J.M., and Little, R.E. (1985) 'Reliability of retrospective estimates of alcohol consumption during pregnancy by recovering alcoholics', *Journal of Studies on Alcohol*, 46: 86–88.

Bochner, S. (1994) 'The effectiveness of same-sex versus opposite-sex role models in advertisements to reduce alcohol consumption in teenagers', *Addictive Behaviors*, 19: 69–82.

Bolen, J.S. (1994) *Crossing to Avalon: A Woman's Midlife Pilgrimage*, New York, HarperCollins Publishers.

Bond, A.H. (1985) 'Virginia Woolf: manic-depressive psychosis and genius. An illustration of separation-individuation theory', *Journal of the American Academy of Psychoanalysis*, 13: 191–210.

Bone, J. (1926) *The Perambulator in Edinburgh*, London, Jonathan Cape.

Boomsma, D.I., Koopmans, J.R., Van Doornen, L.J. and Orlebeke, J.F. (1994) 'Genetic and social influences on starting to smoke: a study of Dutch adolescent twins and their parents', *Addiction*, 89: 219–226.

Boothroyd, W.E. (1980) 'Nature and development of alcoholism in women', in Kalant, O.J. (ed.) *Research Advances in Alcohol and Drug Problems, Volume 5: Alcohol and Drug Problems in Women*, New York, Plenum, 299–329.

Bordahl, P.E. (1984) 'Tubal sterilization. A prospective long term investigation of 218 sterilized women', *Acta Obstetricia Gynecologica Scandinavica*, Supplement 128: 1–56.

Borges, G., Lopez-Cervantes, M., Medina-Mora, M.E., Tapiaconyer, R. and Garrido, F. (1993) 'Alcohol consumption, low birth weight, and preterm delivery in the national addiction survey', *International Journal of the Addictions*, 28: 355–368.

Bos, C. (1950) 'Psychiatry in Obstetrics', *McGill Medical Journal*, 19: 176.

Bouhoutsos, J., Holroyd, J.C., Lerman, H., Forer, B.R. and Greenberg, M. (1983) 'Sexual Intimacy between Psychotherapists and Patients', *Professional Psychology: Research and Practice*, 14: 185–196.

Boyd, C.J., Blow, F. and Orgain, L.S. (1993) 'Gender differences among African-American substance abusers', *Journal of Psychoactive Drugs*, 25: 301–305.

Boyd, D.A., Jr (1942) 'Mental disorders associated with childbearing', *American Journal of Obstetrics and Gynecology*, 43: 148.

Boyle, P.P. and O'Grada, C. (1986) 'Fertility trends, excess mortality, and the Great Irish Famine', *Demography*, 23: 543–562.

Boysen, G., Nyboe, J., Appleyard, M. et al. (1988) 'Stroke incidence and risk factors for stroke in Copenhagen', *Stroke*, 19: 1345–1353.

Brace, K.D. (1991) 'Women's body images: the impact of alcohol/drug abuse on body–cathexis scores', *Psychology: A Journal of Human Behavior*, 28.

Bradford, J.M., Greenberg, D.M. and Motayne, G.G. (1992) 'Substance abuse and criminal behavior', *Psychiatric Clinics of North America*, 15: 605–622.

Bradley, R.H., and Caldwell, B.M. (1984) 'A study of the relationship between home environment and cognitive development during the first 5 years', in Gottfried, A.W. (ed.) *Home Environment and Cognitive Development: Longitudinal Research*, New York, Academy Press, 5–56.

Brady, K.T. and Lydiard, R.B. (1993) 'The association of alcoholism and anxiety', *Psychiatric Quarterly*, 64: 135–149.

Bragan, K. (1996) *Self and Spirit in the Therapeutic Relationship*, London, Routledge.

Branch, C.N. (1962) 'Pregnancy and psychiatry', *Rocky Mountain Medical Journal*, 59: 37.

Brandt, P.A., Goldbohm, R.A., and van de Veer, P. (1995) 'Alcohol and breast cancer: Results from a Netherlands cohort study', *American Journal of Epidemiology*, 141: 907–915.

Bray, R.M., Marsden, M.E. and Peterson, M.R. (1991) 'Standardized comparisons of the use of alcohol, drugs, and cigarettes among military personnel and civilians', *American Journal of Public Health*, 81: 865–869.

Brazier, D. (1993) *Beyond Carl Rogers: Towards Psychotherapy in the 21st Century*, London, Constable and Company Ltd.

Breeze, E. (1985) *Women and Alcohol*, London: HMSO.

Breggin, P. (1993) *Toxic Psychiatry*, London, HarperCollins Publishers.

Brehm, N., Khantzian, E.J. and Dodes, L.M. (1993) 'Psychodynamic approaches', in Galanter, M., (ed.) *Recent Developments in Alcoholism: Vol 11: Ten Years of Progress*, New York, Plenum Press, 453–471.

Brennan A.F., Walfish, S. and Aubuchon, P. (1986) 'Alcohol use and abuse in college students. 1. A review of individual and personality correlates', *International Journal of the Addictions*, 21: 449–474.

Brennan, P.L. and Moos, R.H. (1992) 'Life context, coping responses, and adaptive outcomes: A stress and coping perspective on late-life problem drinking', in Beresford, T.P. and Gomberg, E.S.L. (eds) *Alcohol and Aging*, New York, Oxford University Press, 230–259.

Brennan, P.L., Moos, R.H, and Kim, J.Y. (1993) 'Gender differences in the individual characteristics and life contexts of late-middle-aged and older problem drinkers', *Addiction*, 88: 781–790.

Breslin, F.C. and Baum, A. (1994) 'Effect of stress on perceived intoxication and the blood alcohol curve in men and women', *Health Psychology*, 13: 479–487.

Breslow, E.R. and Enstrom, J.E. (1974) 'Geographic correlations between cancer mortality rates and alcohol–tobacco consumption in the United States', *Journal of the National Cancer Institute*, 53: 631–639.

Bresnahan, K., Zuckerman, B. and Cabral, H. (1992) 'Psychosocial correlates of drug and heavy alcohol use among pregnant women at risk for drug use', *Obstetrics and Gynecology*, 80: 976–980.

Brewers and Licensed Retailers Association (formerly the Brewers Society) (1995) *Statistical Handbook*, London, Brewers and Licensed Retailers Association.

Brewington, V., Smith, M. and Lipton, D. (1994) 'Acupuncture as a detoxification treatment: An analysis of controlled research', *Journal of Substance Abuse Treatment*, 11: 289–307.

Brick, J., Nathan, P.E., Westrick, E., et al. (1986) 'The effect of menstrual cycle on blood alcohol levels and behavior', *Journal of Studies on Alcohol*, 47: 472–477.

Briere, J. (1992) *Child Abuse Trauma: Theory and Treatment of the Lasting Effects*, Newbury Park, Sage.

Brinton, L.A., Hoover, R. and Fraumeni, J.F.J. (1982) 'Interaction of familial and hormonal risk factors for breast cancer', *Journal of the National Institute*, 69: 817–822.

Brinton, L.A., Schairer, C., Stanford, J.L. and Hoover, R.N. (1986) 'Cigarette smoking and breast cancer', *American Journal of Epidemiology*, 123: 614–622.

Briquet, P. (1859) *Traite Clinique et Thérapeutique de l'Hysterie*, Paris: J.B. Bailliere.

Brisbane, F.L. and Womble, M. (eds) (1985) *Treatment of Black Alcoholics*, New York, Haworth.

British Medical Journal (1986) (news item) 'Russia faces demographic crisis', 313: 385.

Broaden, R.N. and Boa, K.L. (1991) 'Flumazenil: A reappraisal of its pharmacological properties and therapeutic efficacy as a benzodiazepine antagonist', *Drugs*, 42: 1061–1089.

Brontë, C. (1989) *Shirley*, reprinted in 1985, London, Penguin.

Brooke, O.G., Anderson, H.R., Bland, J.M., Peacock, J.L. and Stewart, C.M. (1989) 'Effects on birth weight of smoking, alcohol, caffeine, socioeconomic factors, and psychosocial stress', *British Medical Journal*, 298: 795–801.

Brosius (1886) 'The use of alcohol in nervous diseases', *Alienist and Neurologist*, July 7,3: 506.

Brosky, G. (1995) 'Why do pregnant women smoke and can we help them quit?', *Canadian Medical Association Journal*, 152: 163–166.

Browne, A. (1986) 'Impact of child abuse: A review of the research', *Psychological Bulletin*, 99: 66–77.

Browne, A. and Finkelhor, D. (1986) 'Impact of child sexual abuse: A review of the research', *Psychological Bulletin*, 99,1: 66–77.

Brown, G.W., Harris, T.O. and Hepworth, C. (1995) 'Loss, humiliation and entrapment among women developing depression: a patient and non-patient comparison', *Psychological Medicine*, 25: 7–21.

Brown, J., Babor, T.F., Litt, M.D. and Kranzler, H.R. (1994) 'The type A/type B distinction. Subtyping alcoholics according to indicators of vulnerability and severity', *Annals of the New York Academy of Sciences*, 708: 23–33.

Brown, S. (1991) 'Adult children of alcoholics: The history of a social movement and its impact on clinical theory and practice', in Galanter, M. (ed.) *Recent Developments in Alcoholism, Vol. 9*, New York, Plenum, 267–285.

Brown-Sequard (1889) 'Fons Vitae', *Alienist and Neurologist*, 10,4: 651.

Browne, A. (1993) 'Violence against women by male partners', *American Psychologist*, 48: 1077–1087.

Browne-Miller, A. (1993) *Gestalting Addiction: The Addiction-Focused Group Psychotherapy of Dr Richard Louis Miller*, Norwood, New Jersey, Ablex.

Brudevoll, J.E., Liestol, K. and Walloe, L. (1979) 'Menarcheal age in Oslo during the last 140 years', *Annals of Human Biology*, 6: 407–416.

Bruix, J., Barrera, J.M., Calvet, X. et al. (1989) 'Prevalence of antibodies to hepatitis C virus in Spanish patients with heptocellular carcinoma and cirrhosis', *Lancet*, 2: 1004–1006.

Brumbaugh, A.G. (1993) 'Acupuncture: new perspectives in chemical dependency treatment', *Journal of Substance Abuse Treatment*, 10: 35–43.

Brumberg, J.J. (1982) 'Chlorotic girls, 1870–1920: a historical perspective on female adolescence', *Child Development*, 53: 1468–1477.

Brundtland, G.H. and Walloe, L. (1976) 'Menarcheal age in Norway in the 19th century: a re-evaluation of the historical sources', *Annals of Human Biology*, 3: 363–374.

Bruno, F. (1989) 'Buspirone in the Treatment of Alcoholic Patients', *Psychopathology*, 22, Supplement 1: 49–59.

Bruun, K., Edwards, G., Lumio, M., Mäkelä, K., Pan, I., Popham, R.E., Room, R., Schmidt, W., Skog, Ø.-J., Sulkunan, P. and Österberg, E. (1975) *Alcohol Control Policies in Public Health Perspective*, Helsinki, Finnish Foundation for Alcohol Studies.

Bucholz, K.K., Homan, S.M. and Helzer, J.E. (1992) 'When do alcoholics first discuss drinking problems?' *Journal of Studies on Alcohol*, 53: 582–589.

Bucholz, K.K., Sheline, Y.I., and Helzer, J.E. (1992) 'The epidemiology of alcohol use, problems and dependence in elders: A review', in Beresford, T.P. and Gomberg, E. (eds) *Alcohol and Aging*, New York, Oxford University Press, 19–41.

Buckner, J.C., Bassuk, E.L. and Zima, B.T. (1993) 'Mental health issues affecting homeless women: implications for intervention', *American Journal of Orthopsychiatry*, 63: 385–399.

Budd, S. and Sharma, U. (1994) *The Healing Bond: The Patient Practitioner Relationship and Therapeutic Responsibility*, London, Routledge.

Buist, A. (1995) 'Childhood sexual abuse and adult psychopathology, relevant in general practice', *Australian Family Physician*, 24: 1229–1231.

Bulik, C.M. and Brinded, E.C. (1993) 'The effect of food deprivation on alcohol consumption in bulimic and control women', *Addiction*, 88: 1545–1551.

Bulik, C.M. and Brinded, E.C. (1994) 'The effect of food deprivation on the reinforcing value of food and smoking in bulimic and control women', *Physiology and Behavior*, 55: 665–672.

Bulik, C.M. and Sullivan, P.F. (1993) 'Comorbidity of bulimia and substance abuse: perceptions of family of origin', *International Journal of Eating Disorders*, 13: 49–56.

Bulik, C.M., Sullivan, P.F., McKee, M., Weltzin, T.E. and Kaye, W.H. (1994) 'Characteristics of bulimic women with and without alcohol abuse', *American Journal of Drug and Alcohol Abuse*, 20: 273–283.

Bunting, S. and Campbell, J.C. (1990) 'Feminism and nursing: historical perspectives', *Advances In Nursing Science*, 12: 11–24.

Bunzel, R. (1980) 'The role of alcoholism in two central American cultures, *Psychiatry*, 3: 361–387.

Burman, S. (1994) 'The disease concept of alcoholism: Its impact on women's treatment', *Journal of Substance Abuse Treatment*, 11: 121–126.

Burton, F. (1906) 'The causes of melancholy', in Burton, F., (ed.) *The Anatomy of Melancholy*, London, William Tegg.

Bush, T.L. (1990) 'Noncontraptive estrogen use and risk of cardiac disease: overview and critique of the literature', in Koreman, S.C. (ed.) *The Menopause: Proceedings of the Symposium on the Menopause*, Napa, Serano Symposia, 211–223.

Bushman, B.J. and Cooper, H.M. (1990) 'Effects of alcohol on human aggression: An integrative research review', *Psychological Bulletin*, 107: 341–354.

Buss, A.R. (1976) 'Galton and sex differences: an historical note', *Journal of the History of the Behavioral Sciences*, 12: 283–285.

Bustillo, K.W.V. (1995) 'Honduras', in Heath, D.B., (ed.) *International Handbook on Alcohol and Culture*, Connecticut, Greenwood Press, 110–116.

Butcher, R.E. (1985) 'An historical perspective on behavioral teratology', *Neurobehavioral Toxicology and Teratology*, 7: 537–540.

Butler, F.O. (1942) 'The defective delinquent', *American Journal of Mental Deficiency*, 47: 7–13.

Byers, T. and Funch, D.P. (1982) 'Alcohol and breast cancer', *Lancet*, 1: 799–802.

Byers, T. and Graham, S. (1984) 'The epidemiology of diet and cancer', *Advanced Journal of Cancer Research*, 41: 1–69.

Caetano, R. and Weisner, C. (1995) 'The association between DSM–111–R alcohol dependence, psychological distress and drug use', *Addiction*, 90: 351–359.

Caballeria, J., Baraona, E. and Lieber, C.S. (1987) 'The contribution of the stomach to ethanol oxidation in the rat', *Life Science*, 41: 1021–1027.

Caballeria, J., Frezza, M., Hernandez-Munoz, R. et al. (1989) 'The gastric origin of the first pass metabolism of ethanol in man: effect of gastrectomy', *Gastroenterology*, 96: 1205–1209.

Cahalan, D. and Cisin, I.H. (1968) 'American drinking practices: Summary of findings from a national probability sample', *Quarterly Journal of Studies on Alcohol*, 29: 139–151.

Cahalan, D., Cisin, I.H. and Crossley, H.M. (1969) *American Drinking Practices*, New Brunswick, Rutgers Center for Alcohol Studies.

Cain, L.P. (1980) 'Child abuse: historical precedent and legal ramifications', *Health and Social Work*, 5: 61–67.

Cala, L.A., Thickbroom, G.W., Black, J.L., Collins, D.W. and Mastaglia, F.L. (1981) 'Brain density and cerebrospinal fluid spaces on the cranial CT scan in normal volunteers', *American Journal of Neuroradiology*, 2: 41–47.

Camacho, T.C., Kaplan, G.A. and Richard, D. (1987) 'Alcohol consumption and mortality in Alameda County', *Journal of Chronic Diseases*, 40: 229–236.

Camargo, C. (1989) 'Moderate alcohol consumption and stroke. The epidemiological evidence' *Stroke*, 20: 1611–1620.

Camberwell Council on Alcoholism (1980) *Women and Alcohol*, London, Tavistock.

Cameron, D. (1995) *Liberating Solutions to Alcohol Problems: Treating Problem Drinkers Without Saying 'No'*, Northvale, New Jersey, Jason Aronson Inc.

Cameron, N. (1979) 'The growth of London schoolchildren 1904–1966: an analysis of secular trend and intra-county variation', *Annals of Human Biology*, 6: 505–525.

Campbell, D.W. (1993) 'Nursing care of African-American battered women: Afrocentric perspectives', *Clinical Issues in Perinatal Womens Health Nursing*, 4: 407–415.

Canetto, S.S. (1991) 'Gender roles, suicide attempts, and substance abuse', *Journal of Psychology*, 125: 605–620.

Canino, G. (1994) 'Alcohol use and misuse among Hispanic women: selected factors, processes, and studies', *International Journal of the Addictions*, 29: 1083–1100.

Canterbury, R.J., Gressard, C.F., Vieweg, W.V., Grossman, S.J., McKelway, R.B. and Westerman, P.S. (1992) 'Risk-taking behavior of college students and social forces', *American Journal of Drug and Alcohol Abuse*, 18: 213–222.

Cantwell, R. and Chick, J. (1994) 'Alcohol misuse: Clinical features and treatment', in Chick, J. and Cantwell, R., (eds) *Alcohol and Drug Misuse*, London, Royal College of Psychiatrists, 126–155.

Capacchione, L. (1991) *Recovery of Your Inner Child*, New York, Fireside, Simon and Schuster.

Cárdenas, F.M. (1995) 'Chile', in Heath, D.B., (ed.) *International Handbook on Alcohol and Culture*, Connecticut, Greenwood Press, 31–41.

Carey, K.B. (1995) 'Heavy drinking contexts and indices of problem drinking among college students', *Journal of Studies on Alcohol*, 56: 287–292.

Carlson, E.T. (1981) 'The history of multiple personality in the United States: I: The beginnings', *American Journal of Psychiatry*, 138: 666–668.

Carotenuto, A. (1984) *A Secret Symmetry: Sabina Spielrein Between Jung and Freud: The Untold Story of the Woman Who Changed the Early History of Psychoanalysis*, London, Routledge and Kegan Paul.

Carpenter (1880) *Alcoholic Drinks Not Necessaries of Life*, London, British Women's Temperance Association.

Carrol, M.E. and Meisch, R.A. (1980) 'The effects of feeding conditions on drug reinforced behavior: Maintenance at reduced body weight versus availability of food', *Psychopharmacology*, 68: 121–124.

Carson, A.T. and Baker, R.C. (1994) 'Psychological correlates of codependency in women', *International Journal of the Addictions*, 29: 395–407.

Carstenson, R. and O'Grady, L.F. (1980) 'A breast self-examination program for high school students', *American Journal of Public Health*, 70: 1293–1296.

Carter, C.S. (1993) 'Treatment of alcoholic women: The effects of gender-specific intervention on treatment outcome', *Dissertation International Abstracts*, 54,3–A: 1093.

Carter, H. (1919) *The Control of the Drink Trade in Britain: A contribution to national efficiency during the Great War 1915–1918*, London, Longman, Green and Co.

Carver, V., Graham, K., Brett, P.J. and Baron, J. (1994) 'Older women and substance misuse: Recognition and intervention', in Ney, T. (ed.) *Proceedings for Symposium on Innovative Addictions Programming for Women*, BC Ministry of Health and Ministry Responsible for Seniors, Victoria, 116–132.

Cartwright, A. (1979) *The Dignity of Labour? A Study of Childbearing and Induction*, London, Tavistock.

Casey, J.C., Griffin, M.L. and Googins, B.K. (1993) 'The role of work for wives of alcoholics', *American Journal of Drug and Alcohol Abuse*, 19: 119–131.

Casiro, O.G., Stanwick, R.S., Pelech, A. and Taylor, V. (1994) 'Public awareness of the risks of drinking alcohol during pregnancy: the effects of a television campaign. Child health committee, Manitoba Medical Association', *Canadian Journal of Public Health Revue/ Canadienne de Sante Publique*, 85: 23–27.

Cassano, G.B., Akiskal, H.S., Perugi, G., Musetti, L. and Savino, M. (1992) 'The importance of measures of affective temperaments in genetic studies of mood disorders', *Journal of Psychiatric Research*, 26: 257–268.

Cassano, P.A., Koepsell, T.D. and Farwell, J.R. (1990) 'Risk of febrile seizure in childhood in relation to prenatal cigarette smoking and alcohol intake', American Journal of Epidemiology, 132: 462–473.

Casswell, S. (1982) 'Alcohol and youth: Alcohol use by Auckland high school students', *New Zealand Medical Journal, 95: 856–858.*

Casswell, S., Gilmore, L., Silva, P. and Brasch, P. (1983) 'Early experiences with alcohol: A survey of eight and nine year old sample', *New Zealand Medical Journal*, 96: 1001–1003.

Cauley, J.A., Gutai, J.P., Kuller, L.H., LeDonne, D., Powell, J.G. (1989) 'The epidemiology of serum sex hormones in postmenopausal women', *American Journal of Epidemiology*, 129: 1120–1131.

Cauley, J.A., Gutai, J.P., Kuller, L.H., LeDonne, D., Powell, J.G. (1991) 'Reliability and interrelations among serum sex hormones in postmenopausal women', *American Journal of Epidemiology*, 133: 50–57.

Cauley, J.A., Gutai, J.P., Gynn, N.W. et al. (1994) 'Serum estone concentrations and coronary artery disease in postmenopausal women' *Arteriosclerosis and Thrombosis,* 14: 14–18.

Cavallo, F., Russo, R., Zotti, C., Camerlengo, A. and Moiraghi Ruggenini, A. (1995) 'Moderate alcohol consumption and spontaneous abortion', *Alcohol and Alcoholism*, 30: 195–201.

Cavan, S. (1966) *Liquor License: An Ethnography of Bar Behavior*, Chicago, Aldine.

Cayleff, S.E. (1988) '"Prisoners of their own feebleness": Women, nerves and Western medicine – a historical overview', *Social Science and Medicine*, 26: 1199–1208.

Celentano, D.D., McQueen, D.V. and Chee, E. (1980) 'Substance abuse by women: A review of the epidemiologic literature', *Journal of Chronic Diseases*, 33: 383–394.

Center for Disease Control (1983) 'Long term oral contraceptive use and the risk of breast cancer', *Journal of the Amerian Medical Association*, 249: 1591–1595.

Center for Substance Abuse Treatment (1994) *Practical Approaches in the Treatment of Women Who Abuse Alcohol and Other Drugs*, Rockville, Maryland, Department of Health and Human Services, Public Health Service.

Chaddock, C.G. (1892) 'The visual imagery of alcoholic delirium', *Alienist and Neurologist*, January, 13,1: 86–90.

Chandler, L.S., Richardson, G.A., Gallagher, J.D. and Day, N.L. (1996) 'Prenatal exposure to alcohol and marijuana: Effects on motor development of preschool children', *Alcoholism: Clinical and Experimental Research*, 20: 455–461.

Chandy, J.M., Harris, L., Blum, R.W. and Resnick, M.D. (1995) 'Female adolescents of alcohol misusers: disordered eating features', *International Journal of Eating Disorders*, 17: 283–289.

Charette, L., Tate, D.L. and Wilson, A. (1990) 'Alcohol consumption and menstrual distress in women at higher and lower risk of alcoholism', *Alcoholism, Clinical and Experimental Research*, 14: 152–157.

Charles, D. and Larsen, B. (1986) 'Streptococcal puerperal sepsis and obstetric infections: a historical perspective', *Reviews of Infectious Diseases*, 8: 411–422.

Cheng, A.T. and Chen, W.J. (1995) 'Alcoholism among four aboriginal groups in Taiwan: high prevalences and their implications', *Alcoholism, Clinical and Experimental Research*, 19: 81–91.

Chesler, P. (1994a) 'Heroism is our only alternative', *Feminism and Psychology*, 4: 298–305.

Chesler, P. (1994b) 'Extracts from women and madness', *Feminism and Psychology*, 4: 268–279.

Chetwynd, S.J. and Pearson, V. (1983) 'Reported drinking practices amongst women working in the Home', *Community Health Studies*, 11: 278–284.

Cheung, Y.W. and Erickson, P.G. (1995) 'Canada', in Heath, D.B., (ed.) *International Handbook on Alcohol and Culture*, Connecticut, Greenwood Press, 20–30.

Chiapelli, F. and Taylor, A.N. (1995) 'The fetal alcohol syndrome and fetal alcohol effects on immune competence', *Alcohol and Alcoholism*, 30: 259–263.

Chiaramonte, M, Farinati, F., Fagioli, S. et al. (1990) 'Antibody to hepatitis C virus in hepatocellular carcinoma', *Lancet*, 1: 301–302.

Chiauzzi, E.J. (1991) *Preventing Relapse in Addictive Behaviors: A Biopsychosocial Approach*, Elmsford, New York, Pergamon Press.

Chick, J., Badawy, A. and Borg, S. (1993) 'Identification of excessive drinking and alcohol problems', *Alcohol and Alcoholism*, Supplement, 2: 121–125.

Chick, J. and Cantwell, R. (1994) *Alcohol and Drug Misuse*, London, Royal College of Psychiatrists.

Chipfakacha, V.G. (1989) 'Abdominal deliveries in Africa: food for thought to scholars of the history of medicine', *Central African Journal of Medicine*, 35: 333–336.

Chishti, H.G.M. (1988) *The Traditional Healer: A Comprehensive Guide to the Principles and Practice of Unani Herbal Medicine*, Wellingborough, Thorsons Publishers Ltd.

Chodoff, P. (1982) 'Hysteria and women', *American Journal of Psychiatry*, 139: 545–551.

Chodorow, N.J. (1994) *Femininities, Masculinities, Sexualities: Freud and Beyond*, London, Free Association Books Ltd.

Choi, P.Y.L. and Salmon, P. (1995a) 'Stress responsivity in exercisers and non-exercisers during different phases of the menstrual cycle', *Social Science and Medicine*, 41,6: 769–777.

Choi, P.Y.L. and Salmon, P. (1995b) 'Symptom changes across the menstrual cycle in competitive sports women, exercisers and sedentary women', *British Journal of Clinical Psychology*, 34: 447–460.

Choquet, M. and Ledoux, S. (1989) 'France', in M.A. Plant, (ed.) *Alcohol Problems in High Risk Groups*, Copenhagen, World Health Organization, Euro Reports and Studies No. 109, 45–63.

Christensen, E. (1995) 'Families in distress: The development of children growing up with alcohol and violence', *Arctic Medical Journal*, Supplement, 54,1: 53–57.

Christiaens, L., Mizon, J.P. and Delmarle, G. (1960) 'Sur la descendance des alcooliques (on the offspring of alcoholics)', *American Pediatrics*, 36: 37.

Christopherson, W.M and Parker, J.E. (1965) 'Relation of cervical cancer to early marriage and childbearing', *New England Journal of Medicine*, 273: 235–239.

Chrouser, K.R. (1991) 'Critical analysis of the discourse and reconstructed stories shared by recovering female alcoholics in Alcoholics Anonymous', *Dissertation Abstracts International*, 52: 343A.

Church, O.M and Poirier, S. (1986) 'From patient to consumer; from apprentice to professional practitioner', *Nursing Clinics of North America*, 21: 99–109.

Churchill, F. (1850) 'On the mental disorders of pregnancy and childbirth', *American Journal of Insanity*, 7: 297–317.

Clair, D. and Genest, M. (1987) 'Variables associated with the adjustment of offspring of alcoholic fathers', *Journal of Studies on Alcohol*, 48: 345–355.

Clare, A. (1976) *Psychiatry in Dissent: Controversial Issues in Thought and Practice*, Philadelphia, Institute for the Study of Human Issues.

Clark, A. (1992) *Working Life of Women in the Seventeenth Century*, 3rd edn. London, Routledge.

Clark, H.W. and Zweben, J.E. (1994) 'Dual diagnosis, minority populations and women', in Miller, N.S., (ed.) *Treating Coexisting Psychiatric and Addictive Disorders: A Practical Guide*, Center City, Minnesota, Hazelden Educational Materials, 111–126.

Claussen, B. and Aasland, O.G, (1993) 'The alcohol use disorders identification test (AUDIT) in a routine health examination of long-term unemployed', *Addiction*, 88: 363–368.

Clemmons, P. (1991) 'Feminists, spirituality, and the twelve steps of Alcoholics Anonymous', *Women and Therapy*, 11: 97–109.

Cliver, S.P., Goldenberg, R.L., Cutter, G.R., Hogan, H.J., Copper, R.L., Gotlieb, S.J. and Davis, R.O. (1992) 'The relationships among psychosocial profile, maternal size, and smoking in predicting fetal growth retardation', *Obstetrics and Gynecology*, 80: 262–267.

Cloninger, C.R., Sigvardsson, S. and Bohman, M. (1988) 'Childhood personality predicts alcohol abuse in young adults', *Alcoholism*, 12: 494–505.

Closser, M. and Blow, F.C. (1993) 'Special populations: Women, ethnic minorities and the elderly', *Psychiatric Clinics of North America*, 16: 199–209.

Clouston, T.S. (1904) *Clinical Lectures on Mental Diseases*, 6th edn, Edinburgh, Churchill Livingstone.

Cobo, E. (1973) 'Effect of different doses of ethanol on the milk-ejecting reflex in lactating women', *American Journal of Obstetrics and Gynecology*, 115: 817–821.

Coggins, K. (1990) *Alternative Pathways to Healing: The Recovery Medicine Wheel*, Florida, Health Communications Inc.

Cohen, G.D. (1981) 'Perspectives on psychotherapy with the elderly', *American Journal of Psychiatry*, 138: 347–350.

Colditz, G.A., Branch, L.G., Lipnick, R.J. et al. (1985) 'Moderate alcohol and decreased cardiovascular mortality in an elderly cohort', *American Heart Journal*, 109: 886–889.

Colditz, G.A., Giovannuci, E., Rimm, E.B. et al. (1991) 'Alcohol intake in relation to diet and obesity in men and women', *American Journal of Clinical Nutrition*, 54: 49–55.

Coles, C.D., Brown, R.T., Smith, I.E., Platzman, K.A., Erickson, S. and Falek, A. (1991) 'Effects of prenatal alcohol exposure at school age, 1: Physical and cognitive development', *Neurobehavioral Toxicology*, 13: 357–367.

Coles, C.D., Smith, I., Fernhoff, P.M. and Falek, A. (1985) 'Neonatal neurobehavioral characteristics as correlates of maternal alcohol use during gestation', *Alcoholism: Clinical and Experimental Research*, 9,5: 454–460.

Coletti, S.D., Schinka, J.A., Hughes, P.A., Hamilton, N.L., Renard, C.G., Sicilian, D.M., Urmann, C.F. and Neri, R.L. (1995) 'Par village for chemically dependent women – philosophy and program elements', *Journal of Substance Abuse Treatment*, 12.

Colliere, M.F. (1986) 'Invisible care and invisible women as health care providers', *International Journal of Nursing Studies*, 23: 95–112.

Collins, B.A., McCoy, S.A., Sale, S. and Weber, S.E. (1994) 'Descriptions of comfort by substance-using and nonusing postpartum women', *Journal of Obstetric, Gynacologic and Neonatal Nursing*, 23: 293–300.

Collins, J.J.Jr (1982) *Drinking and Crime*, London, Tavistock.

Colman, J. (1870) *Catechism on Alcohol. Revised and Adapted for English Bands of Hope*, London, White and Pike, Moor Street Printing Works.

Colombo, M., Kwo, G., Choo, Q.L., et al. (1989) 'High prevalence of antibody to hepatitis C virus in patients with heptocellular carcinoma', *Lancet*, 2: 1006–1008.

Comas-Diaz (1994) *Women of Color: Integrating Ethnic and Gender Identities in Psychotherapy*, New York, Guilford Press.

Condelli, W.S. (1994) 'Domains of variables for understanding and improving retention in therapeutic communities', *International Journal of the Addictions*, 29: 593–607.

Condran, G.A. (1984) 'An evaluation of estimates of underenumeration in the census and the age pattern of mortality, Philadelphia, 1880', *Demography*, 21: 53–69.

Conn, J.H. (1989) 'Play interview therapy: its history, theory and practice – a fifty year retrospective account', *Child Psychiatry and Human Development*, 20: 3–13.

Connolly, G.M., Casswell, S., Zhang, J.F. and Silva, P.A. (1994) 'Alcohol in the mass media and drinking by adolescents: a longitudinal study', *Addiction*, 89: 1255–1263.

Connors, D.D. (1985) 'Women's "sickness": a case of secondary gains or primary losses', *Advances in Nursing Science*, 7: 1–17.

Conte, H.R., Plutchik, R., Picard, S., Galanter, M. and Jacoby, J. (1991) 'Sex differences in personality traits and coping styles of hospitalized alcoholics', *Journal of Studies on Alcohol*, 52: 26–32.

Cooke, A.R. (1970) 'The simultaneous emptying and absorption of ethanol from the human stomach', *American Journal of Digestive Diseases*, 15: 449–454

Cooke, D.J. and Allan, C.A. (1984) 'Stressful life events and alcohol abuse in women: a general population study', *British Journal of Addiction*, 79: 425–430.

Cooke, K.M., Frost, G.W. and Stokes, G.S. (1983) 'Blood pressure and its relationship to low levels of alcohol consumption', *Clinical and Experimental Pharmacology and Physiology*, 10: 229–233.

Cooke, K.M., Frost, G.W., Thornell, I.R. et al. (1982) 'Alcohol consumption and blood pressure. Survey of the relationship at a health screening clinic', *Medical Journal of Australia*, 1: 65–69.

Cooper, C.L. (1988) *Stress and Breast Cancer*, London, John Wiley and Sons Ltd.

Cooper, C.L., Cooper, R.D. and Eaker, L.H. (1988) *Living with Stress*, London, Penguin Books.

Cooper, D.B. (1994) *Alcohol Home Detoxification and Assessment*, Oxford, Radcliffe Medical Press Ltd.

Cooper, L.Z. (1985) 'The history and medical consequences of rubella', *Reviews of Infectious Diseases*, 7: Supplement 1, S2–10.

Copeland, J. and Hall, W. (1992a) 'A comparison of women seeking drug and alcohol treatment in a specialist women's and two traditional mixed-sex treatment services', *British Journal of Addiction*, 87: 1293–1302.

Copeland, J. and Hall, W. (1992b) 'A comparison of predictors of treatment drop-out of women seeking drug and alcohol treatment in a specialist women's and two traditional mixed-sex treatment services', *British Journal of Addiction*, 87: 883–890.

Copeland, J., Hall, W., Didcott, P. and Biggs, V. (1993) 'A comparison of a specialist women's alcohol and other drug treatment service with two traditional mixed-sex services: client characteristics and treatment outcome', *Drug and Alcohol Dependence*, 32: 81–92.

Coppen, A.J. and Metcalfe, M. (1965) 'Effects of a depressive illness on M.P.I. scores', *British Journal of Psychiatry*, 111: 236

Corbett, K., Mora, J. and Ames, G. (1991) 'Drinking patterns and drinking-related problems of Mexican-American husbands and wives', *Journal of Studies on Alcohol*, 52: 215–223.

Corcoran, K.J. and Parker, P.S. (1991) 'Alcohol Expectancy Questionnaire Tension Reduction Scale as a predictor of alcohol consumption in a stressful situation', *Addictive Behaviors*, 16: 129–137.

Corcos, A.F. (1984) 'Reproduction and heredity beliefs of the Hindus based on their sacred books', *Journal of Heredity*, 75: 152–154.

Cornelius, M.D., Richardson, G.A., Day, N.L., Cornelius, J.R., Geva, D. and Taylor, P.M. (1994) 'A comparison of prenatal drinking in two recent samples of adolescents and adults', *Journal of Studies on Alcohol*, 55: 412–419.

Corrigan, E.M. and Butler, S. (1991) 'Irish alcoholic women in treatment: early findings', *International Journal of the Addictions*, 26,3: 281–292.

Corti, B. and Ibrahim, J. (1990) 'Women and alcohol – trends in Australia', *Medical Journal of Australia*, 152: 625–632.

Coryell, W., Winokur, G., Keller, M., Schetner, W. and Endicott, J. (1992) 'Alcoholism and primary major depression', *Journal of Affective Disorders*, 24: 93–99.

Cotten, N.U., Resnick, J., Browne, D.C., Martin, S.L., McCarraher, D.R. and Woods, J. (1994) 'Aggression and fighting behavior among African-American adolescents: individual and family factors', *American Journal of Public Health*, 84: 618–622.

Cottino, A. (1995) 'Italy', in Heath, D.B., (ed.) *International Handbook on Alcohol and Culture*, Connecticut, Greenwood Press, 157–167.

Cotton, N.S. (1979) 'The family incidence of alcoholism: A review', *Journal of Studies on Alcohol*, 40: 89–116.

Council of Europe, (1995) *Women and Drugs*, Strasbourg, Council of Europe Publishing.

Couzigou, P., Begleiter, H., Kiianmaa, K. And Agarwal, D.P. (1993) 'Genetics and alcohol', in Verschuren, P.M. (ed.), *Health Issues Related to Alcohol Consumption*, Washington, D.C., ILSI Press, 281–329.

Covey, H.C. (1992) 'The definitions of the beginning of old age in history', *International Journal of Aging and Human Development*, 34: 325–337.

Covington, S.S. (1982) *Sexual Experience, Dysfunction, and Abuse: A Descriptive Study of Alcoholic and Non Alcoholic Women*, PhD dissertation, Union Graduate School, Cincinnati, Ohio.

Covington, S.S. (1994) *A Woman's Way Through the Twelve Steps*, Center City, Minnesota, Hazelden Press.

Covington, S.S. and Kohen, J. (1984) 'Women, alcohol, and sexuality', in Stimmel, B., (ed.) *Cultural and Sociological Aspects of Alcoholism and Substance Abuse*, New York, Haworth Press, 41–56.

Cowley, D.S. (1992) 'Alcohol abuse, substance abuse and panic disorder', *American Journal of Medicine*, 92: 41S–47S.

Cox, L.W. (1991) 'The development of infertility treatment in Australia', *Australian and New Zealand Journal of Obstetrics and Gynaecology*, 31: 254–259.

Crabb, D.W. (1993) 'The liver', in Galanter, M. (ed.) *Recent Developments in Alcoholism, Volume 11: Ten Years of Progress*, New York, Plenum, 207–230.

Craig, D., Parrott, A. and Coomber, J.A. (1992) 'Smoking cessation in women: effects of the menstrual cycle', *International Journal of the Addictions*, 27: 697–706.

Cranmer, D. (1994) 'Core energetics', in Jones, D., (ed.) *Innovative Therapy*, Buckingham, Open University Press, 117–130.

Cravens, H. (1992) 'A scientific project locked in time. The Terman genetic studies of genius, 1920s–1950s', *American Psychologist*, 47: 183–189.

Crilly, R.G., Anderson, C., Hogan, D., Delaquerrière-Richardson, L. (1988) 'Bone histomorphology, bone mass, and related parameters in alcoholic males', *Calcified Tissue International*, 43: 269–276.

Criqui, M.H. and Ringel, B.L. (1994) 'Does diet or alcohol explain the French paradox?' *Lancet*, 344: 1719–1723.

Criqui, M.H., Wallace, R.B., et al. (1981) 'Alcohol consumption and blood pressure: the Lipid Research Clinics Prevalence Study', *Hypertension*, 3: 557–565.

Critchley, E.M. and Cantor, H.E. (1984) 'Charcot's hysteria renaissant', *British Medical Journal – Clinical Research*, 289: 1785–1788.

Croft, J.B., Freedman, D.S., Cresenta, J.L., Srinivasan, S.R., Burke, G.L., et al. (1987) 'Adverse influence of alcohol, tobacco and oral contraceptive use on cardiovascular risk factors during transition to adulthood', *American Journal of Epidemiology*, 126: 202–213.

Crompton, L. (1980) 'The myth of lesbian impunity: Capital laws from 1270 to 1791', *Journal of Homosexuality*, 6: 11–25.

Crosby, W.M. (1991) 'Studies in fetal malnutrition', *American Journal of Diseases of Children*, 145: 871–876.

Cross, L.W. (1991) 'Body and self in feminine psychology: as illustrated by delicate self-mutilation and the eating disorders', *Dissertation Abstracts International*, 51: 5570.

Crothers, T.D. (1881) 'What shall be done with the inebriate?' *Alienist and Neurologist*, 2: 166–189.

Crothers, T.D. (1882a) 'Legislative acts for the control and care of inebriates', *Alienist and Neurologist*, April 3: 239–242.

Crothers, T.D. (1882b) 'Inebriate criminals', *Alienist and Neurologist*, January 3: 66–84.

Crothers, T.D. (1886) 'Certain hereditary and psychical phenomena in inebriety', *Alienist and Neurologist*, July 7,3: 566–580.

Crothers, T.D. (1889a) 'Inebriate asylums and their work', *Alienist and Neurologist*, 10: 98–99.

Crothers, T.D. (1889b) 'Medico-legal problems of inebriety, illustrated by "the Swift Case"' *Alienist and Neurologist*, 10,4: 522–534.

Crothers, T.D. (1891) 'The American Medical Temperance Association: Quotation from the Journal of Inebriety', *Alienist and Neurologist*, October 12,4: 637–639.

Crothers, T.D. (1892) 'The law of periodicity in inebriety', *Alienist and Neurologist*, July 13,3: 476–486.

Crowe, L. and George, W.H. (1989) 'Alcohol and human sexuality', *Psychological Bulletin*, 105: 374–386.

Cruikshank, W.H. (1940) 'Psychosis associated with pregnancy and the puerperium', *Canadian Medical Journal*, 43: 571

Cullen, K., Stenhouse, N.S. and Wearne, K.L. (1982) 'Alcohol and mortality in the Bussleton Study', *International Journal of Eidemiology*, 11: 67–70.

Culpepper, N. (1662) *Culpepper's Dictionary for Midwives*, London, Peter Cole.

Curlee, J. (1969) 'Alcoholism and the "empty nest"', *Bulletin of the Menninger Clinic*, 33: 165–171.

Cushway, D. and Sewell, R. (1992) *Counselling with Dreams and Nightmares*, London, Sage Publications Ltd.

Cutrona, C.E., Cadoret, R.J., Suhr, J.A., Richards, C.C., Troughton, E., Schutte, K. and Woodworth, G. (1994) 'Interpersonal variables in the prediction of alcoholism among adoptees: Evidence for gene-environment interactions', *Comprehensive Psychiatry*, 35: 171–179.

Cybulska, E. and Rucinski, J. (1986) 'Gross self-neglect in old age', *British Journal of Hospital Medicine*, 36: 21–25.

D'Archangelo, E. (1993) 'Substance abuse in later life', *Canadian Family Physician*, 39: 1986–1993.

da Costa Pereira, A., Olsen, J. and Ogston, S. (1993) 'Variability of self reported measures of alcohol consumption: implications for the association between drinking in pregnancy and birth weight', *Journal of Epidemiology and Community Health*, 47: 326–330.

Daily Record (Scotland) (1988) 'Cancer risk to boozy women', 6 August, 6.

Daly, M. (1979) *Gyn/Ecology: The Metaethics of Radical Feminism*, London, The Women's Press Ltd.

Daniels, R.S. and Lessow, H. (1964) 'Severe post-partum reactions: An interpersonal view', *Psychosomatics*, 5: 21.

Darby, B.L., Streissguth, A.P. and Smith, D.W. (1981) 'A preliminary follow-up of 8 children diagnosed fetal alcohol syndrome in infancey', *Neurobehavioral Toxicology and Teratology*, 3,2: 157–159.

David, H.P. (1992) 'Abortion in Europe, 1920–91: a public health perspective', *Studies In Family Planning*, 23: 1–22.

Davidson, R., Rollnick, S. and McEwan, I. (1991) *Counselling Problem Drinkers*, London, Routledge.

Davies, J.B. and Stacey, B. (1972) *Teenagers and Alcohol*, London, HMSO.

Davies, P.J.M., Partrige, J.W. and Storrs, C.N. (1982) 'Alcohol consumption in pregancy: How much is safe?' *Archives of Diseases in Childhood*, 57: 940–943.

Davis, D.L. (1989) 'George Beard and Lydia Pinkham: gender, class, and nerves in late 19th century America', *Health Care For Women International*, 10: 93–114.

Davis, D.L. and Whitten, R.G. (1988) 'Medical and popular traditions of nerves', *Social Science and Medicine*, 26: 1209–1221.

Davis, N.S. (1891) 'The American Medical Temperance Association', *Alienist and Neurologist*, October 12,4: 637–639.

Davis, N.Z. and Farge, A. (1993) *History of Women: Renaissance and Enlightenment Paradoxes*, Cambridge, Massachusetts, The Belknap Press of Harvard University Press.

Davis, R.B. (1994) 'Drug and alcohol use in the former Soviet Union: Selected factors and future considerations', *International Journal of the Addictions*, 29: 303–323.

Davis, W.M. (1986) 'Premature mortality among prominent American authors noted for alcohol abuse', *Drug and Alcohol Dependence*, 18: 133–138.

Dawson, D.A. and Grant, B.F. (1993) 'Gender effects in diagnosing alcohol abuse and dependence', *Journal of Clinical Psychology*, 49: 298–307.

Day, N., Sambamoorthi, U., Taylor, P., Richardson, G., Robles, N., Jhon, Y., Scher, M., Stoffer, D., Cornelius, M. and Jasperse, D. (1991) 'Prenatal marijuana use and neonatal outcome', *Neurotoxicology and Teratology*, 13: 329–334.

Day, N.L., Goldschmidt, L., Robles, N. et al. (1991) 'Prenatal exposure and offspring growth at eighteen months of age: The predictive validity of two measures of drinking', *Alcoholism. Clinical and Experimental Research*, 15: 914–918.

Day, N.L., Richardson, G., Robles, N. et al. (1990) 'Effect of prenatal alcohol exposure on growth and morphology of offspring at eight months', *Pediatrics*, 85: 748–752.

Day, N.L., Richardson, G.A., Goldschmidt, L., Robles, N., Taylor, P.M., Stoffer, D.S., Cornelius, M.D. and Geva, D. (1994) 'Effect of prenatal marijuana exposure on the cognitive development of offspring at age three', *Neurotoxicology and Teratology*, 16: 169–175.

Day, N.L., Robles, N., Richardson, G. and et al. (1991) 'The effects of prenatal alcohol use on the growth of Children at Three Years', *Alcoholism: Clinical and Experimental Research*, 15: 67–71.

de Beauvoir, S. (1988) *The Second Sex*, London, Picador Classics, Pan Books Ltd.

de Boer, M.C., Schippers, G.M. and van der Staak, C.P. (1993) 'Alcohol and social anxiety in women and men: pharmacological and expectancy effects', *Addictive Behaviors*, 18: 117–126.

de Boer, M.C., Schippers, O.M. and van der Staak, C.P. (1994) 'The effects of alcohol, expectancy, and alcohol beliefs on anxiety and self-disclosure in women: do beliefs moderate alcohol effects?' *Addictive Behaviors*, 19: 509–520.

De Feo, P., Volpi, E., Lucidi, P., Cruciani, G., Monacchia, F., Reboli, G., Santeusanio, F., Bolli, G.B. and Brunetti, P. (1995) 'Ethanol Impairs Post-Prandial Hepatic Protein Metabolism', *Journal of Clinical Investigation*, 95: 1472–1479.

de Groot, J.M. and Rodin, G. (1994) 'Eating disorders, female psychology, and the self', *Journal of the American Academy of Psychoanalysis*, 22: 299–317.

De Vernejoul, M.C., Bielakof, J., Herve, M. et al. (1983) 'Evidence for defective osteoblastic function. A role for alcohol and tobacco consumption in osteoporosis in middle aged men', *Clinical Orthopedics*, 179: 107–115.

de Vries, H. and Backbier, E. (1994) 'Self-efficacy as an important determinant of quitting among pregnant women who smoke: the phi-pattern', *Preventive Medicine*, 23: 167–174.

De Young, M. (1982) *The Sexual Victimisation of Children*, Jefferson NC, McFarland.

Debooy, V.D., Seshia, M.M., Tenenbein, M. and Casiro, O.G. (1993) 'Intravenous pentazocine and methylphenidate abuse during pregnancy. Maternal lifestyle and infant outcome', *American Journal of Diseases of Children,* 147: 1062–1065.

Decker, K.P. and Ries, R.K. (1993) 'Differential diagnosis and psychopharmacology of dual disorders', *Psychiatric Clinics of North America,* 16: 703–718.

Deckert, J., Muller, T., Becker, T. et al. (1992a) 'Nimodipine and Flunarizine in alcohol withdrawal: An open study', *Psychopathology,* 22: 49–59.

Deckert, J., Muller, T., Becker, T. et al. (1992b) 'Nimodipine and Flunarizine in alcohol withdrawal: An open study', *Journal of Psychopharmacology,* 6: 273–277.

Deevey, S. and Wall, L.J. (1992) 'How do lesbian women develop serenity?' *Health Care For Women International*: 13,2: 199–208.

Degen, H.M., Myers, B.J., Williams-Petersen, M.G., Knisely, J.S. and Schnoll, S.S. (1993) 'Social support and anxiety in pregnant drug abusers and nonusers: unexpected findings of few differences', *Drug and Alcohol Dependence,* 32: 37–44.

Del Boca, F.K. (1994) 'Sex, gender, and alcoholic typologies', *Annals of the New York Academy of Science,* 708: 34–48.

Delacoste, F. and Alexander, P. (1988) *Sex Work. Writings by Women in the Sex Industry*, London, Virago Press.

Department of Transport (1990) *Blood Alcohol Levels in Fatalities in Great Britain 1988*, London, Transport and Road Research Laboratory.

DePetrillo, P.B. and Rice, J.M. (1995) 'Methadone dosing and pregnancy: impact on program compliance', *International Journal of the Addictions,* 30: 207–217.

Dershimer, F. (1936) 'The influence of mental attitudes on childbearing', *American Journal of Obstetrics and Gynecology,* 31: 444.

DeSalvo, L. (1991) *Virginia Woolf: The Impact of Childhood Sexual Abuse on her Life*, London, The Women's Press.

Deutsch, H. (1947) *Psychology of Women: Volume 2: Motherhood*, London, Research Books Ltd.

Deykin, D., Janson, P. and McMahon, L. (1982) 'Ethanol potentiation of aspirin-induced prolongation of the bleeding time', *New England Journal of Medicine,* 306: 852–854.

Di Padova, C., Frezza, M. and Lieber, C.S. (1988) 'Gastric metabolism of ethanol; Implications for its bioavailability in men and women', in Kuriyama, K., Takada, A. and Ishii, H., (eds) *Biomedical and Social Aspects of Alcohol and Alcoholism*, Barking, Elsevier, 81–84.

Diamond, T., Stiel, D., Lunzer, M. et al. (1989) 'Ethanol reduces bone formation and may cause osteoporosis', *American Journal of Medicine,* 86: 282–288.

Dick, R.W., Manson, S.M. and Beals, J. (1993) 'Alcohol use among male and female native American adolescents: patterns and correlates of student drinking in a boarding school', *Journal of Studies on Alcohol,* 54: 172–177.

Diczfalusy, E. (1984) 'The early history of estriol', *Journal of Steroid Biochemistry*, 20: 945–953.

Dillon, G. (1985) *A Delusion of the Australian Culture*, Sydney, New South Wales Temperance Alliance.

Dobkin, P., Dongier, M., Cooper, D. and Hill, J.M. (1991) 'Screening for alcoholism in a psychiatric hospital', *Canadian Journal of Psychiatry/Revue Canadienne De Psychiatric*, 36: 39–45.

Docwra, M.E. (1880) *The Non-Alcoholic Cookery Book*, London, British Women's Temperance Association.

Dodes, L.M. (1984) 'Abstinence from alcohol in long-term individual psychotherapy with alcoholics', *American Journal of Psychotherapy*, 38: 248–256.

Dodes, L.M. (1988) 'The psychology of combining dynamic psychotherapy and Alcoholics Anonymous', *Bulletin of the Menninger Clinic*, 42: 283–293.

Dodes, L.M. (1990) 'Addiction, helplessness and narcissistic rage', *Psychoanalytic Quarterly*, 59: 398–419.

Doherty, W.J. and Needle, R.H. (1991) 'Psychological adjustment and substance use among adolescents before and after a parental divorce', *Child Development*, 62: 328–337.

Doll, R., Forman, D., La Vecchia, C. and Woutersen, R. (1993) 'Alcoholic beverages and cancers of the digestive tract and larynx', in Verschuren, P.M. (ed.) *Health Issues Related to Alcohol Consumption*, Washington, D.C., ILSI Press,125–166.

Domenico, D. and Windle, M. (1993) 'Intrapersonal and interpersonal functioning among middle-aged female adult children of alcoholics', *Journal of Consulting and Clinical Psychology*, 61: 659–666.

Donald, M., Dunne, M. and Raphael, B. (1993) 'Young women and alcohol: psychosocial factors associated with their own drinking, their fathers' drinking, and both', *International Journal of the Addictions*, 28: 959–972.

Donnison, J. (1988) *Midwives and Medical Men: A History of the Struggle for the Control of Childbirth*, London, Historical Publications.

Donovan, C. and McEwan, R. (1995) 'A review of the literature examining the relationship between alcohol use and HIV-related sexual risk taking in young people', *Addiction*, 90: 319–328.

Donovan, D.M. (1988) 'Assessment of addictive behaviors: Implications of an emerging biopsychosocial model', in Donovan, D.M. and Marlatt, G.A., (eds) *Assessment of Addictive Behaviors*, New York, Guilford Press, 3.

Donovan, D.M. and Chaney, E.F. (1985) 'Alcoholic relapse prevention and intervention: Models and methods', in Marlatt, G.A. and Gordon, J.R., (eds) *Relapse Prevention: Maintenance Strategies in the Treatment of Addictive Behaviors*, New York, Guilford Press, 351.

Donovan, D.M. and Marlatt, G.A. (1993) 'Behavioral treatment', in Galanter, M., (ed.) *Recent Developments in Alcoholism: Vol 11: Ten Years of Progress*, New York, Plenum Press, 397–411.

Douglas, R.R. (1990) 'Formulating alcohol policies for community recreation facilities: tactics and problems', in Giesbrecht, N., Conley, P. Denniston, R.W., Gliksman, L. Holder, H., Pederson, A., Room, R., and Shain, M. (eds) *Research, Action, and the Community: Experience in the Prevention of Alcohol and Other Drug Problems*, Rockville, Maryland, US Department of Health and Human Services, OSAP Prevention Monograph number 4, 61–67.

Dover, K.J. (1974) *Greek Popular Morality in the Time of Plato and Aristotle*, Oxford, Blackwell, quoted in Just, R. (1991) *Women in Athenian Law and Life*, London, Routledge.

Downs, W.R., Miller, B.A., Testa, M. and Panek, D. (1992) 'Long-term effects of parent to child violence for women', *Journal of Interpersonal Violence*, 7: 365–382.

Dragadze, T. (1994) 'Gender, ethnicity and alcohol in the former Soviet Union', in McDonald, M., (ed.) *Gender, Drink and Drugs*, Oxford, Berg, 145–152.

Drake, R.E., McHugo, G.J. and Biesanz, J.C. (1995) 'The test–retest reliability of standardized instruments among homeless persons with substance use disorders', *Journal of Studies on Alcohol*, 56: 161–167.

Draper, J. (1882) 'Insanity in Great Britain and upon the Continent of Europe', *Alienist and Neurologist*, July 3,3: 375–411.

Draucker, C.B. (1993) *Counselling Survivors of Childhood Sexual Abuse*, London, Sage Publications Ltd.

Drever, F. (1995) *Occupational Health: Dicennial Supplement*, London, HMSO.

Drossman, D.A. (1995) 'Sexual and physical abuse and gastrointestinal illness', *Scandinavian Journal of Gastroenterology*, Supplement, 208: 90–96.

Drozd, L.M. and Dalenberg, C.J. (1994) 'The self as mediator in the psychopathology of female children of alcoholics', *International Journal of the Addictions*, 29: 1787–1800.

Dryden, W. (1990) *Individual Therapy*, Buckingham, Open University Press.

Dryden, W. and Feltham, C. (1992) *Psychotherapy and its Discontents*, Buckingham, Open University Press.

Dryden, W. and Thorne, B. (1991) *Training and Supervision for Counselling in Action*, London, Sage Publications Ltd.

Duby, G. (1988) *A History of Private Life; Revelations of the Medieval World*, Cambridge, Massachusetts The Belknap Press of Harvard University Press.

Duby, G. and Perrot, M. (1994) 'Writing the history of women', in Schmitt Pantel, P. (ed.) *A History of Women*, Cambridge, Mass., The Belknap Press of Harvard University Press, x–xxi.

Duckert, F. (1993) 'Predictive factors for outcome of treatment for alcohol problems', *Journal of Substance Abuse*, 5: 31–44.

Duckert, F., Amundsen, A. and Johnsen, J. (1992) 'What happens to drinking after therapeutic intervention? *British Journal of Addiction*, 87: 1457–1467.

Duckert, F., Johnsen, J., Amundsen, A., Stromme, J. and Morland, J. (1992) 'Co-variation between biological markers and self-reported alcohol consumption. a two-year study of the relationship between changes in consumption and changes in the biological markers Gamma-Glutamyl Transpeptidase (GGT) and average volume per erythrocyte (MCV) among problem drinkers', *Alcohol and Alcoholism,* 27: 545–555.

Duffin, J. (1992) 'The death of Sarah Lovell and the constrained feminism of Emily Stowe', *Canadian Medical Association Journal*, 146: 881–888.

Dunbar, J.A. (1985) *A Quiet Massacre. A Review of Drinking and Driving in the United Kingdom,* London, Institute of Alcohol Studies, Occasional Paper 7.

Dunbar, J., Pentilla, A. and Pakkarainen, J. (1987) 'Drinking and driving: the success of random breath testing in Finland', *British Medical Journal*, 295: 101–103.

Dunham, R.G. (1986) 'Noticing alcoholism in the elderly and women: A nationwide examination of referral behavior', *Journal of Drug Issues*, 16: 397–406.

Dunkel, L.M. (1983) 'Moral and humane: patients' libraries in early nineteenth-century American mental hospitals', *Bulletin of the Medical Library Association*, 71: 274–281.

Dunne, F.J., Galatopoulos, C. and Schipperheijn, J.M. (1993) 'Gender differences in psychiatric morbidity among alcohol misusers', *Comprehensive Psychiatry*, 34: 95–101.

Durant, R.H., Rickert, V.I., Ashworth, C.S., Newman, C. and Slavens, G. (1993) 'Use of multiple drugs among adolescents who use anabolic steroids', *New England Journal of Medicine*, 328: 922–926.

Dyer, A.R., Cutter, G.R. and Liu, K. et al. (1990) 'Alcohol intake and blood pressure in young adults: the Cardia study', *Journal of Clinical Epidemiology*, 43: 1–13.

Earleywine, M. (1994) 'Cognitive bias covaries with alcohol consumption', *Addictive Behaviors*, 19:539.

Earleywine, M. and Martin, C.S. (1993) 'Anticipated stimulant and sedative effects of alcohol vary with dosage and limb of the blood alcohol curve', *Alcoholism, Clinical and Experimental Research*, 17: 135–139.

East, P. (1995) *Counselling in Medical Settings*, London, Open University Press.

Edwards, G. (1983) 'Alcohol and advice to pregnant women', *British Medical Journal*, 286: 247–248.

Edwards, G., Anderson, P., Babor, T.F., Casswell, S., Ferrence, R., Giesbrecht, N., Godfrey, C., Holder, H.D., Lemmens, P., Mäkelä, K., Midanik, L.T., Norström, T., Österberg, E., Romelsjö, A., Room, R., Simpura, J. and Skog, Ø.J. (1995) *Alcohol Policy and the Public Good*, Oxford, Oxford University Press.

Edwards, R.W. and Thurman, P.J. (1995) 'Patterns of alcohol use among ethnic minority adolescent women', *Recent Developments in Alcoholism*, Vol 12: New York, Plenum Press, 369–386.

Ehrenberg, V. (1974) *The People of Aristophenes*, London, Methuen.

Ehrenreich, B. and English, D. (1979) *For Her Own Good. 150 Years of the Experts' Advice to Women*, London, Pluto Press.

Einstein, S. and Wolfson, E. (1970) 'Alcoholism curricula: How professionals are trained', *International Journal of the Addictions*, 5: 295–312.

Eisenbach-Stangl, I. (1992) 'Treatment seeking and treatment-reluctant alcoholics: A two-class alcohol-treatment system in Austria', in Klingemann, H., Takkala, J. and Hunt, G., (eds) *Cure, Care or Control: Alcoholism Treatment in Sixteen Counties*,. Albany, New York, State University of New York Press, 173–189.

Eisenbach-Stangl, I. (1997) 'Professional treatment and mutual aid: Different offers for female alcoholics or offers for women with different alcohol-related problems?' *European Addiction Research*, 3: 22–29.

Eisenhofer, G., Whiteside, E.A. and Johnson, R.H. (1985) 'Plasma catecholamine responses to changes of posture in alcoholics during withdrawal and after continued abstinence from alcohol', *Clinical Science*, 68: 71–78.

El-Bassell, N., Ivanoff, A., Schilling, R.F., Gilbert, L. and Chen, D-R. (1995) 'Correlates of problem drinking among drug-using incarcerated women', *Addictive Behaviors*, 29: 359–369.

Elderton, E. and Pearson, K. (1910) *A First Study of the Influence of Parental Alcoholism on the Physique and Ability of the Offspring* (Eugenics Laboratory Memoir), London, Cambridge University Press.

Elekes, Z. (1992) 'The development of an alcohol treatment system in Hungary', in Klingemann, H., Takkala, J. and Hunt, G. (eds) *Cure, Care or Control: Alcoholism Treatment in Sixteen Countries*, Albany, New York, State University of New York Press, 23–38.

El-Guebaly, N. (1995) 'Alcohol and polysubstance abuse among women', *Canadian Journal of Psychiatry – Revue Canadienne De Psychiatric*, 40: 73–79.

Ell, S.R. (1989) 'Three days in October of 1630: Detailed examination of mortality during an early modern plague epidemic in Venice', *Reviews of Infectious Diseases*, 11: 128–141.

Ellis, A. (1982) *Rational Emotive Therapy and Cognitive Behavior Therapy*, New York, Springer Publishers.

Ellis, A., McInerney, J.F., DiGiuseppe, R. et al. (1988) *Rational-Emotive Therapy with Alcoholics and Substance Abusers*, Elmsford, New York, Pergamon Press.

Ellis, A. and Whiteley, J.M. (1979) *Theoretical and Empirical Foundations of Rational-Emotive Therapy*, California, Brooks/Cole.

Elsner, J. (1995) 'Neurobehavioral abnormalities induced by prenatal exposure to substances of abuse – stating the problems', *Archives of Toxicology*, Supplement, 17: 221–232.

Emmelkamp, P.M.G. and Heeres, H. (1988) 'Drug addiction and parental rearing style: A controlled study', *International Journal of the Addictions*, 23: 207–216.

Emrick, C.D. (1974) 'A review of psychologically oriented treatment of alcoholism. 1. The use and interrelationships of outcome criteria and drinking behavior following treatment', *Journal of Studies on Alcohol*, 35: 523–549.

Emrick, C.D. (1975) 'A review of psychologically oriented treatment of alcoholism. 2: The relative effectiveness of treatment versus no-treatment', *Journal of Studies on Alcoholism*, 35: 534–549.

Endicott, M. (1993) 'The menstrual cycle and mood disorders', *Journal of Affective Disorders*, 29: 193–200.

Engel, E. (1977) 'One hundred years of cytogenetic studies in health and disease', *American Journal of Mental Deficiency*, 82: 109–116.

Engelstein, L. (1986) 'Syphilis, historical and actual: Cultural geography of a disease', *Reviews of Infectious Diseases*, 8: 1036–1048.

Ericksen, K.P. and Trocki, K.F. (1994) 'Sex, alcohol and sexually transmitted diseases: A national survey', *Family Planning Perspectives*, 26: 257–263.

Eriksen, L., Bjornstad, S. and Gotestam, C. (1986) 'Social skills training in groups for alcoholics: One-year treatment outcome for groups and individuals', *Addictive Behaviors*, 11: 309–329.

Eriksson, B. (1980) 'A lesbian execution in Germany, 1721: The trial records', *Journal of Homosexuality*, 6: 27–40.

Ernhart, C.B., Sokol, R.J., Martier, S., Moron, P., Nadler, D., Ager, J.W. and Wolf, A. (1987) 'Alcohol teratology in the human: A detailed assessment of specificity, critical period,and threshold', *American Journal of Obstetrics and Gynecology*, 156: 33–39.

Ernst, W. (1991) *Mad Tales from the Raj; The European Insane in British India. 1800–1858*, London, Routledge.

Eronen, M. (1995) 'Mental disorders and homicidal behavior in female subjects', *American Journal of Psychiatry*, 152: 1216–1218.

Estes, C.P. (1992) *Women Who Run with the Wolves: Myths and Stories of the Wild Woman Archetype*, New York, Random House Inc.

Ethier, L.S. (1995) 'Childhood adversity, parental stress, and depression of negligent mothers', *Child Abuse and Neglect: The International Journal*, 19: 619–632.

Ettorre, E.M. (1985) 'A study of alcoholism treatment units: some findings on units and staff', *Alcohol and Alcoholism*, 20: 371–378.

Evans, C. and Lacey, J.H. (1992) 'Multiple self-damaging behaviour among alcoholic women. A prevalence study', *British Journal of Psychiatry*, 161: 643–647.

Evenden, D. (1994) 'Mothers and their midwives in Seventeenth Century London', in Marland, H., (ed.) *The Art of Midwifery: Early Modern Midwives in Europe*, London, Routledge, 9–26.

Everett, M.W., Waddell, J.O. and Heath, D.B. (1976) *Cross-Cultural Approaches to the Study of Alcohol: An Interdisciplinary Perspective*, The Hague, Mouton.

Fabrizio, T. (1991) 'Women, youth and alcohol', *Nordisk Medicin*, 106: 328–329.

Faderman, L. (1986) 'Love between women in 1928: Why progressivism is not always progress', *Journal of Homosexuality*, 12: 23–42.

Fagan, J. (1993) 'Interactions among drugs, alcohol, and violence', *Health Affairs*, 12: 65–79.

Farid, B. and Clarke, M.E. (1992) 'Characteristics of attenders to a community based alcohol treatment centre with special reference to sex difference', *Drug and Alcohol Dependence*, 30,1: 33–36.

Farr, A.D. (1980) 'The Marquis de Sade and induced abortion', *Journal of Medical Ethics*, 6: 7–10.

Farrell, M. and Strang, J. (1991) 'Substance use and misuse in childhood and adolescence', *Journal of Child Psychology and Psychiatry and Allied Disciplines*, 32: 109–128.

Fazey, C. (1977) *The Aetiology of Psychoactive Substance Use*, Paris, UNESCO.

Featherstone, M. and Hepworth, M. (1985) 'The history of the male menopause 1848–1936', *Maturitas*, 7: 249–257.

Fee, E. and Greene, B. (1989) 'Science and social reform: Women in public health', *Journal of Public Health Policy*, 10: 161–177.

Feldman, B. (1927) 'Alcohol in ancient Jewish literature', *British Journal of Addiction*, 24: 121–124.

Feldman, F., Susselman, S., Lipetz, B. and Barrera, S.E. (1946) 'Shock treatment of psychosis associated with pregnancy', *Journal of Nervous and Mental Diseases*, 103: 494.

Fendrich, M., Mackesy-Amiti, M.E., Goldstein, P., Spunt, B. and Brownstein, H. (1995) 'Substance involvement among juvenile murderers: Comparisons with older offenders based on interviews with prison inmates', *International Journal of the Addictions*, 30: 1363–1382.

Ferguson, J. (1892) 'The insanity following exhaustion, acute disease, injuries etc.', *Alienist and Neurologist*, July 13,3: 407–438.

Figlio, K. (1978) 'Chlorosis and chronic disease in 19th-century Britain: the social constitution of somatic illness in a capitalist society', *International Journal of Health Services*, 8: 589–617.

File, S.E., Zharkovsky, A. and Hitchcott, P.K. (1992) 'Effects of nitrendipine, chlordiazepoxide, flumazenil and baclofen on the increased anxiety resulting from alcohol withdrawal', *Progress in Neuro-Psychopharmacology and Biological-Psychiatry*, 67: 87–93.

Fillmore, K.M. (1987) 'Women's drinking across the life course as compared to men's', *British Journal of Addiction*, 82: 801–811.

Fillmore, K. (1988) *Alcohol Use Across the Life Course: A Critical Review of Seventy Years of International Longitudinal Research*, Toronto, Addiction Research Foundation.

Fillmore, K.M., Golding, J.M., Kniep, S., Leino, E.V., Shoemaker, C., Ager, C.R., Ferrer, H.P., Ahlström, S., Allebeck, P. and Amundsen, A. (1995) 'Gender differences for the risk of alcohol-related problems in multiple national contexts', *Recent Developments in Alcoholism*, Vol. 12, New York, Plenum Press, 409–439.

Fillmore, K.M., Golding, J.M., Leino, E.V., Motoyoshi, M., Ager, C.R. and Ferrer, H.P. (1994) 'Relationships of measures of alcohol consumption with alcohol-related problems in multiple studies: A research synthesis from the collaborative alcohol-related longitudinal project', *Addiction*, 89: 1143–1156.

Finkelhor, D. (1979) *Sexually Victimised Children*, New York, Free Press.

Finkelstein, N. (1993) 'Treatment programming for alcohol and drug-dependent pregnant women', *Journal of Drug Issues*, 28, 13 1275–1309.

Finkelstein, N. (1994) 'Treatment issues for alcohol and drug-dependent pregnant and parenting women', *Health and Social Work*, 19: 7–15.

Finlayson, R.E. (1992) 'Comorbidity in elderly alcoholics', in Beresford, T.P. and Gomberg, E. (eds) *Alcohol and Aging*, New York, Oxford University Press, 56–69.

Finn, W.F. (1984) 'Maternal welfare – Nassau County, New York, 1957–1981', *Obstetrical and Gynecological Survey*, 39: 127–133.

Finnegan, L.P. (1994) 'Perinatal morbidity and mortality in substance using families: Effects and intervention strategies', *Bulletin on Narcotics*, 46: 19–43.

Finney, J.W., Moos, R.H. and Brennan, P.L. (1991) 'The Drinking Problems Index: A measure to assess alcohol-related problems among older adults', *Journal of Substance Abuse*, 3: 431–440.

Firth, M. (1880) *Brandy: What it Is, What it Does and What it Cannot Do*, London, John Smith and Company.

Fischer, P. (1991) *Alcohol, Drug Abuse and Mental Health Problems Among Homeless Persons: A Review of the Literature, 1980–1990*, Rockville, MD., US Department of Health and Human Services, Alcohol, Drug Abuse, and Mental Health Administration.

Fisher, M. and Gordon, T. (1985) 'The relation of drinking and smoking habits to diet: The Lipid Clinics Prevalence Study', *American Journal of Clinical Nutrition*, 41: 623–630.

Fisher, R.S., Roberts, G.S., Grabowski, C.J. and Cohen, S. (1978) 'Inhibition of lower esophageal sphincter circular muscle by female sex hormones', *American Journal of Physiology*, 234: 243–248.

Fisher, S.E. (1991) 'Ethanol and fetal/postnatal growth', *Alcoholism: Clinical and Experimental Research*, 15: 903–904.

Fisher, S.E. and Karl, P.I. (1988) 'Maternal ethanol use and selective fetal malnutrition', in Glanter, M. (ed.) *Recent Devlopments in Alcoholism, Vol. 6*, New York, Plenum, 277–289.

Fitzpatrick, K.M. and Boldizar, J.P. (1993) 'The prevalence and consequences of exposure to violence among African-American youth', *Journal of the American Academy of Child and Adolescent Psychiatry*, 32: 424–430.

Flaherty, J.A. and Richman, J.A. (1993) 'Substance use and addiction among medical students, residents, and physicians', *Psychiatric Clinics of North America*, 16: 189–197.

Fleming, J. (1996) 'The epidemiology of alcohol use in Australian women: Findings from a national survey of women's drinking', *Addiction*, 91: 1325–1334.

Fleming, P.M., Meyroyan, A. and Klimova, I. (1994) 'Alcohol treatment services in Russia: A worsening crisis', *Alcohol and Alcoholism*, 29: 357–362.

Flores-Ortiz, Y.G. (1994) 'The role of cultural and gender values in alcohol use patterns among Chicana/Latina high school and university students: implications for AIDS prevention', *International Journal of the Addictions,* 29: 1149–1171.

Florey, C., Taylor, T., Bolumar, F. et al. (1992) 'A European concerted action: Maternal alcohol consumption and its relation to the outcome of pregnancy and child development at 18 months', *International Journal of Epidemiology,* 21 (supplement 1).

Floyd, R.L., Rimer, B.K., Giovino, G.A., Mullen, P.D. and Sullivan, S.E. (1993) 'A review of smoking in pregnancy: Effects on pregnancy outcomes and cessation efforts', *Annual Review of Public Health,* 14 ISS: 379–411.

Folsom, C.F. (1890) A comparison of hypnotics, new and old', *Alienist and Neurologist,* 11,3: 608–609.

Foote-Smith, E. and Bayne, L. (1991) 'Joan of Arc', *Epilepsia,* 32: 810–815.

Ford, K. and Norris, A. (1994) 'Urban minority youth: Alcohol and marijuana use and exposure to unprotected intercourse', *Journal of Acquired Immune Deficiency Syndromes,* 7: 389–396.

Forrest, F., Florey, C., Taylor, D., McPherson, F. and Young, J.A. (1991) 'Reported social alcohol consumption during pregnancy and infants' development at 18 months', *British Medical Journal,* 303: 22–26.

Fortenberry, J.D. (1995) 'Adolescent substance use and sexually transmitted diseases risk: A review', *Journal of Adolescent Health,* 16: 304–308.

Fortmann, S.P., Haskell, W.L. Vranizan, K. et al. (1983) 'The association of blood pressure and dietary alcohol: differences by age, sex and estrogen use', *American Journal of Epidemiology,* 118: 497–507.

Fortmann, S.P. and Killen, J.D. (1994) 'Who shall quit? comparison of volunteer and population-based recruitment in two minimal-contact smoking cessation studies', *American Journal of Epidemiology,* 140: 39–51.

Fossey, E. (1993) 'Young children and alcohol: A theory of attitude development', *Alcohol and Alcoholism,* 28: 485–498.

Fossey, E. (1994) *Growing Up with Alcohol,* London, Tavistock/Routledge.

Foster, K., Wilmot, A. and Dobbs, J. (1990) *General Household Survey: 1988,* London, HMSO.

Foster, P. (1995) *Women and the Health Care Industry: An Unhealthy Relationship?* Buckingham, Open University Press.

Foster, R.S. and Costanza, M.C. (1984) 'Breast self-examination practices and breast cancer survival', *Cancer,* 53: 999–1005.

Fosu, G.B. (1995) 'Women's orientation toward help-seeking for mental disorders', *Social Science and Medicine,* 40: 1029–1040.

Fox, K.M. and Gilbert, B.O. (1994) 'The interpersonal and psychological functioning of women who experienced childhood physical abuse, incest, and parental alcoholism', *Child Abuse and Neglect,* 18: 849–858.

Fox, R. (1975) 'Group psychotherapy with alcoholics', in Rosenbaum, M. and Berger, M., (eds) *Group Psychotherapy and Group Function,* New York, Basic Books, 521–543.

Franke, G.H., Jager, H., Thomann, B. and Beyer, B. (1992) 'Assessment

and evaluation of psychological distress in HIV-infected women', *Psychology and Health*, 6: 297–312.
France, A. (1988) *Consuming Psychotherapy*, London, Free Association Books.
Fraser, S. (1989) *My Father's House: A Memoir of Incest and of Healing*, London, Virago Press Ltd.
Freeman, E.M. (1993) *Substance Abuse Treatment: A Family Systems Perspective*, Newbury Park, California, Sage Publications.
French, S.A., Perry, C.L., Leon, G.R. and Fulkerson, J.A. (1994) 'Weight concerns, dieting behavior, and smoking initiation among adolescents: A prospective study', *American Journal of Public Health*, 84: 1818–1820.
Freyberg, J.T. (1980) 'Difficulties in separation-individuation as experienced by offspring of Nazi holocaust survivors', *American Journal of Orthopsychiatry*, 50: 87–95.
Frezza, M., di Padova, C., Pozzato, G. et al. (1990) 'High blood alcohol levels in women. The role of decreased gastric alcohol dehydrogenase activity and first pass metabolism', *New England Journal of Medicine*, 322: 95–99.
Fried, P.A. (1993) 'Prenatal exposure to tobacco and marijuana: Effects during pregnancy, infancy, and early childhood', *Clinical Obstetrics and Gynecology*, 36: 319–337.
Fried, P.A. (1995a) 'The Ottawa Prenatal prospective study (OPPS): methodological issues and findings – it's easy to throw the baby out with the bath water', *Life Sciences*, 56: 2159–2168.
Fried, P.A. (1995b) 'Prenatal exposure to marihuana and tobacco during infancy, early and middle childhood: effects and an attempt at synthesis', *Archives of Toxicology*, Supplement, 17: 233–260.
Fried, P.A. and O'Connell, C.M. (1987) 'A comparison of the effects of prenatal exposure to tobacco, alcohol, cannabis and caffeine on birth size and subsequent growth', *Neurobehavioral Toxicology*, 9: 79–85.
Friedan, B. (1983) *The Second Stage*. London, Abacus.
Friedenreich, C.M., Howe, G.R., Miller, A.B. and Jain, M.G. (1992) 'Cohort study of alcohol consumption and risk of breast cancer', (abstract no 307) Society for Epidemiological Research, 25th Annual Meeting, 9–12 June.
Friedlander, D. (1983) 'Demographic responses and socioeconomic structure: Population processes in England and Wales in the nineteenth century', *Demography*, 20: 249–272.
Friedlander, D. and Ben Moshe, E. (1986) 'Occupations, migration, sex ratios, and nuptiality in nineteenth century English communities: A model of relationships', *Demography*, 23: 1–12.
Friedman, G.D., Klatsky, A.L. and Siegelaub, A.B. (1982) 'Alcohol, tobacco and hypertension', *Hypertension*, 4 (supplement): 143–150.
Friedman, L.A. and Kimbal, A.W. (1986) 'Coronary heart disease mortality and alcohol consumption in Framingham', *American Journal of Epidemiology*, 124: 481–489.
Friman, P.C., Finney, J.W., Glassock, S.G. et al. (1986) 'Testicular self-

examination: Validation of a training strategy for early cancer detection', *Journal of Applied Behavior Analysis*.

Fry, P.S. (1995) 'Perfectionism, humor, and optimism as moderators of health outcomes and determinants of coping styles of women executives', *Genetic, Social and General Psychology Monographs*, 121: 211–245.

Gabert, H.A. and Bey, M. (1988) 'History and development of cesarean operation', *Obstetrics and Gynecology Clinics of North America*, 15: 591–605.

Galanter, M., Castaneda, R. and Franco, H. (1991) 'Group therapy and self-help groups', in Frances, R.J. and Miller, S.J., (eds) *Clinical Textbook of Addictive Disorders*, New York, Guilford Press, 431.

Gallant, S.J., Hamilton, J.A., Popiel, D.A., Morokoff, P.J. and Chakraborty, P.K. (1991) 'Daily mood and symptoms: Effects of awareness of study focus, gender, menstrual cycle phase and day of the week', *Health Psychology*, 10: 180–189.

Galton, F. (1889) *Natural Inheritance*, London, Macmillan.

Gambert, S.R. and Katsoyannis, K.K. (1992) 'Alcohol-related medical disorders of older heavy drinkers', in Beresford, T.P. and Gomberg, E. (eds) *Alcohol and Aging*, New York, Oxford University Press, 70–81.

Gamella, J.F. (1995) 'Spain', in Heath, D.B., (ed.) *International Handbook on Alcohol and Culture*, Connecticut, Greenwood Press, 254–269.

Gannon, J.P. (1989) *Soul Survivors: A New Beginning for Adults Abused as Children*, New York, Prentice Hall Press.

Gapstur, S.M, Potter, J.D., Sellers, T.A. and Folsom, A.R. (1992) 'Interaction of alcohol consumption and estrogen use on risk of breast cancer in post menopausal women', (abstract no 110), Society for Epidemiological Research, 25th Annual Meeting, 9–12 June.

Garcia, J., Osuna, E., Perez-Carceles, M.D. and Luna, A. (1991) 'Attitudes of medical practitioners towards alcohol and alcohol consumption', *Medicine and Law*, 10: 469–475.

Garcia, S.A. (1993) 'Maternal drug abuse: Laws and ethics as agents of just balances and therapeutic interventions', *International Journal of the Addictions*, 28: 1311–1339.

Garcia-Gil, C., Cortes-Majo, M., Nieto-Garcia, A., Rosado Martin, M. and Najera, E. (1989) 'Epidemiological appraisal of the active role of women in the decline of infant mortality in Spain during the twentieth century', *Social Science and Medicine*, 29: 1351–1362.

Gardner, J.F. and Wiedemann, T. (1991) *The Roman Household. A Source Book*, London, Routledge.

Garfinkel, L., Boffelta, P. and Stellman, S.D. (1988) 'Alcohol and Breat Cancer: A cohort study', *Preventative Medicine*, 17: 686–693.

Garland, M.A., Parsons, O.A. and Nixon, S.J. (1993) 'Visual-spatial learning in nonalcoholic young adults with and those without a family history of alcoholism', *Journal of Studies on Alcohol*, 54: 219–224.

Garretsen, H.F.L. and van de Goor, I. (1995) 'The Netherlands', in Heath, D.B., (ed.) *International Handbook on Alcohol and Culture*, Connecticut, Greenwood Press, 190–200.

Garrett, D. (1995) 'Violent behaviors among African-American adolescents', *Adolescence*, 30: 209–216.

Gartner, U. and Ryden, G. (1972) 'The elimination of alcohol in the premature infant', *Acta Paediatrica Scandinavica*, 61: 720–721.

Gary, L.E. and Gary, R.B. (1985) 'Treatment needs of black alcoholic women', in Brisbane, F.L. and Womble, M. (eds) *Treatment of Black Alcoholics*, New York, Haworth.

Gavaler, J.S. (1988) 'Effects of moderate consumption of alcoholic beverages on endocrine function in postmenopausal women: Bases for hypotheses', in Galanter, M., (ed.) *Recent Developments in Alcoholism* Vol. 6, New York, Plenum Press, 229–251.

Gavaler, J.S. (1992) 'Alcohol effects in postmenopausal women: Alcohol and estrogens', in Mendelson, J.H., and Mello, N.K. (eds) *Medical Diagnosis and Treatment of Alcoholism*, New York, McGraw Hill, 623–638.

Gavaler, J.S. (1993) 'Alcohol and nutrition in postmenopausal women', *Journal of the American College of Nutrition*, 12: 349–356.

Gavaler, J.S. (1995) 'Alcohol effects on hormone levels in normal post menopausal women and in post menopausal women with alcohol-induced cirrhosis', in Galanter, M. (ed.) *Recent Developments in Alcoholism: Volume 12, Alcoholism and Women*, New York, Plenum, 199–208.

Gavaler, J.S. and Arria, A.M. (1995) 'Increased susceptibility of women to alcoholic liver disease: Artifactual or real?', In Hall, P. (ed.) *Alcoholic Liver Disease: Pathology and Pathogenisis*, Melbourne, Edward Arnold.

Gavaler, J.S., Deal, S.R., Van Thiel, D.H. et al. (1993) 'Alcohol and estrogen levels in postmenopausal women: The spectrum of effect', *Alcoholism: Clinical and Experimental Research*, 17: 786–790.

Gavaler, J.S., Rizzo, A., Rossaro, L., Van Thiel, D.H., Brezza, E. and Deal, S.R. (1993) 'Sexuality of alcoholic women with menstrual cycle function: Effects of duration of alcohol abstinence', *Alcoholism, Clinical and Experimental Research*, 17, 778–781.

Gavaler, J.S., Rizzo, A., Rossaro, L., Van Thiel, D.H., Brezza, E. and Deal, S.R. (1994) 'Sexuality of alcoholic postmenopausal women: Effects of duration of alcohol abstinence', *Alcoholism, Clinical and Experimental Research*, 18: 269–271.

Gavaler, J.S. and Van Thiel, D.H. (1992) 'The association between moderate alcoholic beverage consumption and serum estradial and testosterone levels in normal postmenopausal women: Relationships to the literature', *Alcoholism; Clinical and Experimental Research*, 16: 87–92.

Gawain, S. (1985) *Creative Visualisation*, New York, Bantam Books Inc.

Gaziano, M.I., Buring, J.E., Breslow, J.L., Goldhaber, S.Z., Rosner, B., Van Der Burgh, M., Willet, W. and Hennekens, C.H. (1993) 'Moderate alcohol intake, increased levels of high-density lipoprotein and its subfractions, and decreased risk of myocardial infarction', *New England Journal of Medicine*, 329: 1829–1834.

Gearhart, J.G., Beebe, D.K., Milhorn, H.T. and Meeks, G.R. (1991) 'Alcoholism in women', *American Family Physician*, 44: 907–913.

Gebhard, P.H., Gagnon, J.H., Pomeroy, W.B. and Christensen C.V. (1965) *Sex Offenders*, New York, Harper and Row.

Gefou-Madianou, D. (1992) 'Exclusion and unity, retsina and sweet wine', in Gefou-Madianou, D. (ed.) *Alcohol, Gender and Culture*, London, Tavistock, 108–136.

Gefou-Madianos, M.D., Richardson, C. and Stefanis, C.N. (1995) 'Factors affecting illicit and licit drug use among adolescents and young adults in Greece', *Acta Psychiatrica Scandinavica*, 91: 258–264.

Geissler, L.S., Bormann, C.A., Kwiatkowski, C.F., Braucht, G., Nicholas, E. et al. (1995) 'Women, homelessness and substance abuse: Moving beyond the stereotypes', *Psychology of Women Quarterly*, 19: 65–83.

Geller, A. (1984) 'The social, psychological and medical management of intoxication', *Journal of Substance Abuse Treatment*, 1: 11–19.

Geller, J.L. (1985) 'Women's accounts of psychiatric illness and institutionalization', *Hospital and Community Psychiatry*, 36: 1056–1062.

Gendlin, E.T. (1981) *Focusing*, 2nd edn. New York, Bantam Books.

Genteel, T. (1994) 'Treatment needs of women offenders with substance abuse histories: A Delphi study', *Dissertation Abstracts International*, 54,7: 3852B.

George, W.H., Cue, K.L., Lopez, P.A. and Crowe, E. C. (1995) 'Self-reported alcohol expectancies and postdrinking sexual inferences about women', *Journal of Applied Social Psychology*, 25: 164–186.

George, W.H., Gournic, S.J. and McAffe, M.P. (1988) 'Perceptions of post-drinking female sexuality: Effects of gender, beverage choice, and drink payment', *Journal of Applied Social Psychology*, 18: 1295–1317.

Gerrein, J.E., Rosenberg, C.M. and Manohar, V. (1973) 'Disulfiram maintenance in outpatient treatment of alcoholism', *Archives of General Psychiatry*, 28: 798–802.

Gershoff, S.N. (1977) 'Science-neglected ingredient of nutrition policy. 10th Martha F. Trulson Memorial Lecture', *Journal of the American Dietetic Association*, 70: 471–478.

Gerstein, D. and Green, L. (eds) (1993) *Preventing Drug Abuse: What Do We Know?* Washington, D.C., National Academy Press.

Giancola, P.R. and Zeichner, A. (1995) 'Alcohol-related aggression in males and females: Effects of blood alcohol concentration, subjective intoxication, personality, and provocation', *Alcoholism, Clinical and Experimental Research*, 19: 130–134.

Gibson, G.T., Baghurst, P.A., and Colley, D.P. (1983) 'Maternal alcohol, tobacco and cannabis consumption and the outcome of pregancy', *Australia and New Zealand Journal of Obstetrics and Gynaecology*, 23: 15–19.

Gibson, W.C. (1980) 'The cost of not doing medical research', *Journal of the American Medical Association*, 244: 1817–1819.

Giesbrecht, N. and Dick, R. (1993) 'Societal norms and risk-taking behaviour: Inter-cultural comparisons of casualties and alcohol consumption', *Addiction*, 88: 867–876.

Giesbrecht, N., Gonzalez, R., Grant, M., Österberg, E., Room, R., Rootman,

I., and Towle, L. (1989) *Drinking and Casualties: Accidents, Poisonings and Violence in an International Perpective*, London, Tavistock/Routledge.

Gilbert, A.N. (1980) 'Conceptions of homosexuality and sodomy in Western history', *Journal of Homosexuality*, 6: 57–68.

Gilbert, M.J., Mora, J. and Ferguson, L.R. (1994) 'Alcohol-related expectations among Mexican-American women', *International Journal of the Addictions*, 29: 1127–1147.

Gill, J. (1997) 'Women, alcohol and the menstrual cycle', *Alcohol and Alcoholism* (in press).

Gill, J.S., Shipley, M.J., Hornby, R.H. et al. (1988) 'A community case control study of alcohol consumption in stroke', *International Journal of Epidemiology*, 17: 542–547.

Gillet, C., Paille, F., Wahl, D., Aubin, H.J., Pirollet, P. and Prime, T. (1991) 'Outcome of treatment in alcoholic women', *Drug and Alcohol Dependence*, 29: 189–194.

Gilligan, S.B., Reich, T. and Cloninger, C.R. (1988) 'Alcohol-related symptoms in heterogeneous families of hospitalised alcoholics', *Alcoholism: Clinical and Experimental Research*, 12: 671–678.

Gillman, C.P. (1981) *The Yellow Wallpaper*, London, Virago.

Gillman, M.W., Cook, N.R., Evans, D.A. Rosner, B. And Hennekens, C.H. (1995) 'Relationship of alcohol intake with blood pressure in young adults', *Hypertension*, 25: 106–1110.

Gindhart, P.S. (1989) 'An early twentieth-century skeleton collection', *Journal of Forensic Sciences*, 34: 887–893.

Ginsburg, E.S., Mello, N.K., Mendelson, J.H., Barbieri, J.W., Teoh, S.K., Rothman, M, Goa, J.W. and Sholar, J.W. (1995) 'Effects of alcohol ingestion on estrogens in postmenopausal women', *Journal of the American Medical Association*, 276: 1747–1751.

Ginsburg, E.S., Walsh, B.W., Shea, B.F., Gao, X., Gleason, R.E. and Barbieri, R.L. (1995) 'The effects of ethanol on the clearance of estradiol in post menopausal women', *Fertility and Sterility*, 63: 1227–1230.

Girdler, S.S., Pedersen, C.A., Stern, R.A. and Light, K.C. (1993) 'Menstrual cycle and premenstrual syndrome: Modifiers of cardiovascular reactivity in women', *Health Psychology*, 12, 180–185.

Giunta, C.T. and Compas, B.E. (1994) 'Adult daughters of alcoholics: Are they unique?' *Journal of Studies on Alcohol*, 55: 600–606.

Glantz, J.C., and Woods, J.R. (1993) 'Cocaine, heroin and phencyclidine: Obstetric perspectives', *Clinical Obstetrics and Gynecology*, 36: 279–301.

Glantz, M.D. (1992) 'Cognitive therapy with elderly alcoholics', in Beresford, T.P. and Gomberg, E.S.L. (eds) *Alcohol and Aging*, New York, Oxford University Press, 211–229.

Glantz, M.D. and Backenheimer, M. (1988) 'Substance use among elderly women', *Clinical Gerontologist*, 8: 3–26.

Glaser, G.H. (1978) 'Epilepsy, hysteria, and "possession". A historical essay', *Journal of Nervous and Mental Disease*, 166: 268–274.

Glass, D.D. (1995) *'All My Fault': Why Women Don't Leave Abusive Men*, London, Virago Press Ltd.

Glass, L. (1993) *He Says, She Says: Closing the Gap Between the Sexes*, New York, Perigee Books, Putnam Publishing Group.

Glass, T.A., Prigerson, H., Kasl, S.V. and Mendes de Leon, C.F. (1995) 'The effects of negative life events on alcohol consumption among older men and women', *Journal of Gerontology Series B, Psychological Sciences and Social Sciences*, 50: 205–216.

Glass-Crome, I.B. (1995) 'Gender related issues in alcohol problems research: a special need group?' in Tabakoff, B. and Hoffman, P.L. (eds) *Biological Aspects of Alcoholism*, Seattle, Hogrefe and Huber, 163–187.

Gleason, N.A. (1994a) 'College women and alcohol: A relational perspective', *Journal of American College Health*, 42: 279–289.

Gleason, N.A. (1994b) 'Preventing alcohol abuse by college women: A relational perspective 2', *Journal of American College Health*, 43: 15–24.

Glendinning, C. and Millar, J. (1992) *Women and Poverty in Britain: The 1990s*, Hertfordshire, Simon and Schuster International Group.

Glenn, S.W. and Nixon, S.J. (1991) 'Applications of Cloninger's subtypes in a female alcoholic sample', *Alcoholism: Clinical and Experimental Research*, 15: 851–857.

Glicksman, L. (1986) 'Alcohol management policies for municipal recreation departments: an evaluation of the Thunder Bay model', in Giesbrecht, N. and Cox, A. (eds) *Prevention and the Environment*, Toronto, Addiction Research Foundation, 198–204.

Glynn, P.M. (1993) 'Critique of coping strategies of abstainers from alcohol up to three years post-treatment', *Nursing Research*, 6: 21–22.

Goddard, E. (1996) *Teenage Drinking in 1994*, London, Office of Population Censuses and Surveys: HMSO.

Godding, W.W. (1874) 'Puerperal insanity', *Boston Medical Journal*, 91: 317

Godfrey, C. (1997) 'Can tax be used to minimise harm? A health economist's perspective', in Plant, M.A., Single, E. and Stockwell, T. (eds) *Alcohol: Minimising the Harm: What Works?*, London, Free Association Books, 29–42.

Goedde, W.H. and Agarwal D.P. (1987) 'Genetics and alcoholism: Problems and perspectives', in Goedde, W.D. and Agarwal, D.P. (1987) *Genetics and Alcoholism*, New York, Alan R. Liss Inc., 3–20.

Goist, K.C. Jr and Sutker, P.B. (1985) 'Acute alcohol intoxication and body composition in women and men', *Pharmacology, Biochemistry and Behavior*, 22: 811–814.

Goldbloom, D.S. (1993) 'Alcohol misuse and eating disorders: Aspects of an association', *Alcohol and Alcoholism*, 28,4: 375–381.

Goldman, D. (1993) 'Genetic transmission', *Recent Developments in Alcoholism*, Vol. 11, New York, Plenum Press. 231–248.

Goldman, M.S., Brown, S.A. and Christiansen, B.A. (1987) 'Expectancy theory: Thinking about drinking', in Blane, H.T. and Leonard, K.E., (eds) *Psychological Theories of Drinking and Alcoholism*, New York, Guilford Press, 181–226.

Goldstein, M.Z. and Perkins, C.A. (1993) 'Mental health and the aging woman', *Clinics in Geriatric Medicine*, 9: 191–196.

Goldstein, P.J. (1979) *Prostitution and Drugs*, Lexington, Lexington Books.

Gomberg, E.S.L. (1976) 'Alcoholism in women', in Kissin, B. and Begleiter, H., (eds) *The Biology of Alcoholism. Vol 4: Social Aspects of Alcoholism*, New York, Plenum Press, 117–166.

Gomberg, E.S.L. (1990) 'Alcoholic women in treatment report of violent events', *Alcoholism: Clinical and Experimental Research*, 14: 312.

Gomberg, E.S.L. (1992) 'Older alcoholics: Entry into treatment', In Bersford, T.P. and Gomberg, E.S.L. (eds) *Alcohol and Aging*, New York, Oxford University Press, 169–185.

Gomberg, E.S.L. (1993a) 'Alcohol, women and the expression of aggression', *Journal of Studies on Alcohol*, Supplement 11: 89–95.

Gomberg, E.S.L. (1993b) 'Women and alcohol: use and abuse', *Journal of Nervous and Mental Disease*, 181: 211–219.

Gomberg, E.S.L. (1993c) 'Gender issues', *Recent Developments in Alcoholism*, 11 ISS: 95–107.

Gomberg, E.S.L. (1994) 'Risk factors for drinking over a woman's life span. special focus: women and alcohol', *Alcohol Health and Research World'* 18: 220–227.

Gomberg, E.S.L. (1995) 'Older Women and Alcohol: Use and Abuse', in Galanter, M., (ed.) *Recent Developments in Alcoholism: Vol 12: Alcoholism and Women*, New York, Plenum Press, 61–79.

Gomberg, E.S.L., Nelson, B.W. and Hatchett, B.F. (1991) 'Women, alcoholism, and family therapy', *Family and Community Health*, 13: 61–71.

Gomberg, E.S.L. and Nirenber, T.D. (1991) 'Women and substance abuse', *Journal of Substance Abuse*, 3: 255–267.

Gonzalez-Calvin, J.L., Garcia-Sanchez, A., Bellot, V. et al. (1993) 'Mineral metabolism, osteoblastic function and bone mass in chronic alcoholism', *Alcohol and Alcoholism*, 28,5: 571–579.

Goodale, T.S. and Stoner, S.B. (1994) 'Sexual abuse as a correlate of women's alcohol abuse', *Psychological Reports*, 75: 1496–1498.

Goode, E. (1972) *Drugs in American Society*, New York, Alfred A. Knopf.

Goodell, W. (1890) 'The abuse of uterine treatment through mistaken diagnosis', *Alienist and Neurologist*, 11,1: 78–88.

Goodison, J. (1995) *The Dreams of Women*, London, The Women's Press.

Goodwin, D.W. (1979) 'Alcoholism and heredity: A review and hypothesis', *Archives of General Psychiatry*, 36: 57–61.

Goodwin, J. (1987) 'Mary Reynolds: a post-traumatic reinterpretation of a classic case of multiple personality disorder', *Hillside Journal of Clinical Psychiatry*, 9: 89–99.

Gordon, A.A. (1898) *The Beautiful Life of Frances E. Willard*, Chicago, Woman's Temperance Publishing Association..

Gordon, G.B. (1991) 'Child sexual abuse and eating disorders: How women understand the experience of both in their lives', *Dissertation Abstracts International*, 51: 4049B.

Gordon, J.E. (1978) 'Epidemiological insights on malnutrition: Some resurrected, others restructured, a few retired', *American Journal of Clinical Nutrition*, 31: 2339–2351.

Gordon, L. (1989) *Heroes of Their Own Lives: The Politics and History of Family Violence Boston 1880–1966*, London, Virago.

Gordon, R. (1993) *The Alarming History of Medicine*, London, Sinclair Stevenson.

Gordon, T. and Kannel, W.B. (1983) 'Drinking and its relation to smoking, blood pressure, blood lipids and uric acid', *Archives of Internal Medicine*, 143: 1366–1374.

Gordon, T., Kannel, W.B., Hjortland, M.C. et al. (1978) 'Menopause and coronary heart disease: The Framingham study', *Annals of Internal Medicine*, 89: 157–161.

Gorelick, D.A. (1991) 'Overview of pharmacological treatment approaches for alcohol and other drug addictions: Intoxication, withdrawal, relapse prevention', *Psychiatric Clinics of North America*, 16: 141–156.

Gorelick, D.A. (1993) 'Recent developments in alcoholism: Pharmacological treatment', in Galanter, M., (ed.) *Recent Developments in Alcoholism*, Vol. 11, New York, Plenum Press, 413–427.

Gorelick, D.A. and Wilkins, J.N. (1986) 'Special aspects of human alcohol withdrawal', in Galanter, M., (ed.) *Recent Developments in Alcoholism*, Vol. 4, New York, Plenum Press, 283–305.

Gorelick, P. (1989) 'The status of alcohol as a risk factor for stroke', *Stroke*, 20: 1607–1610.

Gossop, M., Powis, B., Griffiths, P. and Strang, J. (1994) 'Sexual behaviour and its relationship to drug-taking amongst prostitutes in South London', *Addiction*, 89: 961–970.

Goto, M. (1994) 'Alcohol dependence of women in Japan', *Addiction*, 89: 953–954.

Gottheil, E. and Waxman, H.M. (1982) 'Alcoholism and schizophrenia', in Pattison, F.M. and Kaufnan, E., (eds) *Encyclopedic Handbook of Alcoholism*, New York, Gardner Press, 636–646.

Gourlay, W. (1906) *National Temperance: A Jubilee Biograph of the National Temperance League*, London, Richard James.

Grabowski, J. and Vanderbos, G.R. (1992) *Psychopharmacology: Basic Mechanisms and Applied Intervention*, Washington, D.C.: American Psychological Association.

Grady, K.E., Kegeles, S.S. and Lund, A.K. (unpublished, no date) 'Experimental studies to increase BSE: preliminary findings', cited by Marino and Levy (1986).

Grady, K.E. and Wolk, C.H. (unpublished, no date) 'The disruptive effects of stressful life events on compliance with breast self-examination', cited by Marino and Levy (1986).

Graham, K. (1985) 'Determinants of heavy drinking and drinking problems: The contribution of the bar environment', in Single, E. and

Storm, T., (eds) *Public Drinking and Public Policy*, Toronto, Addiction Research Foundation, 71–84.

Graham, K., Carver, V. and Brett, P.J. (1995) 'Alcohol and drug use by older women: Results of a national survey', *Canadian Journal of Aging*, 14: 769–791.

Graham, K., Clarke, D., Bois, V.C., et al. (1996) 'Addictive behavior in older adults', *Addictive Behaviors*, 21: 33–351.

Graham, K. and Homel, R. (1997) 'Creating safer bars', in Plant, M.A., Single, E. and Stockwell, T., (eds) *Alcohol: Minimising the Harm: What Works?* London, Free Association Books, 172–192.

Graham, K., LaRocque, L., Yetman, R., Ross, T.J., and Guistra, E. (1980) 'Aggression and barroom environments', *Journal of Studies on Alcohol*, 41: 277–292.

Graham, K., Price, B., Brett, P., Baker, A., Bois, A., Boyle, B., Chapman, L., Eliany, M., Gaskin, J., Martin, G., Sobell, L. and Thompson, J. (1995) *Directory of Client Outcome Measures for Addictions Treatment Programs*, Toronto, Addiction Research Foundation.

Graham, K., Wilsnack, R., Dawson, D. and Vogeltanz, N. (1996) 'Should alcohol consumption measures be adjusted for gender differences?' Paper presented at 22nd Alcohol Epidemiology Symposium of the Kettil Bruun Society, Edinburgh.

Grahn, J. (1986) 'Strange country this: Lesbianism and North American Indian tribes', *Journal of Homosexuality*, 12: 43–57.

Grant, C.A. (1995) 'Women who kill: The impact of abuse', *Issues In Mental Health Nursing*, 16: 315–326.

Grant, K.A., Tonigan, J.S. and Miller, W.R. (1995) 'Comparison of three alcohol consumption measures: a concurrent validity study', *Journal of Studies on Alcohol*, 56: 168–172.

Grant, M. (1986) 'Comparative analysis of the impact of alcohol education in North America and Western Europe', in Babor, T. (ed) *Alcohol and Culture-Comparative Perspectives from Europe and North America*, New York, New York Academy of Sciences, 198–210.

Grant, M. and Ritson, E.B. (1983) *The Prevention Debate*, London, Croom Helm.

Graves, T. (1989) *Pendulum Dowsing*, Dorset, Element Books Ltd.

Gravitz, H.L. and Bowden, J.D. (1986) 'Therapeutic issues of adult children of alcoholics: A continuum of developmental stages', in Ackerman, R.J., (ed.) *Growing in the Shadow: Children of Alcoholics*, Pompano Beach, Florida, Health Communication, 187–195.

Gray, J.H. (1982) *Bacchanalia Revisited: Western Canada's Boozy Skid to Social Disaster*, Saskatoon, Western Producer Prairie Books.

Greco, A.V. (1995) 'Alcohol and the liver: Metabolic and nutritional assesment', *Alcologia*, 7: 3–5.

Greenberg, G.S. (1977) 'The family interactional perspective: a study and examination of the work of Don D. Jackson', *Family Process*, 16: 385–412.

Greene, B. (1994) 'Ethnic-minority lesbians and gay men: Mental health and treatment issues', Journal of *Consulting Clinical Psychololgy*, 62: 2: 243–251.

Greene, T., Ernhart, C.B., Ager, J. et al. (1991) 'Prenatal alcohol exposure and cognitive development in preschool years', *Neurobehavioural Toxicology and Teratology*, 13: 57–68.

Greene, T., Ernhardt, C.B., Sokol, R.N., Martier, S., Marler, M.R., Boyd, T.A. and Ager, J. (1991) 'Prenatal alcohol exposure and preschool physical growth', *Alcoholism: Clinical and Experimental Research*, 15: 905–913.

Greenfield, T. (1997) 'Warning labels: Evidence on harm reduction from long-term American surveys', in Plant, M.A., Single, E., and Stockwell, T. (eds) *Alcohol: Minimising the Harm: What Works?* London, Free Association Books, 105–125.

Gregore, T.K. (1996) 'Subtypes of alcohol involvement and their relationships to exits from homelessness', *Substance Use and Misuse*, 31: 1333–1357.

Grimalauskiene, O. (1995) 'Alcohol and drug abusing women in Lithuania', in Council of Europe, *Women and Drugs*, Strasbourg, Council of Europe Publishing, 95–101.

Grimley Evans, J. (1990) 'The significance of osteoporosis' in R. Smith (ed.) *Osteoporosis*, London, Royal College of Physicians.

Grinder, J. and Bandler, R. (1981) *Trance-Formations*, Moab, Utah, Real People Press.

Gripshover, D.L. and Dacey, C.M. (1994) 'Discriminative validity of the MacAndrew scale in settings with a high base rate of substance abuse', *Journal of Studies on Alcohol*, 55: 303–308.

Grønbæk, M., Deis, A., Søresen, T.I.A., Becker, U., Schnor, P. and Jensen, G. (1995) 'Mortality associated with moderate intakes of wine, beer, or spirits', *British Medical Journal*, 310: 1165–1169.

Gross, W.C. (1993) 'Gender and age differences in college students' alcohol consumption', *Psychological Reports*, 72: 211–216.

Groth, N.A. (1979) *Men Who Rape*, New York, Plenum.

Grover, S.M. and Thomas, S.P. (1993) 'Substance use and anger in midlife women', *Issues In Mental Health Nursing*, 14: 19–29.

Guest, A.M. (1981) 'Social structure and U.S. inter-state fertility differentials in 1900', *Demography*, 18: 465–486.

Gullberg, R.G. (1990) 'The mathematical analysis of breath alcohol profiles generated during breath exhalation', *Journal of Analytical Toxicology*, 14: 358–367.

Guõmundsdóttir, Á. (1996) 'An evaluation of alcoholic women. A shattered self image', Paper Presented at the 22nd International Annual Alcohol Epidemiology Symposium of the Kettil Bruun Society, Edinburgh.

Guõdmunsdóttir, Á. (1997) 'The self-image and social situation of alcoholic women: Implications for treatment', *European Addiction Research*, 3: 3–10.

Gurnack, A.M and Thomas, J.L. (1989) 'Behavioral factors related to elderly alcohol abuse: Research and policy issues', *International Journal of the Addictions*, 24: 641–654.

Gusella, J.L. and Fried, P.A. (1984) 'Effects of maternal social drinking and smoking on offspring at 13 months', *Neurobehavioral Toxicology and Teratology*, 6: 13–17.

Gustafson, R. (1985) 'Alcohol and aggression: A validation study of the Taylor Aggression Paradigm', *Psychological Bulletin*, 57: 667–676.

Gustafson, R. (1986) 'Alcohol, aggression and the validity of experimental paradigms in women', *Psychological Bulletin*, 59: 51–56.

Gustafson, R. (1991) 'Aggressive and nonaggressive behavior as a function of alcohol intoxication and frustration in women', *Alcoholism: Clinical and Experimental Research*, 15,5: 886–892.

Gustafson, R. and Engstrom, C. (1991) 'Alcohol-related expectancies for self and others reported by alcoholic men and women', *Psychological Reports*, 68: 555–562.

Gyntelberg, F. and Meyer, J. (1974) 'Relationship between blood pressure and physical fitness, smoking and alcohol consumption in Copenhagen males aged 40–59', *Acta Medica Scandinavica*, 195: 375–380.

Haack, M.R. and Hughes, T.L. (1989) *Addiction in the Nursing Profession*, New York, Springer Publishing Company Inc.

Haavio-Mannila, E. (1991) 'Impact on colleagues and family members of female alcohol use', Paper Presented at the Symposium on Alcohol, Family and Significant Others. Social Research Institute of Alcohol Studies and Nordic Council for Alcohol and Drug Research, Helsinki.

Haffner, S.M., Stern, M.P., Hazuda, H.P. et al. (1986) 'Upper and centralized adiposity in Mexican Americans and non Hispanic whites: Relationship to body mass index and other behavioral and demographic variables', *International Journal of Obesity*, 10: 493–502.

Hagan, T.A., Finnegan, L.P. and Nelson-Zlupko, L. (1994) 'Impediments to comprehensive treatment models for substance-dependent women: Treatment and research questions', *Journal of Psychoactive Drugs*, 26: 163–171.

Haggard, H.W. and Jellinek, E.M. (1942) *Alcohol Explored*, New York, Doubleday.

Haines, M.R. (1977) 'Mortality in nineteenth century America: Estimates from New York and Pennsylvania census data, 1865 and 1900', *Demography*, 14: 311–331.

Haines, M.R. (1979) 'The use of model life tables to estimate mortality for the United States in the late nineteenth century', *Demography*, 16: 289–312.

Halbreich, U. and Tworek, H. (1993) 'Altered serotonergic activity in women with dysphoric premenstrual syndromes', *International Journal of Psychiatry in Medicine*, 23: 1–27.

Haley, J. (1993) *Uncommon Therapy: The Psychiatric Techniques of Milton Erickson*, New York, W.W. Norton.

Hall, J.M. (1993a) 'What really worked? A case analysis and discussion of confrontational intervention for substance abuse in marginalised women', *Archives of Psychiatric Nursing*, 7: 322–327.

Hall, J.M. (1993b) 'Lesbians and alcohol: Patterns and paradoxes in medical notions and lesbians' beliefs', *Journal of Psychoactive Drugs*, 25: 109–119.

Hall, J.M. (1994a) 'The experiences of lesbians in Alcoholics Anonymous', *Western Journal of Nursing Research*, 16: 556–576.

Hall, J.M. (1994b) 'Lesbians recovering from alcohol problems: An ethnographic study of health care experiences', *Nursing Research*, 43: 238–244.

Hall, L. and Lloyd, S. (1990) *Surviving Child Sexual Abuse*, Hampshire, The Falmer Press.

Hall, W. and Hunter, E. (1995) 'Australia', in Heath, D.B., (ed.) *International Handbook on Alcohol and Culture*, Connecticut, Greenwood Press, 7–19.

Halliday, A., Bush, B., Clearly, P., Aronson, M. and Delbranco, T. (1986) 'Alcohol abuse in women seeking gynecologic care', *Obstetrics and Gynecology*, 68: 322–326.

Hallman, J., von Knorring, L., Edman, G. and Oreland, L. (1991) 'Personality traits and platelet Monoamine Oxidase activity in alcoholic women', *Addictive Behaviors*, 16: 533–541.

Halmesmäki, E. (1988) 'Alcohol counselling of 85 pregnant problem drinkers: effect on drinking and fetal outcome', *British Journal of Obstetrics and Gynaecology*, 95: 243–247.

Halmesmäki, E., Välimäki, M. and Roine, R. (1989) 'Maternal and paternal alcohol consumption and miscarriage', *British Journal of Obstetrics and Gynaecology*, 96: 188–191.

Hamilton, C.J. and Collins, J.J. Jr (1982) 'The role of alcohol in wife beating and child abuse. A review of the literature', in Collins, J.J. Jr, (ed.) *Drinking and Crime*, London, Tavistock, 253–287.

Hamilton, D. (1981) *The Healers: A History of Medicine in Scotland*, Edinburgh, Canongate Publishing Ltd.

Hamilton, G. and Volpe, J. (1982) 'How women recover: Experience and research observations', *Alcohol: Health and Research World*, 16: 193–214.

Hamilton, G.J. (1993) 'Further labeling within the category of disability due to chemical dependency: borderline personality disorder', *Women and Therapy*, 14: 153–157.

Hamlin, R.B. (1992) 'Embracing our past, informing our future: A feminist re-vision of health care', *American Journal of Occupational Therapy*, 46: 1028–1035.

Hammarstrom, A. (1994) 'Health consequences of youth unemployment – review from a gender perspective', *Social Science and Medicine*, 38: 699–709.

Hammer, T. and Vaglum, P. (1989) 'The increase in alcohol consumption in women: A phenomenon related to accessibility or stress? A general population study', *British Journal of Addiction*, 84: 767–775.

Hammer, T. and Vaglum, P. (1992) 'Further course of mental health and use of alcohol and tranquilizers after cessation or persistence of cannabis use in young adulthood: a longitudinal study', *Scandinavian Journal of Social Medicine*, 20: 143–150.

Haney, A.F. (1986) 'The "physiology" of the climacterium', *Clinical Obstetrics and Gynecology*, 29: 397–406.

Hankin, J.R., Sloan, J.J., Firestone, I.J., Ager, J.W., Sokol, R.J. and Martier, S.S. (1996) 'Has awareness of the alcohol warning label reached its upper limit?' *Alcoholism: Clinical and Experimental Research*, 20: 440–444.

Hanna, E.Z. (1991) 'Social opportunity and alcohol abuse in women: Temporal and structural differences in drinking contexts of nonclinic and clinic female drinkers', *Journal of Substance Abuse*, 3: 1–11.

Hanna, E.Z, Faden, V.B. and Dufour, M.C. (1994) 'The motivational correlates of drinking, smoking, and illicit drug use during pregnancy', *Journal of Substance Abuse*, 6: 155–167.

Hanna, E.Z., Faden, V.B. and Harford, T.C. (1993) 'Marriage: Does it protect young women from alcoholism?' *Journal of Substance Abuse*, 5: 1–14.

Hanson, D.J. (1995) 'The United States of America', in Heath, D.B., (ed.) *International Handbook on Alcohol and Culture*, Connecticut, Greenwood Press, 300–315.

Harburg, E., Gleiberman, L., Difranceisco, W. and Peele, S. (1994) 'Towards a concept of sensible drinking and an illustration of measure', *Alcohol and Alcoholism*, 29: 439–450.

Harburg, E., Ozgoren, F., Hawthorn, V.M. and Schork, M.A. (1980) 'Community norms of alcohol usage and blood pressure', *American Journal of Public Health*, 70: 813–820.

Hardt, F. (1992) 'Antabuse treatment for excessive users of alcohol', *Acta Psychiatrica Scandinavica*, Supplement, 369: 37–40.

Hare, E. (1991) 'The history of "nervous disorders" from 1600 to 1840, and a comparison with modern views', *British Journal of Psychiatry*, 159: 37–45.

Hare, E.H. (1974) 'The changing content of psychiatric illness', *Journal of Psychiatric Research*, 18: 283–289.

Hare, E.H. (1981) 'The two manias: A study of the evolution of the modern concept of mania', *British Journal of Psychiatry*, 138: 89–99.

Hare, E.H., Moran, P.A. and Macfarlane, A. (1981) 'The changing seasonality of infant deaths in England and Wales 1912–78 and its relation to seasonal temperature', *Journal of Epidemiology and Community Health*, 35: 77–82.

Harford, T.C. and Parker, D.A. (1994) 'Antisocial behavior, family history and alcohol dependence symptoms', *Alcoholism: Clinical and Experimental Research*, 18,2: 265–268.

Harford, T.C., Wechsler, H. and Rohman, M. (1983) 'The structural context of college drinking', *Journal of Studies on Alcohol*, 44: 722–732.

Harlap, S. and Shiono, P.H. (1980) 'Alcohol, smoking and the incidence of spontaneous abortions in the first and second trimester', *Lancet*, 2: 173– 176.

Harley, D. (1994) 'Provincial midwives in England: Lancashire and Cheshire, 1660–1760', in Marland, H., (ed.) *The Art of Midwifery: Early Modern Midwives in Europe*, London, Routledge, 27–48.

Harman, M.J. and Arbona, C. (1991) 'Psychological adjustment among adult children of alcoholics: A cross-cultural study', *Journal of Psychology*, 125: 641–648.

Harris, D. and Brunt, P. (1995) 'Prognosis of alcoholic liver disease – 100 years on and the need for international standards and guidelines', *Alcohol and Alcoholism*, 30,5: 591–600.

Harris, R.E. and Wynder, E.L. (1988) 'Breast cancer and alcohol consumption', *Journal of the American Medical Association*, 259: 2867–2871.

Harris, T.A. (1969) *I'm OK – You're OK. A Practical Guide to Transactional Analysis*, New York, Harper and Row Publishers Inc.

Harris, T.R., Wilsnack, R.W. and Klassen, A.D. (1994) 'Reliability of retrospective self-reports of alcohol consumption among women: Data from a U.S. national sample', *Journal of Studies on Alcohol*, 55: 309–314.

Harrison, E.R., Haaga, J. and Richards, T. (1993) 'Self-reported drug use data: What do they reveal?' *American Journal of Drug and Alcohol Abuse*, 19: 423–441.

Hartman, F.R. (1983) 'A reappraisal of the Emma episode and the specimen dream', *Journal of the American Psychoanalytic Association*, 31: 555–585.

Hartwig, H., Rohloff, P., Huller, H. and Amon, I. (1982) 'Drugs in pregnancy – A prospective study', *Biological Research in Pregnancy*, 3: 51–55.

Harvey, J.M. and Dodd, D.K. (1993) 'Variables associated with alcohol abuse among self-identified collegiate COA's and their peers', *Addictive Behaviors*, 18: 567–575.

Harvey, P. (1994) 'Gender, community and confrontation: Power relations in drunkenness in Ocongate (Southern Peru)', in McDonald, M., (ed.) *Gender, Drink and Drugs*, Oxford, Berg, 209–234.

Harvey, S.M. and Beckman, L.J. (1985) 'Cyclic fluctuation in alcohol consumption among female social drinkers', *Alcoholism: Clinical and Experimental Research*, 9: 465–467.

Haug, K., Fugelli, P., Aaro, L.E. and Foss, O.P. (1994) 'Is smoking intervention in general practice more successful among pregnant than non-pregnant women?' *Family Practice*, 11: 111–116.

Haver, B. and Dahlgren, L. (1995) 'Early treatment of women with alcohol addiction (EWA): A comprehensive evaluation and outcome study. Patterns of psychiatric comorbidity at intake', *Addiction*, 90: 101–109.

Haver, B. and Franck, J. (1997) 'The Karoliska project for early treatment of women with alcohol addiction', *European Addiction Research*, 3: 30–36.

Havey, J.M. and Dodd, D.K. (1993) 'Variables associated with alcohol abuse among self-identified collegiate COAs and their peers', *Addictive Behaviors*, 18: 567–575.

Hawkins, P. and Shohet, R. (1992) *Supervision in the Helping Professions*, Buckingham, Open University Press.

Haworth, A. (1995) 'Zambia', in Heath, D.B., (ed.) *International Handbook on Alcohol and Culture*, Connecticut, Greenwood Press, 316–327.

Hawthorne, G., Garrard, J. and Dunt, D. (1995) 'Does Life Education's drug education programme have a health benefit?' *Addiction*, 90: 205–216.

Hawthorne, G. (1996) 'The social impact of Life Education: Estimates drug use prevalence among Victorian primary school students and the statewide effect of the Life Education programme', *Addiction*, 91: 1151–1160.

Hay, W.M, Nathan, P.E., Heermans, H.W. and Frankenstein, W. (1984) 'Menstrual cycle, tolerance and blood alcohol level discrimination ability', *Addictive Behaviors*, 9: 67–77.

Haynes, R.H. (1987) 'Suicide and social response in Fiji: A historical survey', *British Journal of Psychiatry*, 151: 21–26.

Heap, M. and Dryden, W. (1991) *Hypnotherapy: A Handbook*, Buckingham, Open University Press.

Heath, A.C., Cates, R., Martin, N.G., Meyer, J., Hewitt, J.K., Neale, M.C. and Eaves, L.J. (1993) 'Genetic contribution to risk of smoking initiation: Comparisons across birth cohorts and across cultures', *Journal of Substance Abuse*, 5: 221–246.

Heath, A.C., Jardine, R. and Martin, N.G. (1989) 'Interactive effects of genotype and social environment on alcohol consumption in female twins', *Journal of Studies on Alcohol*, 50,1: 38–48.

Heath, A.C., Meyer, J., Jardine, R. and Martin, N.G. (1991) 'The inheritance of alcohol consumption patterns in a general population twin sample: II. determinants of consumption frequency and quantity consumed', *Journal of Studies on Alcohol*, 52: 425–433.

Heath, D.B. (1987) 'Cultural, social and ethnic factors as they relate to genetics and alcoholism', In *Genetics and Alcoholism*, New York, Alan R. Liss Inc., 22–31.

Heath, D.B. (1991) 'Women and alcohol: Cross-cultural perspectives', *Journal of Substance Abuse*, 3: 175–185.

Heath, D.B. (1993) 'Anthropology', in Galanter, M., (ed.) *Recent Developments in Alcoholism: Vol. 11: Ten Years of Progress*, New York, Plenum Press, 29–43.

Heath, D.B. (1995) *International Handbook on Alcohol and Culture*, Connecticut, Greenwood Press.

Heather, N. (1992) 'Addictive disorders are essentially motivational problems', *British Journal of Addiction*, 87: 828–835.

Heather, N. (1996) 'The effectiveness of treatment for alcohol problems: A matter of interpretation', *Journal of Substance Misuse*, 1: 126–131.

Heather, N. and Robertson, I. (1981) *Controlled Drinking*, London, Methuen.

Heck, E.J. and Williams, M.D. (1995) 'Using the CAGE to screen for drinking-related problems in college students', *Journal of Studies on Alcohol*, 56: 282–286.

Hedrick, J.D. (1994) *Harriet Beecher Stowe. A Life*, Oxford, Oxford University Press.

Heidensohn, F. (1985) *Women and Crime*, London, Macmillan.

Heidensohn, F.M. (1991) 'Women as perpetrators and victims of crime. A sociological perspective', *British Journal of Psychiatry*, Supplement: 50–54.

Heim, K., Alge, A., and Marthe, C. (1991) 'Anaphylactic reaction to ampicillin and severe complication in the fetus', *Lancet*, 337: 859–860.

Heine, M.W. (1981) 'Alcoholism and reproduction', *Progress in Biochemical Pharmacology*, 18: 75–82.

Heiser, K. and Harmann, U. (12987) 'Disorders of sexual desire in a sample of women alcoholics', *Drug and Alcohol Dependence*, 19: 145–157.

Heller, D.A. and McLern, G.E. (1992) 'Alcohol, aging and genetics', in Beresford, T.P. and Gomberg, E. (eds) *Alcohol and Aging*, New York, Oxford University Press, 99–114.

Heller, W. (1993) 'Gender differences in depression: perspectives from neuropsychology', *Journal of Affective Disorders*, 29: 129–143.

Helm, P. and Helm, S. (1987) 'Uncertainties in designation of age at menarche in the nineteenth century: revised mean for Denmark, 1835', *Annals of Human Biology*, 14: 371–374.

Helzer, J.F,. and Pryzbeck, T.R. (1988) 'The co-occurence of alcoholism with other psychiatric disorders in the general population and its impact on treatment', *Journal of Studies on Alcohol*, 49,3: 219–224.

Henderson, G.L. (1988) 'Designer drugs: past history and future prospects', *Journal of Forensic Sciences*, 33: 569–575.

Hendry, J. (1994) 'Drinking and gender in Japan', in McDonald, M., (ed.) *Gender, Drink and Drugs*, Oxford, Berg, 175–190.

Henker, F.O. (1984) 'Joan of Arc and DSM III', *Southern Medical Journal*, 77: 1488–1490.

Henley, N.M. (1986) *Body Politics: Power, Sex and Nonverbal Communication*, New York, Simon and Schuster Inc.

Herd, D. (1985) 'Ambiguity in black drinking norms: An ethnohistorical interpretation', in Bennet, L. and Ames, G. (eds) *American Experience and Alcohol*, New York, Plenum Press, 149–170.

Herd, D. (1993) 'An analysis of alcohol-related problems in black and white women drinkers', *Addiction Research*, 1: 181–198.

Herd, D. (1997) 'Sex ratios of drinking patterns and problems among blacks and whites: Results from a national survey', *Journal of Studies on Alcohol*, 58: 75–82.

Herd, D. and Grube, J. (1993) 'Drinking contexts and drinking problems among black and white women', *Addiction*, 88: 1101–1110.

Herman, B., Scmitz, P.I.M., Letten, A.C.M. et al. (1983) 'Multivariate logistic analysis of risk factors for stroke in Tilburg, the Netherlands', *American Journal of Epidemiology*, 118: 514–525.

Hernandez, A.C., Newcomb, M.D. and Rabow, J. (1995) 'Types of drunk-driving intervention: prevalence, success and gender', *Journal of Studies on Alcohol*, 56: 408–413.

Hertzberg, R. (1985) 'Congenital cataract following German measles in the mother. Abstracts from the publications of the late Sir Norman McAlister

Gregg', *Australian and New Zealand Journal of Ophthalmology*, 13: 303–309.

Hesse-Biber, S. and Marino, M. (1991) 'From high school to college: Changes in women's self-concept and its relationship to eating problems', *Journal of Psychology*, 125: 199–216.

Hesselbrock, M.N. (1991) 'Gender comparisons of anti-social personality disorder and depression in alcoholism', *Journal of Substance Abuse*, 3: 205–219.

Hesselbrock, V., Meyer, R. and Hesselbrock, M. (1992) 'Psychopathology and addictive disorders: the specific case of antisocial personality disorder', *Research Publications, Association for Research in Nervous and Mental Disease*, 70: 179–191.

Hester, R.K. and Millar, W.R. (1989) *Handbook of Alcoholism Treatment Approaches: Effective Alternatives*, New York, Pergamon Press.

Hetzel, B.S., Bruer, B. and Poidevin, L.O.S. (1961) 'A survey of the relations between certain common antenatal complications in primiparae and stressful life situations during pregnancy', *Journal of Psychiatric Research*, 5: 175.

Hiatt, R.A. (1990) 'Alcohol consumption and breast cancer', *Medical Oncology and Tumour Pharmacotherapy*, 7: 143–151.

Hiatt, R.A. and Bawol, R.D. (1984) 'Alcoholic beverage consumption and breast cancer incidence', *American Journal of Epidemiology*, 120: 676–683.

Hiatt, R.A., Klatsky, A. and Armstrong, M.A. (1988) 'Alcohol and breast cancer', *Preventive Medicine*, 17: 683–685.

Hickey, E.H. (1880) *Where There's a Will There's a Way*, London, John Kempster and Company.

Higgins, M.W. and Kjelsberg, M. (1967) 'Characteristics of smokers and nonsmokers in Tecumseh, Michigan', *American Journal of Epidemiology*, 86: 60–77.

Higuchi, S. and Kono, H. (1994) 'Early diagnosis and treatment of alcoholism: The Japanese experience', *Alcohol and Alcoholism*, 29: 363–373.

Higuchi, S., Muramatsu, T., Shigemori, K., Saito, M., Kono, H., Dufour, M.C. and Harford, T.C. (1992) 'The relationship between low Km aldehyde dehydrogenase phenotype and drinking behavior in Japanese', *Journal of Studies on Alcohol*, 53: 170–175.

Higuchi, S., Parrish, K.M., Dufour, M.C., Towle, L.H. and Harford, T.C. (1992) 'The relationship between three subtypes of the flushing response and DSM–111 alcohol abuse in Japanese', *Journal of Studies on Alcohol*, 53: 553–560.

Higuchi, S., Parrish, K.M., Dufour, M.C., Towle, L.H. and Harford, T.C. (1994) 'Relationship between age and drinking patterns and drinking problems among Japanese, Japanese-Americans and Caucasians', *Alcoholism: Clinical and Experimental Research*, 18,2: 305–310.

Higuchi, S., Suzuki, K., Yamada, K., Parrish, K. and Kono, H. (1993) 'Alcoholics with eating disorders: prevalence and clinical course: a study from Japan', *British Journal of Psychiatry*, 162: 403–406.

Hill, E.M., Blow, F.C., Young, J.P. and Singer, K.M. (1994) 'Family history of alcoholism and childhood adversity: Joint effects on alcohol consumption and dependence', *Alcoholism: Clinical and Experimental Research*, 18: 1083–1090.

Hill, E.M., Nord, J.L. and Blow, F.C. (1992) 'Young-adult children of alcoholic parents: Protective effects of positive family functioning', *British Journal of Addiction*, 87: 1677–1690.

Hill, S.Y. (1993) 'Personality characteristics of sisters and spouses of male alcoholics', *Alcoholism: Clinical and Experimental Research*, 17: 733–739.

Hill, S.Y. (1995a) 'Vulnerability to alcoholism in women: Genetic and cultural factors', in Galanter, M. (ed.) *Recent Developments in Alcoholism Vol 12*, New York, Plenum Press, 9–28.

Hill, S.Y. (1995b) 'Mental and physical health consequences', in Galanter, M., (ed.) *Recent Developments in Alcoholism*, Vol. 12, New York, Plenum Press, 181–197.

Hill, S.Y. and Smith, T.R. (1991) 'Evidence of genetic mediation of alcoholism in women', *Journal of Substance Abuse*, 3: 159–174.

Hillman, E.M. (1991) 'Caesarean section: Historical background', *Scottish Medical Journal*, 36: 150–154.

Hillman, J. and Ventura, M. (1992) *We've had a Hundred Years of Psychotherapy and the World's Getting Worse*, New York, HarperCollins.

Hilton, M.E. (1987) 'Drinking patterns and drinking problems in 1984: Results from a general population survey', *Alcoholism: Clinical and Experimental Research*, 11: 167–175.

Hinde, P.R. (1987) 'The population of a Wiltshire village in the nineteenth century: A reconstitution study of Berwick St James, 1841–71', *Annals of Human Biology*, 14: 475–485.

Hinderliter, S.A. and Zelenak, J.P. (1993) 'A simple method to identify alcohol and other drug use in pregnant adults in a prenatal care setting', *Journal of Perinatology*, 13: 93–102.

Hingson, R., Alpert, J.J., Day, N., Dooling, E., Kaine, H., Morelock, S. et al. (1982) 'Effects of maternal drinking and marijuana use on fetal growth and development', *Pediatrics*, 70: 539–546.

Hingson, R. and Howland, J. (1987) 'Alcohol as a risk factor for injury or death resulting from accidental falls: a review of the literature', *Journal of Studies on Alcohol*, 48: 212–219.

Hingson, R., Scotch, N., Day, N. and Culbert, A. (1980) 'Recognising and seeking help for drinking problems. A study in the Boston Metropolitan area', *Journal of Studies on Alcohol*, 41: 1102–1117.

Hingson, R., Strunin, L., Berlin, B. and Heeren, T. (1990) 'Beliefs about AIDS, use of alcohol, drugs and unprotected sex among Massachusetts adolescents', *American Journal of Public Health*, 80: 295–299.

Hinken, C.H. and Kahn, M.W. (1995) 'Psychological symptomatology in spouses and adult children of alcoholics: An examination of hypothesized personality characteristics of codependency', *International Journal of the Addictions*, 30: 843–861.

Hinman, A.R. (1990) '1889 to 1989: A century of health and disease', *Public Health Reports – Hyattsville*, 105: 374–380.

Hippocrates (1886) 'The epidemics in the 4th Century', in Adams, F. (ed.) *The Genuine Works of Hippocrates*, New York, Wood.

Hislop, W.S., Bouchier, I.A.D., Allan, J.G., Brunt, P.W., Eastwood, M., Finlayson, N.D.C., James, O., Russell, R.I. and Watkinson, G. (1983) 'Alcoholic liver disease in Scotland and Northeastern England: Presenting features in 510 patients', *Quarterly Journal of Medicine*, 206: 232–243.

Ho, R. (1994) 'Cigarette advertising and cigarette health warnings – what role do adolescents motives for smoking play in their assessment', *Australian Psychologist*, 29: 49–56.

Hodgins, D.C., El Guebaly, N. and Armstrong, S. (1995) 'Prospective and retrospective reports of mood states before relapse to substance use', *Journal of Consulting and Clinical Psychology*, 63: 400–407.

Hoffman, F. (1994) 'Cultural adaptations of Alcoholics Anonymous to serve Hispanic populations', *International Journal of the Addictions*, 29, 4: 445–460.

Hogberg, U. and Akerman, S. (1990) 'Reproductive pattern among women in 19th century Sweden', *Journal of Biosocial Science*, 22: 13–18.

Hogberg, U., Wall, S. and Brostrom, G. (1986) 'The impact of early medical technology on maternal mortality in late 19th century Sweden', *International Journal of Gynaecology and Obstetrics*, 24: 251–261.

Holderness, C.C., Brooks-Gunn, J. and Warren, M.P. (1994a) 'Eating disorders and substance use: A dancing vs a nondancing population', *Medicine and Science in Sports and Exercise*, 26: 297–302.

Holderness, C.C., Brooks-Gunn, J. and Warren, M.P. (1994b) 'Co-morbidity of eating disorders and substance abuse review of the literature', *International Journal of Eating Disorders*, 16: 1–34.

Holleb, A.I. (1985) 'Guidelines for the cancer-related checkup: Five years later', *Cancer*, 35: 194–196.

Hollender, M.H. (1980) 'The case of Anna O.: A reformulation', *American Journal of Psychiatry*, 137: 797–800.

Holmila, M. (1993) 'Heavy drinking women: Drinking patterns and resources for controlled drinking', *Addiction Research*, 1: 119–130.

Holmila, M. (1995) 'Intoxication and hazardous use of alcohol: Results from the 1992 Finnish drinking habits survey', *Addiction*, 90: 785–792.

Holmila, M. (1997) 'Family roles and being a problem drinker's intimate other', *European Addiction Research*, 3: 37–42.

Holohan, A.M. (1985) 'St Kilda: childbirth and the women of main street', *Scottish Medical Journal*, 30: 50–53.

Holt, S., Stewart, R.D., Adam, RD., et al. (1980) 'Alcohol absorption, gastric emptying and a breathalizer', *British Journal of Clinical Pharmacology*, 9: 205–208.

Homel, R. and Clark, J. et al. (1994) 'The prediction and prevention of violence in pubs and clubs', *Crime Prevention Studies*, 3: 1–46.

Homel, R., Hauritz, M., Wortley, R., Clark, J. and Carvolth, R. (1994) *The Impact of the Surfers' Paradise Safety Action Project: Key Findings of the*

Evaluation, Griffith University, Centre for Crime Policy and Public Safety.

Honglandarom, G. and Porter, S.B. (1981) 'Cancer detection information for high school students', in Mettlin, C. and Murphy, G.P. (eds), *Progress in Cancer Control*, New York, Alan R. Liss Inc., 197–198.

Hook, E. (1976) 'Changes in tobacco smoking and ingestion of alcohol and caffeinated beverages during early pregnancy', in Kelly, S., Hook, E.B., Janerich, D.T. and Porter, I.H. (eds) *Birth Defects: Risks and Consequences*, New York, Academic Press, 173–183.

Hopper, J.L., White, V.M., Macaskill, G.T., Hill. D.J. and Clifford, C.A. (1992) 'Alcohol use, smoking habits and the adult Eysenck personality questionnaire in adolescent Australian twins', *Acta Geneticae Medicae and Gemellologiae*, 41: 311–324.

Hopwood, J.S. (1927) 'Child murder and insanity', *Journal of Mental Science*, 73: 95.

Hore, B.D. and Plant, M.A. (1981) *Alcohol Problems in Employment*, London, Croom Helm.

Horn, T., Paccaud, F., Niquille, M., Koehn, V., Magnenat, P. and Yersin, B. (1992) 'Drinking patterns among medical in-patients with reference to MAST categories: a comparative study', *Alcohol and Alcoholism*, 27: 439–447.

Hornfeldt, C.S. (1992) 'A report of acute ethanol poisoning in a child: Mouthwash versus cologne, perfume and aftershave', *Clinical Teratology*, 30: 115–121.

Horwitz, A.V. and White, H.R. (1991) 'Becoming married, depression, and alcohol problems among young adults', *Journal of Health and Social Behavior*, 32: 221–237.

Houskamp, B. (1994) 'Assessing and treating battered women: A clinical review of issues and approaches', *New Directions for Mental Health Services*, 64: 79–89.

Hover, S. and Gaffney, L.R. (1991) 'The relationship between social skills and adolescent drinking', *Alcohol and Alcoholism*, 26: 207–214.

Howard, B., Harrison, S., Carver, V. and Lightfoot, L. (1993) *Alcohol and Drug Problems: A Practical Guide for Counsellors*, Toronto, Addiction Research Foundation.

Howard, J. (1982) 'Breast self-examination: Issues for research', *Proceedings of the Working Group Meetings to Explore Issues in Breast Self-Examination*, Bethesda, Maryland.

Howe, D. (1993) *On Being a Client: Understanding the Process of Counselling and Psychotherapy*, London, Sage Publications Ltd.

Howe, H.L. (1985) 'Breast self-examination palpation skill; A methodological note', *Journal of Chronic Disease*, 38: 995–1001.

Hubbard, R. (1986) 'Eugenics and prenatal testing', *International Journal of Health Services*, 16: 227–242.

Hubbard, R. (1987) 'Eugenics: New tools, old ideas', *Women and Health*, 13: 225–235.

Huby, G. (1994) 'Drinking and the Management of Problem Drinking

Among the Bari, Southern Sudan', in McDonald, M., (ed.) *Gender, Drink and Drugs*, Oxford, Berg, 235–248.

Hufton, O. (1993) 'Women, work and family', in Duky, G. and Perrot, M., (eds) *A History of Women in the West: Vol 3. Renaissance and Enlightenment Paradoxes*, Cambridge, Massachusetts, The Belknap Press of Harvard University Press, 15–45.

Hughes, C.H. (1882) 'Hyosciamine in insanity following the puerperal state', *St. Louis Medical and Surgical Journal*, 43: 362.

Hughes, C.H. (1882) 'Outline therapeutics of chronic alcoholism', *Alienist and Neurologist*, January 3, 1: 85–87.

Hughes, C.H. (1890) 'The psychopathic sequences of hereditary alcoholic entailment', *Alienist and Neurologist*, 11,3: 544–554.

Hughes J.R., Higgins, S.T. and Bickel, W.K. (1994) 'Nicotine withdrawal versus other drug withdrawal syndromes: similarities and dissimilarities', *Addiction*, 89: 1461–1470.

Humes, D.L. and Humphrey, L.L. (1994) 'A multimethod analysis of families with a polydrug-dependent or normal adolescent daughter', *Journal of Abnormal Psychology*, 103: 676–685.

Humphreys, K., Mavis, B. and Stofflemayr, B. (1991) 'Factors predicting attendance at self-help groups after substance abuse treatment: Preliminary findings', *Journal of Consulting and Clinical Psychology*, 59,4: 591–593.

Hunt, C. and Seeman, J. (1990) 'A study of women's recovery from alcoholism. Special issue: Human inquiry and the person-centered approach', *Person-Centered Review*, 5: 233–248.

Hunter, E. (1991) 'Out of sight, out of mind – 2. Social and historical contexts of self-harmful behaviour among aborigines of remote Australia', *Social Science and Medicine*, 33: 661–671.

Hurley, D.L. (1991a) 'Incest and the development of alcoholism in adult female survivors', *Alcoholism Treatment Quarterly*, 7: 41–56.

Hurley, D.L. (1991b) 'Women, alcohol and incest: An analytical review', *Journal of Studies on Alcohol*, 52: 253–268.

Hurst, L.C. (1982) 'What was wrong with Anna O?' *Journal of the Royal Society of Medicine*, 75: 129–131.

Hurst, M. and Summey, P.S. (1984) 'Childbirth and social class: The case of cesarean delivery', *Social Science and Medicine*, 18: 621–631.

Huselid, R.F. and Cooper, M.L. (1992) 'Gender roles as mediators of sex differences in adolescent alcohol use and abuse', *Journal of Health and Social Behavior*, 33: 348–362.

Hutchinson, J. (1987) 'The age-sex structure of the slave population in Harris County, Texas: 1850 and 1860', *American Journal of Physical Anthropology*, 74: 231–238.

Hutson, W.R., Roehrkasse, R.L. and Wald, A. (1989) 'Influence of gender and menopause on gastric emptying and motility', *Gastroenterology*, 96: 11–17.

Hyman, R.B., Greenwald, U.S. and Hacker, S. (1995) 'Smoking, dietary, and breast and cervical cancer screening knowledge and screening practices of employees in an urban medical center', *Journal of Cancer Education*, 10: 82–87.

Idänpään-Heikilä, J.E., Fritchie, G.E. Ho, B.T. and McIsaac, W.M. (1971) 'Placental transfer of 14C-ethanol', *American Journal of Obstetrics and Gynecology*, 110: 426.

Idänpään-Heiklä, J.E., Joupila, P., Akerblom, W.K., Isoaho, R., Kauppila, E. and Koivisto, M. (1972) 'Elimination and metabolic effects of ethanol in mother, fetus and newborn infant', *American Journal of Obstetrics and Gynecology*, 112: 387–393.

Ihlen, B.M., Amundsen, A. and Tronnes, L. (1993) 'Reduced alcohol use in pregnancy and changed attitudes in the population', *Addiction*, 88: 389–394.

Ikuesan, B.A. (1994) 'Drinking problems and the position of women in Nigeria', *Addiction*, 89: 941–944.

Iliffe, S., Haines, A., Booroff, A., Goldenberg, E., Morgan, P. and Gallivan, S. (1991) 'Alcohol consumption by elderly people: A general practice survey', *Age and Ageing*, 20: 120–123.

Institute of Medicine (1990) *Broadening the Base of Treatment for Alcohol Problems*, Washington, D.C., National Academy Press.

International Center for Alcohol Policies (1996) *ICAP Reports 1 – Supplement*, Washington, D.C., International Center for Alcohol Policies.

Ioffe, S. and Chernick, V. (1987) 'Maternmal alcohol ingestation and the incidence of respiratory distress syndrome', *American Journal of Obstetrics and Gynecology*, 156: 1231–1235.

Iossifides, A.M. (1992) 'Wine: Life's blood and spiritual essence in a Greek Orthodox convent', in Gefou-Madianou, D. (ed.) *Alcohol, Gender and Culture*, London, Routledge, 80–100.

Ireland, T. and Widom, C.S. (1994) 'Childhood victimization and risk for alcohol and drug arrests', *International Journal of the Addictions*, 29: 235–274.

Ireland, W.W. (1894) 'Means of preventing and evading insanity', *Alienist and Neurologist*, 2: 181–208.

Irwin, M., Schuckit, M. and Smith, T.L. (1990) 'Clinical importance of age of onset in type 1 and type 2 primary alcoholics', *Archives of General Psychiatry*, 47: 320–324.

Isaac, N.E., Kennedy, B. and Graham, J.D. (1995) 'Who's in the car? Passengers as potential interveners in alcohol-involved fatal crashes', *Accident Analysis and Prevention*, 27: 159–165.

Isohanni, M., Oja, H., Moilanen, I., Koiranen, M. and Rantakallio, P. (1995) 'Smoking or quitting during pregnancy: Associations with background and future social factors', *Scandinavian Journal of Social Medicine*, 23: 32–38.

Jackson, F.N. and Holle, R.H. (1985) 'Smoking: perspectives 1985. Primary Care', *Clinics In Office Practice*, 12: 197–216.

Jackson, M.S. (1995) 'Afrocentric treatment of African American women and their children in a residential chemical dependency program', *Journal of Black Studies*, 26,1: 17–30.

Jackson, R., Scragg, R. and Beaglehole, R. (1991) 'Alcohol consumption and risk of coronary heart disease', *British Medical Journal*, 303: 211–216.

Jackson, R., Scragg, R. and Beaglehole, R. (1992) 'Does recent alcohol consumption reduce the risk of acute myocardial infarction and coronary death in regular drinkers?' *American Journal of Epidemiology*, 136: 919–824.

Jackson, R., Stewart, A., Beaglehole, R. and Scragg, R. (1985) 'Alcohol consumption and blood pressure', *American Journal of Epidemiology*, 122: 1034–1044.

Jackson, S.W. (1992) 'The listening healer in the history of psychological healing', *American Journal of Psychiatry*, 149: 1623–1632.

Jacobson, J.L. and Jacobson, S.W. (1991) *Assessment of Teratogenic Effects on Cognitive and Behavioral Development in Infancy and Childhood*, NIDA Research Monograph 114: 248–261.

Jacobson, J.L., Jacobson, S.W., Sokol, R.J., Martier, S.S., Ager, J.W. and Kaplan-Estrin, M.G. (1993) 'Teratogenic effects of alcohol on infant development', *Alcoholism: Clinical and Experimental Research*, 17: 174–183.

Jacobson, J.L., Jacobson, S.W., Sokol, R.J., Martier, S.S., Ager, J.W. and Shankaran, S. (1994) 'Effects of alcohol use, smoking, and illicit drug use on fetal growth in black infants', *Journal of Pediatrics*, 124: 757–764.

Jacobson, S.W. and Jacobson, J.L. (1992) 'Breastfeeding and intelligence', *Lancet*, 339: 926.

Jacobson, S.W., Jacobson, J.L. and Sokol, R.J. (1994) 'Effects of fetal alcohol exposure on infant reaction time', *Alcoholism: Clinical and Experimental Research*, 18: 1125–1132.

Jacobson, S.W., Jacobson, J.L., Sokol, R.J., Martier, S.S. and Ager, J.W. (1993) 'Prenatal alcohol exposure and infant information processing ability', *Child Development*, 64: 1706–1721.

Jacobson, S.W., Jacobson, J.L., Sokol, R.J., Martier, S.S., Ager, J.W. and Kaplan, M.G. (1991) 'Maternal recall of alcohol, cocaine, and marijuana use during pregnancy', *Neurotoxicology and Teratology*, Sep–Oct, 13,5: 535–540.

Jahoda, G. and Cramond, J. (1972) *Children and Alcohol*, London, HMSO.

Janikowski, T.P. and Glover, N.M. (1994) 'Incest and substance abuse – Implications for treatment professionals', *Journal of Substance Abuse Treatment*, 11,3: 177–183.

Jarvis, T.J. (1992) 'Implications of gender for alcohol treatment research: A quantitative and qualitative review', *British Journal of Addiction*, 87: 1249–1261.

Jarvis, T.J., Tebbutt, J. and Mattick, R.P. (1995) *Treatment Approaches for Alcohol and Drug Dependence: An Introductory Guide*, London, John Wiley and Sons Ltd.

Jeavons, C.M. and Zeiner, A.R. (1984) 'Effects of elevated female sex steroids on ethanol and acetaldehyde metabolism in humans', *Alcoholism: Clinical and Experimental Research*, 8: 352–358.

Jeffery, R., Jeffery, P. and Lyon, A. (1984) 'Female infanticide and amniocentesis', *Social Science and Medicine,* 19: 1207–1212.

Jeffs, B.W. and Saunders, W. (1983) 'Minimising alcohol-related offences by enforcement of existing legislation', *British Journal of Addiction*, 78: 67–78.

Jehu, D. (1994) *Patients as Victims: Sexual Abuse in Psychotherapy and Counselling,* Chichester, Wiley and Sons Ltd.

Jellinek, E.M. (1945) 'Classics in the alcohol literature', *Quarterly Journal of Studies on Alcohol,* 5, 647–661.

Jellinek, E.M. (1946) 'Phases in the drinking history of alcoholics', *Quarterly Journal of Studies on Alcohol,* 7: 1–88.

Jellinek, E.M. (1960) *The Disease Concept of Alcoholism,* New Haven, Connecticut, College and University Press.

Jellinek, E.M, and Jolliffe, N. (1942) 'Effect of alcohol on the individual: review of the literature of 1939', *Quarterly Journal of Studies on Alcohol,* 1: 110–181.

Jelly, A.C. (1901) 'Puerperal insanity', *Boston Medical and Surgical Journal,* 144: 271.

Jessor, R., Carman, R.S. and Grossman, P.H. (1968) 'Expectations of need satisfaction and drinking patterns of college students', *Quarterly Journal of Studies on Alcohol,* 29: 101–116.

Jessor, R. and Jessor, S.L. (1973) 'Problem drinking in youth: Personality, social and behavioral antecedents and correlates', in Chafetz, M.E. (ed.) *Proceedings of the Second Annual Conference of the National Institute of Alcohol Abuse and Alcoholism: Psychological and Social Factors in Drinking and Treatment and Treatment Evaluation,* Washington D.C., National Institute of Health, US Government Printing Office.

Jessor, R. and Jessor, S.L. (1977) *Problem Behavior and Psychosocial Development: A Longitudinal Study of Youth,* New York, Academic Press.

Jiacheng, X. (1995) 'China', in Heath, D.R., (ed.) *International Handbook on Alcohol and Culture,* Connecticut, Greenwood Press, 42–50.

Jick, H., Dinan, B. and Rothman, K.J. (1978) 'Noncontraceptive estrogens and nonfatal myocardial infarction', *Journal of the American Medical Association,* 239: 1407–1408.

Johnson, D.W. and Johnson, F.P. (1994) *Joining Together: Group Therapy and Group Skills,* 5th edn. Massachusetts, A Paramount Communications Co.

Johnson, E.O., van den Bree, M.B.M. and Pickens, R. (1996) 'Indicators of genetic and environmental influence in alcohol-dependent individuals', *Alcoholism: Clinical and Experimental Research,* 20: 67–74.

Johnson, J.E. (1994) 'Sleep and alcohol use in rural old-old women', *Journal of Community Health Nursing,* 11: 211–218.

Johnson, K.A. and Jennison, K.M. (1992) 'The drinking–smoking syndrome and social context', *International Journal of the Addictions,* 27: 749–792.

Johnson, L., O'Malley, P. and Bachman, J. (1994) *National Survey of Results on Drug Use from the 'Monitoring the Future' Study, Vol 111:*

College Students and young Adults, National Institute on Drug Abuse, USA, National Institute for Health Publication No. 94–3810.

Johnson, M.A. (1985) 'The cervical cap as a contraceptive alternative', *Nurse Practitioner*, 10: 41–32, 45.

Johnson, V. and Pandna, R.J. (1993) 'A longitudinal examination of the relationships among stress, coping strategies and problems associated with alcohol use', *Alcoholism: Clinical and Experimental Research*, 17: 696–702.

Johnson, W.W. (1884) 'Neurasthenia in young women', *Alienist and Neurologist*, July 3,15: 383–384.

Johnstone, C. and Hannifin, J. *(1987) A Review of Drug Treatment Services in New Zealand. The National Drug Treatment Research Project*, Palmerston North: Manawatu Society on Alcohol and Drug Use.

Jones, A. (1991) *Women who Kill*, London, Victor Gollancz Ltd.

Jones, B.M. and Jones, M.K. (1976) 'Intoxication, metabolism and the menstrual cycle', in Greenblatt, M. and Schuckit, M.A., (eds) *Alcoholism Problems in Women and Children*, New York, Grune and Stratton, 103–136.

Jones, B.M, and Jones, M.K. (1977) 'Interaction of alcohol, oral contraceptives and the menstrual cycle with stimulus-response compatibility', in Seixas, F.A. (ed.) *Currents in Alcoholism*, New York, Grune and Stratton.

Jones, B.M. and Jones, M.K. (1984) 'Ethanol metabolism in women taking oral contraceptives', *Alcoholism: Clinical and Experimental Research*, 8: 24–28.

Jones, B.M., Jones, M.K. and Hatcher, E.M. (1980) 'Cognitive deficits in women alcoholics as a function of gynecological status', *Journal of Studies on Alcohol*, 41: 140.

Jones, B.R., Barret-Connor, E., Criqui, M.H. et al. (1982) 'A community study of calorie and nutrient intake in drinkers and non-drinkers of alcohol', *American Journal of Clinical Nutrition*, 35: 135–141.

Jones, D.J. and Zalewski, C. (1994) 'Shame and depression proneness among female adult children of alcoholics', *International Journal of the Addictions*, 29: 1601–1609.

Jones, K.L. and Smith, D.W. (1973) 'Recognition of the Fetal Alcohol Syndrome in early infancy', *Lancet*, 2: 999–1001.

Jones, R. (1902) 'Puerperal insanity', *British Medical Journal*, 1: 579

Jones, S. (1994) *The Language of the Genes*, London, Flamingo.

Jones-Webb, R., Jacobs, D.R. Jr, Flack, J.M. and Liu, K. (1996) 'Relationships between depressive symptoms, anxiety, alcohol consumption and blood pressure: Results from the CARDIA Study', *Alcoholism: Clinical and Experimental Research*, 20: 420–427.

Josham (1891) 'Pilocarpine in alcoholism', *Alienist and Neurologist*, April 12,2: 255.

Jung, J. (1995) 'Parent–child closeness affects the similarity of drinking levels between parents and their college-age children', *Addictive Behaviors*, 20: 1 –67.

Just, R. (1991) *Women in Athenian Law and Life*, London, Routledge.

Kadden, R.M., Litt, M.D. and Cooney, N.L. (1994) 'Matching alcoholics to coping skills or interactional therapies. Role of intervening variables', *Annals of the New York Academy of Science*, 708: 218–219.

Kaklamani, E., Thrichopolus, D., Tzonou, A. et al. (1991) 'Hepatitis B and C viruses and their interaction in the origin of hepatocellular carcinoma', *Journal of the American Medical Association*, 256: 1974–1976.

Kalb, M. (1975) 'The myth of alcoholism prevention', *Preventive Medicine*, 4: 404–416.

Kaminski, M. (1992) 'Relation of findings to other studies', *International Journal of Epidemiology*, 21, Supplement 1: S79–S81.

Kaminski, M., Franc, M., Lebouvier, M., Du Mazaubrun, C. and Rumeau-Rouquette, C. (1981) 'Moderate alcohol use and pregnancy outcome', *Neurobehavioural Toxicology and Teratology*, 3: 173–181.

Kaminski, M., Leborgne, P. and du Mazaubrun, C. (1985) 'Consommation de boisssons alcoolisées chez les femmes enceintes et issue de la grossesse', in Les relations doses effets de l'alcool. Colleque et congrés du haut comité, La documenation Française Paris: 69–81.i

Kaminski, M., Rumeau-Rouquette, C. and Schwartz, D. (1976) 'Consommation d'alcool chez les femmes enceintes et issue de la grossesse', *Revue Epidémiologie Santé Pulbli*, 24: 27–40. English translation by Little, R.E. and Schinzel, A. (1978) 'Alcohol consumption in pregnant women and the outcome of pregnancy', *American Journal of Public Health*, 57: 2071–2075.

Kaminski, M., Rumeau-Rouquette, C. and Schwartz, D. (1978) 'Alcohol consumption in pregnant women and the outcome of pregnancy', *Alcoholism: Clinical and Experimental Research*, 2: 155–163.

Kanas, N. (1982) 'Alcoholism and group psychotherapy', in Pattison, E.M. and Kaufman, E., (eds) *Encyclopedic Handbook of Alcoholism*, New York, Gardner Press, 1011–1021.

Kane, C.C. and Rullo-Cooney, D. (1991) 'Addicted women: Their families meet on treatment outcome', *Journal of Chemical Dependency Treatment*, 4: 111–119.

Kaplan, S. (1991) 'Child abuse and alcoholism in women: A feminist approach to treatment', *Canadian Woman Studies*, 12: 1: 67–70.

Kaprio, J., Viken, R., Koskenvuo, M., Romanov, K. and Rose, R.J. (1992) 'Consistency and change in patterns of social drinking: a 6-year follow-up of the Finnish twin cohort', *Alcoholism: Clinical and Experimental Research*, 16: 234–240.

Karl, P.I. and Fisher, S.E. (1993) 'Ethanol alters hormone production in cultured human placental trophoblasts', *Alcoholism: Clinical and Experimental Research*, 17,4: 816–821.

Karlen, A. (1995) *Plague's Progress. A Social History of Man and Disease*, London, Victor Gollanz.

Kaskutas, L.A. (1992) 'Preliminary results from a survey of Women for Sobriety', Paper Presented at the 18th Annual Alcohol Symposium of The Kettil Bruun Society, Toronto.

Kaskutas, L.A. (1994) 'What do women get out of self-help? Their reasons for attending Women For Sobriety and Alcoholics Anonymous', *Journal of Substance Abuse Treatment*, 11,3: 185–195.

Kaskutas, L.A. (1995) 'Interpretations of risk: The use of scientific information in the development of the alcohol warning label policy', *International Journal of the Addictions*, 30: 1519–1548.

Kaskutas, L.A. and Greenfield, T.K. (1992) 'First effects of warning labels on alcoholic beverage containers', *Drug and Alcohol Dependence*, 31: 1–14.

Kasl, C.D. (1992) *Women, Sex and Addiction: A Search for Love and Power*, London, Cedar.

Kassebaum, G. and Chandler, S.M. (1994) 'Polydrug use and self control among men and women in prisons', *Journal of Drug Education*, 24: 333–350.

Katcher, B.S. (1993) 'The post-repeal eclipse in knowledge about the harmful effects of alcohol', *Addiction*, 88: 729–744.

Katims, D.S. and Zapata, J.T. (1993) 'Gender differences in substance use among Mexican American school-age children', *Journal of School Health*, 63: 397–401.

Kato, I., Muira, S., Yoshida, M. and Tominiga, S. (1986) 'Risk factors of multiple primary cancers in breast cancer patients', *Japanese Journal of Cancer Research*, 77: 296–304.

Kaufman, E. (1994) *Psychotherapy of Addicted Persons*, New York, Guilford Press.

Kaufman, S.E. and Kaye, M.D. (1979) 'Effects of ethanol upon gastric emptying', *Gut*, 20: 688–692.

Kaye, S.A., Folsom, A.R., Prineas, R.J. et al. (1990) 'The association of body fat distribution with lifestyle and reproductive factors in a population study of postmenopausal women', *International Journal of Obesity*, 14: 583–591.

Keating, G.C. (1991) 'Fashionable pride: An ageless concern', *International Journal of Ageing and Human Development*, 33: 187–196.

Keddy, B., Gillis, M.J., Jacobs, P., Burton, H. and Rogers, M. (1986) 'The doctor–nurse relationship: An historical perspective', *Journal of Advanced Nursing*, 11: 745–753.

Keeble, N.H. (1994) *A Cultural Identity of Seventeenth-Century Woman: A Reader*, London, Routledge.

Keeler, M.H. (1982) 'Alcoholism and affective disorder', in Pattison, E.M. and Kaufman, E., (eds) *Encyclopedic Handbook of Alcoholism*, New York, Gardner Press, 618–627.

Kegeles, S.S. (1984) 'Breast self-exam: Current status and concerns', *Patient Education Newsletter*, 7: 1–3.

Keil, U., Chambless, L., Filipiak, B. and Härtel, U. (1991) 'Alcohol and blood pressure and its interaction with smoking and other behavioural variables: results from the MONICA Augsburg Survey 1984/85', *Journal of Hypertension*, 9: 491–498.

Keil, U., Chambless, L. and Remmers, A. (1989) 'Alcohol and blood pressure: Results from the Lübeck Blood Pressure Study', *Preventive Medicine*, 18: 1–10.

Keil, U., Swales, J.D. and Grobbee, D.E. (1993) 'Alcohol intake and its relation to hypertension', in Verschuren, P. (ed.) *Health Issues Related to Alcohol*, New York, ILSI Press, 17–42.

Keller, M. (1955) *How Alcohol Affects the Body*, (Popular Pamphlet No. 3), New Brunswick, Rutgers Center of Alcohol Studies.

Kelley, J.O. and Angel, J.L. (1987) 'Life stresses of slavery', *American Journal of Physical Anthropology*, 74: 199–211.

Kelsey, J.L., and Berkowitz., G.S. (1988) 'Breast cancer epidemiology', *Cancer Research*, 48: 5615–5623.

Kendall, K. (1986) 'From lesbian heroine to devoted wife: Or, what the stage would allow', *Journal of Homosexuality*, 12: 9–22.

Kendler, K.S., Heath, A.C., Neale, M.C., Kessler, R.C. and Eaves, L.J. (1993) 'Alcoholism and major depression in women: A twin study of the causes of comorbidity', *Archives of General Psychiatry*, 50: 690–698.

Kendall-Tackett, K.A., Meyer Williams, L. and Finkelhor, D. (1993) 'Impact of sexual abuse on children: A review and synthesis of recent empirical studies', *Psychological Bulletin*, 113: 164–180.

Kennedy, C.A., Skurnick, J., Wan, S.Y., Quattrone, O., Sheffet, A., Quinones, M., Wang, W. and Louria, D.B. (1993) 'Psychological distress, drug and alcohol use as correlates of condom use in HIV-serodiscordant heterosexual couples', *AIDS*, 7: 1493–1499.

Kennedy, H. (1993) *Eve was Framed: Women and British Justice*, London, Vintage Books.

Kent, R. (1989) *Say When!* London, Sheldon Press.

Kenyon, O. (1993) *800 Years of Women's Letters*, Winchester, Massachusetts, Faber and Faber Inc.

Kerr, J. (1994) *A Most Dangerous Method: The Story of Jung, Freud, and Sabina Spielrein*, London, Sinclair Stevenson.

Key, T.J., Darby, S.C. and Pike, M.C. (1987) 'Trends in breast cancer mortality and diet in England and Wales from 1911 to 1980', *Nutrition and Cancer*, 10: 1–9.

Khantzian, E.J. and Halliday, K.S. (1990) *Addiction and the Vulnerable Self: Modified Dynamic Group Therapy for Substance Abusers*, New York, Guilford Press.

Khantzian, E.J. and Mack, J.E. (1989) 'A.A. and contemporary psychodynamic theory', in Galanter, M., (ed.) *Recent Developments in Alcoholism: Vol 7*, New York, Plenum Press, 67–89.

Khatzian, E.J. and Mack. J.E. (1994) 'How A.A. works and why it is important for clinicians to understand', *Journal of Substance Abuse Treatment*, 1,1: 77–92.

Khaw, K.T., Barrett-Connor, E. (1987) 'Dietary potassium and stroke-associated mortality. A 12-year prospective study', *New England Journal of Medicine*, 316: 235–240.

Kilburn, K.H. (1984) 'Chronic disease in the workplace and the environment. Lung disease: lessons from the past – keys to the future', *Archives of Environmental Health*, 39: 139–143.

Kilpatrick, D.G., Edmonds, C.N. and Seymour, A.K. (1992) *Rape in America: A Report to the Nation*, Arlington, Virginia, National Victim Center.

Kimmel, M.S. and Mosmiller, T.E. (1992) *Against the Tide: Pro-Feminist Men in the United States 1776–1990: A Documentary History*, Boston, Beacon Press Books.

Kinder, B.N., Pape, N.E. and Walfish, S. (1980) 'Drug and alcohol education programs: A review of outcome studies', *International Journal of the Addictions*, 15: 1035–1056.

King, H. (1994) 'The politick midwife: Models of midwifery in the work of Elizabeth Collier', in Marland, H., (ed.) *The Art of Midwifery: Early Modern Midwives in Europe*, London, Routledge, 115–130.

King, J. and Ashworth, A. (1987) 'Historical review of the changing pattern of infant feeding in developing countries: The case of Malaysia, the Caribbean, Nigeria and Zaire', *Social Science and Medicine*, 25: 1307–1320.

King, T.K., Clark, M.M. and Pera, V. (1996) 'History of sexual abuse and obesity treatment outcome', *Addictive Behaviors*, 21: 283–290.

Kingree, J.B. (1995) 'Understanding gender differences in psychosocial functioning and treatment retention', *American Journal of Drug and Alcohol Abuse*, 21: 267–281.

Kirk (1880a) *Women's Medicinal Use of Alcohol*, London, British Women's Temperance Association.

Kirk (1880b) *Alcohol and Health*, London, British Women's Temperance Association.

Kirkpatrick, J. (1986) *Turnabout: Help for a New Life*, 3rd edn. Seattle, Washington, Madrona Press.

Kissin, B. and Beigleiter, H. (1976) *The Biology of Alcoholism: Vol 4: Social Aspects of Alcoholism*, New York, Plenum Press.

Kissin, M.W. (1991) 'The patron saints of breast disease', *Australian and New Zealand Journal of Surgery*, 61: 452–458.

Kitano, H.H., Chi, I., Rhee, S., Law, C.K. and Lubben, J.E. (1992) 'Norms and alcohol consumption: Japanese in Japan, Hawaii and California', *Journal of Studies on Alcohol*, 53: 33–39.

Kitchens, J.A. (1994) *Talking to Ducks*, New York, Fireside, Simon and Schuster Inc.

Kizilay, P.E. (1992) 'Predictors of depression in women', *Nursing Clinics of North America*, 27: 983–993.

Kjellber, G.O. (1892) 'Nicotinic Psychosis', *Alienist and Neurologist*, January 13,1: 155–156.

Kjellgren, O. (1984) 'The development of gynecological oncology in Scandinavia during the last 50 years', *Acta Obstetricia et Gynecologica Scandinavica*, Supplement, 120: 27–34.

Klajner, F., Hartman, L.M. and Sobell, M.B. (1984) 'Treatment of substance abuse by relaxation Training: A review of its rationale, efficacy and mechanisms', *Addictive Behaviors*, 9: 41–55.

Klassen, A. and Wilsnack, S.C. (1986) 'Sexual experiences and drinking among women in a US national survey', *Archives of Sexual Behavior*, 15: 363–392.

Klatsky, A.L., Friedman, G.D. and Siegelaub, A.B. (1974) 'Alcohol consumption before myocardial infarction', *Annals of Internal Medicine*, 81: 294–301.

Klatsky, A.L., Friedman, G.D., Siegalaub, A.B., and Gerard, M.J. (1977) 'Alcohol consumption and blood pressure', *New England Journal of Medicine*, 296: 1194–1200.

Klatsky, A.L., Friedman, G.D. and Siegelaub, A.B. (1981a) 'Alcohol use and cardiovascular disease; the Kaiser–Permanente experience', *Circulation*, 64 (supplement III): 32–41.

Klatsky, A.L., Friedman, G.D. and Siegelaub, M.S. (1981b) 'Alcohol and mortality. A ten year Kaiser–Permanente experience', *Annals of Internal Medicine*, 95: 139–145.

Klatsky, A.L., Armstrong, M.A. and Friedman, G.D. (1986) 'Relation of alcoholic beverage use to subsequent coronary artery disease hospitalization', *American Journal of Cardiology*, 58: 710–714.

Klatsky, A.L., Armstrong, M.A. and Friedman, G.D. (1990) 'Risk of cardiovascular mortality in alcohol drinkers, ex-drinkers and non-drinkers', *American Journal of Cardiology*, 66: 1237–1242.

Klatsky, A.L. and Armstrong, M.A. (1993) 'Alcohol use, other traits, and risk of unnatural death: A prospective study', *Alcoholism: Clinical and Experimental Research*, 17: 1156–1162.

Klee, L., Schmidt, C. and Ames, G. (1991) 'Indicators of women's alcohol problems; what women themselves report', *International Journal of the Addictions*, 26,8: 879–895.

Klein, R.F., Fausti, K.A. and Carlos, A.S. (1996) 'Ethanol inhibits human osteoblastic cell proliferation', *Alcoholism: Clinical and Experimental Research*, 20: 572–578.

Kleinberg, S.J. (1988) *Retrieving Women's History: Changing Perceptions of the Role of Women in Politics and Society*, Providence, Berg Publishers Ltd. Unesco Press.

Klesges, R.C., Klesges, L.M., DeBon, M., Shelton, M.L., Isbell, T.R. and Klem, M.L. (1995) 'Effects of phenylpropanolamine on withdrawal symptoms', *Psychopharmacology*, 119: 85–91.

Klesges, R.C., Mealer, C.Z. and Klesges, L.M. (1994) 'Effects of alcohol intake on resting energy expenditure in young women social drinkers', *American Journal of Clinical Nutrition*, 59: 805–809.

Kline, J., Shrout, P., Stein, Z., Susser, M. and Warburton, D. (1980) 'Drinking during pregnancy and spontaneous abortion', *Lancet*, i: 176–179.

Kline, R.B. (1990) 'The relaxation of alcohol expectancies to drinking patterns among alcoholics: Generalisation across gender and race', *Journal of Studies on Alcohol*, 51,2: 175–182.

Kline, R.B. and Canter, W.A. (1994) 'Can educational programs affect teenage drinking? A multivariate perspective', *Journal of Drug Education*, 24: 139–149.

Klingemann, H. (1992) 'Alcohol treatment in a consensus democracy: The case of the Swiss Confederation', in Klingemann, H., Takkala, J. and

Hunt, G., (eds) *Cure, Care or Control: Alcoholism Treatment in Sixteen Countries*, Albany, New York, State University of New York Press, 151–172.

Kluft, R.P. (1990) 'Incest and subsequent revictimization: The case of therapist–patient sexual exploitation, with a description of the sitting duck syndrome', in Kluft, R.P., (ed.) *Incest-Related Syndromes of Adult Psychopathology*, Washington, D.C., American Psychiatric Press, 263–287.

Knibbe, R.A., Oostveen, T. and van de Goor, I. (1991) 'Young people's alcohol consumption in public drinking places: reasoned behaviour or related to the situation?' *British Journal of Addiction*, 86: 1425–1433.

Knight, B. (1986) 'The history of child abuse', *Forensic Science International*, 30: 135–141.

Knight, R.P. (1937) 'The dynamic and treatment of chronic alcohol addiction', *Bulletin of the Menninger Clinic*, 1: 233–250.

Knodel, J. (1979) 'From natural fertility to family limitation: the onset of fertility transition in a sample of German villages', *Demography*, 16: 493–521.

Knodel, J. (1987) 'Starting, stopping, and spacing during the early stages of fertility transition: The experience of German village populations in the 18th and 19th centuries', *Demography*, 24: 143–162.

Knodel, J. and Hermalin, A.I. (1984) 'Effects of birth rank, maternal age, birth interval, and sibship size on infant and child mortality: evidence from 18th and 19th century reproductive histories', *American Journal of Public Health*, 74: 1098–1106.

Knops, G.G. (1993) 'Postpartum mood disorders. A startling contrast to the joy of birth', *Postgraduate Medicine*, 93: 103–116.

Knupfer, G. (1964) 'Female drinking patterns', in *Selected Papers Presented at the fifteenth Annual Meeting of the North American Association of Alcoholism Programs*, Washington, D.C., 140–160.

Koatailo, P.K., Adger, H., Duggan, A.K. Repke, J. and Joffe, A. (1992) 'Cigarette, alcohol and other drug use by school-age pregnant adolescents: Prevalence, detection and associated risk factors', *Pediatrics*, 90: 328–334.

Kobler, J. (1973) *Ardent Spirits: The Rise and Fall of Prohibition*, London, Michael Joseph.

Kolata, G.B. (1881) 'Fetal Alcohol Advisory debated', *Science*, 214: 642–645.

Konigsberg, L.W. (1988) 'Migration models of prehistoric postmarital residence', *American Journal of Physical Anthropology*, 77: 471–482.

Kopelman, M.D. (1995) 'The Korsakoff Syndrome', *British Journal of Psychiatry*, 166: 154–173.

Korrapati, M.R. and Vestal, R.E. (1992) 'Alcohol and medications in the elderly: Complex interactions', in Beresford, T.P. and Gomberg, E. (eds) *Alcohol and Aging*, New York, Oxford University Press, 42–55.

Kosson, D.S., Steuerwald, B.L., Newman, J.P. and Widom, C.S. (1994) 'The relation between socialization and antisocial behavior, substance use, and family conflict in college students', *Journal of Personality Assessment*, 63: 473–488.

Kosten, T.R., Rounsaville, B., Kosten, T.A. and Merikangas, K. (1991) 'Gender differences in the specificity of alcoholism transmission among the relatives of opioid addicts', *Journal of Nervous and Mental Disease*, 179: 392–400.

Kottler, J.A. (1993) *On Being a Therapist*, San Francisco, Jossey-Bass Inc. Publishers.

Kozaric-Kovacic, D. (1996) *Alcohol Intoxication and Road Traffic Accidents in Croatia in 1995*, (Unpublished).

Krahn, D., Kurth, C., Demitrack, M. and Drewnowski, A. (1992) 'The relationship of dieting severity and bulimic behaviors to alcohol and other drug use in young women', *Journal of Substance Abuse*, 4: 341–353.

Krasner, N., Davis, M., Portmann, B. and Williams, R. (1977) 'Changing patterns of alcoholic liver disease in Great Britain: Relation to sex and signs of autoimmunity', *British Medical Journal*, 1: 497–500.

Krausz, M., Haasen, C., Mass, R., Wagner, H.B., Peter, H. and Freyberger, H.J. (1996) 'Harmful use of psychotropic substances by schizophrenics: Coincidence, patterns of use and motivation', *European Addiction Research*, 2: 11–16.

Kreek, M.J. (1992) *Effects of Drugs of Abuse and Treatment Agents in Women*, NIDA Research Monograph, 119: 106–10.

Kretschmann, H.J., Schleicher, A., Wingert, F., Zilles, K. and Loblich, H.J. (1979) 'Human brain growth in the 19th and 20th century', *Journal of the Neurological Sciences*, 40: 169–188.

Kristenson, H. (1992) 'Long-term Antabuse treatment of alcohol-dependent patients', *Acta Psychiatrica Scandinavia*, 369: 41–45.

Kroft, C.L., Gescuk, B., Woods, B.T. et al. (1991) 'Brain ventricular size in female alcoholics: A MRI study', *Alcohol*, 8: 31–34.

Kroll, J. and De Ganck, R. (1986) 'The adolescence of a thirteenth-century visionary nun', *Psychological Medicine*, 16: 745–756.

Kua, E.H. (1994) 'Chinese women who drink', *Addiction*, 89: 956–958.

Kua, E.H. (1995) 'A profile of Chinese alcoholics in Singapore', *Addiction*, 90: 51–56.

Kubicka, L., Csemy, L. and Kozeny, J. (1991) 'The sociodemographic, microsocial, and attitudinal context of Czech women's drinking', Paper presented at the Symposium on Alcohol, Family and Significant Others. Social Research Institute of Alcohol Studies and Nordic Council for Alcohol and Drug Research, Helsinki.

Kubicka, L., Csemy, L., Kozeny, J. and Nespor, K. (1993) 'The substance specificity of psychosocial correlates of alcohol, tobacco, coffee and drug use by Czech women', *Addiction*, 88: 813–820.

Kuper, A. and Stone, A.A. (1982) 'The dream of Irma's injection: A structural analysis', *American Journal of Psychiatry*, 139: 1225–1234.

Kuzma, J. and Sokol, R. (1982) 'Maternal drinking behavior and decreased intra uterine growth', *Alcoholism: Clinical and Experimental Research*, 6: 396–402.

La Grange, L., Anton, R.F., Garcia, S. and Herrbold, C. (1995) 'Carbohydrate-deficient transferrin levels in a female population', *Alcoholism: Clinical and Experimental Research*, 19: 100–103.

La Grange, L., Jones, T.D., Erb, L. and Reyes, E. (1995) 'Alcohol consumption: Biochemical and personality correlates in a college student population', *Addictive Behaviors*, 20: 93–103.

La Rosa, J.H. (1990) 'Executive women and health: Perceptions and practices', *American Journal of Public Health*, 80: 1450–1454.

La Vecchia, C., Decarli, A., Franceschi, S. et al. (1985) 'Alcohol consumption and the risk of breast cancer in women', *Journal of the National Cancer Institute*, 75,1: 61–65.

La Vecchia, C. (1986) 'Smoking in Italy, 1949–1983', *Preventive Medicine*, 15: 274–281.

La Vecchia, C., Decarli, A., Farnceschi, S., Gentile, A., Negri, E. and Parazzini, F. (1987) 'Dietary factors and the risk of breast cancer', *Nutrition and Cancer*, 10: 205–214.

La Vecchia, C., Negri, E., Parazinni, F. et al. (1989) 'Alcohol and breast cancer: update from an Italian case control study', *European Journal of Cancer and Clinical Oncology*, 25: 1711–1717.

La Vecchia, C., Negri, E., D'Avanzo, B., Franceschi, S. and Boyle, P. (1991) 'Risk factors for gallstone disease requiring surgery', *International Journal of Epidemiology*, 20: 209–215.

La Vecchia, C., Decarli, A., Ferraroni, M. and Negri, E. (1994) 'Alcohol drinking and prevalence of self-reported gallstone disease in the 1983 Italian National health survey', *Epidemiology*, 5,5: 533–536.

LaChat, M.R. (1988) 'Religion's support for the domination of women – breaking the cycle', *Nurse Practitioner*, 13: 31–34.

Lahelma, E., Kangas, R. and Manderbacka, K. (1995) 'Drinking and unemployment: Contrasting patterns among men and women', *Drug and Alcohol Dependence*, 37: 71–82.

Laidlaw, T.A., Malmo, C. et al. (1990) *Healing Voices: Feminist Approaches to Therapy for Women*, California, Jossey-Bass Inc. Publishers.

Laitinen, K., Valimäki, M. and Keto, P. (1991) 'Bone mineral density measured by dual-energy X-ray absorptiometry in healthy Finnish women', *Calcified Tissue International*, 48: 224–231.

Laitinen, K. and Valimäki, M. (1993) 'Bone and the comforts of life', *Annals of Medicine*, 25,4: 413–425.

Lambert, W.R. (1983) *Drink and Sobriety in Victorian Wales 1820–c.1895*, Cardiff, University of Wales Press.

Lammers, S.M.M., Mainzer, D.E.H. and Breteler, M.H.M. (1995) 'Do alcohol pharmacokinetics in women vary due to the menstrual cycle', *Addiction*, 90: 23–30.

Lammers, S.M.M., Schippers, G.M. and van der Staak, C. (1995) 'Submission and rebellion: excessive drinking of women in problematic heterosexual partner relationships', *International Journal of the Addictions*, 30: 901–917.

Lancelot, C. and Kaslow, N.J. (1994) 'Sex role orientation and disordered eating in women: A review', *Clinical Psychology Review*, 14: 139–157.

Landesman-Dwyer, S., Ragozin, A.S. and Little, R. (1981) 'Behavioral correlates of prenatal alcohol exposure: A four-year follow-up study', *Neurobehavioral Toxicology and Teratology*, 3: 187–193.

Landis, J. (1956) 'Experiences of 500 children with adult sexual deviation', *Psychiatric Quarterly*, supplement, 30: 91–109.

Lang, A.R. (1992) 'Person perception as a function of drinking behavior, gender and sex role stereotypes', *Journal of Studies on Alcohol*, 53: 225–232.

Lang, A.R. and Stritzke, W.G. (1993) 'Children and alcohol', in Galanter, M. (ed.), *Recent Developments in Alcoholism*, Vol. 11, New York, Plenum Press, 73–85.

Lang, H. and Srdar, J. (1992) 'Therapeutic communities and aftercare clubs in Yugoslavia', in Klingemann, H., Takkala, J. and Hunt, G., (eds) *Cure, Care or Control: Alcoholism Treatment in Sixteen Countries*, Albany, New York, State University of New York Press, 53–63.

Lang, T., Degoulet, P., Aime, F. et al. (1987) 'Relationship between alcohol consumption and hypertension prevalence and control in a French population', *Journal of Chronic Diseases*, 40: 713–720.

Langanfox, J. and Poole, M.E. (1995) 'Occupational stress in Australian business and professional women', *Stress Medicine*, 11: 113–122.

Lanier, D. (1995) *Absinthe: The Cocaine of the Nineteenth Century*, Jefferson, North Carolina, McFarland and Company.

Lansky, D., Nathan, P.E. and Lawson, D.M. (1978) 'Blood alcohol level discrimination by alcoholics: The role of internal and external cues', *Journal of Consulting and Clinical Psychology*, 46: 953–960.

Lapham, S.C., Skipper, B.J., Owen, J.P., Kleyboecker, K., Teaf, D., Thompson, B. and Simpson, G. (1995) 'Alcohol abuse screening instruments: normative test data collected from a first DWI offender screening program', *Journal of Studies on Alcohol*, 56: 51–59.

Lapidus, L., Bengtosson, C., Hallström, T., and Björntorp, P. (1989) 'Obesity, adipose tissue distribution and health in women', *Appetite*, 12: 25–35.

Larimore, H. (1992) *Older Women in Recovery*, Florida, Health Communications Inc.

Larroque, B. (1992) 'Alcohol and the fetus', *International Journal of Epidemiology*, 21, supplement 1: S8–S16.

Larson, E.W., Olincy, A., Rummans, T.A. et al. (1992) 'Disulfiram treatment of patients with both alcohol dependence and other psychiatric disorders', *Alcoholism: Clinical and Experimental Research*, 16: 125–130.

Latimer, P.R. and Sweet, A.A. (1984) 'Cognitive versus behavioral procedures in cognitive-behavioral therapy: A critical review of the evidence', *Journal of Behavioral Therapy and Experimental Psychiatry*, 15: 9–22.

Lavik, N.J., Clausen, S.E. and Pedersen, W. (1991) 'Eating behaviour, drug use, psychopathology and parental bonding in adolescents in Norway', *Acta Psychiatrica Scandinavica*, 84: 387–390.

Lawrence, S.C. and Bendixen, K. (1992) 'His and hers: Male and female anatomy in anatomy texts for U.S. medical students, 1890–1989', *Social Science and Medicine*, 35: 925–934.

Lawson, D.H., Jink, H. and Rothman, K.J. (1981) 'Coffee and tea consumption and breast cancer', *Surgery*, 90: 801–803.

Lazoritz, S. (1990) 'Whatever happened to Mary Ellen?' *Child Abuse and Neglect*, 14: 143–149.

Lê, M.G., Moulton, L.H., Hill, C. and Kramer, A. (1986) 'Consumption of dairy produce and alcohol in a case-control study of breast cancer', *Journal of the National Cancer Institute*, 77: 633–636.

Lecomte, M. (1950) 'Eléments d'hérédopathologie', *Scalper*, 103: 1133–1145.

Lehfeldt, H. (1986) 'Felix A. Theilhaber – pioneer sexologist', *Archives of Sexual Behavior*, 15: 1–12.

Lehto, J. (1995) 'Trends in alcohol policy', Paper presented at the 21st Alcohol Epidemiology Symposium of the Kettil Bruun Society, Oporto, Portugal.

Lehto, J. and Moskalewicz, J. (1994) *Alcohol Policy During Extensive Socio-Economic Change*, Copenhagen, World Health Organization.

Leibenluft, E. (1993) 'Do gonadal steroids regulate circadian rhythms in humans?' *Journal of Affective Disorders*, 29: 175–181.

Leiber, C.S. (1983) 'Precursor lesions of cirrhosis', *Alcohol and Alcoholism*, 18: 5–20.

Leiber, C.S. (1991) 'Hepatic, metabolic and toxic effects of ethanol: 1991 update', *Alcoholism: Clinical and Experimental Research*, 15: 573–592.

Leiber, C.S. (1992) 'Alcoholic liver injury', *Current Opinions in Gastroenterology*, 8: 449–457.

Leigh, B. (1990a) 'The relationship of substance use during sex to high risk behavior', *Journal of Sex Research*, 27: 199–213.

Leigh, B. (1990b) 'The relationship of sex-related expectancies to alcohol consumption and sexual Behaviour', *British Journal of Addiction*, 85: 919–928.

Leigh, B.C. (1993) 'Alcohol consumption and sexual activity as reported with a diary technique', *Journal of Abnormal Psychology*, 102: 490–493.

Leigh, B.C. and Stall, R. (1993) 'Substance use and risky sexual behavior for exposure to HIV: Issues in methodology, interpretation, and prevention', *American Psychology*, 48: 1035–1045.

Lejoyeux, M. and Ades, J. (1993) 'Evaluation of lithium treatment in alcoholism', *Alcohol and Alcoholism*, 28,3: 273–279.

Lele, A.S. (1982) 'Fetal Alcohol Syndrome: Other effects of alcohol on pregnancy', *New York State Journal of Medicine*, July: 1225–1227.

Lelong, N., Kaminski, M., Chwalow, J., Bean, K. and Subtil, D. (1995) 'Attitudes and behavior of pregnant women and health professionals towards alcohol and tobacco consumption', *Patient Education and Counseling*, 25: 39–49.

Lemere, F. and Voegtlin, W. (1950) 'An evaluation of the aversive treatment of alcoholism', *Quarterly Journal of Studies on Alcohol*, 11: 100–204.

Lemmens, P. (1994) 'The alcohol content of self-report and 'standard' drinks', *Addiction*, 89: 593–601.

Lemoine, P. (1994) 'An historical note about the foetal alcohol syndrome', *Addiction*, 89: 1021–1023.

Lemoine, P., Harronsseau, H., Borteyru, J.P. and Menuet, J.C. (1968) 'Les enfants de parents alcooliques: Anomalies observées à propos 127 cas', *Ouest Médicale*, 25: 475–482.

Lemoine, P. and Lemoine, P.H. (1992) 'Avenir des enfants de mères alcooliques (Etude des 105 cas retrouvés a l'âge adulte) et quelques constations, intérêt prophylactique. (Outcome of the offspring of alcoholic mothers (study of 105 adults) and considerations with a view to prevention)', *Annales de Pediatries*, 39: 226–235, (Paris).

Lender, M.E. (1981) 'Women alcoholics: Prevalence estimates and their problems reflected in turn-of-the-century institutional data', *International Journal of the Addictions*, 16: 443–448.

Lender, M.E. (1984) *Dictionary of the American Temperance Biography*, Westport, Connecticut, Greenwood Press.

Lender, M.E. and Karnchanapee, K.R. (1977) '"Temperance tales": Antiliquor fiction and American attitudes toward alcoholics in the late 19th and early 20th centuries', *Journal of Studies on Alcohol*, 38: 1347–1370.

Lerner, G. (1993) *The Creation of Feminist Consciousness: From the Middle Ages to Eighteen-Seventy*, Oxford, Oxford University Press.

Lerner Croft, C., Gesuk, B. and Woods, B.T. (1991) 'Brain ventricular size in female alcoholics: An MRI study', *Alcohol*, 8: 31–34.

Lenz, H.J., Ferrari-Taylor, J. and Isenberg, J.I. (1983) 'Wine and five per cent ethanol are potent stimulants of gastric acid secretion in humans', *Gastroenterology*, 85: 1082–1087.

Lesch, O.M. and Walter, H. (1996) 'Subtypes of alcoholism and their role in therapy', *Alcohol and Alcoholism*, 31: 63–67.

Leung, P.K., Kinzie, J.D., Boehnlein, J.K. and Shore, J.H. (1993) 'A prospective study of the natural course of alcoholism in a native American village', *Journal of Studies on Alcohol*, 54: 733–738.

Levy, S.T. and Inderbitzin, L.B. (1992) 'Neutrality, interpretation, and therapeutic intent', *Journal of the American Psychoanalytic Association*, 40: 989–1011.

Lewis, C. (1993) 'Factors contributing to alcoholism among homosexual women: A psychosocial approach to treatment', *Dissertation Abstracts International*, 53: 5448B.

Lewis, C.E. and Bucholz, K.K. (1991) 'Alcoholism, antisocial behavior and family history', *British Journal of Addiction*, 86: 177–194.

Lewis, H.B. (1971) *Shame and Guilt in Neurosis*, New York, International Universities Press.

Lewis, M. (1985) 'Older women and health: an overview', *Women and Health*, 10: 1–16.

Lewis, M.J. (1978) 'Obstetrics: Education and practice in Sydney, 1870–1939: part 1', *Australian and New Zealand Journal of Obstetrics and Gynaecology*, 18: 161–164.

Lex, B.W. (1991) 'Some gender differences in alcohol and polysubstance users', *Health Psychology*, 10: 121–132.

Lex, B.W., Goldberg, M.E., Mendelson, J.H., Lawler, N.S. and Bower, T. (1994) 'Components of antisocial personality disorder among women convicted for drunken driving', *Annals of the New York Academy of Sciences*, 28: 49–58.

Lex, B.W., Rhoades, E.M., Teoh, S.K. and Mendelson, J.K.L. (1991) *Divided Attention Task Performance in Women With and Without Familial Alcoholism*, NIDA Research Monograph, 105 ISS, 321.

Lex, B.W., Rhoades, E.M., Teoh, S.K., Mendelson, J.H. and Greenwald, N.E. (1994) 'Divided attention task performance and subjective effects following alcohol and placebo: differences between women with and without a family history of alcoholism', *Drug and Alcohol Dependence*, 35: 95–105.

Lex, B.W., Teoh, S.K., Lagomasino, I., Mello, N.K. and Mendelson, J. (1990) 'Characteristics of women receiving mandatory treatment for alcohol and polysubstance dependence in Massachusetts', *Drug and Alcohol Dependence*, 25: 13–20.

Lhuintre, J.P., Moore, N., Tran, G. et al. (1990) 'Acamprosate appears to decrease alcohol intake in weaned alcoholics', *Alcohol and Alcoholism*, 25: 613–622.

Liao, L-M., K., Hunter, M. and Weinman, J. (1995) 'Health-related behaviours and their correlates in a general population sample of 45-year-old women', *Psychology and Health*, 10: 171–184.

Licata, S.J. (1980) 'The homosexual rights movement in the United States: a traditionally overlooked area of American history', *Journal of Homosexuality*, 6: 161–189.

Lieber, C.S. (1984) 'Alcohol and the liver: 1984 Update', *Hepatology*, 6: 1234–1260.

Lieber, C.S. (1992) 'Alcoholic liver injury', *Current Opinions in Gastroenterology*, 8: 449–457.

Ligon, R.E., Stevenson, D.R., Diner, W., Westbrook, K.C. and Lang, N.P. (1980) 'Breast masses in young women', *American Journal of Surgery*, 140: 779–782.

Likeman, R.K. (1992) 'The boldest procedure possible for checking the bleeding – a new look at an old operation, and a series of 13 cases from an Australian hospital', *Australian and New Zealand Journal of Obstetrics and Gynaecology*, 32: 256–262.

Lillie-Blanton, M., Mackenzie, E. and Anthony, J.C. (1991) 'Black–white differences in alcohol use by women: Baltimore survey findings', *Public Health Reports*, 106: 124–133.

Lindenberg, C.S., Gendrop, S.C., Nencioli, M. and Adames, Z. (1994) 'Substance abuse among inner-city Hispanic women: exploring resiliency', *Journal of Obstetric, Gynecologic and Neonatal Nursing*, 23: 609–616.

Lindenberg, C.S., Gendrop, S.C. and Reiskin, H.K. (1993) 'Empirical evidence for the social stress model of substance abuse', *Research in Nursing and Health*, Oct 16: 351–362.

Lindenberg, C.S. and Keith, A.B. (1993) 'Opiate abuse in pregnancy', *Annual Review of Nursing Research,* 11 ISS: 249–279.

Lindenberg, C.S., Reiskin, H.K. and Gendrop, S.C. (1994) 'The social stress model of substance abuse among childbearing-age women: A review of the literature', *Journal of Drug Education,* 24: 253–268.

Lindegard, B. (1987) 'Alcohol and breast cancer', *New England Journal of Medicine,* 317: 20.

Lindstrom, L. (1992) *Managing Alcoholism: Matching Clients to Treatment,* New York, Oxford University Press.

Lindqvist, P. (1991) 'Homicides commited by abusers of alcohol and illicit drugs', *British Journal of Addiction,* 86: 321–326.

Liskow, B.I. and Goodwin, D.W. (1987) 'Pharmacological treatments of alcohol intoxication withdrawal and dependence', *Journal of Studies on Alcohol,* 48: 356–370.

Lister Sharp, D. (1994) 'Underage Drinking in the United Kingdom since 1979: Public policy, the law and adolescent drinking behaviour', *Alcohol and Alcoholism,* 29: 555–563.

Litten, R.Z. and Allen, J.P. (1991) 'Pharmacotherapies for alcoholism: Promising agents and clinical Issues', *Alcoholism: Clinical and Experimental Research,* 15: 620–633.

Little, R.E. (1976) 'Alcohol consumption in pregnancy as reported to the obstetrician and to an independent interviewer', *Annals of the New York Academy of Sciences,* 273: 588–592.

Little, R.E. and Singh, C.F. (1987) 'Father's drinking and infant birthweight: Report of an association', *Teratology,* 36: 59–65.

Littlewood, R. (1994) 'Symptoms, struggles and functions: What does the overdose represent?' in McDonald, M., (ed.) *Gender, Drink and Drugs,* Oxford, Berg, 77–98.

Littlewood, R. (1995) 'Psychopathology and personal agency: Modernity, culture change and eating disorders in South Asian societies', *British Journal of Medical Psychology,* 68: 45–63.

Loftus, E.F. (1994) 'Memories of childhood sexual abuse: Remembering and repressing', *Psychology of Women Quarterly,* 18: 67–84.

Lomas, P. (1981) *The Case for a Personal Psychotherapy,* Oxford, Oxford University Press.

Lomnitz, L. (1976) 'Alcohol and culture: The historical evolution of drinking patterns among the Mapuohe', in Everett, M.W., Waddell, J.O. and Heath, D.B., (eds) *Cross-Cultural Approaches to the Study of Alcohol: An Interdisciplinary Perspective,* The Hague, Mouton, 177–198.

Long, A. and Mullen, B. (1994) 'An exploration of women's perceptions of the major factors that contributed to their alcohol abuse', *Journal of Advanced Nursing,* 19: 623–639.

Longabaugh, R., McCrady, B., Fink, E., Stout, R., McAuley, T., Doyle, C. and McNeil, D. (1983) 'Cost effectiveness of alcoholism treatment in partial *vs* inpatient settings: Six month outcomes', *Journal of Studies on Alcohol,* 44: 1049–1071.

Longabaugh, R., Wirtz, P.W., DiClemente, C.C. and Litt, M. (1994) 'Issues in the development of client-treatment matching hypotheses', *Journal of Studies on Alcohol*, Supplement, 12: 46–59.

Longnecker, MP., Berlion, J.A., Orza, M.J. and Chalmers, T.S. (1988) 'A meta-analysis of alcohol consumption in relation to risk of breast cancer', *Journal of the American Medical Association*, 260: 652–656.

Loretto, W. (1994) 'Youthful drinking in Northern Ireland and Scotland: Preliminary results from a comparative study', *Drugs: Education, Prevention and Policy*, 1: 143–152.

Lorion, R.P. and Saltman, W. (1993) 'Children's exposure to community violence: following a path from concern to research to action', *Psychiatry*, 56: 55–65.

Loughlin, N. (1992) 'A trial of the use of psychodrama for women with alcohol problems', *Nursing Practice*, 5: 14–19.

Love, I.N. (1891) 'Coffee: Its use and abuse', *Alienist and Neurologist*, July 12, 3: 475.

Low, K.G., Thoresen, C.E., Pattillo, J.R., King, A.C. and Jenkins, C. (1994) 'Anxiety, depression, and heart-disease in women', *International Journal of Behavioral Medicine*, 1: 305–319.

Lowe, G. (1994) 'Group differences in alcohol-creativity interactions', *Psychological Reports*, 75: 1635–1638.

Lozina, C., Russell, M. and Mudar, P. (1995) 'Correlates of alcohol-related problems in African-American and white gynecologic patients', *Alcoholism: Clinical and Experimental Research*, 19: 25–30.

Lubkin, S.R., Gullberg, R.G., Logan, B.K., Maini, P.K. and Murray, J.D. (1996) 'Simple versus sophisticated models of breath Alcohol exhalation profiles', *Alcohol and Alcoholism*, 31: 61–67.

Lucas-Champonniere (translated by Nelson, E.M.) (1882) 'Idiocy and imbecility – insanity in an infant – moral insanity', *Alienist and Neurologist*, July 3, 3: 434–439.

Lucey, M.R., Egerer, G., Young, J. et al. (1993) 'The interplay of age, sex and gastric function on ethanol metabolism', *Gastroenterology*, 104: A945.

Ludwig, A.M. (1985) 'Cognitive processes associated with "spontaneous" recovery from alcoholism', *Journal of Studies on Alcohol*, 46: 53–58.

Lumeng, L. and Crabb, D.W. (1994) 'Genetic aspects and risk factors in alcoholism and alcoholic liver disease', *Gastroenterology*, 107: 572–578.

Lumey, L.H. (1992) 'Decreased birthweights in infants after maternal in utero exposure to the Dutch famine of 1944–1945', *Paediatric and Perinatal Epidemiology*, 6: 240–253.

Lumley, J., Correy, J.F., Newman, N.M., and Curran, J.T. (1985) 'Cigarette smoking, alcohol consumption and fetal outcome in Tasmania 1981–82', *Australia and New Zealand Journal of Obstetrics and Gynaecology*, 25: 33–40.

Lynch, W.D., Glass, G.V. and Tran, Z.V. (1988) 'Diet, tobacco, alcohol and stress as causes of coronary artery heart disease: An ecological trend analysis of national data', *Yale Journal of Biology and Medicine*, 61: 413–426.

Lyon, D. and Greenberg, J. (1991) 'Evidence of codependency in women with an alcoholic parent: helping out Mr. Wrong', *Journal of Personality and Social Psychology*, 61: 435–439.

Lyvers, M.F. and Maltzman, I. (1991) 'Selective sects of alcohol on Wisconsin card sorting test performance', *British Journal of Addiction*, 86: 399–407.

McBride, C.M., and Pirie, P.L. (1990) 'Postpartum smoking relapse', *Addictive Behaviors*, 15: 165–168.

McCaghy, C., (1968) 'Drinking and deviance disavowal: The case of child molesters', *Social Problems*, 16: 43–49.

McCartney, J. (1994) 'Understanding and helping the children of problem drinkers: A systems-psychodynamic perspective', *Journal of Substance Abuse Treatment*, 11: 155–166.

McCarty, D., Argeriou, M., Huebner, R.B. and Lubran, B. (1991) 'Alcoholism, drug abuse, and the homeless', *American Psychologist*, 46: 1139–1148.

McCool, W.F. and McCool, S.J. (1989) 'Feminism and nurse-midwifery. Historical overview and current issues', *Journal of Nurse-Midwifery*, 34: 323–334.

McCrady, B., Longabaugh, R., Fink, E., Stout, R., Beattie, M. and Ruggieri-Authelet, A. (1986) 'Cost effectiveness of alcoholism treatment in partial hospital versus inpatient settings after brief inpatient treatment: 12-month outcomes', *Journal of Consulting and Clinical Psychology*, 54: 708–713.

McCrady, B.S. (1994) 'Alcoholics Anonymous and Behavior Therapy: Can habits be treated as diseases? Can diseases be treated as habits?' *Journal of Consulting and Clinical Psychology*, 62: 1159–1166.

McCusker, K. (1988) 'Landmarks of tobacco use in the United States', *Chest*, 93: 34S–36S.

McDonald, A.M. (1972) *Chambers Twentieth Century Dictionary*, Edinburgh, W. and R. Chambers Ltd.

Macdonald, D. (1847) 'Puerperal insanity', *American Journal of Insanity*, 4: 113

Macdonald, D.I. (1987) 'Patterns of alcohol and drug use among adolescents', *Pediatric Clinics of North America*, 34: 275–288.

Macdonald, E. (1991) *Shoot the Women First*, London, Fourth Estate Ltd.

Macdonald, I., Debry, G. and Westerterp, K. (1993) 'Alcohol and overweight', in Verschuren, P.M. (ed.) *Health Issues Related to Alcohol Consumption*, Washington, D.C., ILSI Press, 263–279.

McDonald, M. (1994a) *Gender, Drink and Drugs*, Oxford, Berg.

McDonald, M. (1994b) 'Drinking and social identity in the West of France', in McDonald, M., (ed.) *Gender, Drink and Drugs*, Oxford, Berg, 99–124.

McDonald, M. (1994c) 'A social-anthropological view of gender, drink and drugs', in McDonald, M., (ed.) *Gender, Drink and Drugs*, Oxford, Berg, 1–32.

MacDonald, S. (1994) 'Whisky, women and the Scottish drink problem. A view from the Highlands', in McDonald, M., (ed.) *Gender, Drink and Drugs*, Oxford, Berg, 125–144.

MacFarlane, K. and Korbin, J. (1983) 'Confronting the incest secret long after the fact: A family study of multiple victimization with strategies for intervention', *Child Abuse and Neglect*, 7: 225–237.

McGashum, N.D. and Mather, H.S. (1984) 'Cancer pathologic regions: A Rajastham example', *Geographical Medicine*, 14: 4–19.

McGee, R. and Stanton, W.R. (1994) 'Smoking in pregnancy and child development to age 9 years', *Journal of Paediatrics and Child Health*, 30: 263–268.

McGovern, P.E., Glusker, D.L. and Exner, L. (1996) 'Neolothic resinated wine', *Nature*, 381: 480 481.

McGue, M., Pickens, R.W. and Svikis, D.S. (1992) 'Sex and age effects on the inheritance of alcohol problems: a twin study', *Journal of Abnormal Psychology*, 101: 3–17.

McKay, J.R., Longabaugh, R., Beattie, M.C., Maisto, S.A. and Noel, N.E. (1992) 'The relationship of pretreatment family functioning to drinking behavior during follow-up by alcoholic patients', *American Journal of Drug and Alcohol Abuse*, 18,4: 445–460.

McKirnan, D.J. and Peterson, P.L. (1989) 'Alcohol and drug use among homosexual men and women: Epidemiology and population characteristics', *Addictive Behaviors*, 14: 545–553.

McKnight, A.J. (1993) 'Server intervention: Accomplishments and needs', *Alcohol, Health and Research World*, 17: 76–83.

McLane Hamilton, A. (1881) 'Significance of facial hairy growths among insane women', *Alienist and Neurologist*, 2,3: 417–418.

MacLeod (1886) 'An address on puerperal insanity', *British Medical Journal*, 2: 239.

McLeod, D.R., Foste, G.V., Hoehn-Saric, R., Svikis, D.S. and Hipsley, P.A. (1994) 'Family history of alcoholism in women with generalized anxiety disorder who have premenstrual syndrome: Patient reports of premenstrual alcohol consumption and symptoms of anxiety', *Alcoholism: Clinical and Experimental Research*, 18: 664–670.

McLeod, E. (1982) *Women Working: Prostitution Now*, London, Croom Helm.

MacLure, K.M., Hayes, K.C., Colditz, G.A. Stampfer, M.J., Speirer, F.E. and Willett, W.C. (1989) 'Weight, diet, and the risk of symptomatic gallstones in middle aged women', *New England Journal of Medicine*, 321: 563–569.

MacMahon, S.W., Blacket, R.B., Macdonald, G.J. and, Hall, W. (1984) 'Obesity, alcohol consumption and blood pressure in Australian men and women: The National Heart Foundation of Australia risk factor prevalence study', *Journal of Hypertension*, 2: 85–91.

McMahon, J. and Jones, B.T. (1992) 'The change process in alcoholics: client motivation and denial in the treatment of alcoholism within the context of contemporary nursing', *Journal of Advanced Nursing*, 17: 173–186.

McMahon, R.C. and Davidson, R.S. (1986) 'An examination of depressed vs. nondepressed alcoholics in inpatient treatment', *Journal of Clinical Psychology*, 42: 177–184.

McManus, A. (1993) *They said I was Dead: The Complete Alternative Cure for Addiction*, London, Scarlett Press.

McMichael, A.J. (1988) 'Breast cancer in Australia', *Medical Journal of Australia*, 148: 422.

McMichael, A.J. and Armstrong, B.K. (1988) 'Breast cancer in Australia: Occurrence, risk factors, preventability and screening', *Medical Journal of Australia*, 148: 86–88.

McMillan, J. and Baldwin, S. (1993) 'A pilot study of an alcohol education course for young women offenders: What's good for the goose?' *Alcohol and Alcoholism*, 28: 499–504.

MacMillan, M. (1988) *Women of the Raj*, German Democratic Republic, Thames and Hudson.

McNally, E.B. and Finnegan, D.G. (1992) 'Lesbian recovering alcoholics: A qualitative study of identity transformation. A report on research and applications to treatment', *Journal of Chemical Dependency Treatment*, 5: 93–103.

McPherson, K., Engelsman, E., and Conning, D. (1993) 'Breast cancer', in Verschuren, P.M. (ed.) *Health Issues Related to Alcohol Consumption*, Washington, D.C., ILSI Press, 221–244.

Macrae, D. (1877) *Temperance Catechism; or Band of Courage Conversations*, Glasgow, Scottish Temperance League.

McSherry, J.A. (1985) 'Was Mary, Queen of Scots, anorexic?' *Scottish Medical Journal*, 30: 243–245.

Mace, C.J. (1992) 'Hysterical conversion. I: A history', *British Journal of Psychiatry*, 161: 369–377.

Madame De La Tour Du Pin (1985) *Memoirs of Madame De La Tour Du Pin*, London, Century Publishing Co. Ltd.

Madden, J.S. (1994) 'Psychiatric syndromes associated with alcohol and substance misuse', in Chick, J. and Cantwell, R., (eds) *Alcohol and Drug Misuse*, London, Royal College of Psychiatrists, 174–201.

Madianos, M.G., Gefu-Madianou, D. and Stefanis, C. (1994) 'Adolescent drinking and alcohol-related problems in a nationwide general population', *International Journal of the Addictions*, 29,12: 1581–1599.

Madigan, L. and Gamble, N. (1989) *The Second Rape: Society's Continued Betrayal of the Victim*, New York, Lexington Books.

Madrigal, L. (1992) 'Differential sex mortality in a rural nineteenth-century population: Escazu, Costa Rica', *Human Biology*, 64: 199–213.

Magnan, M.V. (1884) 'Clinical lecturers on dipsomania: Lecture one, history and etiology', *Alienist and Neurologist*, October 5,4: 691–694.

Magnan, M.V. (1886) 'Clinical lectures on dipsomania', *Alienist and Neurologist*, January 7, 1: 58–72.

Mahdihassan, S. (1989) 'The five cosmic elements as depicted in Indian and Chinese cosmologies', *American Journal of Chinese Medicine*, 17: 245–252.

Maheswaran, R., Gill, J.S., Davies, P. and Beevers, D.G. (1991) 'High blood pressure due to alcohol. A rapidly reversible effect', *Hypertension*, 17: 787–792.

Mai, F.M. and Merskey, H. (1981) 'Briquet's concept of hysteria: an historical perspective', *Canadian Journal of Psychiatry / Revue Canadienne de Psychiatrie*, 26, 57–63.

Majewski, F. (1981) 'Alcohol embryopathy: Some facts and speculations about pathogenesis', *Neurobehavioral Toxicology*, 3: 129–144.

Makari, G.J. (1991) 'German philosophy, Freud, and the riddle of the woman', *Journal of the American Psychoanalytic Association*, 39: 183–213.

Mäkelä, K. (1991) 'Social and cultural preconditions of Alcoholics Anonymous (AA) and factors associated with the strength of AA', *British Journal of Addiction*, 86: 1405–1413.

Malatesta, V.J., Pollack, R.H., Crotty, T.D. et al. (1982) 'Acute alcohol intoxication and female orgasmic response', *Journal of Sex Research*, 15: 101–107.

Malcolm, E. (1986) *Ireland Sober, Ireland Free: Drink and Temperance in Nineteenth-Century Ireland*, Dublin, Gill and Macmillan.

Malcolm, R., Anton, R.F., Randall, C.L., Johnston, A., Brady, K. and Thevos, A. (1992) 'A placebo-controlled trial of Buspirone in anxious inpatient alcoholics', *Alcoholism: Clinical and Experimental Research*, 16: 1007–1013.

Maletta, G.J. (1982) 'Alcoholism and the aged', in Pattison, E.M. and Kaufman, E., (eds) *Encyclopedic Handbook of Alcoholism*, New York, Gardner Press, 779–791.

Mancini, L. (1993) 'Dissociation in female adolescents who had been sexually abused as children', *Dissertation Abstracts International*, 54: 1105.

Mann, K., Batra, A., Gunthner, A. and Schroth, G. (1992) 'Do women develop alcoholic brain damage more readily than men?' *Alcoholism: Clinical and Experimental Research*, 16: 1052–1056.

Mann, L.I., Bhakthavathsalan, A., Liu, M. and Malinowski, P. (1975) 'Placental transport of alcohol and its effects on maternal and fetal acid-base balance', *American Journal of Obstetrics and Gynaecology*, 122: 845–851.

Manniche, E. (1983) 'Age at menarche: Nicolai Edvard Ravn's data on 3385 women in mid-19th century Denmark', *Annals of Human Biology*, 10: 79–82.

Manning, W.G., Blumberg, L. and Moulton, L.H. (1995) 'The demand for alcohol: The differential response to price', *Journal of Health Economics*, 14: 123–148.

Mantel, N. (1988) 'An analysis of two recent epidemiologic reports in the *New England Journal of Medicine* associating breast cancer in women with moderate alcohol consumption', *Preventive Medicine*, 17: 672–675.

Manton, W.P. (1892) 'Puerperal hysteria (insanity?)', *Journal of the American Medical Association*, 3: 61

Marbury, M.C., Linn, S., Monson, R., Schoenbaum, S., Stubblefield, P.G. and Ryan, K.J. (1983) 'The association of alcohol consumption with outcome of pregnancy', *American Journal of Public Health*, 73: 1165–1168.

Marcus, B.H., Albrecht, A.E., Niaura, R.S., Taylor, E.S., Simkin, L.R., Feder, S.I., Abrams, D.B. and Thompson, P.D. (1995) 'Exercise enhances the maintenance of smoking cessation in women', *Addictive Behaviors*, 20: 87–92.

Marin, B.V. and Flores, E. (1994) 'Acculturation, sexual behavior, and alcohol use among Latinas', *International Journal of the Addictions*, 29: 1104–1114.

Marino, L.B. and Levy, S.M. (1986) 'Primary and secondary prevention of cancer in children and adolescents: Current status and issues', *Pediatric Clinics of North America*, 4: 975–993.

Markham, U. (1989) *The Elements of Visualisation*, Shaftesbury, Dorset, Element Books Ltd.

Marks, J.L., Hair, C.S., Klock, S.C., Ginsburg, B.E. and Pomerleau, C.S. (1994) 'Effects of menstrual phase on intake of nicotine, caffeine, and alcohol and nonprescribed drugs in women with late luteal phase dysphoric disorder', *Journal of Substance Abuse*, 6: 235–243.

Marland, H. (1994a) 'Introduction', in Marland, H., (ed.) *The Art of Midwifery: Early Modern Midwives in Europe*, London, Routledge, 1–8.

Marland, H. (1994b) *The Art of Midwifery: Early Modern Midwives in Europe*, London, Routledge.

Marland, H. (1994c) 'The "burgerlijke" midwife: The stadsvroedvrouw of Eighteenth Century Holland', in Marland, H., (ed.) *The Art of Midwifery: Early Modern Midwives in Europe*, London, Routledge, 192–213.

Marlatt, G.A. (1992) 'Substance abuse: Implications of a biopsychosocial model for prevention, treatment and relapse prevention', in Grabowski, J. and Vanderbos, G.R., (eds) *Psychopharmacology: Basic Mechanisms and Applied Intervention*, Washington, D.C., American Psychological Association, 127.

Marlatt, G.A. and Gordon, J.R. (1985) *Relapse Prevention: Maintenance Strategies in the Treatment of Addictive Behaviors*, New York, Guilford Press.

Marr, D.D. (1993) 'A problem-solving strategy and self-esteem in recovering chemically dependent women', *Alcoholism Treatment Quarterly*, 10: 171–186.

Marsh, A., Dobbs, J. and White, A. (1986) *Adolescent Drinking*, London, HMSO.

Marshall, A.W., Kingstone, D., Boss, M. and Morgan, M.Y. (1983) 'Ethanol elimination in males and females, relationship to menstrual cycle and body composition', *Hepatology*, 3: 701–706.

Martin, C.S., Earleywine, M., Musty, R.E., Perrine, M.W. and Swift, R.M. (1993) 'Development and validation of the biphasic alcohol effects scale', *Alcoholism: Clinical and Experimental Research*, 17: 140–146.

Martin, D.C., Martin, J.C., Streissguth, A.P., and Lund, C.A. (1979) 'Sucking frequency and amplitude in newborns as a function of maternal drinking and smoking', in Galanter, M. (ed.) *Currents in Alcoholism*, Volume V, New York, Grune and Stratton.

Martin, S.E. (1993) *Alcohol and Interpersonal Violence: Fostering Multidisciplinary Perspectives,* Rockville, Maryland, National Institute on Alcohol Abuse and Alcoholism, Monograph 24.

Mason, L.D. (1882) 'Hereditary alcoholic insanity', *Alienist and Neurologist*, October 3, 4: 655.

Mason, M. (1991) 'Women and shame. Kin and culture', in Bepko, C., (ed.) *Feminism and Addiction,* New York, The Howarth Press.

Mason, M.F. and Dubowski, K.M. (1976) 'Breath-alcohol analysis: Uses, methods and some forensic problems – Review and opinions', *Journal of Forensic Sciences*, 21: 9–41.

Massey, J.M. and Massey, E.W. (1984) 'Ergot, the "jerks," and revivals', *Clinical Neuropharmacology*, 7: 99–105.

Masson, J. (1990) *Against Therapy*, London, Fontana Press.

Masson, J. (1992) *The Assault on Truth: Freud and Child Sexual Abuse*, London, Fontana Press.

Mathew, R.J., Mathew, V.G., Wilson, W.H. and Georgi, J.M. (1995) 'Measurement of materialism and spiritualism in substance abuse research', *Journal of Studies on Alcohol*, 56: 470–475.

Mathews, J.J. and Zadak, K. (1991) 'The alternative birth movement in the United States: history and current status', *Women and Health*, 17: 39–56.

Mau, G. and Netter, P. (1974) 'Kaffee und alkoholonsum riskofactoren in der schwangerschaft?' (Are coffeee and alcohol consumption risk factors in pregnancy?) *Geburtschulfe Frauenheilkd*, 34: 1018–1022.

Maurer, K.R., Everhart, J.E., Knowler, W.C., Shawker, T.H. and Roth, H.P. (1990) 'Risk factors for gallstone disease in the Hispanic populations of the United States', *American Journal of Epidemiology*, 131: 836–844.

May, C. (1991) 'Research on alcohol education for young people: A critical review of the literature', *Health Education Journal*, 50: 195–199.

May, C. (1992) 'A burning issue? Adolescent alcohol use in Britain 1970–1991', *Alcohol and Alcoholism*, 27: 109–115.

May, P.A. (1995) 'A multiple-level, comprehensive approach to the prevention of Fetal Alcohol Syndrome (FAS) and other alcohol-related birth defects (ARBD)', *International Journal of the Addictions*, 30: 1549–1602.

May, R. (1991) *The Cry For Myth*, London, Souvenir Press.

May, R.R. (1976) 'Moods shifts and the menstrual cycle', *Journal of Pyschosomatic Research*, 20: 125–130.

Mays, V.M., Beckman, L.J., Oranchak, E. and Harper, B. (1994) 'Perceived social support for help-seeking behaviors of black heterosexual and homosexually active women alcoholics', *Psychology of Addictive Behaviors*, 8,4: 235–242.

Meadows, K. (1992) *Earth Medicine: A Shamanic Way to Self-Discovery*, 4th edn. Dorset, Element Books Ltd.

Mearns, J. and Lees-Haley, P.R. (1993) 'Discriminating neuropsychological sequelae of head injury from alcohol-abuse-induced deficits: A review and analysis', *Journal of Clinical Psychology*, 49: 714–720.

Medina Cárdenas, E. (1995) 'Chile', In Heath, D.B. (ed.) *International Handbook on Alcohol and Culture*, Westport, Connecticut, Greenwood Press, 31–41.

Medina-Mora, E. (1994) 'Drinking and the oppression of women: the Mexican experience', *Addiction*, 89, 958–960.

Medora, N.P. and Woodward, J.C. (1991) 'Factors associated with loneliness among alcoholics in rehabilitation centers', *Journal of Social Psychology*, 131: 769–779.

Meek, G.W. (1986) *Healers and the Healing Process*, 4th edn. Wheaton, Illinois, Quest Books.

Meilman, P.W., von Hippel, F.A. and Gaylor, M.S. (1991) 'Self-induced vomiting in college women: Its relation to eating, alcohol use, and Greek life', *Journal of American College Health*, 40: 39–41.

Meirik, O., Lund, E., Adami, H.O., et al. (1986) 'Oral contraceptive use and breast cancer in young women', *Lancet*, 2: 650.

Mello, N.K. (1980) 'Some behavioral and biological aspects of alcohol problems in women', in Kalant, O.J., (ed.) *Alcohol and Drug Problems in Women*, New York, Plenum Press, 263–298.

Mello, N.K., Medelson, J.H. and Teoh, S.K. (1989) 'Neuroendocrine consequences of alcohol abuse in women', *Annals of the New York Academy of Sciences*, 562:211–240.

Mendel, M.P. (1995) *The Male Survivor: The Impact of Sexual Abuse*, London, Sage Publications Ltd.

Mendelson, J.H., Lukas, S.E., Mello, N.K., Amass, L., Ellingboe, J. and Skupny, A. (1988) 'Acute alcohol effects on plasma estradiol levels in women', *Psychopharmacology*, 94: 464–467.

Mendelson, J.H., Mello, N.K., Cristofara, P., Ellingboe, J., Skupny, A., Palmieri, S.L., Benedikt, R. and Schiff, I. (1987) 'Alcohol effects on naloxone-stimulated luteinizing hormone, prolactin and estradiol in women', *Journal of Studies on Alcohol*, 48: 287–294.

Mender, D. (1994) *The Myth of Neuropsychiatry: A Look at Paradoxes, Physics, and the Human Brain*, New York, Plenum Press.

Menzies, W.F. (1893) 'Puerperal insanity – an analysis of 140 consecutive cases', *American Journal of Insanity*, 50: 147.

Merrier, C. and Racine, G. (1995) 'Case management with homeless women: A descriptive study', *Community Mental Health Journal*, 31: 25–37.

Mercy, H.E. (1991) 'The effect of response to father–daughter incest on psychological well-being among alcoholic and nonalcoholic women', *Dissertation Abstracts International*, 51:98.

Merikangas, K.R. and Gelenter, C.S. (1990) 'Comorbidity for alcoholism and depression', *Psychiatric Clinics of North America*, 13: 613–632.

Merikangas, K.R., Risch, N.J. and Weissman, M.M. (1994) 'Comomorbidity and co-transmission of alcoholism, anxiety and depression', *Psychological Medicine*, 24: 69–80.

Merrill, J., Milner, G., Owens, J. and Vale, A. (1992) 'Alcohol and attempted suicide', *British Journal of Addiction*, 87: 83–89.

Merskey, H. (1992) 'Anna O. had a severe depressive illness', *British Journal of Psychiatry*, 161: 185–194.

Metcalf, M.G. and Mackenzie, J.A. (1980) 'Incidence of ovulation in young women', *Journal of Biosocial Sciences*, 12: 345–352.

Metsch, L.R., Rivers, J.E., Miller, M., Bohs, R., McCoy, C.B., Morrow, C.J., Bandstra, E.S., Jackson, V. and Gissen, M. (1995) 'Implementation of a family-centered treatment program for substance-abusing women and their children: Barriers and resolutions', *Journal of Psychoactive Drugs*, 27: 1: 73–83.

Meyer, L.C., Peacock, J.L., Bland, J.M. and Anderson, H.R. (1994) 'Symptoms and health problems in pregnancy: their association with social factors, smoking, alcohol, caffeine and attitude to pregnancy', *Paediatric and Perinatal Epidemiology*, 8: 145–155.

Meyers, A.R., Hingson, R., Mucatel, M. and Goldman, E. (1982) 'Social and psychologic correlates of problem drinking in old age', *Journal of the American Geriatric Society*, 30: 452–456.

Midanik, L. (1982a) 'The validity of self-reported alcohol consumption and alcohol-related problems. A literature review', *British Journal of Addiction*, 77: 357–382.

Midanik, L. (1982b) 'Over reports of recent alcohol consumption in a clinical population: A validity study', *Drug and Alcohol Dependence*, 9: 101–110.

Milgram, G.G. (1993) 'Adolescents, alcohol and aggression', *Journal of Studies on Alcohol*, Supplement no. 11: 53–61.

Miller, A. (1990) *The Untouched Key: Tracing Childhood Trauma in Creativity and Destructiveness*, London, Virago Press Ltd.

Miller, A. (1991a) *Thou Shall Not Be Aware: Society's Betrayal of the Child*, London, Pluto Press.

Miller, A. (1991b) *For Your Own Good: The Roots of Violence in Child-Rearing*, London, Virago Press Ltd.

Miller, A. (1991c) *Banished Knowledge: Facing Childhood Injuries*, London, Virago Press Ltd.

Miller, A. (1992) *Breaking Down the Wall of Silence: To Join the Waiting Child*, London, Virago Press Ltd.

Miller, B.A. and Downs, W.R. (1993) 'The impact of family violence on use of alcohol by women', *Alcohol: Health and Research World*, 17: 137–143.

Miller, B.A. and Downs, W.R. (1995) 'Violent victimisation among women with alcohol problems', in Galanter, M., (ed.) *Recent Developments in Alcoholism: Vol. 12: Alcoholism and Women*, New York, Plenum Press, 81–101.

Miller, B.A., Downs, W.R. and Gondoli, D.M. (1989) 'Spousal violence among alcoholic women as compared to a random household sample of women', *Journal of Studies on Alcohol*, 50: 533–540.

Miller, B.A., Downs, W.R. and Testa, M. (1993) 'Interrelationships between victimization experiences and women's alcohol/drug use', *Journal of Studies on Alcohol*, 11: 109–117.

Miller, E. (1988) 'Behaviour modification mid-19th century style: Robert Brudenell Carter and the treatment of hysteria', *British Journal of Clinical Psychology*, 27: 297–301.

Miller, E. (1990) 'Single case experimentation: A seventeenth century example', *British Journal of Clinical Psychology*, 29: 433–434.

Miller, K.J. (1994) 'The co-dependency concept: Does it offer a solution for the spouses of alcoholics?' *Journal of Substance Abuse Treatment*, 11: 339–345.

Miller, N.S., Belkin, B.M. and Gold, M.S. (1991) 'Alcohol and drug dependence among the elderly: Epidemiology, diagnosis and treatment', *Comprehensive Psychiatry*, 32,2: 153–165.

Miller, N.S., Giannini, A.J. and Gold, M.S. (1992) 'Suicide risk associated with drug and alcohol addiction', *Cleveland Clinic Journal of Medicine*, 59: 535–538.

Miller, P. and Plant, M.A. (1996) 'Drinking, smoking and illicit drug use among 15–16 year olds in the United Kingdom', *British Medical Journal*, 313: 394–397.

Miller, W.R., Benefield, R.G. and Tonigan, J.S. (1993) 'Enhancing motivation for change in problem drinking: A controlled comparison of two therapist styles', *Journal of Consulting and Clinical Psychology*, 61: 455–461.

Miller, W.R. and Rollnick, S. (1991) *Motivational Interviewing: Preparing People to Change Addictive Behavior*, New York, Guilford Press.

Miller, W.R. and Taylor, C.A. (1980) 'Relative effectiveness of bibliotherapy, individual and group self-control training in the treatment of problem drinkers', *Addictive Behaviors*, 5: 13–24.

Mills, D. (ed.) (1992) *The Chester Mystery Cycle*, East Lansing, Michigan, Colleagues Press.

Mills, J. (1991) *Womanwords: A Vocabulary of Culture and Patriarchal Society*, London, Virago Press Ltd.

Mills, J.K. (1992) 'Locus of control orientation of obese adolescent girls and children of alcoholics in outpatient treatment', *Psychological Reports*, 70: 1184–1186.

Milner, J.S. (1980) *The Child Abuse Potential Inventory Manual* (2nd editon), DeKalb, Illinois, Psytec Inc.

Mindell, A. (1982) *Dreambody*, London, Penguin.

Minkowski, W.L. (1992) 'Women healers of the middle ages: Selected aspects of their history', *American Journal of Public Health*, 82: 288–295.

Minor, M.J. and Van Dort, B. (1982) 'Prevention research on the teratogenic effects of alcohol', Preventative Medicine, 11: 346–359.

Minton, H.L. (1986) 'Femininity in men and masculinity in women: American psychiatry and psychology portray homosexuality in the 1930s', *Journal of Homosexuality*, 13: 1–21.

Minton, J.P., Foecking, M.K., Webster, D.J.T. and Matthews, R.H. (1979) 'Caffeine, cyclic nucleotides and breast disease', *Surgery*, 86: 105–108.

Mintz, L.B. (1995) 'Relations among parental alcoholism, eating disorders, and substance abuse in nonclinical college women: Additional evidence against the uniformity myth', *Journal of Counseling Psychology*, 42: 65–70.

Mitchell, J.E., Pyle, R., Eckhart, E.D. and Hatsukami, I. (1990) 'Influence of prior alcohol and drug abuse problems on bulimia nervosa treatment outcome', *Addictive Behaviors*, 15: 169–173.

Mitchell Wardrop, M. (1992) *Complexity: The Emerging Science at the Edge of Order and Chaos*, London, Penguin Books.

Mohan, D. and Sharma, H.K. (1995) 'India', in Heath, D.B., (ed.) *International Handbook on Alcohol and Culture*, Connecticut, Greenwood Press, 128–141.

Monck, E. (1991) 'Patterns of confiding relationships among adolescent girls', *Journal of Child Psychology and Psychiatry and Allied Disciplines*, 32: 333–345.

Money, J. (1990) 'Androgyne becomes bisexual in sexological theory: Plato to Freud and neuroscience', *Journal of the American Academy of Psychoanalysis*, 18: 392–413.

Monforte, E., Estruch, R., Graus, F. et al. (1990) 'High ethanol consumption as a risk factor for intracerebral hemorrhage in young and middle-aged people', *Stroke*, 21: 1529–1532.

Montague, A. (1965) *Life Before Birth*, New York, Signet.

Monter, E.W. (1980) 'Sodomy and heresy in early modern Switzerland', *Journal of Homosexuality*, 6: 41–55.

Montgomery, P. and Johnson, R. (1992) 'The stress of marriage to an alcoholic', *Journal of Psychosocial Nursing and Mental Health Services*, 30: 12–16.

Montgomery, R.L., Benedicto, J.A. and Haemmerlie, F.M. (1993) 'Personal vs social motivations of undergraduates for using alcohol', *Psychological Reports*, 73: 960–962.

Monti, P.M., Abrams, D.B., Kadden, R.M. and Cooney, N.L. (1989) *Treating Alcohol Dependence: A Coping Skills Training Guide*, New York, Guilford Press.

Moore, J.G., Christian, P.E., Datz, F.L. and Coleman, R.E. (1981) 'Effect of wine on gastric emptying in humans', *Gastroenterology*, 81: 1072–1075.

Moore, R.H. (1994) 'Underage female DUI offenders: Personality characteristics, psychosocial stressors, alcohol and other drug use, and driving-risk', *Psychological Reports*, 74, 435–445.

Moorhouse, M. (1882) *The Effects of Alcohol on the Blood*, London, British Women's Temperance Association.

Moos, R.H., Brennan, P.L. and Moos, B. (1991) 'Short-term processes of remission and nonremission among late-life problem drinkers', *Alcoholism: Clinical and Experimental Research*, 15: 948–955.

Moreno, A. and Parés, X. (1990) 'Purification and characterization of a new alcohol dehydrogenase from the human stomach', *Journal of Biological Chemistry*, 266: 1128–1133.

Morgan, M. (1996) Personal Communication.

Morgan, M.Y. and Sherlock, S. (1977) 'Sex-related differences among 100 patients with alcoholic liver disease', *British Medical Journal*, 1: 939–941.

Morgan-Thomas, R. (1990) 'AIDS risk, alcohol, drugs and the sex industry: A Scottish study', in Plant, M.A., (ed.) *AIDS, Drugs and Prostitution*, London, Tavistock/Routledge, 88–108.

Morgan-Thomas, R., Plant, M.A. and Plant, M.L. (1989) 'Risk of AIDS among workers in the "sex industry", some initial results from a Scottish study', *British Medical Journal*, 299: 148–149.

Morris, S.K. and Schinke, S.P. (1990) 'Treatment needs and services for mothers with a dual diagnosis: substance abuse and mental illness', *Journal of Offender Counselling, Services and Rehabilitation*, 15: 65–84.

Morrison, A.S., Kirshner, J. and Molho, A. (1977) 'Life cycle events in 15th century Florence: Records of the Monte delle doti', *American Journal of Epidemiology*, 106: 487–492.

Morrison, C.L., Ruben, S.M. and Wakefield, D. (1994) 'Female street prostitution in Liverpool', *AIDS*, 8: 1194–1195.

Moscarello, R. (1992) 'Victims of violence: aspects of the "victim-to-patient" process in women', *Canadian Journal of Psychiatry/ Revue Canadienne de Psychiatrie*, 37: 497–502.

Mosher, J. (1984) 'The impact of legal provisions on bar-room behavior: Toward an alcohol-problems prevention policy', *Alcohol*, 1: 205–211.

Moskalewicz, J. and Zielinski, A. (1995) 'Poland', in Heath, D.B., (ed.) *International Handbook on Alcohol and Culture*, Connecticut, Greenwood Press, 224–235.

Moskowitz, J. (1989) 'The primary prevention of alcohol problems: A critical review of the research literature', *Journal of Studies on Alcohol*, 50: 54–88.

Moss, H.B., Kirisci, L., Gordon, H.W. and Tarter, R.E. (1994) 'A neuropsychologic profile of adolescent alcoholics', *Alcoholism, Clinical and Experimental Research*, 18: 159–163.

Moss, V.A. (1991) 'Battered women and the myth of masochism', *Journal of Psychosocial Nursing and Mental Health Services*, 29: 18–23.

Moulton, A.R. (1890) 'Care of the insane in local institutions', *Boston Medical and Surgical Journal*, August, 3.

Mphi, M. (1994) 'Female alcoholism problems in Lesotho', *Addiction*, 89: 945–949.

Mumme, D. (1991) 'Aftercare: Its role in primary and secondary recovery of women from alcohol and other drug dependence', *International Journal of the Addictions*, 26: 549–564.

Mundal, L.D., Van De Weele, T., Berger, C. and Fitsimmons, J. (1991) 'Maternal–infant separation at birth among substance using pregnant women: Implications for attachment', *Social Work in Health Care*, 16: 133–143.

Murphy, G.E. (1992) *Suicide in Alcoholism*, New York, Oxford University Press.

Murphy, G.E., Wetzel, R.D., Robins, E. and McEvoy, L. (1992) 'Multiple risk factors predict suicide in alcoholism', *Archives of General Psychiatry*, 49: 459–463.

Murphy, T.J., Pagano, R.R. and Marlatt, A. (1986) 'Lifestyle modification with heavy alcohol drinkers: Effects of aerobic exercise and meditation', *Addictive Behaviors*, 11: 175–186.

Murra, J.B. (1994) 'Dimensions of multiple personality disorder', *Journal of Genetic Psychology*, 155: 233–246.

Murray, M. and McMillan, C. (1993) 'Problem drinking in Northern Ireland: Results of a community survey using the CAGE questionnaire', *Alcohol and Alcoholism*, 28: 477–483.

Murray, R.M., Clifford, C.A. and Gurling, H.M.D. (1983) 'Twin and adoption studies: How good is the evidence for a genetic role?' in Galanter, M., (ed.) *Recent Developments in Alcoholism*, Vol. 1, New York, Plenum Press, 25–48.

Murray, R.P., Istvan, J.A., Voelker, H.T., Rigdon, M.A. and Wallace, M.D. (1995) 'Level of involvement with alcohol and success at smoking cessation in the lung health study', *Journal of Studies on Alcohol*, 56: 74–82.

Musto, D. (1996) 'Alcohol in American history', *Scientific American*, 274: 64–69.

Mutti, P. and Trevisan, M. (1996) 'Endogenous sex hormones and cardiovascular disease in postmenopausal women', *British Medical Journal*, 312: 777.

Nadeau, L. and Harvey, K. (1995) 'Women's alcoholic intoxication: The origins of the double standard in Canada', *Addiction Research*, 2: 279–290.

Nagoshi, C.T., Wilson, J.R. and Rodriguez, L.A. (1991) 'Impulsivity, sensation seeking, and behavioral and emotional responses to alcohol', *Alcoholism: Clinical and Experimental Research*, 15: 661–667.

Nahoum-Grappe, V. (1995) 'France', in Heath, D.B. (ed.) *International Handbook on Alcohol and Culture*, Connecticut, Greenwood Press, 75–87.

Nair, M., Schwartz, S.A. and Kronfol, Z.A. (1992) 'Alcohol, aging, infections and immunity', in Beresford, T.P. and Gomberg, E. (eds) *Alcohol and Aging*, New York, Oxford University Press, 128–135.

Najavits, L.M. and Weiss, R. (1994) 'The role of psychotherapy in the treatment of substance use Disorders', *Harvard Review of Psychiatry*, 2: 84–96.

Najavits, L.M., Weiss, R. and Leise, B.S. (1996) 'Group cognitive-behavioral therapy for women with PTSD and substance-abuse disorder', *Journal of Substance Abuse Treatment*, 13: 13–22.

Nanji, A.A. and French, S.W. (1984) 'Increased susceptibility of women to alcohol: Is beer the reason?' *New England Journal of Medicine*, 311: 1075–1080.

Naranjo, C.A., Kadlec, K.E., Sanhueza, P., Woodley-Remus, D. and Sellers, E.M. (1991) 'Enalapril effects on alcohol intake and other consummatory behaviors in alcoholics', *Clinical Pharmacology and Therapeutics*, 50: 96–106.

Naranjo, C.A., Poulos, C.X., Lanctot, K.L., Bremner, K.E., Kwok, M. and Umana, M. (1995) 'Ritanserin, a central 5-HT2 antagonist, in heavy social drinkers: desire to drink, alcohol intake and related effects', *Addiction*, 90: 893–905.

Nardi, D.A. (1994) 'Parent–infant interaction during perinatal addiction treatment', *Issues in Comprehensive Pediatric Nursing*, 17: 161–175.

Neff, J.A. and Burge, S.K. (1995) 'Alcohol use, liberal/conservative orientations, and ethnicity as predictors of sexual behaviors', *Journal of Acquired Immune Deficiency Syndromes and Human Retrovirology*, 8: 302–312.

Nelson, H.D., Nevitt, M.C., Scott, J.C., Stone, K.C., Cummins, S.R. and the Study of Osteoporotic Fractures Research Group, (1994) 'Smoking, alcohol and older women', *Journal of the American Medical Association*, 272: 1825–1831.

Nelson-Zlupko, L., Dore, M.M., Kauffman, E. and Kaltenbach, K. (1996) 'Women in recovery: Their perceptions of treatment effectiveness', *Journal of Substance Abuse Treatment*, 13,1: 51–59.

Nelson-Zlupko, L., Kauffman, E. and Dore, M.M. (1995) 'Gender differences in drug addiction and treatment: Implications for social work intervention with substance-abusing women', *Social Work*, 40: 45–54.

Nero, J. (1977) *If Only My Wife Could Drink Like A Lady*, Minnesota, Compcare Publications.

Nespor, K. (1990) 'Treatment needs of alcohol-dependent women', *International Journal of Psychosomatics*, 18,6: 1317–1321.

Nevels, L.A. and Coche, J.M. (1993) *Powerful Wisdom: Voices of Distinguished Women Psychotherapists*, California, Jossey-Bass Inc. Publishers.

Newcomb, M.D. (1994) 'Drug use and intimate relationships among women and men: Separating specific from general effects in prospective data using structural equation models', *Journal of Consulting and Clinical Psychology*, 62: 463–476.

Ney, T. (ed.) (1994) *Proceedings for Symposium on Innovative Addictions Programming for Women*, Victoria, British Columbia Ministry of Health and Ministry Responsible for Seniors.

Nicholson, J. (1980) *What Society Does to Girls*, London, Virago Press.

Nixon, S.J. (1993) 'Typologies in women', in Galanter, M., (ed.) *Recent Developments in Alcoholism: Vol. 11: Ten Years of Progress*, New York, Plenum Press, 305–323.

Nixon, S.J. (1994) 'Cognitive deficits in alcoholic women', *Alcohol Health and Research World*, 18: 228–232

Nixon, S.J. and Glenn, S.W. (1995) 'Cognitive psychosocial performance and recovery in female alcoholics', in Galanter, M. (ed.), *Recent Developments in Alcoholism Vol. 12*, New York, Plenum Press, 287–307.

Niyogi, S.K. (1980) 'Historic development of forensic toxicology in America up to 1978', *American Journal of Forensic Medicine and Pathology*, 1: 249–264.

Noble, A.L. (1993) *Law, Medicine and Women's Bodies: The Social Control of Pregnant Drug Users* (Unpublished).

Noel, N.E., Lisman, S.A., Schare, M.L. and Maisto, S.A. (1992) 'Effects of alcohol consumption on the prevention and alleviation of stress-reactions', *Addictive Behaviors*, 17: 567–577.

Nolen-Hoeksema, S. and Girgus, J.S. (1994) 'The emergence of gender differences in depression during adolescence', *Psychological Bulletin*, 115,3: 424–443.

Nordberg, L., Rydelius, P.A. and Zetterstrom, R. (1994) 'Parental alcoholism and early child development', *Acta Paediatrica Scandinavica*, 404: 14–18.

North, C.S. and Smith, E.M. (1993) 'A comparison of homeless men and women: different populations, different needs', *Community Mental Health Journal*, 29: 423–431.

Northern Ireland Statistics and Research Agency (1996) Personal communication.

Norton, R., Batey, R., Dwyer, T. and MacMahon, S. (1987) 'Alcohol consumption and the risk of alcohol-related cirrhosis in women', *British Medical Journal*, 295: 80–82.

Novey, R. (1983) 'Otto Rank: Beginnings, endings, and current experience', *Journal of the American Psychoanalytic Association*, 31: 985–1002.

Nunes-Dinis, M.C. and Lowe, L. (1992) 'Summary of results of a comparative study of alcohol problems and solutions: Spain and Portugal', *International Journal of the Addictions*, 27, 649–664.

Nurco, D.N., Stephenson, P.E. and Hanlon, T.E. (1991) 'Aftercare/relapse prevention and the self-help movement', *International Journal of the Addictions*, 25: 1179–1200.

Nyberg, K. and Allebeck, P. (1995) 'Sweden', in Heath, D.B., (ed.) *International Handbook on Alcohol and Culture*, Connecticut, Greenwood Press, 280–288.

O'Campo, P., Faden, R.R., Brown, H. and Gielen, A.C. (1992) 'The impact of pregnancy on women's prenatal and postpartum smoking behavior', *American Journal of Preventive Medicine*, 8: 1: 8–13.

O'Connell, D.F. (1991) 'The use of transcendental meditation in relapse prevention counselling', *Alcoholism Treatment Quarterly*, 8,1: 53–68.

O'Conner, D.L, Hulka, B.S., Chambless, L.E., Wilkinson, W.E. and Deubner, D. (1987) 'Cigarette smoking, alcohol consumption and breast cancer', *Journal of the National Cancer Institute*, 78: 229–234.

O'Connor, L.E., Berry, J.W., Inaba, D., Weiss, J. and Morrison, A. (1994) 'Shame, guilt and depression in men and women in recovery from addiction', *Journal of Substance Abuse Treatment*, 11: 503–510.

O'Connor, M.J., Brill, N.J. and Sigman, M. (1986) 'Alcohol use in primiparous women older than thirty years of age: Relation to infant development', *Pediatrics*, 78: 444–450.

O'Connor, P.O., Horwitz, R.I., Gottlieb, L.D., Kraus, M.L. and Segal, S.R. (1993) 'The impact of gender on clinical characteristics and outcome in alcohol withdrawal', *Journal of Substance Abuse Treatment*, 10: 59–61.

O'Connor, T.A., Kilbride, H.W. and Hayen, L.K. (1993) 'Incidence of Fetal Alcohol Syndrome among infants with intrauterine cocaine exposure', *Journal of Maternal-Fetal Investigation*, 3: 29–31.

O'Donnell, M. (1985) 'Research on drinking locations of alcohol-impaired drivers: Implication for prevention policies', *Journal of Public Health Policy*, 6: 510–525.

O'Donnell, W.E., De Soto, C.B. and De Soto, J.L. (1994) 'Neuropsychological symptoms in a cross-sectional sample of abstinent alcoholics', *Psychological Reports*, 5: 1475–1484.

O'Farrell, T.J. (1993) *Treating Alcohol Problems: Marital and Family Interventions*, New York, Guilford Press.

O'Farrell, T.J. and Cowles, K.S. (1989) 'Marital and family therapy', in Hester, R.K. and Miller, W.R., (eds) *Handbook of Alcoholism Treatment Approaches: Effective Alternatives*, New York, Pergamon Press, 183–205.

O'Gorman, P. (1993) 'Codependency explored: A social movement in search of definition and treatment', *Psychiatry Quarterly*, 64: 199–212.

O'Malley, S.S., Carey, K.B. and Maisto, S.A. (1986) 'Validity of young adults' reports of parental drinking practices', *Journal of Studies on Alcohol*, 47: 433–435.

O'Malley, S.S., Jaffe, J.J., Chang, G., Schottenfeld, R.S., Meyer, R. and Rounsaville, B. (1992) 'Naltrexone and coping skills therapy for alcohol dependence: A controlled study', *Archives of General Psychiatry*, 49: 881–887.

Oakley-Browne, M.A., Joyce, P.R., Wells, J.E., Bushnell, J.A. and Hornblow, A.R. (1995) 'Adverse parenting and other childhood experience as risk factors for depression in women aged 18–44 years', *Journal of Affective Disorders*, 34: 13–23.

Odujinrin, O. (1993) 'Wife battering in Nigeria', *International Journal of Gynaecology and Obstetrics*, 41: 159–164.

Office for National Statistics (1996) Personal communication.

Ogborne, A.C. and Smart, R.G. (1995) 'People with physical disabilities admitted to a residential addiction treatment program', *American Journal of Drug and Alcohol Abuse*, 21: 137–145.

Ogston, S.A. and Parry, G.J. (1992) 'Results-strategy of analysis of pregnancy outcome', *International Journal of Epidemiology*, 21, Supplement 1: S45–S71.

Ohannessian, C.M. and Hesselbrock, V.M. (1993) 'The influence of perceived social support on the relationship between family history of alcoholism and drinking behaviors', *Addiction*, 88: 1651–1658.

Ohannessian, C.M. and Hesselbrock, V.M. (1995) 'Temperament and personality typologies in adult offspring of alcoholics', *Journal of Studies on Alcohol*, 56: 318–327.

Ohannessian, C.M., Hesselbrock, V.M., Tennen, H. and Affleck, G. (1994) 'Hassles and uplifts and generalized outcome expectancies as moderators on the relation between a family history of alcoholism and drinking behaviors', *Journal of Studies on Alcohol*, 55: 754–765.

Ohannessian, C.M., Stabenau, J.R. and Hesselbrock, V.M. (1995) 'Childhood and adulthood temperament and problem behaviors and adulthood substance use', *Addictive Behaviors*, 20: 77–86.

Ojehagen, A., Berglund, M. and Appel, C.P. (1993) 'Long-term outpatient treatment in alcoholics with previous suicidal behavior', *Suicide and Life-Threatening Behavior*, 23: 320–328.

Ojehagen, A., Berglund, M., Appel, C.P., Andersson, K., Nilson, B., Skjaerris, A. and Wedlin-Toftenow, A.M. (1992) 'A randomized study of long-term out-patient treatments in alcoholics: Psychiatric treatment versus multi-modal behavioral therapy, during one versus two years of treatment', *Alcohol and Alcoholism*, 27,6: 649–658.

Ojehagen, A., Berglund, M., Appel, C.P., Nilsson, B. and Skjaerris, A. (1991) 'Psychiatric symptoms in alcoholics attending outpatient treatment', *Alcoholism: Clinical and Experimental Research*, 15: 640–646.

Okada, H., Horibe, H., Ohno, Y. et al. (1976) 'A prospective study of cerebrovascular disease in Japanese rural communities', *Stroke*, 7: 599–607.

Oleckno, W.A. (1988) 'The risk of stroke in young adults: an analysis of the contribution of cigarette smoking and alcohol consumption', *Public Health*, 102: 45–55.

Olenick, N.L. and Chalmers, D.K. (1991) 'Gender-specific drinking styles in alcoholics and nonalcoholics', *Journal of Studies on Alcohol*, 52: 325–330.

Oliver, J. (1889) 'Menstruation, its nerve origin – Not a shedding of mucous membrane', *Alienist and Neurologist*, 73–79.

Olsen, J. (1993) 'Predictors of smoking cessation in pregnancy', *Scandinavian Journal of Social Medicine*, 21: 197–202.

Olsen, J. (1994) 'Effects of moderate alcohol consumption during pregnancy on child development at 18 and 42 months', *Alcoholism: Clinical and Experimental Research*, 18: 1109–1113.

Olsen, J., Rachootin, P., and Schiodt, A.V. (1983) 'Alcohol use, conception time, and birthweight', *Journal of Epidemiology and Community Health*, 37: 63–65.

Olson, R.P., Ganley, G., Devine, V.T. and Dorsey, G.C. (1981) 'Long-term effects of behavioral versus insight-oriented therapy with in-patient alcoholics', *Journal of Consulting and Clinical Psychology*, 49: 6: 866–877.

Omae, T. and Ueda, K. (1982) 'Risk factors of cerebral stroke in Japan. Prospective epidemiological study in Hisayama community', in Katsuki, S., Tsubai, T. and Toyokura, Y. (eds) *Proceedings of the 12th World Congress of Neurology, Kyoto, Japan*, Amsterdam, Exerpta Medica, 119–135.

Omoluabi, P.F. (1995) 'A review of the incidence of nonprescription psychoactive substance use/misuse in Nigeria', *International Journal of the Addictions*, 30: 445–458.

Oppenheimer, E. (1991) 'Alcohol and drug misuse among women – an overview', *British Journal of Psychiatry*, Supplement, 36–44.

Orford, J. and Velleman, R. (1991) 'The environmental intergenerational transmission of alcohol problems: a comparison of two hypotheses', *British Journal of Medical Psychology*, 64: 189–200.

Orland, R.M., Orland, F.J. and Orland, P.T. (1990) 'Psychiatric assessment of Cleopatra – a challenging evaluation', *Psychopathology*, 23: 169–175.

Orlebeke, J.F., Boomsma, D.I., Van Baal, G.C. and Bleker, O.P. (1994) 'Effect of maternal smoking on birth weight of twins: A study from the Dutch twin register', *Early Human Development*, 37: 161–166.

Orozco, S. and de Castro, J.M. (1994) 'Effect of spontaneous alcohol intake on heart rate and dietary intake of free-living women', *Pharmacology, Biochemistry and Behavior*, 49: 629–638.

Osborn, J.A., Harris, S.R. and Weinberg, J. (1993) 'Fetal alcohol syndrome: Review of the literature with implications for physical therapists', *Physical Therapy*, 73: 599–607.

Oshodin, O.G. (1995) 'Nigeria', in Heath, D.B., (ed.) *International Handbook on Alcohol and Culture*, Connecticut, Greenwood Press, 213–223.

Osterling, A. and Berglund, M. (1994) 'Elderly first time admitted alcoholics: A descriptive study on gender differences in a clinical population', *Alcoholism: Clinical and Experimental Research*, 18,6: 1317–1321.

Osterling, A., Berglund, M., Nilsson, L.H. and Kristenson, H. (1993) 'Sex differences in response style to two self-report screening tests on alcoholism', *Scandinavian Journal of Social Medicine*, 21: 83–89.

Otto, M.W., Pollack, M.H., Sachs, G.S., O'Neil, C.A. and Rosenbaum, J.F. (1992) 'Alcohol dependence in panic disorder patients', *Journal of Psychiatric Research*, 26: 29–38.

Otto, S. (1981) Alcohol and Social Control. in Hutter, B. and Williams, G., (eds) *Controlling Women*, London, Croom Helm, 154–167.

Owsley, D.W., Orser, C.E. Jr, Mann, R.W., Moore-Jansen, P.H. and Montgomery, R.L. (1987) 'Demography and pathology of an urban slave population from New Orleans', *American Journal of Physical Anthropology*, 74: 185–197.

Oyemade, U.J., Cole, O.J., Johnson, A.A., Knight, E.M., Westney, O.E., Laryea, H., Hill, G., Cannon, E., Fomufod, A. and Westney, L.S. (1994) 'Prenatal substance abuse and pregnancy outcomes among African American women', *Journal of Nutrition*, 124: 994–999.

Pacurucu-Castillo, S. (1994) 'Drinking and drinking problems among women: Different stages of a fading taboo', *Addiction*, 89: 951–952.

Padgett, D.K. and Struening, E.L. (1992) 'Victimization and traumatic injuries among the homeless: associations with alcohol, drug, and mental problems', *American Journal of Orthopsychiatry*, 62: 525–534.

Paganini-Hill, A. and Ross, R.K. (1983) 'Breast cancer and alcohol consumption', *Lancet*, 2: 626–627.

Paganini-Hill, A., Ross, R.K. and Henderson, B.E. (1988) 'Postmenopausal oestrogen treatment and stroke: A prospective study', *British Medical Journal*, 297: 519– 522.

Pahl, K.P. (1981) 'Life expectancy in ancient and modern man', *Acta Anthropogenetica*, 5: 119–128.

Pam, A., Inghilterra K., Munson C., et al. (1994) 'Agoraphobia: The interface between anxiety and personality disorder', *Bulletin of the Menninger Clinic*, 58: 242–261.

Pan, H.S. (1994) 'Predicting mild and severe husband-to-wife physical aggression', *Journal of Consulting and Clinical Psychology*. 62: 975–981.

Papagaroufali, E. (1992) 'Uses of alcohol among women: games of resistance, power and pleasure', in Gefu-Madianou, D. (ed.) *Alcohol, Gender and Culture*, London, Routledge.

Parazzini, F., Bocciolone, L.A., La Vecchia, C., Negri, E., and Fedele, L, (1990) 'Maternal and paternal daily alcohol consumption and unexplained miscarriages', *British Journal of Obstetrics and Gynaecology*, 97: 618–622.

Parfitt, W. (1990) *The Elements of Psychosynthesis*, Shafstbury, Element Books Ltd.

Pariser, S.F. (1993) 'Women and mood disorders. Menarche to menopause', *Annals of Clinical Psychiatry*, 5: 249–254.

Park, J. (1991) 'Beyond stereotypes: A study of some New Zealand women alcohol drinkers', *Australian Journal of Public Health*, 15: 202–206.

Park, J. (1995) 'New Zealand', in Heath, D.B., (ed.) *International Handbook on Alcohol and Culture*, Connecticut, Greenwood Press, 201–212.

Parker, D.A. and Harford, T.C. (1992) 'Gender-role attitudes, job competition and alcohol consumption among women and men', *Alcoholism: Clinical and Experimental Research*, 16: 159–165.

Parker, D.A., Harford, T.C. and Rosenstock, I.M. (1994) 'Alcohol, other drugs, and sexual risk-taking among young adults', *Journal of Substance Abuse*, 6: 87–93.

Parkinson, C.E., Wallis, S. and Harvey, D. (1981) 'School achievement and behaviour of children who were small-for-dates at birth', *Developmental Medicine and Child Neurology*, 23: 41–50.

Parrish, K.M., Higuchi, S., Stinson, F.S., Towle, L.H., Dufour, M.C. and Harford, T.C. (1992) 'The association of drinking levels and drinking attitudes among Japanese in Japan and Japanese-Americans in Hawaii and California', *Journal of Substance Abuse*, 4: 165–177.

Parry, G.J. and Ogston, S.A. (1992) 'Results – child development at age 18 months', *International Journal of Epidemiology*, (supplement) 21,4: 572–578.

Parssinen, T.M. (1983) *Secret Passions, Secret Remedies: Narcotic Drugs in British Society 1820–1930*, Philadephia, Institute for the Study of Human Issues.

Partanen, J. (1991) *Sociability and Intoxication*, Helsinki, The Finnish Foundation for Alcohol Studies.

Patterson, D.G. (1995) 'Alcoholism – treating "the second sex"', *Irish Journal of Psychological Medicine*, 12: 46–47.

Pattison, E.M. and Kaufman, E. (1982) *Encyclopedic Handbook of Alcoholism*, New York, Gardner Press.

Patton, D., Barnes, G.E. and Murray, R.P. (1994) 'The reliability and construct validity of two measures of addictive personality', *International Journal of the Addictions*, 29: 8: 999–1014.

Patton, L.H. (1995) 'Adolescent substance abuse, risk factors and protective factors', *Pediatric Clinics of North America*, 42: 283–293.

Paul, J.P., Stall, R. and Bloomfield, K.A. (1991) 'Gay and alcoholic: Epidemiologic and clinical issues', Alcohol: Health and Research World, 15: 151–160.

Paulin, J.M., Simpson, F.O. and Waal-Manning, H.J. (1985) 'Alcohol consumption and blood pressure in a New Zealand community study', *New Zealand Medical Journal*, 98: 425–428.

Paykel, E.S. (1991) 'Depression in women', *British Journal of Psychiatry*, Supplement: 22–29.

Peace, A. (1992) 'No fishing without drinking', in Gefou-Madianou, D. (ed.) *Alcohol, Gender and Culture*, London, Tavistock, 167–180.

Peachey, J.E., Armis, H.M., Bornstein, E.R., Sykora, K., Maglan, M.S. and Shamai, S. (1989) 'Calcium Carbimide in alcoholism treatment. Part 1: A placebo-controlled, double-blind clinical trial of short term efficacy', *British Journal of Addiction*, 84: 881–887.

Peacock, C. (1992) 'International policies on alcohol-impaired driving', *International Journal of the Addictions*, 27: 187–208.

Peacock, P.B., Riley, C.P. and Lampton, T.D. et al. (1972) 'The Birmingham stroke, epidemiology and rehabilitation study', in Stewart, G. (ed.) *Trends in Epidemiology: Applications to Health Service Research and Training*, Springfield, Illinois, Charles C. Thomas, 231–345.

Pearce, E.J. and Lovejoy, F.H. (1995) 'Detecting a history of childhood sexual experiences among women substance-abusers', *Journal of Substance Abuse Treatment*, 12,4: 283–287.

Pearson, F.G. (1986) 'Lung cancer. The past twenty-five years', *Chest*, (Supplement) 89: 200S–205S.

Pendergrast, R.A., DuRant, R.H. and Gaillard, G.L. (1992) 'Attitudinal and behavioral correlates of condom use in urban adolescent males', *Journal of Adolescent Health*, 13: 133–139.

Pepersack, T., Fuss, M., Otero, J., Bergmann, P., Valsamis, J. and Corvilaain, J. (1992) 'Longitudinal study of bone metabolism after ethanol withdrawal in alcoholic patients', *Journal of Bone and Mineral Research*, 7: 383–387.

Periti, M., Salvaggio, A., Qualglia, G. and Di Marzio, L. (1988) 'Alcohol consumption and blood pressure: An Italian study', *European Journal of Epidemiology*, 4: 477–481.

Perkins, K.A., Epstein, L.H., Fonte, C., Mitchell, S.L. and Grobe, J.E. (1995) 'Gender, dietary restraint, and smoking's influence on hunger and the reinforcing value of food', *Physiology and Behavior*, 57: 675–680.

Perkins, K.A., Rohay, J., Meilahn, E.N., Wing, R.R., Matthews, K.A. and Kuller, L.H. (1993) 'Diet, alcohol, and physical activity as a function of smoking status in middle-aged women', *Health Psychology*, 12: 410–415.

Perkins, K.A., Sexton, J.E., DiMarco, A., Orobe, J.E., Scierka, A. and Stiller, R.L. (1995) 'Subjective and cardiovascular responses to nicotine combined with alcohol in male and female smokers', *Psychopharmacology*, 119: 205–212.

Perls, F. (1969) *Ego Hunger and Aggression: The Beginning of Gestalt Therapy*, New York, Random House.

Perls, F., Hefferline, R.F. and Goodman, P. (1974) *Gestalt Therapy*, Harmondsworth, Penguin.

Pernanen, K. (1991) *Alcohol and Human Violence*, New York, Guilford Press.

Perola, M., Vuori, E. and Penttila, A. (1994) 'Abuse of alcohol in sudden out-of-hospital deaths in Finland', *Alcoholism: Clinical and Experimental Research*, 18,2: 255–260.

Perper, M.M., Breitkopf, L.J., Breitstein, R., Cody, R.P. and Manowitz, P. (1993) 'MAST scores, alcohol consumption, and gynecological symptoms in endometriosis patients', *Alcoholism: Clinical and Experimental Research*, 17: 272–278.

Persson, E., Hanson, B.S. and Rastam, A.S. (1994) 'Alcohol habits among teenagers in Sweden: Factors of importance', *Journal of Studies on Alcohol*, 55: 719–725.

Peters, T.J., Martin, F., and Ward, K. (1985) 'Chronic alcoholic skeletal myopathy – common and reversible, *Alcohol*, 2: 485–489.

Petersen, J., Skinhoj, P. and Thorsen, T. (1986) 'An epidemic of cirrhosis in Danish women revisited', *Scandinavian Journal of Social Medicine*, 14: 171–178.

Peterson, J., Hartsock, N. and Lawson, D. (1984) 'Sexual dissatisfaction of female alcoholics', *Psychological Reports*, 55: 744–751.

Petitti, D.B., Wingerd, J. Pellegrin, F. and Ramcharan, S. (1979) 'Risk of vascular disease in women: Smoking, oral contraceptives, noncontraceptive estrogens, and other factors', *Journal of the American Medical Association*, 242: 1150–1154.

Petraitis, J., Flay, B.R. and Miller, T.Q. (1995) 'Reviewing theories of adolescent substance use: Organizing pieces in the puzzle', *Psychological Bulletin*, 117: 67–86.

Petrie, T.A. (1993) 'Disordered eating in female collegiate gymnasts: Prevalence and personality/attitudinal correlates', *Journal of Sport and Exercise Psychology*, 15: 424–436.

Petticrew, M., McKee, M. and Jones, J. (1993) 'Coronary heart surgery: Are women discriminated against?' *British Medical Journal*, 306: 1164–1166.

Petty, F. (1992) 'The depressed alcoholic: Clinical features and medical management', *General Hospital Psychiatry*, 14: 258–264.

Pfeiffer, A., Högel, B. and Kaess, H. (1992) 'Effect of ethanol and commonly ingested alcoholic beverages on gastric emptying and gastrointestinal transit', *Clinical Investigator*, 70: 487–491.

Pffeifer, R.I., Whipple, G.H., Kurosaki, T.T. and Chapman, J.M. (1978) 'Coronary risk estrogen use in postmenopausal women', *American Journal of Epidemiology*, 107: 479–487.

Pharoah, P.O. and Alberman, E.D. (1981) 'Mortality of low birthweight infants in England and Wales 1953 to 1979', *Archives of Disease in Childhood*, 56: 86–89.

Phelps, L. and Grabowski, J.A. (1990) 'Fetal Alcohol Syndrome: Diagnostic features and psychoeducational risk factors', *School Psychology Quarterly*, 7: 112–128.

Phillips, R.C. (1975) 'Role of life style and dietary habits in risk of cancer among Seventh-Day Adventists', *Cancer Research*, 35: 3513–3522.

Phyu, T.T. (1994) 'Women and drinking problems in the developing world: A note from Myanmar', *Addiction*, 89: 1021.

Piazza, N.J. (1996) 'Dual diagnosis and adolescent psychiatric patients', *Substance Use and Misuse*, 31: 215–223.

Pihl, R.O. and Peterson, J.B. (1991) 'Attention-deficit hyperactivity disorder, childhood conduct disorder, and alcoholism', *Alcohol Health and Research World*, 15: 25–31.

Pinhas, V. (1980) 'Sex guilt and sexual control in women alcoholics in early sobriety', *Sexual Disability*, 3: 256.

Pinhas, V. (1987) 'Sexual dysfunction in women alcoholics', *Medical Aspects of Human Sexuality*, 21: 97–101.

Piper, J.M. and Kennedy, D.L. (1987) 'Oral contraceptives in the United States: Trends in content and potency', *International Journal of Epidemiology*, 16: 215–221.

Pitt, B. (1965) *A Study of Emotional Disturbance Associated with Childbearing, with Particular Reference to Depression Arising in the Puerperium*, MD thesis (unpublished).

Pittman, D.J. and Snyder, C.R. (1962) *Society, Culture and Drinking Patterns*, New York, Wiley.

Pittman, D.J. and White, H.R. (1991) *Society, Culture and Drinking Patterns Revisited*, New Brunswick, New Jersey, Rutgers Center of Alcohol Studies.

Plant, M.A. (1975) *Drugtakers in an English Town*, London, Tavistock.

Plant, M.A. (1979) *Drinking Careers*, London, Tavistock.

Plant, M.A. (ed.) (1982) *Drinking and Problem Drinking*, London, Junction.

Plant, M.A. (ed.) (1990) *AIDS, Drugs and Prostitution*, London, Tavistock/Routledge.

Plant, M.A. (1995) 'United Kingdom', in Heath, D.B., (ed.) *International Handbook on Alcohol and Culture*, Connecticut, Greenwood Press, 289–299.

Plant, M.A. (1996) 'Contemporary Research – Alcohol, drugs, HIV/AIDS and risk taking', *Journal of Substance Misuse*, 1, 32–37.

Plant, M.A., Bagnall, G., Foster, J. and Sales, J. (1991) 'Young people and drinking: Results from an English national survey', *Alcohol and Alcoholism*, 25: 685–690.

Plant, M.A. and Dickson, M.L. (1974) 'Working with alcoholics', *Nursing Week*, 50: 7.

Plant, M.A. and Foster, J. (1991) 'Teenagers and alcohol: Results of a Scottish national survey', *Drug and Alcohol Dependence*, 28: 203–210.

Plant, M.A., Miller, P., Plant, M.L. and Nichol, P. (1994) 'No such thing as a safe glass', (letter), *British Medical Journal*, 308: 1237–1238.

Plant, M.A. and Mills, D. (1994/95) 'Glass conscious: Safer glasses – fewer injuries?' *Scientist, The Faculty of Science and Engineering News*, Edinburgh, The University of Edinburgh, Spring edition.

Plant M.A., Orford, J. and Grant, M. (1989) 'The effects on children and adolescents of parents' excessive drinking: An international review', *Public Health Reports*, 104: 433–442.

Plant, M.A., Peck, D.F. and Samuel, E. (1985) *Alcohol, Drugs and School Leavers*, London, Tavistock.

Plant, M.A. and Plant, M.L. (1986) 'Alcohol and alcohol problems research. 8. Scotland', *British Journal of Addiction*, 81: 17–21.

Plant, M.A. and Plant, M.L. (1992) *Risk-takers: Alcohol, Drugs, Sex and Youth*, London, Tavistock/ Routledge.

Plant, M.A. and Plant, M.L. (1997) 'Alcohol education and harm minimisation', in Plant, M.A., Single, E. and Stockwell, T. (eds) *Alcohol: Minimising the Harm: What Works?* London, Free Association Books, 193–210.

Plant, M.A., Plant, M.L. and Vernon, B. (1996) 'Ethics, funding and alcohol research', *Alcohol and Alcoholism*, 31: 17–26.

Plant, M.A., Single, E. and Stockwell, T. (eds) (1997) *Alcohol: Minimising the Harm: What Works?* London, Free Association Books.

Plant, M.L. (1983) 'Alcohol In pregnancy. Is it safe?' *Nursing Mirror*, 2–3.

Plant, M.L. (1984) 'Alcohol consumption during pregnancy. Baseline data from a Scottish prospective Study', *Alcohol and Alcoholism*, 19,2: 153–157.

Plant, M.L. (1987) *Women, Drinking and Pregnancy*, 2nd edn. London, Tavistock/Routledge.

Plant, M.L. (1990) *Women and Alcohol: A Review of the International Literature of the Use of Alcohol by Females*, Copenhagan, World Health Organization.

Plant, M.L. (1992) 'Alcohol and breast cancer', *International Journal of the Addictions*, 27: 107–128.

Plant, M.L. and Plant, M.A. (1979) 'Self-reported alcohol consumption and other characteristics of 100 patients attending a Scottish alcohol treatment unit', *British Journal of Alcohol and Alcoholism*, 14: 197–207.

Plant, M.L., Plant, M.A. and Foster, J. (1991) 'Alcohol, tobacco and illicit drug use amongst nurses: A Scottish study', *Drug and Alcohol Dependence*, 28: 195–202.

Plant, M.L., Plant, M.A. and Morgan-Thomas, R. (1990) 'Alcohol, AIDS risks and commercial sex: results from a Scottish study', *Drug and Alcohol Dependence*, 25: 51–55.

Plant, M.L., Sullivan, F.M., Guerri, C. and Abel, E.L. (1993) 'Alcohol and pregnancy', in Verschuren, P.M., (ed.) *Health Issues Related to Alcohol Consumption*, Brussels, International Life Sciences Institute, 245–262.

Platt, S. and Robinson, A. (1991) 'Parasuicide and alcohol: a 20 year survey of admissions to a regional poisoning treatment centre', *International Journal of Social Psychiatry*, 37: 159–172.

Pochin, E.E. (1976) 'Alcohol and cancer of breast and thyroid', *Lancet*, 1, 1137.

Podolsky, E. (1963) 'The woman alcoholic and menstrual tension', *Journal of the American* Medical *Women's Association*, 18: 816–818.

Pohorecky, L.A. (1991) 'Stress and alcohol interaction: An update of human research', *Alcoholism: Clinical and Experimental Research*, 15: 438–459.

Poikolainen, K., Reunala, T. and Karvonen, J. (1994) 'Smoking, alcohol and life events related to psoriasis among women', *British Journal of Dermatology*, 130: 473–477.

Poland, M.L., Dombrowski, M.P., Ager, J.W. and Sokol, R.J. (1993) 'Punishing pregnant drug users: Enhancing the flight from care', *Drug and Alcohol Dependence*, 31: 199–203.

Polich, J.M., Armor, D.J. and Braiker, H.B. (1980) *The Course of Alcoholism: Four Years After Treatment,* Santa Monica, CA, Rand.

Polivy, J., Schueneman, A.L. and Carlson, K. (1976) 'Alcohol and tension reduction: Cognitive and physiological effects', *Journal of Abnormal Psychology*, 85: 595–600.

Pomerleau, C.S., Cole, P.A., Lumley, M.A., Marks, J.L. and Pomerleau, O.F. (1994) 'Effects of menstrual phase on nicotine, alcohol, and codeine intake in smokers', *Journal of Substance Abuse*, 6: 227–234.

Pomerleau, C.S., Ehrlich, E., Tate, J.C., Marks, J.L., Flessland, K.A. and Pomerleau, O.F. (1993) 'The female weight-control smoker: A profile', *Journal of Substance Abuse*, 5: 391–400.

Pomerleau, C.S., Teuscher, F., Goeters, S. and Pomerleau, O.F. (1994) 'Effects of nicotine abstinence and menstrual phase on task performance', *Addictive Behaviors*, 19: 357–362.

Pomerleau, O.F. (1982) 'Current behavioural therapies in the treatment of alcoholism', in Pattison, E.M. and Kaufman, E., (eds) *Encyclopedic Handbook of Alcoholism*, New York, Gardner Press Inc, 1054–1067.

Pomeroy, S.B. (1975) *Goddesses, Whores, Wives and Slaves*, London, Pimlico.

Popay, J., Bartley, M. and Owen, C. (1993) 'Gender inequalities in health: Social position, affective disorders and minor physical morbidity', *Social Science and Medicine*, 36: 21–32.

Pope, K. and Bouhoutsos, J. (1986) *Sexual Intimacy between Therapists and Patients*, New York, Praeger.

Pope, K.S. and Vetter, V.A. (1991) 'Prior therapist–patient sexual involvement among patients seen by Psychologists', *Psychotherapy*, 28: 429–438.

Pope, S.K., Smith, P.D., Wayne, J.B. and Kelleher, K.J. (1994) 'Gender differences in rural adolescent drinking patterns', *Journal of Adolescent Health*, 15: 359–365.

Porter, R. (1987) *Mind-Forg'd Manacles*, London, Penguin.

Potter, J.F. and Beevers, D.G. (1984) 'Pressor effect of alcohol in hypertension', *Lancet*, 1: 119–122.

Powell, K.C. (1988) *Drinking and Alcohol in Colonial Australia 1788–1901 in the Eastern Colonies,* National Campaign Against Drug Abuse Monograph no. 3, Canberra, Australian Government Publishing Service.

Powell, R.R., Zehm, S.J. and Kottler, J.A. (1995) *Classrooms Under the Influence: Addicted Families/Addicted Students*, Thousand Oaks, California, Corwin Press Inc.

Powers, M. (1995) 'Women and public drinking 1890–1920', *History Today*, February, 52: 46–53.

Premo, T. (1984) '"A blessing to our declining years:" Feminine response to filial duty in the new republic', *International Journal of Aging and Human Development*, 20: 69–74.

Prendergast, M.L. (1994) 'Substance use and abuse among college students: A review of recent literature', *Journal of American College Health*, 43: 99–113.

Prentice, D.A. and Miller, D.T. (1993) 'Pluralistic ignorance and alcohol use on campus: some consequences of misperceiving the social norm', *Journal of Personality and Social Psychology*, 64: 243–256.

Prescott, C.A., Hewitt, J.K., Heath, A.C., Truett, K.R., Neale, M.C. and Eaves, L.J. (1994) 'Environmental and genetic influences on alcohol use in a volunteer sample of older twins', *Journal of Studies on Alcohol*, 55: 18–33.

Preston-Shoot, M. (1987) *Effective Groupwork*, London, Macmillan.

Pribor, E.F. and Dinwiddie, S.H. (1992) 'Psychiatric correlates of incest in chidhood', *American Journal of Psychiatry*, 149: 52–56.

Pristach, C.A., Smith, C.M. and Perkins, C. (1993) 'Reliability of the self-administered alcoholism screening test (SAAST) in psychiatric inpatients', *Journal of Addictive Diseases*, 12: 77–88.

Probert, C.S.J., Emmett, P.M. and Heaton, K.W. (1995) 'Some determinants of whole gut transit time: A population based study', *Quarterly Journal of Medicine*, 88: 311–315.

Prochaska, J.O. and DiClemente, C.C. (1986) 'Toward a comprehensive model of change', in Miller, W.R. and Heather, N., (eds) *Treating Addictive Behaviors: Processes of Change*, New York, Plenum Press.

Prochaska, J.O., DiClemente, C.C., Velicer, W.F. and Rossi, J.S. (1992) 'Criticisms and concerns of the transtheoretical model in light of recent research', *British Journal of Addiction*, 87: 825–835.

Project Match Research Group, (1997) 'Matching alcoholism treatments to client heterogeneity: Project MATCH posttreatment outcomes', *Journal of Studies on Alcohol*, 58: 7–29.

Prytz, H. and Anderson, H. (1988) 'Underreporting of alcohol-related mortality from cirrhosis is declining in Sweden and Denmark', *Scandinavian Journal of Gastroenterology*, 23: 1035–1043.

Prytz, H. and Skinhoj, P. (1980) 'Morbidity, mortality and incidence of cirrhosis in Denmark, 1976–1978', *Scandinavian Journal of Gastroenterology*, 16: 839–844.

Puddey, I.B., Jenner, D.A., Beilin, L.J. and Vandongen, R. (1985) 'An appraisal of the effects of usual vs recent alcohol intake on blood pressure', *Clinical and Experimental Pharmacology and Physiology*, 15: 261–264.

Pulkkinen, L. and Pitkanen, T. (1994) 'A prospective study of the precursors to problem drinking in young adulthood', *Journal of Studies on Alcohol*, 55: 578–587.

Punton, J. (1894) 'Treatment and prophylaxis of insanity', *Alienist and Neurologist*, 1: 52–66.

Purcell, N. (1994) 'Women and wine in ancient Rome', in McDonald, M., (ed.) *Gender, Drink and Drugs*, Oxford, Berg, 191–208.

Quinby, P.M. and Graham, A.V. (1993) 'Substance abuse among women', *Primary Care: Clinics In Office Practice*, 20: 131–140.

Rabinowitz, N.S. and Richlin, A. (1993) *Feminist Theory and the Classics*, London, Routledge.

Rada, R. (1982) 'Alcoholism and sociopathy. Diagnostic and treatment implications', in Pattison, E.M. and Kaufman, E., (eds) *Encyclopedic Handbook of Alcoholism*, New York, Gardner Press, 647–654.,

Rada, R.T. (1975) 'Alcohol and rape', *Medical Aspects of Human Sexuality*, 9: 48–65.

Radbill, S.X. (1976) 'Reared in adversity: Institutional care of children in the 18th century', *American Journal of Diseases of Children*, 130: 751–761.

Radomsky, N.A. (1992) 'The association of parental alcoholism and rigidity with chronic illness and abuse among women', *Journal of Family Practice*, 35: 54–60.

Rajan, L. and Oakley, A. (1993) 'No pills for heartache: The importance of social support for women who suffer pregnancy loss', *Journal of Reproductive and Infant Psychology*, 11: 75–87.

Ramanathan, S. (1996) 'Violence against women', *International Medical Journal*, 3: 145–148.

Rapaport, M.H., Dow, B.M., Kelsoe, J.R., Golshan, S. and Gillin, J.C. (1996) 'Comparison of mood ratings and comorbid diagnoses in research subjects with major depression or stimulant dependence', *European Addiction Research*, 2: 24–28.

Raskin, V.D. (1992) 'Maternal bereavement in the perinatal substance abuser', *Journal of Substance Abuse Treatment*, 9: 149–152.

Raskin, V.D. (1993) 'Psychiatric aspects of substance use disorders in childbearing populations', *Psychiatric Clinics of North America*, 16,1: 157–165.

Rathbun, T.A. (1987) 'Health and disease at a South Carolina plantation: 1840–1870', *American Journal of Physical Anthropology*, 74: 239–253.

Rather, L.J. (1965) *Mind and Body in Eighteenth Century Medicine*, London, Wellcome History of Medicine Library.

Ravndal, E. and Vaglum, P. (1994) 'Treatment of female addicts: The importance of relationships to parents, partners and peers for the outcome', *International Journal of the Addictions*, 29: 115–125.

Razel, M. (1988) 'Call for a follow-up study of experiments on long-term deprivation of human infants', *Perceptual and Motor Skills*, 67: 147–158.

Reed, B.G. (1991) 'Linkages: Battering, sexual assault, incest, child abuse, teen pregnancy, dropping out of school and the alcohol and drug connection', in Roth, P., (ed.) *Alcohol and Drugs are Women's Issues*,

Metuchen, New Jersey, Women's Action Alliance and Scarecrow Press, 130–149.

Reed, B.G. (1994) 'Women and alcohol, tobacco and other drugs: The need to broaden the base within EAP's', *Employee Assistance Quarterly*, 9: 179–201.

Registrar General for Scotland (1996) Personal Communication.

Rehm, J., Fichter, M.M. and Elton, M. (1993) 'Effects on mortality of alcohol consumption, smoking, physical activity, and close personal relationships', *Addiction*, 88: 101–112.

Rehman, A.U. (1986) *Puerperal Insanity in the Nineteenth and Twentieth Centuries*, MD thesis, (unpublished).

Rehman, A.U., St Clair, D. and Platz, C. (1990) 'Puerperal insanity in the 19th and 20th centuries', *British Journal of Psychiatry*, 156: 861–865.

Reich, W. (1951) *Ether, God and the Devil*, New York, Orgone Institute Press.

Reich, W. (1972) *Character Analysis*, New York, Farrar, Straus and Giroux.

Renaud, S., Criqui, M.H., Farchi, G. and Veenstra, J. (1993) 'Alcohol drinking and coronary heart disease', in Verschuren, P.M. (ed.) *Health Issues Related to Alcohol Consumption*, Washington, D.C., ILSI Press, 81–123.

Renaud, S., de Lorgeril, M. (1992) 'Wine, alcohol, platelets and the French paradox for coronary heart disease', *Lancet*, 339: 1523–1536.

Research Institute on Addictions (1995) 'Impact of father's alcoholism on child development is focus of new study', *RIA Report*, Research Institute on Addictions, Buffalo, 9: 4.

Rey, G. N. (1995) 'Mexico', in Heath, D.B., (ed.) *International Handbook on Alcohol and Culture*, Connecticut, Greenwood Press, 179–189.

Reynolds, K.D., Coombs, D.W., Lowe, J.B., Peterson, P.L. and Gayoso, E. (1995) 'Evaluation of a self-help program to reduce alcohol consumption among pregnant women', *International Journal of the Addictions*, 30: 427–443.

Rhodes, T. (1996) 'Culture, drugs and unsafe sex: Confusion about causation', *Addiction*, 91: 753–758.

Richards, T. (1983) 'Weather, nutrition, and the economy: Short-run fluctuations in births, deaths, and marriages, France 1740–1909', *Demography*, 20: 197–212.

Richardson, D., Vinsel, A. and Taylor, S.P. (1980) 'Female aggression as a function of attitudes towards women', *Sex Roles*, 6: 265–271.

Richman, J.A., Flaherty, J.A. and Pyskoty, C. (1992) 'Shifts in problem drinking during a life transition: Adaptation to medical school training', *Journal of of Studies on Alcohol*, 53: 17–24.

Richman, J.A, and Rospenda, K.M. (1992) 'Gender roles and alcohol abuse. costs of noncaring for future physicians', *Journal of Nervous and Mental Disease*, 180: 619–626.

Riddle, J.M. (1992) *Contraception and Abortion from the Ancient World to the Renaissance*, Cambridge, Massachusetts, Harvard University Press.

Ridge, J.J. (1880) *Nursing Without Alcohol*, London, British Women's Temperance Association.

Ridlon, F.V. (1988) *A Fallen Angel: The Status Insularity of the Female Alcoholic*, London, Associated University Presses Inc.

Rienzi, H.M. (1992) 'Prevalence of undetected alcohol dependence in the mental health diagnostic interview', *Psychological Reports*, 70: 913–994.

Ries, R. (1993) 'Clinical treatment matching models for dually diagnosed patients', *Psychiatric Clinics of North America*, 16: 167–187.

Rimm, E.B., Klatsky, A., Grobbee, D. and Stampfer, M.J. (1996) 'Review of moderate alcohol consumption and reduced risk of coronary heart disease: is the effect due to beer, wine or spirits?' *British Medical Journal*, 312: 731–736.

Rissanen, A.M., Heliovarra, M., Knekt, P. et al. (1991) 'Determinants of weight gain and overweight in adult Finns', *European Journal of Clinical Nutrition*, 45: 419–430.

Ritson, E.B. (1995) *Community and Municipal Action on Alcohol*, Copenhagen, World Health Organization Regional Publications, European Series No. 63.

Roazen, P. (1981) 'Two cases of induced insanity', *International Journal of Psycho-Analysis*, 62: 139–150.

Robbins, C.A. (1991) 'Social roles and alcohol abuse among older men and women', *Family and Community Health*, 13: 37–48.

Roberts, E.M. (1995) *A Woman's Place. An Oral History of Working-Class Women 1890–1940*, Oxford, Blackwell Publishers.

Roberts, I. (1988) 'Legal aspects involved in the development of anti-progesterones for fertility control', *Human Reproduction*, 3: 815–817.

Roberts, J.E. (1979) 'Maternal positions for childbirth: A historical review of nursing care practices', *Journal of Gerontological Nursing*, 8: 24–32.

Roberts, J.S. (1984) *Drink, Temperance and the Working Class in Nineteenth Century Germany*, 12th edn. Boston, Allen and Unwin.

Robertson, J.A. and Plant, M.A. (1988) 'Alcohol, sex and risk of HIV infection', *Drug and Alcohol Dependence*, 22: 75–78.

Robertson, M.J. (1991) 'Homeless women with children. The role of alcohol and other drug abuse', *American Psychology*, 46: 1198–1204.

Robinson, D. and Robinson, Y. (1979) *From Self-Help to Health: A Guide to Self-Help Groups*, London, Concord Books.

Robinson, D., Rollnick, S. and MacEwan, I. (1991) *Counselling Problem Drinkers*, London, Routledge.

Robinson, J. (1994) *How to Handle Your Drink*, London, Cedar.

Robinson, J.O. (1986) 'Treatment of breast cancer through the ages', *American Journal of Surgery*, 151: 317–333.

Robles, N., Flaherty, D.G. and Day, N.L. (1994) 'Retention of resistant subjects in longitudinal studies: description and procedures', *American Journal of Drug and Alcohol Abuse*, 20: 87–100.

Rocha-Silva, L., de Miranda, S. and Erasmus, R. (1996) *Alcohol, Tobacco and Other Drug Use Among Black Youth*, Pretoria, HSRC Publishers.

Rodés, J., Salaspuro, M. and Sorensen, T.I.A. (1993) 'Alcoholic liver diseases', in Verschuren, P.M. (ed.), *Health Issues Related to Alcohol Consumption*, Washington, D.C, ILSI Press, 167–220.

Rodin, A.V. (1981) 'Infants and gin mania in 18th-century London', *Journal of the American Medical Association*, 245: 1237–1239.

Rodney, H.E. (1996) 'Inconsistencies in the literature on collegiate adult children of alcoholics: Factors to consider for African Americans', *Journal of American College Health*, 45,1: 19–25.

Rodriguez, L.A., Wilson, J.R. and Nagoshi, C.T. (1993) 'Does psychomotor sensitivity to alcohol predict subsequent alcohol use?' *Alcoholism: Clinical and Experimental Research*, 17: 155–161.

Rogers, A. (1990) 'The UK breast cancer screening programme: An expensive mistake', *Journal of Public Health Science*, 12: 197–204.

Rogers, C.R. (1951) *Client-Centred Therapy*, Boston, Houghton Mifflin.

Rogers, C.R. (1957) 'The necessary and sufficient conditions of therapeutic personality change', *Journal of Consulting Psychology*, 21: 95–103.

Rogers, C.R. (1961) *On Becoming a Person*, Boston, Houghton Mifflin.

Rogers, P.D., Speraw, S.R. and Ozbek, I. (1995) 'The assessment of the identified substance-abusing adolescent', *Pediatric Clinics of North America*, 42: 351–370.

Rohan, T.A. and McMichael, A.J. (1988) 'Alcohol consumption and the risk of breast cancer', *International Journal of Cancer*, 41: 695–699.

Roine, R.P., Gentry, R.G., Hernandez-Munoz, R., Baroana, E. and Lieber, C.S. (1990) 'Aspirin increases blood alcohol concentrations in humans after ingestion of ethanol', *Journal of the American Medical Association*, 264: 2406–2408.

Roine, R.P., Gentry, T. and Lim, R.T. et al. (1991) 'Effect of concentration of ingested ethanol on blood alcohol levels', *Alcoholism: Clinical and Experimental Research*, 15: 734–738.

Rolls, J.A. (1995) 'The recovering female alcoholic – A family affair', *Contemporary Family Therapy*, 17: 317–329.

Roman, L. (1985) 'State strategies for prevention of alcohol-related birth defects', *Alcohol Health and Research World*, 10; 60–65.

Roman, P.M. and Blum, T.C. (1992) 'Life transitions, work, and alcohol: An overview and preliminary data', *Alcoholism: Clinical and Experimental Research*, 16: 149–158.

Romans-Clarkson, S.E., Walton, V.A., Herbison, G.P. and Mullen, P.E. (1992) 'Alcohol-related problems in New Zealand women', *Australian and New Zealand Journal of Psychiatry*, 26: 175–182.

Romelsjö, A., Hasin, D., Hilton, M., Boström, G., Diderichsen, F., Haglund, B., Hallqvist, J., Karlsson, G. and Svanstrom, L. (1992) 'The relationship between stressful working conditions and high alcohol consumption and severe alcohol problems in an urban general population', *British Journal of Addiction*, 87: 1173–1183.

Romelsjö, A. and Lunberg, M. (1996) 'The changes in the social class distribution of moderate and high alcohol consumption and of alcohol-related disabilities over time in Stockholm County and in Sweden', *Addiction*, 91: 1307–1323.

Romm, S. (1987) 'Art, love, and facial beauty', *Clinics in Plastic Surgery*, 14: 579–583.

Room, R. (1989) 'Alcoholism and Alcoholics Anonymous in U.S. films, 1945–1962: The party ends for the "wet generations"', *Journal of Studies on Alcohol*, 50: 368–383.

Room, R. (1992) 'The impossible dream? – Routes to reducing alcohol problems in a temperance culture', *Journal of Substance Abuse*, 4: 91–106.

Room, R. and Collins, G. (eds) (1983) *Alcohol and Disinhibition: Meaning and Nature of the Link*, Washington, D.C., NIAAA, Research Monograph 12, US Department of Health and Human Services.

Roper, E. et al. (1958) 'Public see alcoholism as an illness', *The Public Pulse: Chigago National News Syndicate*. January 4.

Rorabaugh, W.R. (1979) *The Alcoholic Republic: An American Tradition*, New York, Oxford University Press.

Rørstad, P. and Checinski, K. (1996) *Dual Diagnosis: Facing the Challenge, the Care of People with a Dual Diagnosis of Mental Illness and Substance Abuse*, Surrey, Wynne Howard Publications.

Rose, L. (1992) 'The moral journey of the first Viennese psychoanalysts', *Psychoanalytic Quarterly*, 61: 590–623.

Rosen, A. (1981) 'Psychotherapy and Alcoholics Anonymous: Can they be coordinated?' *Bulletin of the Menninger Clinic*, 45: 229–246.

Rosenberg, L., Schwingl, P.J., Kaufman, D.W. et al. (1984) 'Breast cancer and cigarette smoking', *New England Journal of Medicine*, 310: 92–94.

Rosenberg, L., Slone, D., Shapiro, S. et al. (1981) 'Alcoholic beverage and myocardial infarction in young women', *American Journal of Public Health*, 71: 82–85.

Rosenberg, L., Slone, D., Shapiro, S. et al. (1982) 'Breast cancer and alcoholic beverage consumption', *Lancet*, 1: 267–271.

Rosenberg, L., Palmer, J.R., Miller, D.R., et al. (1990) 'A case-control study of alcoholic beverage, consumption and breast cancer', *American Journal of Epidemiology*, 131,1: 6–14.

Rosenberg, M. (1965) *Society and the Adolescent Self-Image*, Princeton, New Jersey, Princeton University Press.

Rosenberg, M. (1988) 'Birth weights in three Norwegian cities, 1860–1984. Secular trends and influencing factors', *Annals of Human Biology*, 15: 275–288.

Rosenberg, M. (1989) 'Breast-feeding and infant mortality in Norway 1860–1930', *Journal of Biosocial Science*, 21: 335–348.

Rosenqvist, P. and Kurube, N. (1992) 'The Swedish alcohol-treatment system', in Klingemann, H., Takkala, J. and Hunt, G., (eds) *Cure, Care or Control: Alcoholism Treatment in Sixteen Countries*, Albany, New York, New York State University Press, 65–86.

Rosenzweig, S. (1987) 'Sally Beauchamp's career: a psychoarchaeological key to Morton Prince's classic case of multiple personality', *Genetic, Social, and General Psychology Monographs*, 113: 5–60.

Rosette, H.L., Oulette, E.M. and Weiner, L. (1976) 'A pilot prospective study of the Fetal Alcohol syndrome at the Boston City Hospital (1) maternal drinking', *Annals of the New York Academy of Science*, 273: 118–122.

Rosette, H.L. and Weiner, L. (1984) *Alcohol and the Fetus: A Clinical Perspective*, New York, Oxford University Press Inc.

Rosette, H.L., Weiner, L., Zuckerman, B., McKinlay, S. and Edelin, K.C. (1980) 'Reduction of alcohol consumption during pregnancy with benefits to the newborn', *Alcoholism: Clinical and Experimental Research*, 4: 178–184.

Rosette, H.L, Weiner, L., Lee, A., Zuckerman, B., Dooling, E. and Oppenheimer, E. (1983) 'Patterns of alcohol consumption and fetal development', *Journal of the American College of Obstetricians and Gynecologists*, 61: 539–546.

Rosoff, J.I. (1988) 'The politics of birth control', *Family Planning Perspectives*, 20: 312–320.

Ross, H. (1997) 'Life-time problem drinking and psychiatric comorbidity among Ontario women', *Addiction*, 92: 183–196.

Ross, H.E. (1989) 'Alcohol and drug abuse in treated alcoholics: A comparison of men and women', *Alcoholism: Clinical and Experimental Research*, 13: 810–816.

Ross, H.E. (1993) 'Benzodiazepine use and anxiolytic abuse and dependence in treated alcoholics', *Addiction*, 88: 209–218.

Ross, H.E., Glaser, F.B. and Germanson, T. (1988) 'The prevalence of psychiatric disorders in patients with alcohol and other drug problems', *Archives of General Psychiatry*, 45: 1023–1031.

Ross, L.J. (1992) 'African-American women and abortion', *Journal of Health Care for the Poor and Underserved*, 3: 274–284.

Ross, R.K., Mack, T.M., Paganini-Hill, A. et al. (1981) 'Menopausal estrogen therapy and protection from death from ischaemic heart disease', *Lancet*, 1: 858–861.

Rossi, A.S. and Sitaraman, H. (1988) 'Abortion in context: Historical trends and future changes', *Family Planning Perspectives*, 20: 273–81.

Rossi, P.H. (1990) 'The old homeless and the new homelessness in historical perspective', *American Psychology*, 45: 954–959.

Rossow, I. and Wichstrom, L. (1994) 'Parasuicide and use of intoxicants among Norwegian adolescents', *Suicide and Life-Threatening Behavior*, 24: 174–183.

Rostand, A., Kaminski, M., LeLong, N. et al. (1990) 'Alcohol use in pregnancy, craniofacial features, and fetal growth', *Journal of Epidemiological Community Health*, 44: 302–306.

Roth, L. and James, P. (1994) 'Peer support groups for women in treatment and aftercare', in Watson, R.R., (ed.) *Addictive Behaviors in Women: Drug and Alcohol Abuse Reviews:* Vol. 5, Totowa, New Jersey, Humana Press, 159–175.

Rothberg, B.P. and Kidder, D.M. (1992) 'Double trouble: Lesbians emerging from alcoholic families', *Journal of Chemical Dependency Treatment*, 5: 77–92.

Rouquette, P.C. (1957) *The Influence of Parental Toxicomania on the Physical and Mental Development of Young Children*, MD thesis, University of Paris.

Rouse, B.A., Carter, J.H. and Rodriguez-Andrew, S. (1995) 'Race/ethnicity and other sociocultural influences on alcoholism treatment for women', in Galanter, M., (ed.) *Recent Developments in Alcoholism: Vol. 12: Alcoholism and Women*, New York, Plenum Press, 343–367.

Rousselle, A. (1994) 'Body politics in ancient Rome', in Schmitt Pantel, P., (ed.) *A History of Women in the West: 1) From Ancient Goddesses to Christian Saints*, Cambridge, Massachusetts, The Belknap Press of Harvard University Press, 296–336.

Rowland, R. (1993) *Living Laboratories: Women and Reproductive Technology*, London, Cedar.

Roy, A., Delong, J., Lamparski, D. et al. (1991) 'Depression among alcoholics: Relationships to clinical and cerebrospinal fluid variables', *Archives of General Psychiatry*, 48: 428–432.

Royal College of Psychiatrists (1986) *Alcohol: Our Favourite Drug*, London, Tavistock.

Rubington, A. (1995) 'Elderly homeless alcoholic careers', in Beresford, T.P. and Gomberg, E.S.L. (eds) *Alcohol and Aging*, New York, Oxford University Press, 293–306.

Ruble, D.N., Greulich, F., Pomerantz, E.M. and Gochberg, B. (1993) 'The role of gender-related processes in the development of sex differences in self-evaluation and depression', *Journal of Affective Disorders*, 29: 97–128.

Rubonis, A.V., Colby, S.M., Monti, P.M., Rohsenow, D.J., Gulliver, S.B. and Sirota, A.D. (1994) 'Alcohol cue reactivity and mood induction in male and female alcoholics', *Journal of Studies on Alcohol*, 55: 487–494.

Rush, B. (1889) 'The place for chronic inebriates', *Alienist and Neurologist*, 10,2: 339–340.

Rush, B.R. and Ogborne, A.C. (1992) 'Alcoholism treatment in Canada: History, current status and emerging issues', in Klingemann, H., Takkala, J. and Hunt, G. (eds) *Cure, Care or Control: Alcoholism Treatment in Sixteen Countries*, Albany, New York, State University of New York, 253–268.

Russ, J. (1986) 'To write "like a woman": transformations of identity in the work of Willa Cather', *Journal of Homosexuality*, 12: 77–87.

Russel, G.W. (1880) 'What shall be done with the inebriate?' *Alienist and Neurologist*, 1: 285–314.

Russel, I. (1881) 'The psychological aspects of alcoholism', *Alienist and Neurologist*, January 2,1: 61–66.

Russel, J. (1993) *Out of Bounds*, London, Sage Publications.

Russell, M., Czarnecki, D.M., Cowan, R., McPherson, E. and Mudar, P.J. (1991) 'Measures of maternal alcohol use as predictors of development in early childhood', *Alcoholism: Clinical and Experimental Research*, 15: 991–1000.

Russell, M., Kang, G. and Uhleg, I. (1983) 'Evaluation of an educational program on the fetal alcohol syndrome of a health professional', *Journal of Alcohol and Drug Education*, 29,1: 48–61.

Russell, M., Martier, S.S., Sokol, R.J., Mudar, P., Bottoms, S., Jacobson, S. and Jacobson, J. (1994) 'Screening for pregnancy risk-drinking', *Alcoholism: Clinical and and Experimental Research*, 18: 1156–1161.

Russell, M. and Skinner, J.B. (1988) 'Early measures of maternal alcohol use as predictors of adverse pregnancy outcomes', *Alcoholism: Clinical and Experimental Research*, 12: 824–930.

Rutter, M. (1986) 'Meyerian psychobiology, personality development, and the role of life experiences', *American Journal of Psychiatry*, 143: 1077–1087.

Rutter, P. (1990) *Sex in the Forbidden Zone*, London, Mandala.

Sacco, R.L., Wolf, P.A., Bhararucha, N.E. et al. (1984) 'Subarachnoid and cerebral hemorrhage: Natural history, prognosis, and precursive factors in the Framingham study', *Neurology*, 34: 847–854.

Sagan, C. and Druyan, A. (1993) *Shadows of Forgotten Ancestors: A Search for Who We Are*, London, Arrow Books.

Sagan, F. (1988) *Freud, Women and Morality: The Psychology of Good and Evil*, New York, Basic Books Inc.

Saltstone, R., Halliwell, S. and Hayslip, M.A. (1994) 'A multivariate evaluation of the Michigan Alcoholism Screening Test and the drug abuse screening test in a female offender population', *Addictive Behaviors*, 19: 455–462.

Saltz, R.F. (1997) 'Prevention where alcohol is sold and consumed: Server intervention and responsible beverage service', in Plant, M.A., Single, E. and Stockwell, T. (eds) *Alcohol: Minimising the Harm: What Works?*, London, Free Association Books, 72–84.

Saltz, R.F. and Hennessy, M. (1990) *Reducing Intoxication in Commercial Establishments: An Evaluation of Responsible Beverage Service Practices*, Berkeley, Prevention Research Center.

Samarasinghe, D. (1995) 'Sri Lanka'. in Heath, D.B., (ed.) *International Handbook on Alcohol and Culture*, Connecticut, Greenwood Press, 270–279.

Sampson, P.D., Bookstein, F.L., Barr, H.M. and Streissguth, A.P. (1994) 'Prenatal alcohol exposure, birthweight, and measures of child size from birth to age 14 years', *American Journal of Public Health*, 84: 1421–1428.

Sanchez-Craig, M., Spivak, K. and Davila, R. (1991) 'Superior outcome of females over males after brief treatment for the reduction of heavy drinking: Replication and report of therapist effects', *British Journal of Addiction*, 86: 867–876.

Sanderson, W.C. (1979) 'Quantitative aspects of marriage, fertility and family limitation in nineteenth century America: another application of the Coale specifications', *Demography*, 16: 339–358.

Sandmaier, M. (1981) *The Invisible Alcoholics: Women and Alcohol Abuse in America*, New York, McGraw-Hill Book Company.

Sanford, I.T. (1991) *Strong at the Broken Places: Overcoming the Trauma of Childhood Abuse*, London, Virago Press Ltd.

Saulnier, C.F. (1996) 'African-American women in an alcohol intervention group address personal and political issues', *Substance Use and Misuse*, 31,10: 1259–1278.

Saunders, B. (1994) 'The cognitive-behavioural approach to the management of addictive behaviour', in Chick, J. and Cantwell, R., (eds) *Alcohol Use and Misuse*, London, Royal College of Psychiatrists, 156–173.

Saunders, B., Baily, S., Phillips, M. and Allsop, S. (1993) 'Women with alcohol problems: do they relapse for reasons different to their male counterparts?' *Addiction*, 88: 1413–1422.

Saunders, J.B., Beevers, D.G. and Paton, A. (1981) 'Alcohol-induced hypertension', *Lancet*, 2: 653–656.

Saunders, J.B., Davis, M. and Williams, R. (1981) 'Do women develop alcoholic liver disease more readily than men?' *British Medical Journal*, 282: 1140–1143.

Savage, G.H. (1875) 'Observations on the insanity of pregnancy and childbirth', London, Guy's Hospital Reports, (unpublished).

Savage, G.H. (1889) 'Septic puerperal insanity', Proceedings of the Medical Society of London, (nupublished).

Savage, G.H. (1896) 'Prevention and treatment of insanity of pregnancy and the puerperal period', *Lancet*, 1: 164–165.

Savin Williams, R. (1994) 'Verbal and physical abuse as stressors in the lives of lesbian, gay male, and bisexual youths: association with school problems, running away, substance abuse, prostitution, and suicide', *Journal of Consulting and Clinical Psychology*, 62: 26–269.

Savitz., D.A., Schwingl, P.J. and Keele, M.A. (1991) 'Influence of paternal age, smoking, and alcohol consumption on congenital abnormalities', *Teratology*, 44: 429– 440.

Sayegh, R., Schiff, I., Wurtman, J., Spiers, P., McDermott, J. and Wurtman, R. (1995) 'The effect of a carbohydrate-rich beverage on mood, appetite, and cognitive function in women with premenstrual syndrome', *Obstetrics and Gynecology*, 86: 520–528.

Sayette, M.A., Breslin, F.C., Wilson, G.T. and Rosenblum, O.D. (1994) 'Parental history of alcohol abuse and the effects of alcohol and expectations of intoxication on social stress', *Journal of Studies on Alcohol*, 55: 214–223.

Savoy-Moore, R.T., Dombrowski, M.P., Cheng, A., Abel, E.A. and Sokol, R.J. (1989) 'Low dose alcohol contracts human umbilical artery', *Alcoholism: Clinical and Experimental Research*, 13: 40–42.

Schaef, A.W. (1986) *Co-Dependence: Misunderstood – Mistreated*, New York, Harper and Row Publishers.

Schaefer, S., Evans, S. and Sterne, M. (1985) 'Incest among women in recovery from drug dependency: Correlation and implication for treatment', *Proceedings of the 34th Congress on Alcoholism and Drug Dependence, Calgary, Alberta*, August 1985, 268–269.

Schandler, S.L., Thomas, C.S. and Cohen, M.J. (1995) 'Spatial learning deficits in preschool children of alcoholics', *Alcoholism: Clinical and Experimental Research*, 19: 1067–1072.

Schaps, E., Dibartolo, R., Moskowitz, J., Balley, C.G. and Churgin, G. (1981) 'A review of 127 drug abuse prevention program evaluations', *Journal of Drug Issues*, 11: 17–43.

Schatzkin, A., Carter, C., Green, S.B. et al. (1989) 'Is alcohol consumption related to breast cancer? Results from the Framingham Health Study', *Journal of the National Cancer Institute*, 81: 31–35.

Schatzkin, A., Jones, D.Y., Hoover, R.N. et al. (1987) 'Alcohol consumption and breast cancer in the epidemiologic follow-up of the First National Health and Nutrition Survey', *New England Journal of Medicine*, 316: 1169–1173.

Scheid, J. (1994) 'The religious roles of Roman women', in Schmitt Pantel, P. (ed.) *A History of Women*, Cambridge, Massachusetts, The Belknap Press of Harvard University Press, 377–408.

Scheidt, D.M. and Windle, M. (1995) 'The alcoholics in treatment HIV risk (ATRISK) study: Gender, ethnic and geographic group comparisons', *Journal of Studies on Alcohol*, 56: 300–308.

Schermer, V.L. and Pines, M. (1994) *Ring of Fire: Primitive Affects and Object Relations in Group Psychotherapy*, London, Routledge.

Schinke, S.P., Gilchrist, L.D., Snow, W.H. and Schilling, R.F. (1985) 'Skills-building methods to prevent smoking by adolescents', *Journal of Adolescent Health Care*, 6: 439–444.

Schiøler, P. (1995) 'Denmark', in Heath, D.H., (ed.) *International Handbook on Alcohol and Culture*, Connecticut, Greenwood Press, 51–62.

Schissel, B. (1993) 'Coping with adversity: testing the origins of resiliency in mental health', *International Journal of Social Psychiatry*, 39: 34–46.

Schliebner, C.T. (1994) 'Gender-sensitive therapy: An alternative for women in substance abuse', *Journal of Substance Abuse Treatment*, 11: 6: 511–515.

Schmidt, L. and Weisner, C. (1993) 'Developments in alcoholism treatment', in Galanter, M., (ed.) *Recent Developments in Alcoholism: Vol. 11: Ten Years of Progress*, New York, Plenum Press, 370–391.

Schmidt, L. and Weisner, C. (1995) 'The emergence of problem-drinking women as a special population in need of treatment', in Galanter, M., (ed.) *Recent Developments in Alcoholism Vol. 12, Woman and Alcohol*, New York, Plenum Press, 309–334.

Schmitt Pantel. P (1994) *A History of Women in the West: From Ancient Goddesses to Christian Saints*, Cambridge, Massachusetts, The Belknap Press of Harvard University.

Schmitz, J., DeJong, J., Roy, A., Garnett, D., Moore, V., Lamparski, D., Waxman, R. and Linnoila, M. (1993) 'Substance abuse among subjects screened out from an alcoholism research program', *American Journal of Drug and Alcohol Abuse*, 19: 359–368.

Schneider, K.M., Kviz, F.J., Isola, M.L. and Filstead, W.J. (1995) 'Evaluating multiple outcomes and gender differences in alcoholism treatment', *Addictive Behaviors*, 20: 1–21.

Schoeffel, P. (1984) 'Dilemmas of modernization in primary health care in Western Samoa', *Social Science and Medicine*, 19: 209–216.

Schoeneman, T.J. (1977) 'The role of mental illness in the European witch hunts of the sixteenth and seventeenth centuries: an assessment', *Journal of the History of the Behavioral Sciences*, 13: 337–351.

Schroedel, J.R. and Peretz, P. (1994) 'A gender analysis of policy formation: The case of fetal abuse', *Journal of Health Politics, Policy and Law*, 19: 335–360.

Schroeder, E.D. (1991) 'Family therapy and twelve-step programmes: Complementary process', *Journal of Chemical Dependency Treatment*, 4: 87–109.

Schroff (1891) 'Nicotine psychosis', *Alienist and Neurologist,* April 12,2: 248–249.

Schuckit, M.A., Anthenelli, R.M., Bucholz, K.K., Hesselbrock, V.M. and Tipp, J. (1995) 'The time course of development of alcohol-related problems in men and women', *Journal of Studies on Alcohol*, 56: 218–225.

Schuckit, M.A., Hesselbrock, V., Nurnberger, J.I.J., Anthenelli, R.M. and Crowe, R.R. (1995) 'The prevalence of major anxiety disorders in relatives of alcohol dependent men and women', *Journal of Studies on Alcohol*, 56: 309–317.

Schuckit, M.A., Morrissey, E.R. and O'Leary, M.R. (1978) 'Alcohol problems in elderly men and women', *Addictive Diseases*, 3: 405–416.

Schuckit, M.A., Tipp, J.E. and Kelner, E. (1994) 'Are daughters of alcoholics more likely to marry alcoholics?' *American Journal of Drug and Alcohol Abuse*, 20: 237–245.

Scully, D. and Marolla, J. (1984) 'Convicted rapists' vocabulary of motive: Excuses and justification', *Social Problems*, 31: 530–544.

Schwaber, E.A. (1992) 'Psychoanalytic theory and its relation to clinical work', *Journal of the American Psychoanalytic Association,* 40: 1039–1057.

Schwarz, J.C. and Wheeler, D.S. (1992) 'Dependency conflict, marital threat, and alcohol consumption in a middle-aged sample', *Journal of Genetic Psychology*, 153: 249–267.

Schwoon, D.R. and Saake, G. (1997) 'Female alcoholism: Approaches towards a differential diagnosis', *European Addiction Research*, 3: 11–21.

Scida, J. and Vannicelli, M. (1979) 'Sex-role conflict and women's drinking', *Journal of Studies on Alcohol*, 40: 28–44.

Sclare, A.B. (1970) 'The female alcoholic', *British Journal of Addiction*, 65: 99–107.

Scott, K.G., Urbano, J.C. and Boussy, C.A. (1991) 'Long-term psychoeducational outcome of prenatal substance exposure', *Seminars in Perinatology*, 15: 317–323.

Scott, M.J. and Stradling, S.G. (1994) *Counselling for Post-Traumatic Stress Disorder*, London, Sage Publications Ltd.

Scragg, R.K.R., McMichael, A.J., and Baghurst, P.A. (1984) 'Diet, alcohol and relative weight in gallstone disease', *British Medical Journal*, 288: 1113–1119.

Scull, A. (1981) (ed.) *Madhouses, Mad-Doctors and Madmen*, Philadelphia, University of Pennsylvania Press/London, Athlone.

Scully, D. and Marolla, J. (1984) 'Convicted rapists' vocabulary of motice: excuses and justifications', *Social Problems*, 31,5: 30–544.

Seppala, M., Raiha, N.C.R. and Tamminen, V. (1971) 'Ethanol elimination in a mother and her premature twins', *Lancet*, 1188–1189.

Searles, J.S., Alterman, A.I. and Miller, S.M. (1993) 'Comparability of self-report of familial alcoholism among male and female college students', *Journal of Studies on Alcohol*, 54: 730–732.

Seda-Mendoza, L., Agosto-Rodriguez, J., Pagan-Agostini, W. and Ramos-Valencia, G. (1992) 'Prevalence of alcohol and drug use in a medical sciences campus freshman class', *Puerto Rico Health Sciences Journal*, 11: 13–18.

Sedney, M.A. and Brooks, B. (1984) 'Factors associated with a history of childhood sexual experience in a nonclinical female population', *Journal of the American Academy of Child Psychiatry*, 123: 215–218.

Seidman, H., Stellerman, S.D. and Mushinski, M.H. (1982) 'A different perspective on breast cancer risk factors', *Cancer Journal for Clinicians*, 32: 301–313.

Seitz., H. Egerer, G., Oertal, U., Xu, Y., Simanowski, U.A., Wermuth, B. and Wartburg, J.P. (1990) 'Biochemical and histological studies on alcohol dehydrogenase in the human stomach', *Gastroenterology*, 98: A629.

Seitz, H., Egerer, G., Simanowski, U. et al. (1993) 'Human gastric alcohol dehydrogenase activity: Effects of age, sex and alcoholism', *Gut*, 34: 1433–1437.

Sellars, C. (1996) 'Dance, dance, wherever you may be', *Human Potential*, Spring: 17–19.

Seppä, K., Koivula, T. and Sillanaukee, P. (1992) 'Drinking habits and detection of heavy drinking among middle aged women', *British Journal of Addiction*, 87: 777–83.

Seppä, K., Laippala, P. and Sillanaukee, P. (1996) 'High diastolic blood pressure: Common among women who are heavy drinkers', *Alcoholism: Clinical and Experimental Research*, 20: 47–51.

Seppä, K. and Mäkelä, R. (1993) 'Heavy drinking in hospital patients', *Addiction*, 88: 1377–1382.

Seppälä, M., Raiha, N.C.R. and Tamminen, V. (1971) 'Ethanol elimination in a mother and her premature twins', *Lancet*, June: 1188–1189.

Shain, R.N. (1986) 'A cross-cultural history of abortion', *Clinics In Obstetrics and Gynaecology*, 13: 1–17.

Shaw, G.K., Waller, S., Alberts, J.L., Latham, C.J. and Dunn, G. (1994) 'Tiapride in the prevention of relapse in recently detoxified alcoholics', *British Journal of Psychiatry*, 165: 515–523.

Shaw, S., Cartwright, A., Sprately, T. and Harwin, J. (1978) *Responding to Drinking Problems*, London, Croom Helm.

Sheehan, M.F. (1993) 'Dual diagnosis', *Psychiatry Quarterly*, 64: 107–134.

Shepherd, J.P., Brickley, M.R., Gallaghar, D. and Walker, R.V. (1994) 'Risk of occupational glass injury to bar staff', *Injury*, 25: 219–220.

Shepherd, J.P., Huggett, R.H. and Kidner, G. (1994) 'Impact resistance of bar glasses', *The Journal of Trauma*, 35: 936–938.

Shepherd, J.P., Price, M. and Shenfine, P. (1990) 'Glass abuse and urban licensed premises', *Journal of the Royal Society of Medicine*, 83: 276–277.

Shepherd, J.P., Shapland, M., Pearce, N.X. and Scully, C. (1990) 'Pattern, severity and aetiologies of injury in victims of assault', *Journal of the Royal Society of Medicine*, 83: 75–80.

Sher, K.J. (1987) 'Stress response dampening', in Blanc, H.T. and Leonard, K.E., (eds) *Psychological Theories of Drinking and Alcoholism*, New York, Guilford Press, 227.

Sher, K.J. (1993) 'Children of alcoholics and the intergenerational transmission of alcoholism: A biopsychosocial perspective', in Baer, J.S., Marlatt, G.A. and McMahon, R.J., (eds) *Addictive Behaviors Across the Lifespan*, London, Sage Publications Ltd, 3–33.

Sher, K.J., Walitzer, K.S., Wood, P.K. and Brent, E.E. (1991) 'Characteristics of children of alcoholics: putative risk factors, substance use and abuse, and psychopathology', *Journal of Abnormal Psychology*, 100: 427–448.

Sheridan, M.J. (1995a) 'A psychometric assessment of the children of alcoholics screening test (CAST)', *Journal of Studies on Alcohol*, 56: 156–160.

Sheridan, M.J. (1995b) 'A proposed intergenerational model of substance abuse, family functioning, and abuse/neglect', *Child Abuse and Neglect*, 19: 519–530.

Sherlock, S. (1982) *Alcohol and Disease*, London, Churchill Livingstone.

Shifren, K., Bauserman, R. and Carter, D.B. (1993) 'Gender-role orientation and physical health – a study among young-adults', *Sex Roles*, 29: 421–432.

Shirali, K.A. and Bharti, S.P. (1993) 'Hysteria in hill women: life stress and personality', *Indian Journal of Clinical Psychology*, 20: 93–102.

Shope, J.T., Copeland, L.A., Maharg, R., Dielman, T.E. and Butchart, A.T. (1993) 'Assessment of adolescent refusal skills in an alcohol misuse prevention study', *Health Education Quarterly*, 20: 373–390.

Shore, E.R. (1993) 'Outcomes of a primary prevention project for business and professional women', *Journal of Studies on Alcohol*, 55: 657–659.

Shore, E.R. and Batt, S. (1991) 'Contextual factors related to the drinking behaviors of American business and professional women', *British Journal of Addiction*, 86: 171–176.

Shore, E.R. and Pieri, S.A. (1992) 'Drinking behaviors of women in four occupational groups', *Women and Health*, 19: 55–64.

Shorkey, C.T. and Armendariz, J. (1985) 'Personal worth, self-esteem, anomie, hostility and irrational thinking of abusing mothers: A multivariate approach', *Journal of Clinical Psychology*, 41: 414–421.

Showalter, E. (1985) *The Female Malady: Women, Madness and English Culture, 1830–1980*, New York, Pantheon.

Showalter, E. (1988) *A Literature of Her Own: British Women Novelists from Brontë to Lessing*, London, Virago.

Shumaker, S.A. and Hill, D.R. (1991) 'Gender differences in social support and physical health', *Health Psychology*, 10: 102–111.

Sidorov, P.I. (1995) 'Russia', in Heath, D.B., (ed.) *International Handbook on Alcohol and Culture*, Connecticut, Greenwood Press, 237–253.

Silverman, W.K., La Greca, A.M. and Wasserstein, S. (1995) 'What do children worry about? Worries and their relation to anxiety', *Child Development*, 66: 671–686.

Silverstein, B. and Perlick, D. (1991) 'Gender differences in depression: Historical changes', *Acta Psychiatrica Scandinavica*, 84: 327–331.

Silvia, L.Y., Sorell, G.T. and Busch-Rossnagel, N.A. (1988) 'Biopsychosocial discriminators of alcoholic and nonalcoholic women', *Journal of Substance Abuse*, 1: 55–65.

Simkin, P. (1989) 'Childbearing in social context', *Women and Health*, 15: 5–21.

Simmons, H.G. (1987) 'Psychosurgery and the abuse of psychiatric authority in Ontario', *Journal of Health Politics, Policy and Law*, 12: 537–550.

Simon, H. (1992) '"Incest – see under Oedipus complex": The history of an error in psychoanalysis', *Journal of the American Psychoanalytic Association*, 40: 955–988.

Simon, M.S., Carman, W., Wolfe, R. et al. (1991) 'Alcohol consumption and the risk of breast cancer: a report from the Tecumseh Community Health Study', *Journal of Clinical Epidemiology*, 44: 755–761.

Simpson, T.L., Westerberg, V.S., Little, L.M. and Trujillo, M. (1994) 'Screening for child physical and sexual abuse among outpatient substance-abusers', *Journal of Substance Abuse Treatment*, 11: 347–358.

Singer, L., Farkas, K. and Kliegman, R. (1992) 'Childhood medical and behavioral consequences of maternal cocaine use', *Journal of Pediatric Psychology*, 17: 389–406.

Singer, M.V., Teyssen, S. and Eysselein, V.E. (1991) 'Action of beer and its ingredients on gastric acid secretion and release of gastrin in humans', *Gastroenterology*, 101:935–942.

Singer, P. (1993) *Practical Ethics*, Cambridge, Massachusetts, Cambridge University Press.

Single, E., Robson, L., Xie, X. and Rehm, J. (1996a) *The Costs of Substance Abuse in Canada*, (Main Report), Toronto, Canadian Centre on Substance Abuse.

Single, E., Robson, L., Xie, X. and Rehm, J. (1996b) *The Costs of Substance Abuse in Canada*, (Highlights) Toronto, Canadian Centre on Substance Abuse.

Single, E. and Wortley, S. (1993) 'Drinking in various settings as it relates to demographic variables and levels of consumption: Findings from a national survey in Canada', *Journal of Studies on Alcohol*, 54: 590–599.

Sinha, R., Bernardy, N. and Parsons, O.A. (1992) 'Long-term test–retest reliability of event-related potentials in normals and alcoholics', *Biological Psychiatry*, 32: 992–1003.

Sinnett, E.K., Holen, M.C. and Albott, W.L. (1995) 'MMPI scores of female victims', *Psychological Reports*, 70: 139–144.

Sitharthan, T. and Kavanagh, D.J. (1991) 'Role of self-efficacy in predicting outcomes from a programme for controlled drinking', *L. ug and Alcohol Dependence*, 27: 87–94.

Skodra, E.E. (1992) 'Families and abuse of prescribed medication: A psychological analysis of women's and children's experiences in the family and other social institutions', *Counselling Psychology Quarterly*, 5: 315–324.

Smart, R.G. and Adlaf, E.M. (1988) 'Alcohol and drug use among the elderly: Trends in use and characteristics of users', *Canadian Journal of Public Health*, 79: 236–242.

Smart, R.G. and Liban, C.B. (1981) 'Predictors of problem drinking among elderly, middle-aged and youthful drinkers', *Journal of Psychoactive Drugs*, 13: 153–163.

Smith, C. and Nutbeam, D. (1992) 'Adolescent drug use in Wales', *British Journal of Addiction*, 87: 227–233.

Smith, C., Nutbeam, D., Moore, L., Roberts, C. and Catford, J. (1994) 'Current changes in smoking attitudes and behaviours among adolescents in Wales, 1986–1992', *Journal of Public Health Medicine*, 16: 165–171.

Smith, D.L. (1991) *Hidden Conversations: An Introduction to Communicative Psychoanalysis*, London, Routledge.

Smith, E.M., North, C.S. and Spitznagel, E.L. (1993) 'Alcohol, drugs, and psychiatric comorbidity among homeless women: an epidemiologic study', *Journal of Clinical Psychiatry*, 54: 82–87.

Smith, G.T., McCarthy, D.M. and Goldman, M.S. (1995) 'Self-reported drinking and alcohol-related problems among early adolescents: dimensionality and validity over 24 months', *Journal of Studies on Alcohol*, 56: 383–394.

Smith, K.J. and Eckhardt, M.J. (1991) 'The effects of prenatal alcohol on the central nervous system', in Galanter, M. (ed.) *Recent Developments in Alcoholism*, Vol. 9, Children of Alcoholics, New York, Plenum, 151–164.

Smith, L. (1992) 'Help seeking in alcohol-dependent females', *Alcohol and Alcoholism*, 27: 3–9.

Smith, P.M., Przybeck, T.R., Bradford, S.E., Gogineni, A. and Spitznagel, E.L. (1994) 'Adult offspring of alcoholic women as family history informants', *Alcoholism: Clinical and Experimental Research*, 18: 1354–1360.

Snow, M.G., Prochaska, J.O. and Rossi, J.S. (1994) 'Processes of change in Alcoholics Anonymous: Maintenance factors in long-term sobriety', *Journal of Studies on Alcohol*, 55: 362–371.

Sobell, L.C., Cunningham, J.A., Sobell, M.B. and Toneatto, T. (1993) 'A life-span perspective on natural recovery (self-change) from alcohol problems across the life-span', in Baer, J.S., Marlatt, G.A. and McMahon, R.J., (eds) *Addictive Behaviors Across the Lifespan: Prevention, Treatment and Policy*, London, Sage Publications, 34–66.

Sobell, L.C., Sobell, M.B. and Nirenberg, T.D. (1988) 'Behavioral asessment and treatment planning with alcohol and drug abusers: A review with an emphasis on clinical application', *Clinical Psychological Review*, 8: 19–54.

Sobell, L.C., Sobell, M.B. and Toneatto, T. (1996) 'Recovery from alcohol problems without treatment', in Miller, W.R. and Greeley, J., (eds) *Self-Control and Addictive Behaviors*, Elmsford, New York, Pergamon Press.

Sobell, M.B. and Sobell, L.C. (1993) *Problem Drinkers: Guided Self-Change Treatment*, New York, Guilford Press.

Sokol, R.J., Ager, J.W. and Martier, S.S. (1992) *Methodological Issues in Obtaining and Managing Substance Abuse Information from Prenatal Patients*, NIDA Research Monograph 117, 80–97.

Sokol, R.J., Martier, S.S., Ager, J.W. et al. (1993) 'Paternal drinking may affect intrauterine growth', *Society of Perinatal Obstetricians Abstracts*, (cited in Plant et al. 1993).

Sokol, R.J., Miller, S.I. and Reed, G. (1980) 'Alcohol abuse during pregnacy: An epidemiologic study', *Alcoholism: Clinical and Experimental Research*, 4: 135–145.

Solomon, R. and Payne, J. (1996) *Alcohol, Liability in Canada and Australia: Sell, Serve and be Sued*, Perth, Western Australia, National Centre for Research into the Prevention of Drug Abuse.

Sorell, G.T., Silvia, L.Y. and Busch-Rossnagel, N.A. (1993) 'Sex-role orientation and self-esteem in alcoholic and nonalcoholic women', *Journal of Studies on Alcohol*, 54: 566–573.

Soueif, M.I. and Hannourah, M.A. (1987) 'The use of psycho-active substances by female Egyptian university students', *Drug and Alcohol Dependence*, 19: 233–247.

South, N. (1995) *Drugs, Crime and Criminal Justice* Vol. I, Aldershot, Dartmouth Publishing Company.

Spacarelli, S., Sandler, I.N. and Roosa, M. (1994) 'History of spouse violence against mother: Correlated risks and unique effects in child mental health', *Journal of Independent Social Work*, 4: 27–34.

Spaulding, J.M. (1986) 'The Canton Asylum for insane Indians: An example of institutional neglect', *Hospital and Community Psychiatry*, 37: 1007–1011.

Speckens, A.E., Heeren, T.J. and Rooijmans, H.G. (1991) 'Alcohol abuse among elderly patients in a general hospital as identified by the Munich alcoholism test', *Acta Psychiatrica Scandinavica*, 83: 460–462.

Spencer, H., Rubio, N., Burio, E. et al. (1986) 'Chronic alcoholism: Frequently overlooked cause of osteoporosis in men', *American Medical Journal*, 80: 393–397.

Spender, D. (1983) *Feminist Theorists: Three Centuries of Women's Intellectual Traditions*, London, The Women's Press Ltd.

Spender, D. (1994) 'Women and madness: A justifiable response', *Feminism and Psychology*, 4: 280–283.

Spitzack, C. (1987) 'Confession and signification: The systematic inscription of body consciousness', *Journal of Medicine and Philosophy*, 12: 356–369.

Spivak, K., Sanchez-Craig, M. and Davila, R. (1994) 'Assisting problem drinkers to change on their own: effect of specific and non-specific advice', *Addiction*, 89: 1135–1142.

Spoh, H-L., and Steinhausen, H-C. (1984) 'Clinical, psychopathological and developmental aspects in children with the fetal alcohol syndrome: A four-year follow-up study', in Porter, R., O'Conner, M. and Whelan, J. (eds) *Mechanisms of Alcohol Damage in Utero*, London, Pitman, 197–217.

St Leger, A.S., Cochrane, A.L. and Moore, F. (1979) 'Factors associated with cardiac mortality in developed countries with particular reference to the consumption of wine', *Lancet*, 1: 1017–1020.

Stabenau, J.R. and Hesselbrock, V, (1984) 'Genetic precursors and consequences in alcoholism', in Hemmei, A. and Tuhkanen, K., (eds) *Regional Symposium of the World Psychiatric Association: Book of Abstracts*, Copenhagen, Munksgaard International Publishers.

Stall, R. and Leigh, B. (1994) 'Understanding the relationship between drug or alcohol use and high risk sexual activity for HIV transmission: where do we go from here?' *Addiction*, 89: 131–134.

Stall, R., McKusick. L., Wiley, J. et al. (1986) 'Alcohol and drug use during sexual activity and compliance with safe sex guidelines for AIDS: the AIDS Behavioral Research Project', *Health Education Quarterly*, 13: 359–371.

Stampfer, M.J. and Colditz, G.A. (1991) 'Estrogen replacement therapy and coronary disease: a quantitative assessment of the epidemiologic evidence', *Preventive Medicine*, 20: 47–63.

Stampfer, M.J., Colditz, G.A., Willet, W.C. et al. (1988) 'A prospective study of moderate alcohol consumption and the risk of coronary disease and stroke in women', *New England Journal of Medicine*, 319: 267–273.

Stampfer, M.J., Colditz, G.A., Willet, W.C. et al. (1991) 'Postmenopausal estrogen therapy and cardiovascular diseases; follow-up from the nurses' health study', *New England Journal of Medicine*, 325: 756–762.

Stamfer, M.J., Willett, W.C., Colditz, G.A., Ropsner, B., Speizer, F.E. and Hennekens, C.H. (1985) 'A prospective study of postmenopausal estrogen therapy and coronary heart disease', *New England Journal of Medicine*, 313: 1044–1049

Stanton, M.E. and Spear, L.P. (1990) 'Workshop on the qualitative and quantitative comparability of human and animal developmental neurotoxicity, Work Group 1 Report: Comparability of measures of developmental neurotoxicity in humans and laboratory animals', *Neurobehavioral Toxicity*, 12: 261–267.

Stark, E. and Flitcraft, A. (1995) 'Killing the beast within: Woman battering and female suicidality', *International Journal of the Health Services*, 25: 43–65.

Stason, W.B., Neff, R.K., Miettinen, O.S. and Jick, H. (1976) 'Alcohol consumption and non-fatal myocardial infarction', *American Journal of Epidemiology*, 104: 603–608.

Steegmann, A.T. Jr (1991) 'Stature in an early mid-19th century poorhouse population: Highland Park, Rochester, New York', *American Journal of Physical Anthropology*, 85: 261–268.

Steinberg, J. and Goodwin, P.J. (1991) 'Alcohol and breast cancer risk', *Breast Cancer Research and Treatment*, 19: 221–231.

Steiner, C. (1971) *Games Alcoholics Play*, New York, Grove Press Inc.

Steiner, M. (1992) 'Female-specific mood disorders', *Clinical Obstetrics and Gynecology*, 35: 599–611.

Steingart, R.M, Packer, M., Ham, P. et al. (1991) 'Sex differences in the management of coronary disease', *New England Journal of Medicine*, 325: 226–230.

Stephens, C.J. (1985) 'Alcohol consumption during pregnancy among southern city women', *Drug and Alcohol Dependence*, 16: 19–29.

Stephens, C.J. (1987) 'The effects of social support on alcohol consumption during pregnancy: Situational and ethnic/cultural considerations', *International Journal of the Addictions*, 223: 609–619.

Stephenson, M. (1990) 'Evaluating the impact of incest on the recovery of alcohol/drug dependent women in residential care', *Dissertation Abstracts International*, 51: 1514B.

Stern, S.L., Dixon, K.N., Sansone, R.A., Lake, M.D., Nemzer, E. and Jones, D. (1992) 'Psychoactive substance use disorder in relatives of patients with anorexia nervosa', *Comprehensive Psychiatry*, 33: 207–212.

Stevens, M., Youells, F., Whaley, R. and Linsey, S. (1991) 'Prevalence and correlates of alcohol use in a survey of rural elementary school students: the New Hampshire study', *Journal of Drug Education*, 21: 333–347.

Stevens, P.E. and Hall, J.M. (1991) 'A critical historical analysis of the medical construction of lesbianism', *International Journal of Health Services*, 21: 291–307.

Stevens, S.J. and Arbiter, N. (1995) 'A therapeutic community for substance-abusing pregnant women and women with children: Progress and outcome', *Journal of Psychoactive Drugs*, 27: 49–56.

Stevens, S.J. and Gilder, P.J. (1994) 'Therapeutic communities: Substance abuse treatment for women', in Tims, F.M., De Leon, G. and Jainchill, N., (eds) *Therapeutic Community: Advances in Research and Application*. NIDA Research Monograph: 144, Rockville, Maryland, National Institute on Drug Abuse, 162–180.

Stewart, I. and Jones, V. (1991) *T.A. Today: A New Introduction to Transactional Analysis*, Nottingham, Lifespace Publishing.

Stewart, K. and Sweedler, B.M. (1997) 'Driving under the influence of alcohol', in Plant, M.A., Single, E. and Stockwell, T. (eds) *Alcohol: Minimising the Harm: What Works?* London, Free Association Books, 126–142.

Stewart, L. and Casswell, S. (1992) 'Treating alcohol problems in New Zealand', in Klingemann, H., Takkala, J. and Hunt, G., (eds) *Cure, Care or Control: Alcoholism Treatment in Sixteen Countries*, Albany, New York, State University of New York Press, 131–149.

Stewart, M. (1992) 'I can't drink wine, I've just drunk water', in Gefou-

Madianou, D. (ed.) *Alcohol, Gender and Culture,* London, Tavistock, 137–156.

Stimmel, E. (1982) *The Effects of Maternal Alcohol and Drug Abuse on the Newborn, Advances in Alcohol and Substance Abuse,* Vol. 1, New York, Haworth Press.

Stinchfield, R.D., Niforopulos, L. and Feder, S.H. (1994) 'Follow-up contact bias in adolescent substance abuse treatment outcome research', *Journal of Studies on Alcohol,* 55: 285–289.

Stockwell, T., Masters, L., Philips, M., Daly, A., Gahegan, M., Midford, R. and Philp, A. (1996) 'Consumption of different alcoholic beverages as predictors of local rates of assault, road crash and hospital admissions', (unpublished).

Stockwell, T., Rydon, P., Lang, E. and Beel, A. (1993) *An Evaluation of the 'Freo Respects You' Responsible Alcohol Project,* Perth, Western Australia, National Centre for Research into the Prevention of Drug Abuse, Curtin University.

Stockwell, T. and Single, E. (1997) 'Standard unit labelling of alcoholic containers', in Plant, M.A., Single, E., and Stockwell, T. (eds) *Alcohol: Minimising the Harm: What Works?* London, Free Association Books, 85–104.

Stockwell, T., Single, E., Hawks, D. and Rehm, J. (1996) 'Sharpening the focus of alcohol policy from aggregate consumption to harm and risk reduction', paper presented at 22nd Annual Alcohol Epidemiology Symposium, Kettil Bruun Society, 7 June.

Stone, A.B. and Pearlstein, T.B. (1994) 'Evaluation and treatment of changes in mood, sleep, and sexual functioning associated with menopause',. *Obstetrics and Gynecology Clinics of North America,* 21: 391–403.

Stone, L. (1977) *The Family, Sex and Marriage in England 1500–1800,* New York, Harper and Row.

Stoney, C.M., Owens, F., Matthews, K.A., Davis, M.C. and Caggiula, A. (1990) 'Influences of the normal menstrual cycle on physiologic functioning during behavioural stress', *Psychophysiology,* 27: 125.

Strassberg, D.S., Ross, S. and Todt, E.H. (1995) 'MMPI performance among women with bulimia: a cluster-analytic study', *Addictive Behaviors,* 20: 137–140.

Strasser, T.J., Pike, K.M. and Walsh, B.T. (1992) 'Impact of prior substance abuse on treatment outcome for bulimia nervosa', *Addictive Behaviors,* 17: 387–395.

Streissguth, A.P. (1977) 'Maternal drinking and the outcome of pregnancy: Implications for child mental health', *American Journal of Orthopsychiatry,* 47: 422–431.

Streissguth, A.P. (1992) 'Fetal Alcohol Syndrome: Early and long-term consequences', *NIDA Research Monograph* 119, 126–130.

Streissguth, A.P., Aase, J.M., Clarren, S.K., Randels, S.P., LaDue, R.A. and Smith, D.F. (1991) 'Fetal alcohol syndrome in adolescents and adults', *Journal of the American Medical Association,* 265: 1961–1967.

Streissguth, A.P., Barr, H.M., Olson, H.C., Sampson, P.D., Bookstein, F.L. and Burgess, D.M. (1994) 'Drinking during pregnancy decreases word attack and arithmetic scores on standardized tests: adolescent data from a population-based prospective study', *Alcoholism: Clinical and Experimental Research*, 18: 248–254.

Streissguth, A.P., Barr, H.M. and Sampson, P.D. (1990) 'Moderate prenatal alcohol exposure: effects on child IQ and learning problems at age seven and a half', *Alcoholism: Clinical and Experimental Research*, 14: 622–669.

Streissguth, A.P., Grant, T.M., Barr, H.M., Brown, Z.A., Martin, J.C., Maycock, D.E., Landesman Ramey, S. and Moore, L. (1991) 'Cocaine and the use of alcohol and other drugs during pregnancy', *American Journal of Obstetrics and Gynecology*, 164: 1239–1243.

Streissguth, A.P., Martin, D.C. and Buffington, V.E. (1977) 'Identifying heavy drinkers: a comparison of eight alcohol scores obtained on the same sample', in Seixas, F.A. (ed.) *Currents in Alcoholism* Vol. 11, New York, Grune and Stratton.

Streissguth, A.P., Martin, D.C., Martin, J.C. and Barr, H.M. (1981) 'The Seattle Longitudinal Prospective Study on Alcohol and Pregnancy', *Neurobehavioral Toxicology and Teratology*, 3: 223–233.

Strickland, T.L., James, R., Myers, H., Lawson, W., Bean, X. and Mapps, J. (1993) 'Psychological characteristics related to cocaine use during pregnancy: a postpartum assessment', *Journal of the National Medical Association*, 85: 758–760.

Striegel-Moore, R.H. and Huydic, E.S. (1993) 'Problem drinking and symptoms of disordered eating in female high school students', *International Journal of Eating Disorders*, 14: 417–425.

Striegel-Moore, R.H., Silberstein, L.R. and Rodin, J. (1993) 'The social self in bulimia nervosa: public self-consciousness, social anxiety, and perceived fraudulence', *Journal of Abnormal Psychology*, 102: 297–303.

Struening, E.L. (1991) 'A typology based on measures of substance abuse and mental disorder', *Journal of Addictive Diseases*, 11: 99–117.

Sulaiman, N.D., Florey, C. du V., Taylor, D.J. et al. (1988) 'Alcohol consumption in Dundee primigravidas and its effects on outcome of pregnancy', *British Medical Journal*, 296: 1500–1503.

Sullivan, E.J. and Handley, S.M. (1993) 'Alcohol and drug abuse', *Annual Review of Nursing Research*, 11: 281–297.

Sulloway, F.J. (1986) 'Freud and biology: The hidden legacy', *Acta Psychiatrica Belgica*, 86: 760–788.

Sulloway, F.J. (1992) *Freud: Biologist of the Mind. Beyond the Psychoanalytic Legend*, Cambridge, Massachusetts, Harvard University Press.

Sulsky, S.I., Jacques, P.F., Otradovec, C.L., Hartz, S.C., Russell, R.M. and Jacques (1990) 'Descriptors of alcohol consumption among noninstitutionalised nonalcoholic elderly', *Journal of the American College of Nutrition*, 9: 326–331.

Sutherland, L.A., Weaver, S.N., McPeake, J.D. and Quimby, C.D. (1993) 'The Beech Hill Hospital eating disorders treatment program for drug dependent females: program description and case analysis', *Journal of Substance Abuse Treatment*, 10: 473–481.

Sutker, P.B., Allain, A.N., Brantley, P.J. and Randall, C. (1982) 'Acute intoxication, negative affect, and autonomic arousal in women and men', *Addictive Behaviours*, 7: 17–25.

Sutker, P.B., Goist, K.C. and King, A.R. (1987) 'Acute alcohol intoxication in women: Relationship to dose and menstrual cycle phase', *Alcoholism: Clinical and Experimental Research*, 11: 74–79.

Suzuki, K., Takeda, A. and Matsushita, S. (1995) 'Coprevalence of bulimia with alcohol abuse and smoking among Japanese male and female high school students', *Addiction*, 90: 971–975.

Svanum, S. and McAdoo, W.G. (1991) 'Parental alcoholism: An examination of male and female alcoholics in treatment', *Journal of Studies on Alcohol*, 52: 127–132.

Svenson, L.W., Jarvis, G.K. and Campbell, R.L. (1994) 'Gender and age differences in the drinking behaviors of university students', *Psychological Reports*, 75: 395–402.

Swett, C. and Halpert, M. (1994) 'High rates of alcohol problems and history of physical and sexual abuse among women inpatients', *American Journal of Drug and Alcohol Abuse*, 20: 263–272.

Swett, C.J., Cohen, C., Surrey, J., Compaine, A. and Chavez, R. (1991) 'High rates of alcohol use and history of physical and sexual abuse among women outpatients', *American Journal of Drug and Alcohol Abuse*, 17: 49–60.

Swiatkiewicz, G. (1995) 'Regulating unregulated markets', paper presented at European Conference on Health, Society and Alcohol, Paris, 12–14 December.

Tagney, J.P. (1990) 'Assessing individual differences in proneness to shame and guilt: Development of the self-conscious affect and attribution inventory', *Journal of Personality and Social Psychology*, 61: 598–607.

Takkala, J. and Lehto, J. (1992) 'Finland: The non-medical model reconsidered', in Klingemann, H., Takkala, J. and Hunt, G. (eds) *Cure, Care or Control: Alcoholism Treatment in Sixteen Countries*, Albany, New York, State University of New York, 87–110.

Talamini, R., La Vecchia, C., Decarli, A. et al. (1984) 'Social factors, diet and breast cancer in a northern Italian population', *British Journal of Cancer*, 49: 723–729.

Tamburini (translated by Workman, J). (1890) 'On motor hallucinations', *Alienist and Neurologist*, July 1,2: 382–383.

Tanaka, H., Ueda, Y., Hayashi, M. et al. (1982) 'Risk factors for cerebral hemorrhage and cerebral infarction in a Japanese rural community', *Stroke*, 13: 62–73.

Tannen, D. (1992) *You Just Don't Understand: Men and Women in Conversation*, London, Virago Press Ltd.

Tarter, R.E. (1992) 'Cognition, aging and alcohol', in Beresford, T.P. and Gomberg, E. (eds) *Alcohol and Aging*, New York, Oxford University Press.

Tarter, R.E. (1995) 'Genetics and primary prevention of drug and alcohol abuse', *International Journal of the Addictions*, 30: 1479–1484.

Tarter, R.E., Arria, A.M. and Van Thiel, D.H. (1991) 'Hepatic encephalopathy coexistent with alcoholism', in Galanter, M., (ed.) *Recent Developments in Alcoholism*, Vol. 9, New York, Plenum Press, 205–224.

Tarter, R.E., McBride, H., Buopane, N. and Schneider, D.U. (1977) 'Differentiation of alcoholics: Childhood history of minimal brain dysfunction, family history and drinking pattern', *Archives of General Psychiatry*, 34: 761–768.

Tate, D.L. and Charette, L. (1991) 'Personality, alcohol consumption, and menstrual distress in young women', *Alcoholism: Clinical and Experimental Research*, 15. 647–652.

Tatum, H.J. and Connell-Tatum, E.B. (1981) 'Barrier contraception: A comprehensive overview', *Fertility and Sterility*, 36: 1–12.

Taylor, A.V., Peveler, R.C., Hibbert, G.A. and Fairbairn, C.G. (1993) 'Eating disorders among women receiving treatment for an alcohol problem', *International Journal of Eating Disorders*, 14: 147–151.

Taylor, J. and Jackson, B.B. (1991) 'Evaluation of a holistic model of mental health symptoms in African American women', *Journal of Black Psychology*, 18: 19–45.

Taylor, J.R. and Combs-Orme, T. (1985) 'Alcohol and strokes in young adults', *American Journal of Psychiatry*, 142: 116–168.

Taylor, L., Zuckerman, B., Harik, V. and Groves, B.M. (1994) 'Witnessing violence by young children and their mothers', *Journal of Deviant Behavior and Pediatrics*, 5: 120–123.

Taylor, M.E. and Qi Wang, M. (1988) 'Educational implications of alcohol use patterns among employed women', *Health Education*, October/November: 78–82.

Taylor, S.P. and Chermack, S.T. (1993) 'Alcohol, drugs and human aggression', *Journal of Studies on Alcohol*, Supplement. 11: 78–88.

Taylor, S.P. and Leonard, K.E. (1983) 'Alcohol and human physical aggression', in Green, R.G. and Donnerstein, E.I., (eds) *Aggression: Theoretical and Empirical Reviews*, 2nd edn. San Diego, California, Academic Press Inc.

Taylor, S.P. and Sears, J.D. (1988) 'The effects of alcohol and persuasive social pressure on human physical aggression', *Aggressive Behavior*, 14: 237–243.

Tebaldi, A. (1892) 'Sentiment', *Alienist and Neurologist*, October 13,4: 633–649.

Temple, M. and Leigh, B. (1990) 'Alcohol and sexual behavior in discrete events, 1. Characteristics of sexual encounters involving and not involving alcohol', Paper presented at the Kettil Bruun Society Meeting, Budapest.

Temple, M.T., Fillmore, K.M., Hartka, E., Johnstone, B., Leino, E.V. and Motoyoshi, M. (1991) 'A meta-analysis of change in marital and employment status as predictors of alcohol consumption on a typical occasion', *British Journal of Addiction*, 86: 1269–1281.

ten Bensel, R.W. and Berdie, J. (1976) 'The neglect and abuse of children and youth: The scope of the problem and the school's role', *Journal of School Health*, 46: 453–461.

Tennes, K. and Blackard, C. (1980) 'Maternal alcohol consumption, birth weight and minor physical anomalies', *American Journal of Obstetrics and Gynecology*, 138: 774–780.

Tether, P. and Robinson, D. (1986) *Preventing Alcohol Problems: A Guide to Local Action*, London, Tavistock.

Teufel, N.I. (1994) 'Alcohol consumption and its effect on the dietary patterns of Hualapai Indian women', *Medical Anthropology*, 16: 79–97.

Thacker, S.B. (1988) 'Meta Analysis: A quantitative approach to research integration', *Journal of the American Medical Association*, 258: 1685–1689.

Thearle, M.J. (1985) 'Infant feeding in colonial Australia 1788–1900', *Australian Paediatric Journal*, 21: 75–79.

Theriot, N.M. (1993) 'Women's voices in nineteenth-century medical discourse: A step toward deconstructing science', *Signs*, 19: 1–31.

Thom, B. (1986) 'Sex differences in help-seeking for alcohol problems, 1: The barriers to help-seeking', *British Journal of Addiction*, 81: 777–788.

Thom, B. (1987) 'Sex differences in help-seeking for alcohol problems, 2: Entry into treatment', *British Journal of Addiction*, 82: 989–997.

Thom, B. (1994a) 'Women and alcohol: The emergence of a risk group', in MoDonald, M., (ed.) *Gender, Drink and Drugs*, Oxford, Berg, 33–54.

Thom, B. (1994b) *Alcohol Treatment Since 1983: A Review of the Research Literature*, London, Centre for Research on Drugs and Health Behaviour.

Thom, B. (1995) 'Treatment issues', Report from the Conference on Women and Substance Abuse, Brighton, England, May 1995.

Thom, B., Browne, C., Drummond, D.C., Edwards, G., and Mullan, M. (1992) 'Engaging patients with alcohol problems in treatment: the first consultation', *British Journal of Addiction*, 87: 601–611.

Thomasson, H.R. (1995) 'Gender differences in alcohol metabolism', in Galanter, M., (ed.) *Recent Developments in Alcoholism*, Vol. 12, New York, Plenum Press, 163–179.

Thombs, D.L., Beck, K.H. and Mahoney, C.A. (1993) 'Effects on social context and gender on drinking patterns of young adults', *Journal of Counselling Psychology*, 1: 115–119.

Thombs, D.L., Beck, K.H., Mahoney, C.A. Bromley, M.D. and Bezon, K.M. (1994) 'Social context, sensation seeking and teenage alcohol abuse', *Journal of School Health*, 64: 73–79.

Thombs, D.L. Beck, K.H. and Pleace, D.J. (1993) 'The relationship of social context and expectancy factors to alcohol use intensity among 18 to 22-year-olds', *Addiction Research*, 1: 59–68.

Thompson, G. (1889) 'Bromomania', *Alienist and Neurologist*, October 10,4: 649.

Thompson, M.S. (1988) 'The wages of sin: The problem of alcoholism and general paralysis in Nineteenth Century Edinburgh', in Bynum, W.F.,

Porter, R. and Shepherd, M., (eds) *The Anatomy of Madness*, Vol. 3, London, Routledge, 316–340.

Tims, F.M., De Leon, G. and Jainchill, N. (1994) *Therapeutic Community: Advances in Research and Application*, MD Monograph 144, Rockville, Maryland, National Institute on Drug Abuse.

Tisserand, M. (1986) *Aromatherapy for Women*, Wellingborough, Thorsons Publishing Group.

Titus, M.A. and Smith, W.H. (1992) 'Contemporary issues in the psychotherapy of women', *Bulletin of the Menninger Clinic*, 56: 48–61.

Tobin, M.B. (1994) 'Reported alcohol use in women with premenstrual syndrome', *American Journal of Psychiatry*, 151: 1503–1504.

Tobler, N. (1986) 'Meta-analyisis of 143 adolcscent drug abuse prevention programs: Quantitative outcome results of program participants compared to a control or comparison group', *Journal of Drug Issues*, 16: 537–567.

Tofler, A.B., Sake, B.M., Rollo, K.A. et al. (1969) 'Electrocardiogram of the social drinker in Perth, Western Australia', *British Heart Journal*, 31: 306–313.

Tolnay, S.E. (1981) 'Trends in total and marital fertility for black Americans, 1886–1899', *Demography*, 18: 443–463.

Tolstrup, K. (1990) 'Incidence and causality of anorexia nervosa seen in a historical perspective', *Acta Psychiatrica Scandinavica*, Supplementum, 361: 1–6.

Tomlinson, C. (1992) G.C. 'Lichtenberg: dreams, jokes, and the unconscious in eighteenth-century Germany', *Journal of the American Psychoanalytic Association*, 40: 761–799.

Toneatto, A., Sobell, L.C. and Sobell, M.B. (1992) 'Gender issues in the treatment of abusers of alcohol, nicotine and other drugs', *Journal of Substance Abuse*, 4: 209–218.

Tongue, A. (1978) 'Five-thousand years of drinking', in Ewing, J.A. and Rouse, B.A., (eds) *Drinking: Alcohol and American Society – Issues in Current Research*, Chicago, Nelson-Hall.

Toren, C. (1994) 'The drinker as chief or rebel: Kava and alcohol in Fiji', in McDonald, M., (ed.) *Gender, Drink and Drugs*, Oxford, USA.: Berg, 153–174.

Tosi, D.J., Eshbaugh, D.M. and Murphy, M.A. (1993) *A Clinician's Guide to the Personality Profiles of Alcohol and Drug Abusers: Typological Descriptions Using the MME*, Springfield, Illinois, Charles C. Thomas.

Toussaint-Samat, M. (1994) *History of Food*, Cambridge, Massachusetts, Blackwell Publishers.

Trad, P.V. (1993) 'Substance-abuse in adolescent mothers – strategies for diagnosis, treatment and prevention', *Journal of Substance Abuse Treatment*, 10: 421–431.

Trad, P.V. (1994) 'Developmental vicissitudes that promote drug abuse in adolescents', *American Journal of Drug and Alcohol Abuse*, 20: 459–481.

Traeen, B. and Lewin, B. (1992) 'Casual sex among Norwegian adolescents', *Archives of Sexual Behavior*, 21: 253–269.

Traeen, B. and Kvalem, I. (1996) 'Sex under the influence of alcohol among Norwegian adolescents', *Addiction*, 91: 995–1006.

Tredrea, D. (1983) 'What price the next drink?' (unpublished).

Treno, A.J., Parker, R.N. and Holder, H.D. (1993) 'Understanding U.S. alcohol consumption with social and economic factors: A multivariate time series analysis, 1950–1986', *Journal of Studies on Alcohol*, 54: 146–156.

Trevisan, M., Krogh, V. and Farinaro, E. (1987) 'Alcohol consumption, drinking pattern and blood pressure: Analysis of data from the Italian national research council study', *International Journal of Epidemiology*, 16: 520–527.

Trimpey, J. (1989) *Rational Recovery from Alcohol: The Small Book*, Lotus, California, Lotus Press.

Trotter, T. (1981) *An Essay, Medical, Philosophical, and Chemical, on Drunkenness*, 2nd edn, New York, Arno Press Inc.

Tschann, J.M., Adler, N.E., Irwin, C.E.J., Millstein, S.G., Turner, R.A. and Kegeles, S.M. (1994) 'Initiation of substance use in early adolescence: The roles of pubertal timing and emotional distress', *Health Psychology*, 13: 326–333.

Tu, E.J. (1979) 'Cohort maternal mortality: New York, 1917–1972', *American Journal of Public Health*, 69: 1052–1055.

Tuchfeld, B. (1981) 'Spontaneous remission in alcoholics: Empirical observations and theoretical implications', *Journal of Studies on Alcohol*, 41: 626–641.

Tucker, J.A. and Gladsjo, J.A. (1993) 'Help seeking and recovery by problem drinkers: Characteristics of drinkers who attended A.A. or formal treatment or who recovered without assistance', *Addictive Behaviors*, 18: 529–542.

Tucker, J.A. and Sobell, L.C. (1992) 'Influences on help-seeking for drinking problems and on natural recovery without treatment', *Behavior Therapy*, 15: 12–14.

Turnbull, J.E. and Gomberg, E.S. (1991) 'The structure of drinking-related consequences in alcoholic women', *Alcoholism: Clinical and Experimental Research*, 15: 29–38.

Turner, C. and Anderson, P. (1990) 'Alcohol and cancer', *Lancet*, 335: 634.

Turner, J., Roy, D., Irwin, G. et al. (1984) 'Does a booklet on breast self-examination improve subsequent detection rates?' *Lancet*, ii: 337–339.

Turner, T.B. and Bennett, V.L. (1993) *Forward Together: Industry and Academia*, Baltimore, Maryland, Alcoholic Beverage Medical Research.

Turner, T.H. (1992) 'A diagnostic analysis of the Casebooks of Ticehurst House Asylum, 1845–1890', *Psychological Medicine*, Monograph Supplement, 21: 1–70.

Turnure, C. and Young, P. (1994) 'Chemical abuse and family violence', *Minnesota Medicine*, 77: 24–26.

Tuttle, J. (1993) 'Adolescent substance abuse: Psychosocial factors', *Journal of School Nursing*, 3: 22–25.

Tweed, S.H. and Ryff, C.D. (1991) 'Adult children of alcoholics: Profiles of wellness amidst distress', *Journal of Studies Alcohol*, 52: 133–141.

Ulfelder, H. (1980) 'The stilbestrol disorders in historical perspective', *Cancer*, 45: 3008–3011.

Ulleland, C.N. (1972) 'The offspring of alcoholic mothers', *Annals of the New York Academy of Science*, 197: 167–169.

Ullman, A.D. and Orenstein, A. (1994) 'Why some children of alcoholics become alcoholics: Emulation of the drinker', *Adolescence*, 29: 1–11.

Underhill, B.L. (1991) 'Recovery needs of lesbian alcoholics in treatment', in Van Den Bergh, N., (ed.) *Feminist Perspectives on Addictions*, New York, Springer Publishing Company, 73–86.

United States Surgeon General (1981) 'Advisory on alcohol and pregnancy', *Food and Drug Administration Bulletin*, 1: 9–10.

Urbana-Márquez, A., Estruch, R., Fernández-Solá, J., Nicolás, J.M., Paré, J.C. and Rubin, E. (1995) 'The greater risk of alcoholic cardiomyopathy in women compared with men', *Journal of the American Medical Association*, 274: 149–154.

Urquiza, A., Wyatt, G.E. and Root, M.P. (1994) 'Violence against women of color', Violence and Victims 9: 203–206.

Ussher, J. (1991) *Women's Madness: Misogyny or Mental Illness?* Hertfordshire, Harvester Wheatsheaf, Simon and Schuster International Group.

Ussher, J.M. (1992) 'Research and theory related to female reproduction: Implications for clinical psychology', *British Journal of Clinical Psychology*, 31: 129–151.

Ussher, J.M. (1994) 'Women and madness: a voice in the dark of women's despair', *Feminism and Psychology*, 4: 288–292.

Ussher, J.M. and Wilding, J.M. (1991) 'Performance and state changes during menstrual cycle, conceptualised within a broad band testing framework', *Social Science and Medicine*, 32: 525–534.

Ussher, J.M. and Wilding, J.M. (1992) 'Interaction between stress and performance during the menstrual cycle in relation to the premenstrual syndrome', *Journal of Reproduction and Infant Psychology*, 10: 83.

Valbo, A. and Schioldborg, P. (1993) 'Smoking in pregnancy: A follow-up study of women unwilling to quit, *Addictive Behaviors*, 18: 253–257.

Välimäki, M., Härkonen, H. and Ylikahri, R. (1983) 'Acute effects of alcohol on female sex hormones', *Alcoholism: Clinical and Experimental Research*, 7: 289–293.

van de Goor, I. (1990) *Situational Aspects of Adolescent Drinking Behavior*, Rijksuniversiteit Limburg, Faculuteit der Gezonheidswetenschappen (Netherlands).

Van den Brandt, P.A., Goldbohm, R.A. and van t'Veer (1995) 'Alcohol and breast cancer: Results from the Netherlands cohort study', *American Journal of Epidemiology*, 141: 907–913.

Van den Bergh, N. (1991) *Feminist Perspectives on Addictions*, New York, Springer.

Van der Molen, G.M., Merckelbach, H. and Van Den Hout, M.A. (1988) 'The possible relation of the menstrual cycle to susceptibility to fear acquisiton', *Journal of Behavioral Therapy and Experimental Psychiatry*, 19: 127–133.

van Gijn, J., Stampfer, M.J., Wolfe, C. and Algra, A. (1993) 'The association between alcohol and stroke', in Verschuren, P.M. (ed.) *Health Issues Related to Alcohol Consumption*, Washington, D.C., ILSI Press, 43–79.

Van Hasselt, V.B., Null, J.A., Kempton, T. and Bukstein, O.G. (1993) 'Social skills and depression in adolescent substance abusers', *Addictive Behaviors*, 18: 9–18.

Van Nieuwkerk, K. (1992) 'Female entertainers in Egypt', in Gefou-Madianou, D. (ed.) *Alcohol, Gender and Culture*, London, Tavistock, 35–47.

van Roosmalen, E.H. and McDaniel, S.A. (1992) 'Adolescent smoking intentions: Gender differences in peer context', *Adolescence*, 27: 87–105.

Van Thiel, D.H. and Gavaler, J.S. (1988) 'Ethanol metabolism and hepatotoxicity: Does sex make a difference?' in Galanter, M., (ed.) *Recent Developments in Alcoholism*, Vol. 6, New York, Plenum Press, 291–304.

Van Thiel, D.H., Gavaler, J.S. and Stremple, J.F. (1979) 'Lower esophageal sphincter pressure during the normal menstrual cycle', *American Journal of Obstetrics and Gynecology*, 134: 64–69.

Van Thiel, D.H., Gavaler, J.S. and Tarter, R.E. (1988) 'The effects of alcohol on sexual behavior and function', in Sitsen, J.M.A. (ed.) *Handbook of Sexology. Vol 6. The Pharmacology and Endocrinology of Sexual Function*, New York, Elsevier Science Publishers, 478–498.

Van t'Veer, P., Kok, F.J., Hermus, R.J. and Sturmans, F. (1989) 'Alcohol dose, frequency and age at first exposure in relation to the risk of breast cancer', *International Journal of Epidemiology*, 18: 511–517.

Vandereycken, W. and Lowenkopf, E.L. (1990) 'Anorexia nervosa in 19th century America', *Journal of Nervous and Mental Disease*, 178: 531–535.

Vannicelli, M. (1984) 'Treatment outcome of alcoholic women: The state of the art in relation to sex bias and expectancy effects', in Wilsnack, S.C, and Beckman, L.J., (eds) *Alcohol Problems in Women*, New York, Guilford Press.

Vannicelli, M. (1989) *Group Psychotherapy with Adult Children of Alcoholics: Treatment Techniques and Countertransference Considerations*, New York, Guilford Press.

Vannicelli, M. (1992) *Removing the Roadblocks*, New York, Guilford Press.

Varvasovsky, Z. (1996) 'Alcohol policy and prevention in Hungary', paper presented at 41st Scottish Alcohol Problems Research Symposium, Pitlochry, April.

Velleman, R. (1992a) 'Intergenerational effects – a review of environmentally oriented studies concerning the relationship between parental alcohol problems and family disharmony in the genesis of alcohol and other problems. I: the intergenerational effects of alcohol problems', *International Journal of the Addictions*, 27: 253–280.

Velleman, R. (1992b) 'Intergenerational effects – a review of environmentally oriented studies concerning the relationship between parental alcohol problems and family disharmony in the genesis of alcohol and other problems. II. the intergenerational effects of family disharmony', *International Journal of the Addictions*, 27: 367–389.

Velleman, R. (1996) 'Setting up and developing a new statutory service: a personal view', *Journal of Substance Misuse*, 1: 205–209.

Verga (1881) 'Proceedings of the 3rd Congress of Italian Alienists', *Alienist and Neurologist*, January 2,1: 113–114.

Verschuren, P. (ed.) (1993) *Health Issues related to Alcohol Consumption*, Washington, D.C., ILSI.

Verkerk, P.H. (1992) 'The impact of alcohol misclassification on the relationship between alcohol and pregnancy outcome', *International Journal of Epidemiology*, Supplement 21: 4: 33–37.

Vertinsky, P. (1988) '"Of no use without health": late nineteenth century medical prescriptions for female exercise through the life span', *Women and Health*, 14: 89–115.

Vicinus, M. and Nergaard, B. (1989) *Ever Yours, Florence Nightingale. Selected Letters*, London, Virago Press.

Vincent, A.L., Bradham, D.D., Urena Rajas, C.A. and Fisher, S.K. (1993) 'The Dominican Republic and the Marlboro brand: A cigarette smoking survey and status report', *Bulletin of the Pan American Health Organization*, 27: 370–381.

Vinson, J.S. (1984) 'Sexual contact with psychotherapists: A study of client reactions and complaint procedures', Doctoral dissertation, California School of Professional Psychology,

Vogt, I. (1987) 'Female alcoholics: Results of an interview study', Paper presented at Alcohol Epidemiology Symposium, the Kettil Bruun Society, Aix en Provence.

Vogt, I. (1990) 'Governing images of alcoholism in Germany, 1870–1920', *International Journal of Law and Psychiatry*, 13: 149–154.

Vogt, I. (1995a) 'Women and addiction: A frame of reference for theory and practice', in Council of Europe, *Women and Drugs*, Strasburg, Council of Europe Publishing, 1–21.

Vogt, I. (1995b) 'Germany', in Heath, D.B., (ed.) *International Handbook on Alcohol and Culture*, Connecticut, Greenwood Press, 88–98.

Volpicelli, J.R., Alterman, A.I., Hayashida, M. et al. (1992) 'Naltrexone in the treatment of alcohol dependence', *Archives of General Psychiatry*, 49: 876–880.

Von Arbin, M., Britton, M., de Faire, U. and Tisell, A. (1985) 'Circulatory manifestations and risk factors in patients with cerebrovascular disease and in matched controls', *Acta Medica Scandinavica*, 218: 373–380.

Wagenaar, A.C., Toomey, T.L., Murray, D.M., Short, B.J., Wolfson, M and

Jones-Webb, R. (1996) 'Sources of alcohol for underage drinkers', *Journal of Studies on Alcohol*, 57: 325–333.

Wagenaar, A.C., Zobeck, T.S., Williams, G.D. and Hingson, R. (1995) 'Methods used in studies of drug control effects: A meta-analysis of the literature from 1960 to 1991', *Accidents: Annals of Prevention*, 27: 307–316.

Wald, A., Van Thiel, D.H. and Hoechstetter, L. (1982) 'Effects of pregnancy on gastrointestinal transit', *Digestive Diseases and Sciences*, 27: 1015–1018.

Walfish, S., Stenmark, D.E., Sarco, D., Shealy, J.S. and Krone, A.M. (1992) 'Incidence of bulimia in substance misusing women in residential treatment', *International Journal of the Addictions*, 27: 425–433.

Walker, E.A., Gelfand, A.N., Gelfand, M.D., Koss, M.P. and Katon, W.J. (1995) 'Medical and psychiatric symptoms in female gastroenterology clinic patients with histories of sexual victimization', *General Hospital Psychiatry*, 17: 85–92.

Walkowitz, J.R. (1992) *City of Dreadful Delight. Narratives of Sexual Danger in Late-Victorian London*, London, Virago.

Wallen, J. (1992) 'A comparison of male and female clients in substance abuse treatment', *Journal of Substance Abuse Treatment*, 9: 243–248.

Wallen, J. and Berman, K. (1992) 'Possible indicators of childhood sexual abuse for individuals in substance abuse treatment', *Journal of Child Sexual Abuse*, 1: 63–74.

Walpole, I., Zubrick, S. and Pontré, J. (1990) 'Is there fetal effect with low to moderate alcohol use before or during pregnancy?' *Journal of Epidemiology and Community Health*, 44: 297–301.

Walpole, I., Zubrick, S., Pontré, J. and Lawrence, C. (1991) 'Low to moderate maternal alcohol use before and during pregnancy and neurobehavioral outcome in the newborn infant', *Developmental Medicine and Child Neurology*, 33: 875–883.

Walter, G. (1992) 'The psychiatrist in American cartoons, 1941–1990', *Acta Psychiatrica Scandinavica*, 85: 167–172.

Waltman, R. and Iniquez, E.S. (1972) 'Placental transfer of ethanol and its elimination at term', *Obstetrics and Gynaecology*, 40: 180–185.

Walton, M.A. and Gomberg, E.S. (1994) 'Determinants of early alcohol and drug use among young women in alcoholism treatment', *Journal of Substance Abuse*, 6: 367–379.

Wang, M.Q., Nicholson, M.E., Richardson, M.T., Fitzhugh, E.C., Reneau, P., and Westerfield, C.R. (1995) 'The acute effect of moderate alcohol consumption on cardiovascular responses in women', *Journal of Studies on Alcohol*, 56: 16–20.

Ward, M. and Goodman, C. (1995) *Alcohol Problems in Old Age*, Surrey, Wynne Howard Publications.

Ware, V. (1992) *Beyond the Pale: White Women, Racism and History*, London, Verso.

Warner, J. (1992) 'North, South, male, female: Levels of alcohol consumption in late medieval Europe', Personal communication. Cited by Plant,

M.A. (1995) 'The United Kingdom', in Heath, D. (ed.) *International Handbook on Alcohol and Culture*, Westport, Greenwood Press, 290.

Warner, J. (1994) '"Resolv'd to drink no more": addiction as a preindustrial construct', *Journal of Studies on Alcohol*, 55: 685–691.

Warner, M. (1985) *Monuments and Maidens: The Allegory of the Female Form*, London, Picador.

Warner, R.H. and Rosett, H.L. (1975) 'The effects of drinking on offspring: An historical survey of the American British literature', *Journal of Studies on Alcohol*, 36: 1395–1420.

Waterson, E.J. and Murray-Lyon, I.M. (1990) 'Preventing alcohol-related birth damage; a review', *Social Science and Medicine*, 30: 349–364.

Wartski, S.G. (1993) 'Married women with eating disorders: An explorative study of a neglected subgroup', *Dissertation Abstracts International*, 54: 1116.

Watson, H.E., Kershaw, P.W. and Davies, J.B. (1991) 'Alcohol problems among women in a general hospital ward', *British Journal of Addiction*, 86: 889–894.

Watson, P.E., Watson, I.D. and Batt, R.D. (1980) 'Total body water volumes for adult males and females estimated from simple anthropometric measurements', *American Journal of Clinical Nutrition*, 33: 27–39.

Watson, R.R. (1995) *Alcohol, Cocaine and Accidents*, New Jersey, Humana Press Inc.

Watterson, P.A. (1988) 'Infant mortality by father's occupation from the 1911 census of England and Wales', *Demography*, 25: 289–306.

Wattley, L.A. (1983) 'Male physicians and female health and sexuality in 19th century English and American society', *Journal of Advanced Nursing*, 8: 423–428.

Webb, E. (1880) *Temperance in the Home*, London, British Women's Temperance Association.

Webster, L.A., Layde, P.M., Wingo, P.A. and Ory, H.W. (1983) 'Alcohol consumption and risk of breast cancer', *Lancet*, 2: 724–726.

Webster, R.A., Hunter, M. and Keats, J.A. (1994) 'Personality and sociodemographic influences on adolescents' substance use: a path analysis', *International Journal of the Addictions*, 29: 941–956.

Weeks, J. (1980) 'Inverts, perverts, and Mary-Annes. Male prostitution and the regulation of homosexuality in England in the nineteenth and early twentieth centuries', *Journal of Homosexuality*, 6: 113–134.

Weibel-Orlando, J. (1989) 'Hooked on healing: anthropologists, alcohol and intervention', *Human Organization*, 48: 148–155.

Weidner, G., Connor, S.L., Chesney, M.A., Burns, J.W., Connor, W.E., Matarazzo, J.D. and Mendell, N.R. (1991) 'Sex differences in high density lipoprotein cholesterol among low-level alcohol consumers', *Circulation*, 83: 176–180.

Weidner, G. and Helmig, L. (1990) 'Cardiovascular stress reactivity and mood during the menstrual cycle', *Women and Health*, 16: 5–7.

Weinberg, N.Z., Dielman, T.E., Mandell, W. and Shope, J.T. (1994)

'Parental drinking and gender factors in the prediction of early adolescent alcohol use', *International Journal of the Addictions*, 29: 89–104.

Weiner, D.B. (1992) 'Philippe Pinel's "Memoir on Madness" of December 11, 1794: A fundamental text of modern psychiatry', *American Journal of Psychiatry*, 149: 725–732.

Weisberg, D.K. (1985) *Children of the Night: A Study of Adolescent Prostitution*, Lexington, Lexington Books.

Weisner, C. (1993) 'Toward an alcohol treatment entry model: A comparison of problem drinkers in the general population and in treatment', *Alcoholism: Clinical and and Experimental Research*, 17: 746–752.

Weisner, C. and Morgan, P. (1992) 'Rapid growth and bifurcation: Public and private alcohol treatment in the United States', in Klingemann, H., Takkala, J. and Hunt, G., (eds) *Cure, Care or Control: Alcoholism Treatment in Sixteen Countries*, Albany, New York, State University of New York Press, 223–251.

Weisner, C. and Schmidt, L. (1992) 'Gender disparities in treatment for alcohol problems', *Journal of the American Medical Association*, 268: 1872–1876.

Weisner, C. and Schmidt, L. (1995) 'The community epidemiology laboratory: Studying alcohol problems in community and agency-based populations', *Addiction*, 90: 329–341.

Weiss, G. (1991) 'The death of Charlotte Brontë', *Obstetrics and Gynecology*, 78: 705–708.

Weiss, S. (1991) 'Adult women's drinking in Israel: A review of the literature', *Alcohol and Alcoholism*, 26: 277–283.

Weiss, S. (1993) 'Alcohol and the elderly: An overlooked phenomenon in the literature in developing countries', *Drug and Alcohol Review*, 12: 217–224.

Weiss, S. (1995) 'Israel', in Heath, D.B., (ed.) *International Handbook on Alcohol and Culture*, Connecticut, Greenwood Press, 142–155.

Weisz, J.R., Weiss, B., Han, S.S., Granger, A. and Morton, T. (1995) 'Effects of psychotherapy with children and adolescents revisited: A meta-analysis of treatment outcome studies', *Psychogical Bulletin*, 117: 450–468.

Welldon, E.V. (1991) 'Psychology and psychopathology in women – a psychoanalytic perspective', *British Journal of Psychiatry*, Supplement: 85–892.

Welsh, D.M. (1996) 'Alcohol and sexuality', *Alcohol Health and Research World*, 15: 2.

Welte, J.W. and Mirand, A.L. (1992) *Alcohol Use by the Elderly: Patterns and Correlates. Report on the Erie County Elder Drinking Survey*, Buffalo, New York, Research Institute on Addictions.

Werch, C.E. (1991) 'How much is enough? Willingness to participate in alcohol interventions', *Journal of American College Health*, 39: 269–274.

Werkerk, P., van Noord-Zaadstra, B.M., Florey, C.D., de Jonge, G.A. and

Verloove-Vanhorick, S.P. (1993) 'The effect of moderate maternal alcohol consumption on birth weight and gestational age in a low risk population', *Early Human Development*, 32: 121–129.

Werner, L.J. and Broida, J.P. (1991) 'Adults self-esteem and locus of control as a function of familial alcoholism and dysfunction', *Journal of Studies on Alcohol*, 52: 249–252.

Werner, M.J., Walker, L.S. and Greene, J.W. (1995) 'Relationship of alcohol expectancies to problem drinking among college women', *Journal of Adolescent Health*, 16: 191–199.

Wesson, J. (1992) *The Vintage Years: Older People and Alcohol*, Birmingham, Aquarius.

West, W. (1994) 'Post-Reichian therapy', in Jones, D., (ed.) *Innovative Therapy*, Buckingham, Open University Press, 131–145.

Westoft; C.F. (1986) 'Fertility in the United States', *Science*, 234: 554–559.

Whitby, J.D. (1980) 'Alcohol in anaesthesia and surgical resuscitation', *Anaesthesia*, 35: 502–505.

White, H.R. (1993) 'Sociology', in Galanter, M., (ed.) *Recent Developments in Alcoholism: Vol. 11: Ten Years of Progress*, New York, Plenum Press, 7–27.

White, H.R., Brick, J. and Hansell, S. (1993) 'A longitudinal investigation of alcohol use and aggression in adolescence', *Journal of Studies on Alcohol*, Supplement 11: 62–77.

Whitfield, C.L. (1989) *Healing the Child Within*, Deerfield Beach, Florida, Health Communications Inc.

Whitfield, J.B. and Martin, N.G. (1994) 'Alcohol consumption and alcohol pharmacokinetics: Interactions within the normal population', *Alcoholism: Clinical and Experimental Research*, 18: 238–243.

Whitmore, D. (1991) *Psychosynthesis Counselling in Action*, London, Sage Publications Ltd.

Widom, C.S., Ireland, T. and Glynn, P.J. (1995) 'Alcohol abuse in abused and neglected children followed-up; Are they at increased risk?' *Journal of Studies on Alcohol*, 56: 207–217.

Wiers, R.W., Sergeant, J.A. and Gunning, W.B. (1994) 'Psychological mechanisms of enhanced risk of addiction in children of alcoholics: A dual pathway?' *Acta Paediatrica*, Supplement, 404: 9–13.

Wiese, P.R. (1995) 'Efficacy of addiction treatment in a correctional setting for female offenders as measured by the Addiction Severity Index', *Dissertation Abstracts International*, 55: 4136B.

Wiggins, B. and Wiggins, J.A. (1992) 'Specification of the association between sociability and drinking level among college students', *Journal of Studies on Alcohol*, 53: 137–141.

Wilbush, J. (1988a) 'Menorrhagia and menopause: A historical review', *Maturitas*, 10: 5–26.

Wilbush, J. (1988b) 'Menopause and menorrhagia: A historical exploration', *Maturitas*, 10: 83–108.

Wilcoxon, L.A., Schrader, S.L. and Sherif, C.W. (1976) 'Daily self-reports on activities, life events, moods and somatic changes during the menstrual cycle', *Psychosomatic Medicine*, 38: 399–417.

Wilke, D. (1994) 'Women and alcoholism: How a male-as-norm bias affects research, assessment, and treatment', *Health and Social Work*, 19: 29–35.

Wilkins, R.H. (1974) *The Hidden Alcoholic in General Practice*, London: Elek Science.

Wilkinson, P. (1980) 'Sex differences in morbidity of alcoholics', in Kalant, O.J., (ed.) *Alcohol and Drug Problems in Women*, New York, Plenum Press, 331–364.

Wilkinson, S. (1994) 'Phyllis Chesler: "Amazon warrior": Then and now', *Feminism and Psychology*, 4: 261–267.

Williams, G.D. and DeBakey, S.F. (1992) 'Changes in levels of alcohol consumption in the United States, 1983–1988', *British Journal of Addiction*, 87: 643–648.

Williams, L.M. (1994) 'Recall of childhood trauma: a prospective study of women's memories of child sexual abuse', *Journal of Consulting and Clinicla Psychology*, 62,6: 1167–1176.

Williams, J.G. and Morris, A. (1992) 'Measuring drinking patterns among college students', *Psychological Reports*, 70: 231–238.

Williams, J.G. and Smith, J.P. (1993) 'Alcohol and other drug use among adolescents: Family and peer influences', *Journal of Substance Abuse*, 5: 289–294.

Williams, R.R. and Horn, J.W. (1977) 'Association of cancer sites with tobacco and alcohol consumption and socioeconomics status of patients: interview study from the Third National Cancer Survey', *Journal of the National Cancer Institute*, 58: 525–547.

Williams, R.R., Stegens, N.L. and Goldsmith, J.R. (1977) 'Associations of cancer site and type with occupation and industry from the Third National Cancer survey interview', *Journal of the National Cancer Research Institute*, 59: 1147–1185.

Williams-Petersen, M.G., Myers, B.J., Degen, H.M., Knisely, J.S., Elswick, R.K.J. and Schnoll, S.S. (1994) 'Drug-using and nonusing women: Potential for child abuse, child-rearing attitudes, social support, and affection for expected baby', *International Journal of the Addictions*, 29: 1631–1643.

Williamson, D.F., Forman, M.R., Binkin, N.J. et al. (1987) 'Alcohol and body weight in United States adults', *American Journal of Public Health*, 77: 1324–1330.

Williston, G. and Johnstone, J. (1983) *Discovering your Past Lives*, London, HarperCollins Publishers.

Willett, W.C., Stampfer, M.J., Colditz, G.A. et al. (1987) 'Moderate alcohol consumption and the risk of breast cancer', *New England Journal of Medicine*, 316: 1174–1180.

Wilsnack, R.W. and Wilsnack, S.C. (1992) 'Women, work, and alcohol: Failures of simple theories', *Alcoholism: Clinical and Experimental Research*, 16: 172–179.

Wilsnack, S.C. (1984) 'Drinking, sexuality, and sexual dysfunction in women', in Wilsnack, S.C. and Beckman, L.J., (eds) *Alcohol Problems in Women: Antecedents, Consequences and Interventions,* New York, Guilford Press, 189–227.

Wilsnack, S.C., Klassen, A.D., Schur, B.E. and Wilsnack, R.W. (1991) 'Predicting onset and chronicity of women's problem drinking: A five-year longitudinal analysis', *American Journal of Public Health*, 81: 305–318.

Wilsnack, S.C., Klassen, A.D., Vogeltanz, N.D. and Harris, T.R. (1994) 'Childhood sexual abuse and women's substance abuse: National survey findings, Paper presented at the American Psychological Association Conference, Washington, D.C.

Wilsnack, S.C. and Wilsnack, R. (1995) 'Drinking and problem drinking in US women', in Galanter, M. (ed) *Recent Developments in Alcoholism, Volume 12: Women and Alcoholism,* New York, Plenum Press, 29–60.

Wilsnack, S.C., Vogeltanz, N.D., Diers, L.E. and Wilsnack, R.W. (1995) 'Drinking and problem drinking in older women', in Beresford, T.P. and Gomberg, E.S.L. (eds) *Alcohol and Aging,* New York, Oxford University Press, 263–292.

Wilson, A., Davidson, W.J., Blanchard, R. and White, J. (1978) 'Disulfiram implantation: A placebo-controlled trial with two-year follow-up', *Journal of Studies on Alcoholism*, 39: 809–819.

Wilson, D.M., Killen, J.D., Hayward, C., Robinson, T.N., Hammer, L.D., Kraemer, H.C., Varady, A. and Taylor, C.B. (1994) 'Timing and rate of sexual maturation and the onset of cigarette and alcohol use among teenage girls', *Archives of Pediatrics and Adolescent Medicine,* 148: 789–795.

Wilson, G.T., Brick, J., Adler, J., Coco, K. and Breslin, C. (1989) 'Alcohol and anxiety, reduction in female social drinkers', *Journal of Studies on Alcohol*, 50: 226–235.

Wilson, G.T. and Lawson, D.M. (1976) 'Effects of alcohol on sexual arousal in women', *Journal of Abnormal Psychology*, 85: 489–497.

Wilson, G.T. and Lawson, D.M. (1978) 'Expectancies, alcohol and sexual arousal in women', *Abnormal Psychology,* 87: 358–367.

Wilson, J.M. (1992) 'Breast feeding and the chemically dependent woman', NAACOGS Clinical Issues in Perinatal and Womens Health Nursing, 3,4: 667–672.

Windle, M. (1994a) 'Substance use, risky behaviors, and victimization among a US national adolescent sample', *Addiction,* 89: 175–182.

Windle, M. (1994b) 'Coexisting problems and alcoholic family risk among adolescents', *Annals of the New York Academy of Sciences,* 28: 157–164.

Windle, M., Windle, R.C., Scheidt, D.M. and Miller, G.H. (1995) 'Physical and sexual abuse and associated mental disorders among alcoholic in-patients', *American Journal of Psychiatry*, 152: 1322–1328.

Winefield, H.R., Ooldney, R.D., Winefield, A.H. and Tiggemann, M. (1992) 'Psychological correlates of the level of alcohol consumption in young adults', *Medical Journal of Australia*, 156: 755–759.

Winick, C., Levine, A. and Stone, W.A. (1992) 'An incest survivors' therapy group', *Journal of Substance Abuse Treatment*, 9: 311–318.
Winkelstein, W. Jr (1995) 'Spontaneous abortion and coronary heart disease', *Journal of Clinical Epidemiology*, 48,4: 500–501.
Winternitz, M.C. and Bunting, H. (1992) 'The law and planned parenthood case report. 1942', *Connecticut Medicine*, 56: 100.
Wiseman, P.M. (1882) 'Asylums in Great Britain. Notes of a visitor', *Alienist and Neurologist*, October 3,4: 505–516.
Witmer, A.H. (1891) 'Insanity in the coloured races in the United States', *Alienist and Neurologist*, January 12,1: 19–30.
Witterman, J.C.M., Willett, W.C., Stampfer, M.J., et al. (1989) 'A prospective study of nutritional factors and hypertension among US women', *Circulation*, 80: 1320–1327.
Wolf, N. (1990) *The Beauty Myth*, London, Chatto and Windus Ltd.
Wolf, P.A., D'Agostino, R.B., Odell, P. et al. (1988) 'Alcohol consumption as a risk factor in stroke. The Framingham study', (abstract) *Annals of Neurology*, 24: 177.
Wolff, L. (1988) *Child Abuse in Freud's Vienna*, New York, New York University Press.
Wool, C.A. and Barsky, A.J. (1994) 'Do women somatize more than men? Gender differences in somatization', *Psychosomatics*, 35: 445–452.
Woolf, V. (1984) *A Room of One's Own*, London, Chatto and Windus.
Workman, M. and Beer, J. (1992) 'Aggression, alcohol dependency, and self-consciousness among high school students of divorced and nondivorced parents', *Psychological Reports*, 71: 279–286.
World Health Organization (1994a) *Alcohol and HIV/AIDS*, Copenhagen, World Health Organization Regional Office for Europe.
World Health Organization (1994b) *World Health Statistics*, Geneva, World Health Organization.
World Health Organization (1994c) *European Alcohol Action Plan*, Copenhagen, World Health Organization.
World Health Organization (1994d) *Alcohol and HIV/AIDS*, Copenhagen, World Health Organization.
World Health Organization (1994e) *World Health Statistics*, Geneva, World Health Organization.
World Health Organization (1996) *Alcohol – Less is Better*, Copenhagen, WHO Regional Publications, European Series, No. 70.
Wright, J.T., Barrison, I.G., Lewis, I.G., Macrae, K.D., Waterson, E.J., Toplis, P.J., Gordon, M.G. and Morris, N.F. (1983) 'Alcohol consumption, pregnancy and low birthweight', *Lancet*, March: 663–665.
Wright, T.L. (1881) 'Observations on the origin, character and treatment of oinomania', *Alienist and Neurologist*, October, 2,4: 631–648.
Wright, T.L. (1882a) 'Inebriety – A study upon alcohol and its relation to mind and conduct', *Alienist and Neurologist*, April 3,2: 155–239.
Wright, T.L. (1882b) 'The physical basis of moral insanity viewed in relation to alcoholic impressions', *Alienist and Neurologist*, October 3,4: 542–550.

Wright, T.L. (1886) 'Inebrietism: A psychological and pathological study', *Alienist and Neurologist*, July 7,3: 714

Wright, T.L. (1889) 'Distinctive forms of drunkenness', *Alienist and Neurologist,* April 10,2: 265–284.

Wright, T.L. (1890a) 'The unexpected in drunkenness. A study of inebriate responsibility', *Alienist and Neurologist,* 11,1: 46

Wright, T.L. (1890b) 'Drunkenness and its influence on morality', *Alienist and Neurologist,* 11,2: 297–304.

Wright, T.L. (1891a) 'Observations on the criminal status of inebriety', *Alienist and Neurologist,* January 12,1: 1–18.

Wright, T.L. (1891b) 'The human constitution in its relations with the alcoholic crave', *Alienist and Neurologist,* October, 12,4: 548–555.

Wyatt, G.E. and Riederle, M. (1994) 'Sexual harassment and prior sexual trauma among African-American and white American women', *Violence and Victims,* 9: 233–247.

Wynder, E.L. (1984) 'Nutrition, diet and cancer – an evaluation', *Current Concepts in Nutrition,* 13: 171–193.

Yalom, I.D. (1985) *The Theory and Practice of Group Psychotherapy,* 3rd edn. New York, Basic Books. Inc.

Yama, M.F., Fogas, B.S., Teegarden, L.A. and Hastings, H. (1993) 'Childhood sexual abuse and parental alcoholism: Interactive effects in adult women', *American Journal of Orthopsychiatry,* 63: 300–305.

Yama, M.F., Tovey, S.L., Fogas, B.S. and Teegarden, L.A. (1992) 'Joint consequences of parental alcoholism and childhood sexual abuse, and their partial mediation by family environment', *Violence and Victims,* 7: 313–325.

Yamamoto, J., Silva, J.A., Sasao, T., Wang, C. and Nguyen, L. (1993) 'Alcoholism in Peru', *American Journal of Psychiatry,* 150: 1059–1062.

Yeager, R.D., Piazza, N.J. and Yates, J.W. (1992) 'Testing the progressive nature of alcoholism', *International Journal of the Addictions,* 27: 947–959.

Yersin, B., Nicolet, J.F., Dercrey, H., Burnier, M., van Melle, G. and Pecoud, A. (1995) 'Screening for excessive alcohol drinking. Comparative value of carbohydrate-deficient transferrin, gamma-glutamyltransferase, and mean corpuscular volume', *Annals of Internal Medicine,* 155: 1907–1911.

Yokoyama, A., Takagi, T., Ishii, H., Wada, N., Marayama, K., Takagi, S. and Hayshida, M. (1995) 'Gastroectomy enhances vulnerability to the development of alcoholism', *Alcohol,* 12: 213–216.

York, J.L. (1995) 'Progression of alcohol consumption across the drinking career in alcoholics and social drinkers', *Journal of Studies on Alcohol,* 56: 328–336.

York, J.L. and Biederman, I. (1991) 'Hand movement speed and accuracy in detoxified alcoholics', *Alcoholism: Clinical and Experimental Research,* 15: 982–990.

York, J.L. and Welte, J.W. (1994) 'Gender comparisons of alcohol consumption in alcoholic and non alcoholic populations', *Journal of Studies on Alcohol*, 55: 743– 750.

Young, M. (1994) 'The police, gender and the culture of drug use and addiction', in Mcdonald, M., (ed.) *Gender, Drink and Drugs*, Oxford, Berg, 55–76.

Young, R. (ed.) (1992) *Women and Alcohol*, London, HMSO.

Young, T.H. (1989) 'A case-control study of breast cancer and alcohol consumption habits', *Cancer*, 64: 552–558.

Zaluska, M., Bronowski, P., Cendrowski, K., Piotrowski, A. and Stelmachow, J. (1993) 'Alcohol, drugs and the newborn', *International Journal of Prenatal and Perinatal Psychology and Medicine*, 5: 157–167.

Zambarana, R.E., Hernandez, M. Dunkel-Schetter, C. and Scrimshaw, S.C.M. (1991) 'Ethnic differences in the substance use patterns of low income pregant women', *Family and Community Health*, 13: 1–11.

Zeichner, A., Allen, J.D., Giancola, P.R. and Lating, J.M. (1994) 'Alcohol and aggression: Effects of personal threat on human aggression and affective arousal', *Alcoholism: Clinical and Experimental Research*, 18: 657–663.

Zeiner, A.R. and Kegg, P.S. (1981) 'Menstrual cycle and oral contraceptive effects on alcohol pharmokinetics in Caucasian females', *Alcoholism: Clinical and Experimental Research, 8: 47–56.*

Zeitlin, H. (1994) 'Children with alcohol misusing parents', *British Medical Bulletin*, 50: 139–151.

Zlotnick, C., Shea, M.T., Zakriski, A., Costello, E., Begin, A., Pearlstein, T. and Simpson, E. (1995) 'Stressors and close relationships during childhood and dissociative experiences in survivors of sexual abuse among inpatient psychiatric women', *Comprehensive Psychiatry*, 36: 207–212.

Zucker, R.A. and Gomberg, E.S.L. (1986) 'Etiology of alcoholism reconsidered: The case for a biopsychosocial process', *American Psychologist*, 41: 783–793.

Zucker, R.A., Kincaid, S.B., Fitzgerald, H.E. and Bingham, C.R. (1995) 'Alcohol schema acquisition in preschoolers: differences between children of alcoholics and children of non-alcoholics', *Alcoholism: clinicla and Experimental Research*, 19,4: 1011–1017.

Zuriek, M and Ducimetière, P. (1996) 'High alcohol-related premature mortality in France: Concordant estimates from a prospective cohort study and national mortality statistics', *Alcoholism: Clinical and Experimental Research*, 20: 428–433.

Zwerling, I. and Rosenbaum, M. (1959) 'Alcohol addiction and personality', in Arieti, S. (ed.) *American Handbook of Psychiatry*, New York, Basic Books, 623–644.

Name Index

Index by Judith Lavender

Subject Index